ReFocus: The Films of John Waters

ReFocus
The Films of John Waters

Edited by Michelle E. Moore and Brian Brems

EDINBURGH
University Press

Edinburgh University Press is one of the leading university presses in the UK. Publishing new research in the arts and humanities, EUP connects people and ideas to inspire creative thinking, open new perspectives and shape the world we live in. For more information, visit www.edinburghuniversitypress.com.

Edinburgh University Press Ltd
13 Infirmary Street, Edinburgh EH1 1LT

First published in hardback by Edinburgh University Press 2025

Typeset in 10/12 Ehrhardt MT by
IDSUK (DataConnection) Ltd, and
Printed and bound in the UK using 100% renewable electricity by
CPI Group (UK) Ltd

A CIP record for this book is available from the British Library

ISBN 978 1 3995 4390 3 (hardback)
ISBN 978 1 3995 4393 4 (paperback)
ISBN 978 1 3995 4391 0 (webready PDF)
ISBN 978 1 3995 4392 7 (epub)

Contents

List of Figures vii
Acknowledgments x
Notes on Contributors xi

Introduction: Meeting John Waters 1
Michelle E. Moore

Part I Authorial Identity, Aesthetics, and Style

1. Multiple Melodramas: Melodramatic Influences and Their Uses in the Cinema of John Waters 13
Jamie Hook
2. John Waters in the 1980s: Publication, Performance, and the Redefinition of Authorial Identity 31
Matt Connolly
3. The Bloodless 1990s: From *Serial Mom* to Wes Craven's *Scream* 48
Fernando Gabriel Pagnoni Berns and Canela Ailen Rodriguez Fontao
4. Artsy Fartsy: *Pecker* and the Guilty Pleasures of John Waters' "Bad" Art Habits 63
Kristen Galvin
5. "Full of Grace": John Waters as Auteur with the Semiautobiographical Film *Pecker* 81
John P. Bray
6. "Technique Is Failed Style": John Waters, Style, and *Cecil B. Demented* 97
Brian Brems
7. Little Movies: John Waters and the Visual Arts 110
Nicholas Morgan

Part II Collaboration, Subversion, and Queering the Family

8. Once Upon a Time in Dreamland: 2015 Recollections and Reflections 131
Chris Holmlund
9. Family Values: Charles Manson and John Waters' Cult Cinema 151
Kate J. Russell
10. Queer Moms, Trash Aesthetics, and Suburban Filth: The Portrayal of Maternal Abject in John Waters' Cinema 168
Sony Jalarajan Raj and Adith K. Suresh
11. Fame! Fortune! Glamour!: John Waters Remembers Midcentury TV 184
Hollis Griffin
12. An Audience with John Waters 200
Jane Giles

Part III Interview

13. Interview with John Waters Conducted by Michelle E. Moore and Brian Brems at His Home in Baltimore, November 2 2023 219

Filmography 241
Selected Writing by John Waters 242
Bibliography 243
Index 254

Figures

Figure 1.1 Dawn, Chicklette, and Concetta are defined as "bad girls" through costuming, behavior, and attitude in *Female Trouble* (1974). 20
Figure 1.2 Hellcats Connie, Meg, and Dolly smoke and argue in the school lavatory before class in the teen melodrama *High School Hellcats* (1958). 21
Figure 1.3 *Polyester* (1981) announces its intertextual engagement with Douglas Sirk's *All That Heaven Allows* (1955) from the opening credits. 24
Figure 2.1 Waters takes a luxurious drag off a cigarette while insisting (with a wink) that theatergoers abstain in a PSA shot for the Nuart Theatre in Los Angeles. 39
Figure 2.2 Waters cameos as a sleazy used-car salesman looking for some quick cash in Jonathan Demme's *Something Wild* (1986). 41
Figure 3.1 Horror is the most salient genre in Chip's video rental shop. 58
Figure 3.2 Gore and disgust is made prominent by Waters amidst a sanitized era. 59
Figure 4.1 Film still of Pecker on the cover of *New York Magazine*, *Pecker* (1998, Waters). 70
Figure 4.2 Film still of the final queer dance party scene, *Pecker* (1998, Waters). 74
Figure 4.3 John Waters, . . . *And Your Family Too*, 2009, c-print (edition of 5), 11 x 14 inches, © John Waters, courtesy of the artist and Marianne Boesky Gallery, New York and Aspen. 77
Figure 5.1 Pecker photographs a cockroach in a plate of French Fries in *Pecker* (1998). 88
Figure 5.2 Jean Schertler as Memama in *Pecker* (1998). 89
Figure 5.3 Shelley and Pecker in *Pecker* (1998). 90

Figure 6.1 Mirror images in *Cecil B. Demented*; the film camera watches the film camera. 102
Figure 6.2 Radical filmmaker Cecil B. Demented leads a hostile takeover of a soundstage, assuming the commanding heights of the crane. 104
Figure 7.1 In his first work of visual art, Waters returns to his own archive, using an amateur point-and-shoot camera to re-present a moment from *Multiple Maniacs*. John Waters, *Divine in Ecstasy*, 1992, 10 × 13 inches. © John Waters. Courtesy of the artist and Marianne Boesky Gallery, New York and Aspen. 111
Figure 7.2 This installation, comprised of speakers, painted wood, synthetic velour, and an iPod, pokes fun at the strange conventions for collecting and exhibiting moving-image-based work in the art world, which are utterly distinct from cinematic modes of distribution. John Waters, *Faux Video Room*, 2006, 110 3/4 × 96 × 6 inches. © John Waters. Courtesy of the artist and Marianne Boesky Gallery, New York and Aspen. 117
Figure 7.3 Waters strips away the smoke and mirrors of Hollywood film, reducing Taylor to the part objects of primary interest to a small body of fetishistic spectators. John Waters, *Liz Taylor's Hair and Feet*, 1996, Each image: 5 × 7 inches. © John Waters. Courtesy of the artist and Marianne Boesky Gallery, New York and Aspen. 125
Figure 8.1 Art designer Vincent Peranio ("Freak" in the Cavalcade of Perversions; here, a sleeping disciple) and George Figgs (a junkie in the Cavalcade; here, "Jesus Christ") reenact Jesus' prayers in the Garden of Gethsemane. (*Multiple Maniacs* DVD © Criterion Collection, 2017). 139
Figure 8.2 Mink Stole's "Connie Marble" scathingly dismisses a job applicant: "I guess there's just two kinds of people, Miss Sandstone. My kind of people, and assholes. It's rather obvious which category you fit into. Have a nice day." (*Pink Flamingos/ Female Trouble* 25th anniversary edition DVD © New Line Home Entertainment, 2001.) 145
Figure 8.3 In simple black suit and rakish black hat, the elegant Mary Vivian Pearce ("Donna Dasher") testifies against the grotesque and increasingly insane "Dawn Davenport" (Divine) in *Female Trouble*. (*Female Trouble* DVD © Alliance Atlantis, 2004). 149
Figure 9.1 The Marbles' residence in *Pink Flamingos* (1972). 157
Figure 9.2 Queen Carlotta's castle in *Desperate Living* (1977). 158
Figure 9.3 The opening credits to *Female Trouble* (1974). 159
Figure 10.1 Babs Johnson's trailer, located on the outskirts of Phoenix, Maryland, is seen with a gazing ball and a pair of plastic pink flamingos in front of it, capturing the kitsch aesthetic central to John Waters' *Pink Flamingos*. 172

Figure 10.2 Babs Johnson sits next to her mother, Edie, in a playpen, sharing a moment over a basket of hard-boiled eggs in John Waters' *Pink Flamingos.* 176
Figure 10.3 Babs Johnson and her son Crackers break into the home of their rivals, Connie and Raymond Marble. In an act of revenge, Babs begins licking objects to spread their "filth," showcasing the film's outrageous and rebellious spirit in *Pink Flamingos.* 177
Figure 11.1 In *Hairspray*, teenage protagonist Tracy Turnblad and her friend dance in the family living room while watching an afternoon variety program that targets teen audiences. 187
Figure 11.2 Francine Fishpaw, the long-suffering mother and housewife in *Polyester*, is the quintessential "ideal mother" of television soap operas. 192
Figure 11.3 Beverly Sutphin meets actress Suzanne Somers (playing herself) as she is interviewed by a television journalist after being acquitted of murder charges in *Serial Mom.* 194
Figure 12.1 John Waters onstage at the Scala, May 1988. 203
Figure 12.2 *Female Trouble* flyer, February 1980. 208
Figure 12.3 May 1982 ("10 Days of Trash"). 210
Figure 13.1 John Waters in Baltimore, November 2023, interviewed by the editors. © Mark Weissburg, 2023. 221
Figure 13.2 John Waters in conversation. © Mark Weissburg, 2023. 239

Acknowledgments

We would like to first express our gratitude to John Waters, without whom this volume would not exist. His films have provided a lifeline and are a source of inspiration for those who exist on the edges of society. He is a consummate artist and his work provides a way forward to those trying to be true to a vision over a lifetime. His kindness and generosity during our interview with him was unparalleled and we are forever grateful for his time and insights that afternoon. We also would like to thank Trish Shweers and Jen Berg for their immeasurable help coordinating with us that day and afterwards.

We would like to thank our editor at Edinburgh University Press, Gillian Leslie, for her enthusiastic encouragement of this project and the series editors, Alicia Kozma, Gary D. Rhodes, Robert Singer, and Frances Smith, for their unflagging support. Their comments, editing, and advice provided insights that made this book much stronger. We would also like to express our appreciation for the wonderful writers included in this volume, who produced insightful and important work while meeting tight deadlines.

We would also like to express our gratitude to Jay Bliznick and Richard Knight Jr. for helping bring the underground to light, and us to John Waters.

We would also like to thank our partners, Genna Brems and Mark Weissburg, without whose patience and support this volume would certainly have not happened.

Notes on Contributors

Fernando Gabriel Pagnoni Berns is Professor at the Universidad de Buenos Aires (UBA)—Facultad de Filosofía y Letras, where he teaches courses on international horror film. He is director of the research group on horror cinema "Grite," has authored *Historias para no Dormir* (2020), and edited books on the Frankenstein bicentennial, James Wan and Wes Craven, the Italian *giallo* film, and horror comics.

John Patrick Bray is an associate professor and Graduate Coordinator/PhD Area Head in the Department of Theatre and Film Studies at the University of Georgia. His essays have been published in various journals; and he has contributed book chapters to *The Composer on Screen*, *Embodied Playwriting*, *The Routledge Companion to Absurdist Literature*, and a co-authored chapter to *Mapping Smallville*. His monograph *Jack Gelber: Consider This* is under contract. His plays have been produced around the U.S. and are published with Next Stage Press, Original Works Publishing, and in anthologies and journals. His screenplays include the co-written feature *Liner Notes* (Woodstock Film Festival), and the shorts *Barflies* (Horror Realm Con) and *Escapism* (in festivals). He has edited anthologies of plays for Applause Theatre and Cinema Books.

Brian Brems is a Professor of English at the College of DuPage, where he teaches film studies. He is the author of *The Films of Walter Hill: Another Time, Another Place* (2022), and the co-editor of *ReFocus: The Films of Paul Schrader* (2020, Edinburgh University Press), with other publications appearing in several edited collections on Westerns and horror films. He is also a regular contributor to a variety of online publications, including Vague Visages.

Matt Connolly is an associate professor of film studies in the Department of Creative Arts at Minnesota State University, Mankato. He is the co-author (with Dr. Chelsea McCracken) of *100 Queer Films Since Stonewall*. His scholarly work has been published in *JCMS*, *The Velvet Light Trap*, and *Spectator*, as well as in current and forthcoming edited collections. He is the editor-in-chief of *New Review of Film and Television Studies* and has previously served on the board of the SCMS Queer and Trans Caucus.

Canela Ailen Rodriguez Fontao holds a degree in Arts at the Facultad de Filosofía y Letras, Universidad de Buenos Aires (UBA), Argentina. She integrates the research group on cinema CIyNE and has published articles on Argentinian and international cinema and television in publications such as *lafuga*, and in books such as *Cine y Revolución en America Latina*, *Bullying in Popular Culture: Essays on Film, Television and Novels*, *Romancing the Zombie: Essays on the Undead as Significant Other and Clint Eastwood's Cinema of Trauma: Essays on PTSD in the Director's Films*, among others. She is co-founder of the collective La Monstrua, dedicated to researching the presence of women in horror films.

Kristen Galvin's research in contemporary American visual culture explores intersections across film and media, art history, popular music, gender and sexuality, and memory studies. Her current book project examines media 'hypernostalgias' in the twenty-first century that reprocess and repurpose cultures of the 1980s and 1990s to articulate fraught constructions of Americanness within the ongoing culture wars. She is currently an Assistant Professor in the Visual Cultures Program in the Department of Visual and Performing Arts at the University of Colorado at Colorado Springs.

Jane Giles is a London based film writer and director with a background in cinema exhibition and distribution. Her film journalism has appeared in newspapers and magazines including *The Guardian*, *Time Out*, *Sight & Sound*, and *Artforum*. She has contributed chapters to books including *The Routledge Companion to British Cinema History* (eds. IQ Hunter, Laraine Porter, Justin Smith, 2017); *Love: A BFI Compendium* (2015); *Shock Express* (ed. Stefan Jaworzyn, Titan) volume 2 (1993) and volume 3 (1996). Her books include *Un Chant d'amour: The Cinema of Jean Genet* (1990), *The Crying Game* (1997), *Criminal Desires* (2002), and *Scala Cinema 1978–1993* (2018), winner of the 2019 Kraszna-Krausz award for Excellence in Moving Image Book Publication. Her co-directed documentary feature filmmaking debut *SCALA!!!* (2023) was released by the BFI in the UK and Severin Films in the US in 2024.

Hollis Griffin is Associate Professor in the Department of Communication and Media at the University of Michigan, where he teaches and researches television, new media, and cultural politics, particularly as they intersect with questions of sexuality, affect and emotion, and space/place. His book, *Feeling Normal: Sexuality and Media Criticism in the Digital Age* (2017), was named an Outstanding Academic Title for 2017 by *Choice*. He is also the editor of *Television Studies in Queer Times* (2023). He is currently at work on a monograph about the relationship between television and the gentrification of New York City, tentatively titled *Securing the Big Apple: Television and the Rise of New York, 1975–2001*.

Chris Holmlund is Professor Emerita at the University of Tennessee-Knoxville. Her most recent anthology, co-edited with Lisa Purse and Yvonne Tasker, is *Action Cinema since 2000* (2024). Her books include (as author) *Female Trouble* (2017) and *Impossible Bodies* (2002). She has also edited *The Ultimate Stallone Reader* (2014) and *American Cinema of the 1990s* (2008), and co-edited *Contemporary American Independent Film* (2004) and *Between the Sheets, In the Streets: Queer, Lesbian, Gay Documentary* (1997).

Jamie Hook earned his Ph.D. from the Department of Communication & Culture at Indiana University, Bloomington, where he currently serves as a Lecturer in Communication & Professional Skills in the Kelley School of Business. His research interests include media adaptation practices across film, literature, and theatre; stigmatized genres and spectators; representations of gender and sexuality; and camp. He has published chapters in various anthologies including entries in *Palgrave Studies in Adaptation and Visual Culture*, *ReFocus: The American Directors Series* from Edinburgh University Press, and Routledge's *Screening Cinema* series.

Michelle E. Moore is Professor of English at the College of Dupage, where she teaches courses in film studies and literature. She is the author of *Chicago and the Making of American Modernism: Cather, Hemingway, Faulkner and Fitzgerald in Conflict* (2019) and co-editor of *Refocus: The Films of Paul Schrader* (Edinburgh University Press, 2020). She has published articles in *Faulkner Studies*, *Cather Studies*, and *Literature/Film Quarterly*, in addition to contributing chapters to *Modernism in Wonderland: Legacies of Lewis Carroll*, *Rape in Art Cinema*, and *Hemingway in the Digital Age*.

Nicholas C. Morgan is Assistant Professor of Fine Arts at Hampden-Sydney College in Farmville, Virginia. A historian and critic of modern and contemporary art, he teaches and writes on gender and sexuality, artists' film and video, and the relations between aesthetics and politics.

Sony Jalarajan Raj is an Assistant Professor at the Department of Communication, MacEwan University, Edmonton, Canada. Raj is a professional journalist turned academic who has worked in different demanding positions as a reporter, special correspondent, and producer in several news media channels like BBC, NDTV, Doordarshan, AIR, and Asianet News. Raj served as the Graduate Coordinator and Assistant Professor of Communication Arts at the Institute for Communication, Entertainment and Media at St. Thomas University Florida, USA. He was a full-time faculty member in Journalism, Mass Communication, and Media Studies at Monash University, Australia, Curtin University, Mahatma Gandhi University and University of Kerala. He was the recipient of Reuters Fellowship and is a Thomson Foundation (UK) Fellow in Television Studies with the Commonwealth Broadcasting Association Scholarship.

Kate J. Russell has a Ph.D. in Cinema Studies from the University of Toronto, where she wrote her dissertation on John Waters and cult cinema. Her writing appears in *Monstrum*, *The Velvet Light Trap*, *Discourse*, and *ReFocus: The Films of William Castle*. She is also a co-managing editor for *Discourse: Journal for Theoretical Studies in Media and Culture*.

Adith K. Suresh is currently associating as a research assistant at the Department of Communication, MacEwan University, Canada. Adith holds a Master's Degree in English Language and Literature from Mahatma Gandhi University. His research interests include Film Studies, Literary Criticism, and South Asian Cultural Studies.

Introduction: Meeting John Waters

Michelle E. Moore

We arrived at John Waters' house in Baltimore. There had been an accidental double booking with another interview and he graciously offered to take an early train down from NYC to meet us at 8:30AM. He wasn't there yet and his assistant let us into the parlor that had already been featured in so many pictures and interviews: the velvet couch, the books on art, rows of pulp fiction, and an early copy of *John Waters: The Pope of Trash* displayed on top of a stack on the coffee table. Over the last year, he had opened it all up for the curators of his retrospective exhibit, and I wondered what in the room remained from before and what had been rearranged and added to fill in the gaps left by everything shipped out to LA. On the floor by the door was a medium-size white carboard box with dents and tears, wrapped with a fierce-looking chain and heavy padlock. It looked like something dangerous had been trying to get out, or get in, and someone had tried to contain it in the most bizarre way. Then Waters was suddenly there saying: "I was talking to Paul Schrader about you last night at dinner!"

Later, I found an interview where he spoke about Paul Gabrielli's 2012 art piece: "What lunatic would have a box and put these kinds of locks on it that anybody could break in—a cardboard box? This is obviously a crazy person's secret that I love!"[1] Waters has written and directed twelve full length films and four shorts, and written seven bestselling books all about the secrets of crazy people that he loves. He has recently written a novel, *Liarmouth*. He writes articles in and journalists interview him regularly for the international and domestic press, magazines such as the *Artforum*, *Artnews*, *Variety*, *Vanity Fair*, *The New Yorker*, *Interview*, *Time Out New York*, *Slate*, and most recently for the Academy Museum Retrospective of his work. He has been interviewed for documentaries ranging from *Lynch/Oz* and *the Andy Warhol Diaries* to the

BBC Queens of Disco and those about his own work: *Divine Waters* and *Divine Trash*. He has taught classes at the Patuxent Institution, a correctional facility. He acts and does cameos and voices in films and cartoons. Each year, he lists the best films for the Vulture section of *New York*. He tours in one-man shows, has released a Christmas Album, did the audio commentary on *Mommie Dearest* and *Christmas Evil*, and routinely appears "in conversation" at colleges and public humanities festivals. He hosts "Camp John Waters," "The All-Inclusive Dreamland Sleepaway Weekend" in upstate NY each summer.[2]

The Film Society of Lincoln Center presented the first retrospective of Waters' sixteen films in the U.S. in 2014: "Fifty Years of John Waters: How Much Can You Take?" In 2017, the Criterion Collection released a deluxe restored version of *Multiple Maniacs* (1970) on Blu-ray and DVD, the first time the film had been available in a home format in thirty years. Criterion has since released editions of *Pink Flamingos* (1972), *Female Trouble* (1974), and *Polyester* (1981). The Library of Congress added his films *Pink Flamingos* and *Hairspray* (1988) to the U.S. National Film Registry in 2021 and 2022. In 2023, the American Film Academy honored Waters, "whose bold sensibility and keen understanding of the zeitgeist have cemented his exalted position in cinematic history," with the first comprehensive exhibition of his work.[3]

In many ways, Waters has already received a great deal of attention and it would seem that his place in film history has been cemented. However, because his films are deliberately provocative, often seeking to dismantle the conventions of Hollywood and trash filmmaking through outright parody, absurdist dialogue, and their open trafficking in smashing cultural taboos and confrontational material, they have received relatively little scholarly attention. The 2023 Academy Museum Exhibition catalog lists only twenty-two critical analyses of Waters published in the last thirty-five years, the majority of which are single chapters and articles. *Refocus: The Films of John Waters* is the first academic collection to consider Waters' contributions to cinematic history as a director with a singular point of view and style. It is only over the last decade that he has even been considered for these kinds of studies, which had been previously reserved for a certain kind of filmmaker—which Waters is not. Examining all of the films together allows the linkages and parallels between his films and his contemporaries to emerge, as well as showing new influences and purposes behind his filmmaking. This volume seeks to begin new conversations about Waters, which positions him as a highly formidable and important filmmaker and artist.

Waters was born on April 22, 1946 to John Samuel and Patricia Ann Waters in Baltimore, the city that figures prominently in all of his work and where he still lives. He grew up Catholic, because his mother was Catholic, with his three siblings in Lutherville, a suburb of Baltimore. In high school, he met Glen Milstead, who would later become known as the bombshell actress Divine, and Waters' artistic muse and great friend. He briefly attended film school in New York, dropping out and returning home after one semester, where he continued making films until his early twenties. He moved out to Fells Point to be with his friends, and with them, established Dreamland Productions in his house.

While Waters was making his early rough and shocking films with his friends in Baltimore, New York-based artists were simultaneously exploring similar cultural taboos in music, painting, and other media. His first shorts and films, *Hag in a Black Leather Jacket* (1964), *Roman Candles* (1966), *Eat Your Makeup* (1968), *Mondo Trasho* (1969), *Multiple Maniacs* (1970), and *The Diane Linkletter Story* (1970) seem to have the most in common with the experimental filmmaking of the NY downtown scene because of their all-out attack on traditional aesthetics, Hollywood moviemaking, and heteronormative values, which was fueled from not having much of a budget.

Waters and Dreamland Productions screened their third film, *Eat Your Makeup*, on February 23 and 24, 1968 in the Great Hall of the Emmanuel Church in Baltimore for a donation of ninety-nine cents. The handwritten flier announces the film as "An Underground Film Premiere."[4] Manny Farber first used the word Underground in 1957 to describe what he considered those "male masters of the action film" like Howard Hawks, who produced a tremendous amount of B-roll film, and positioned themselves in in the "anti-art role in Hollywood."[5] What he called "perceptive trash" no longer had an audience. In 1961, Stan VanDerBeek asked: "Meanwhile, what of the artists, poets, experimenters in America, who must work as if they were secret members of the underground?"[6] He recycles the word "underground" to now link it to the new and secret experimental art and filmmaking in the U.S. and its audiences. Waters and the Dreamlanders, too, were positioning themselves as secret members and asking for their work to be seen as experimental, new, and a kind of uncommercial anti-art.

The bottom of the flier reads: "Also: 'Short Circuit' by the Eight Year Old David Wise," with an excerpt from Jonas Mekas' review of the then five-year-old *Short Circuit* (1963), praising the film as a "Wonderland."[7] Waters credits Jonas Mekas with inspiring him to make films, going so far as to say "I owe my career to Jonas Mekas." He has told the story many times over the last decade that as a young boy in Baltimore, "he'd read his film column in *The Village Voice* every week and in *Film Culture* magazine, and it was all about underground movies and that's what I wanted to be. I'd go to New York on weekends and see underground movies at [places] like the Film-makers' Cooperative, and that's really all I wanted to do."[8]

But the flier also shows an early theatrical juxtaposition of Waters' third film short with the kind of underground filmmakers Waters didn't seem to usually associate himself with at the time, like David Wise, VanDerBeek,

Mekas, Kenneth Anger, Stan Brakhage, and Maya Deren. David Wise, at the age of eight, had already been mentored by VanDerBeek, and by 1968 was an internationally recognized experimental filmmaker whom Mekas called "the Mozart of Cinema." The term "underground" should be seen simultaneously as an umbrella term for both kinds of alternative and independent filmmaking outside of the studio system, and as a measure of the distance the Dreamlanders were placing between themselves and those other kinds of filmmakers. By 1968, the New York group tended to refer to themselves as experimental or even avant-garde, to differentiate themselves from the new generation of artists who became the hippie underground, with its emphasis on mind expansion and psychedelics. Waters and the Dreamlanders in Baltimore fit into neither place or definition.

When I asked him what he thought about Maya Deren in the interview for this book, Waters separated himself from these experimental filmmakers who are conjured up by the early flier. He said: "she was part of that Jonas Mekas club, but that was more the experimental side. I liked Kenneth Anger, the Kuchar Brothers, Warhol. As far as the whole other crowd, Stan VanDerBeek and all that, I like them today more than I liked them then. They were the other ones. We didn't sit with them. They didn't sit with us. I mean emotionally." When asked what changed, he explained: "Because people look at—I didn't know what I was doing when I made those movies, but if you like them, you call it raw. If you don't, you say amateur. It's the same thing."

Waters mentioned VanDerBeek again when asked if he considered himself part of the avant-garde. He answered quickly: "No, that word always sounds pretentious to me, and it always sounds—I mean, that word, if people use it again—no, to me, avant-garde would be Stan VanDerBeek, that kind of thing. Or—no, I don't think I'm part of the avant-garde. I'm a commercial." Waters stresses the difference in being that he is now "commercial" separating himself from someone like VanDerBeek, despite sharing many commonalities with him: living in Baltimore, not attending film school, being an outsider, being an underground artist. He has been far more open about his admiration for those NY artists at the time who played out the tensions between commercial and high art, such as Andy Warhol. Waters told *Interview* magazine in 2014: "I think *Chelsea Girls* (1966) is a complete masterpiece, and I think Andy's films are equally as good as the art." He then added: "I think one day they will be considered equal. They aren't yet. They will be."[9]

Waters' next film, *Pink Flamingos* (1972), made for $12,000, launched his career as an underground cult filmmaker. The film ends with a performance piece, where Divine infamously eats dogshit. Waters takes pains to show the audience that it is really happening, not a filmic magic trick, and so we even witness the dog shitting beforehand. *Female Trouble* (1974) and *Desperate Living* (1977) follow, and together the three films will become known as the Trash

Trilogy. *The Trash Trilogy* began to be noticed by fans of cult movies and critics who were working at removing the line between art and trash films over the next two decades.[10] By the early 1980s, it had become commonplace in academic journals to attack art cinema with trash cinema. It was as much a dispute over how to think about what cinema is and how that related to aesthetics as it was a conversation about what could be acceptably watched and discussed. It was a discussion about film tastes, which Pierre Bourdieu said was actually about class,[11] and a revision of Pauline Kael's ideas about good and bad movies.[12] The binaries of high and low art were leveled, hierarchies bulldozed, and now that trash cinema was becoming acceptable, Waters got an offer from New Line cinema to make *Polyester* (1981), with a budget of $300,000. "I always wanted to be a sellout," he wrote in 1983's *Crackpot: The Obsessions of John Waters*.[13]

Waters' Hollywood films hit big: *Hairspray* (1988), which would go on to be an extremely successful Broadway show, leading to a mainstream remake in 2007, and *Crybaby* (1990), starring a young Johnny Depp. Bigger budgets meant bigger stars, which in turn allowed for more success. Just as Waters became a director of some notice in Hollywood and his older films had obtained cult status, film studies began following Michel Foucault and Roland Barthes in dismantling the idea of authorship. Kaja Silverman has argued that the post-structuralist dismantling of auteurship in film studies happened at the exact moment that those outside of the white, heteronormative canon were starting to gain access it to it.[14] There would be brief considerations of Waters' individual films by critics, and as examples of poststructural and postmodern work, but it was no longer acceptable to do longform monographs on a single director.

By the 1990s, Waters had become a popular part of U.S. popular culture and extremely recognizable. Generation X came of age and would use the word "underground" to describe a certain kind of convention-defying, subversive filmmaking that was by and for what were now known as subcultures. The films would now be shown as part of underground film festivals, including the Chicago Underground Film Festival founded in 1993. Critics made his films into examples of postmodern style and he would critique this ironic stance in his next three films: *Serial Mom* (1994), *Pecker* (1998), and *Cecil B. Demented* (2000). Waters returned to his over-the-top style with *A Dirty Shame* (2004), a sexploitation romp starring Tracey Ullman, seemingly critiquing his critique. In the twenty years since, at the time of writing he has never taken a break: writing the screenplays for multiple films, working on obtaining development deals, and publishing his first novel *Liarmouth*.

He also works in visual art, making sculpture, photographs, photomontage and collage. The American Fine Arts Co. mounted his first show, *My Little Movies*, in 1995 and he has had a show almost every year in the U.S. and abroad to the present day. He has been represented by C. Grimaldis Gallery in Baltimore, Maryland, since 2002,[15] and by Marianne Boesky Gallery in

New York since 2006.[16] Through this work, he has become part of the art world of galleries, openings, and auctions and the press associated with it. He inhabits the world as an interdisciplinary artist, though he is most associated with his filmmaking.

Waters' films and art circulate in what Linda Hutcheon calls the cultural relevance of recycled, parodic narratives. She proposes that the parodic form "is not nostalgic; it is always critical. . . .Instead, through a double process of installing and ironizing, parody signals how present representations come from past ones and what ideological consequences derive from both continuity and difference."[17] If a film pastiche, filled with kitsch, signals to the viewer to respond nostalgically and with great feeling, then the parodic film teaches the viewer how to read the reassemblage critically, as signifying past, present, and future simultaneously, at once critiquing the past and showing how the present has been built on such unsteady foundations. Pastiche yearns for an auratic past; parody plays in the fissures and cracks that result from showing how kitschy objects are arbitrary and lose their cultural meanings. In Waters' films, a tension arises in the viewer, who must negotiate between the nostalgia caused by seeing the kitsch of the past that litters the background of his films and the parody caused by the critical recycling of Hollywood narratives about that world. Waters' films are so difficult and cause their viewers to not always know how to respond, because they are simultaneously pastiche and parody.

The films' engagement with and parodic reworking of Hollywood melodramas and popular culture narratives create what Walter Metz has called a "queering effect"[18] and Emmanuel Levy has, following Barbara Klinger, labeled "mass camp." Levy explains:

> From the start, Waters politicized camp, using it as a deliberate assault on mainstream culture. He employed gay camp as a counter-cultural means, as an oppositional standpoint and active force. For him, camp attacks acceptable values, normal physical appearances, and conventional modes of behavior. It could be either a mild or a radical rejection of essential tenets of traditional aesthetics. Waters' brand of camp thrives on exaggeration, theatricality, and travesty, as is evident in the glorification of the characters in his texts and the particular actors who play them. The elements of his aesthetics are deemed cheap, sleazy, vulgar, and crude because the plots of his features transgress the bourgeois sense of decency and morality. Instead, they loudly extol bizarre and grotesque sexuality that's considered appalling by standards of middle-class taste.[19]

The political attack extends to the realm of film analysis itself. When we watch a Waters film, we feel that we're in another place, outside the realm where film criticism and theory usually resides.

How, then, does one go about categorizing these campy, parodic films that defy categorization and queer even the idea of the auteur's overarching vision? This collection challenges conventional methods of structuring the work of filmmakers, by organizing the collection thematically with a long gaze at the films' camp and queering effects that thwart attempts at classification. It draws on and expands upon well-established and less established threads about how Waters uses his awareness of film conventions, genres, and stylistic features in creating artistic identity and narratives, expressing and defining his own version of filmmaking. Chapters cover the films' intersections with other arts and his adoption of the storytelling tropes of melodrama. Other chapters assess Waters' personal filmmaking practice, whether through his use of visual style or sound, or in his reliance on autobiography. Still others place the films in conversation with the work of other filmmakers, including those he admires and his contemporaries. Where appropriate, chapters have considered the reception of the films outside of a traditional U.S. context, which culminates in the collection's final chapter, which examines the audience for Waters in a London theater. Finally, a series of interviews with Waters and the Dreamlanders allows the filmmakers to speak on their own conception of their work and creative processes. As such, *Refocus: The Films of John Waters* offers a collection of chapters that surround the topic of the films of John Waters, considering them from a variety of thematic, stylistic, and contextual approaches.

The first section of the book, "Authorial Identity, Aesthetics, and Style," places Waters' films in a larger context of the art form itself; to this end, the chapters examine how Waters uses his awareness of film conventions, genres, stylistic features, and the very idea of practice. The volume opens with Jamie Hook's consideration of the influence of melodrama—in many ways the most pervasive and representative of Hollywood genres—across the films. He shows how Waters incorporates not only Hollywood A-list pictures, but also juvenile delinquent exploitation melodramas and auteur productions that would go on to be evaluated in the terms of art cinema, and, finally, studio melodramas made during the fall of the Hays Code. In Chapter 2, Matt Connolly highlights the broader value of extratextual analysis of a director's career, underscoring how seemingly "secondary" materials can prove as foundational to a filmmaker's identity and development as the "primary" filmic texts that so often occupy scholarly study. He considered how an analysis of Waters' 80s-era extratextual output redefines the commercial success of *Hairspray* as an extension of (and not a break from) his work throughout the decade. Chapter 3 shows how *Serial Mom* mocks how horror was slowly turned safe and sanitized in the 1980s. Gabriel Fernando Pagnoni Berns and Canela Ailen Rodriguez Fontao argue that he resorts to a double strategy, privileging gory horror and using a meta approach to discuss the collapse of a certain type of horror during that era.

Chapters 4, 5, and 6 examine the ways the later films reflect on Waters' status as artist and commercially successful filmmaker. In Chapter 4, Kristen Galvin takes *Pecker* (1998) as departure point and examines Waters' unusual navigation between, and fluid crossing of, the contemporary art world and Hollywood through tactics of camp humor that poke fun at both, as his own "life as art/art as life" strategy of "guilty pleasure." Chapter 5, by John Bray, asserts that *Pecker* is a deeply personal film which considers the complexities of auteurship and stands between the then-and-now for Waters: the yesteryear life of a young man who has not yet experienced fame, and Waters as the celebrated icon he has become. In Chapter 6, Brian Brems considers how *Cecil B. Demented* (2000) examines the role that film style plays in Waters' work both in his early independent films and in his studio work. The chapter offers detailed stylistic analysis of Waters' film practice, including insights about how *A Dirty Shame* provides insight both into stable features of his style and those that evolve over time and according to varying budgetary limitations. In Chapter 7, the final chapter of the section, Nicholas Morgan analyzes the underground, camp, and queer dimensions of Waters' cinematic output through the lens of his writings on visual art and his own efforts in sculpture and photography. Morgan considers photocollages like *Illusion-O* (2014) to make his claim about subcultural and marginal forms of cinema explicit, appropriating stills from William Castle's *13 Ghosts* (1960) in a way that both exacerbates and celebrates the film's gimmicky, over-the-top brand of camp horror.

The second section of the book, "Collaboration, Subversion, and Queering the Family" considers how Waters collaborates with culture, placing the filmmaker in the context of community, his "Gang." It positions Waters as a collaborator, a not-auteur, and someone who deliberately and carefully undermines the idea of the auteur by queering the very structures it relies on to have meaning. Chris Holmland's Chapter 8 centers around interviews conducted with *Female Trouble*'s cast and crew in 2015. Mink Stole, George Figgs, Pat Moran, Mary Vivian Pearce, and Vincent Peranio and Delores Deluxe. She points out the collaborative filmmaking process of the early years and that "Waters has no problem admitting that he does not and never did have all the answers." In Chapter 9, Kate Russell takes on the difficult subject of Waters' engagement with the Manson Family. She does so "not to open old wounds, but to read it through Waters' evolving attitude and preoccupations, and to situate his work within the wider sociohistorical contexts in which it was produced." In Chapter 10, Sony Jalarajan Raj and Adith K. Suresh explore Waters' depiction of motherhood in his films and examine how distinct characters, with their complex gender identity and sexual preferences, negotiate with the universal identity of the mother. They argue that in doing so, the films create a form of revulsion by differentiating the abject mother from the normative mother, which is emblematic of the arbitrary existence of established popular identities that in themselves are embodiments of a conservative dominant ideology.

In Chapter 11, Hollis Griffin illustrates how Waters' movies feature familiar stock characters and plots, well-established syntactic arrangements in shot sequences, and strategic use of sound and music to provide metacommentary on midcentury television and the social mores associated with the medium during that era. In bringing television to the fore in this way, the chapter complicates common understandings of Waters' work and his influences. The section ends with Jane Giles' analysis in Chapter 12 of the Scala! theater, considering the broader question of how audience group behavior can contribute to the meaning of the film itself, using Waters' work as a prism to explore the idea that our future filmmakers and artists are inspired and influenced by the experience of watching in a heightened environment.

The third and final section will feature the interview the editors conducted with John Waters at his home in Baltimore, Maryland on November 2, 2023. The substantive discussion sheds additional light on the subjects covered in each of the book's preceding chapters, and allows Waters himself the opportunity to comment on many of the same areas of focus chosen by the chapters' authors. Its organizational placement gives Waters the final word on his own career and serves as a valuable complement to the work done in the other sections of the book.

This volume is the first to focus solely on the iconoclastic director, writer, and artist's contributions to cinema, with academic work on the entirety of his filmography. *Refocus: The Films of John Waters* aims to correct the long-standing critical overlooking of Waters' work. In this effort, the volume joins The Academy Museum of Motion Pictures exhibit—*The Pope of Trash*—and The Criterion Collection, which has recently restored editions of many of Waters' most challenging films. Waters' long career deserves more attention than we have devoted in these pages, and it is my co-editor's and my hope that these collected chapters are not the final word on this important filmmaker.

NOTES

1. Rita Braver, "John Waters, Conoisseur of Quirky Art," *CBS News.com* (March 12, 2023), https://www.cbsnews.com/news/john-waters-art-collector-baltimore-museum-of-art/
2. "Camp John Waters 2024," *Events.com*, https://events.com/r/en_US/registration/camp-john-waters-2024-kent-september-915361
3. Jenny He and Dara Jaffe, eds., *John Waters: Pope of Trash* (Academy Museum of Motion Pictures, Los Angeles: Delmonico Books, 2023), 5.
4. "John Waters New Film *Eat Your Makeup* Also *Short Circuit. . . .*" *Boohooray*, https://www.boo-hooray.com/pages/books/6477/john-waters/john-waters-new-film-eat-your-makeup-also-short-circuit-teenage-mutant-ninja-turtles?soldItem=true
5. Manny Farber, "Underground Films; A Bit of Male Truth," *Commentary* (November, 1957) https://www.commentary.org/articles/manny-farber/underground-filmsa-bit-of-male-truth/.
6. Stan VanDerBeek, "The Cinema Delimina: Films from the Underground Author," *Film Quarterly* 14, no. 4 (Summer 1961): 8.

7. "John Waters New Film *Eat Your Makeup* Also *Short Circuit. . . .*"
8. Brian Brooks, "John Waters Looks Back and Forward Prior to His Film Society Retrospective," *FilmlincDaily* (September 5, 2014), https://www.filmlinc.org/daily/john-waters-interview-retrospective-film-society-2014/
9. Oliver Shaw, "That Time John Waters and Andy Warhol Unknowingly Parodied JFK's Assassination at the Same Time," *Interview* (August 21, 2019) https://www.interviewmagazine.com/film/that-time-john-waters-and-andy-warhol-unknowingly-parodied-jfks-assassination-at-the-same-time
10. See Joan Hawkins, "Sleaze Mania, Euro-Trash, and High Art: The Place of European Art Films in American Low Culture," *Film Quarterly* 53, no. 2 (1999): 14–29.
11. See Pierre Bourdieu, *Distinction: A Social Critique of the Judgement of Taste* (New York: Routledge, 1984) and Lawrence Levine, *Highbrow, Lowbrow: The Emergence of Cultural Hierarchy in America* (Cambridge, MA: Harvard University Press, 1990).
12. Pauline Kael, "Trash Art and the Movies," In *Going Steady: Film Writings, 1968–1969* (London: Marion Boyars, 1970), 87–129. Originally Published in *Harper's Magazine* (February 1969).
13. John Waters, *Crackpot* (New York: Scribner, 1983), 138.
14. Kaja Silverman, "The Female Authorial Voice," in *The Acoustic Mirror: The Female Voice in Psychoanalysis and Cinema* (Bloomington: Indiana University Press, 1988).
15. "John Waters," C. Grimaldis Gallery, https://www.cgrimaldisgallery.com/john-waters
16. "John Waters" Marianne Boesky Gallery, https://marianneboeskygallery.com/artists/64-john-waters/biography/
17. Linda Hutcheon, *The Politics of Postmodernism* (London: Routledge, 1989), 93.
18. Walter Metz, "John Waters Goes to Hollywood: A Poststructural Authorship Study," in *Authorship and Film*, edited by David A. Gerstner and Janet Staiger, 157–174 (New York: Routledge, 2003), 173.
19. Emanuel Levy, *Gay Directors, Gay Films?: Pedro Almodóvar, Terrence Davies, Todd Haynes, Gus Van Sant, John Waters* (New York, Columbia University Press, 2015), 289–290.

PART I

Authorial Identity, Aesthetics, and Style

CHAPTER 1

Multiple Melodramas: Melodramatic Influences and Their Uses in the Cinema of John Waters

Jamie Hook

Two blockbuster melodramas of the late 1950s feature scenes in which eruptions of domestic violence end in the devastation of the highly charged symbol of the Christmas tree. In the 1957 adaptation of Grace Metalious' scandalous bestseller *Peyton Place* (directed by Mark Robson), a recently decorated tree is upended when Selena Cross (Hope Lange) fights off before eventually killing her sexually abusive stepfather (Arthur Kennedy) when he unexpectedly returns to the small home she shares with her younger brother. A "solid plastic" tree that "should last at least ten years" is also toppled during an instance of familial discord in *A Summer Place* (Delmer Daves, 1959) when young Molly Jorgenson (Sandra Dee) is forcefully slapped by her mother (Constance Ford) during an argument after Molly returns from meeting the boyfriend she is forbidden from seeing. These scenes are not at all dissimilar to that which catalyzes the action of John Waters' *Female Trouble* (1974), a film that camps the domestic melodrama and the generational anxieties often depicted in films of the genre; in all three, the destruction of the tree represents a true crisis not only in the familial sphere, but also the larger social order for which it is metonymic.

In *Female Trouble*'s yuletide furor, it is no longer a young woman who bears the brunt of the Christian familial order as it comes literally crashing down around her, but rather the parents of delinquent high schooler Dawn Davenport (Divine, né Harris Glenn Milstead), who refused their daughter the one present she most coveted: cha-cha heels. No longer the result of parental abuse, here it is the daughter's serious fury over the disgracefully frivolous that brings down the tree. "Not on Christmas!" is all Mrs. Davenport (Betty Woods) can moan from beneath as Dawn flees her family home forever. Here Waters taps into the cultural semiotics of the 1950s family melodrama and transposes its values in a way that can open a cathartic interpretative path for queer or otherwise counterculturally positioned viewers, those whose own lived experiences of family politics and the Christian holiday are potentially quite different from the cultural norm the original symbolism presumes, and which is necessary for its dramatic and moral authority to be sustained.[1]

This particular scene highlights several aspects of Waters' cinema germane to this chapter: its tone and style are highly emblematic of Waters' filmmaking sensibilities at large; it continues to enjoy recognition and cultural circulation within queer media ecosystems (including internet memes and a 2015 episode of *RuPaul's Drag Race* [MTV, 2009–]); and, most relevant here, it vividly demonstrates how Waters regularly *made use of* lavish Hollywood melodrama in his independent, underground filmmaking, even before he began working with larger budgets and so-called Indiewood studios like New Line Cinema. Indeed, the influence of melodrama – in many ways the most pervasive and representative of Hollywood genres – across Waters' oeuvre is robust. What follows will examine how Waters' early feature films reveal an egalitarian understanding of this vexed term and some of the ends to which it has been put by one of cinema's true iconoclasts. While the domestic melodrama as illustrated above is understandably the most common reference point in the work of Waters (and this is when it is acknowledged as a noteworthy influence on his filmmaking at all), there is value in tracing out how a more variegated range of melodramatic influences manifest themselves across his filmography in terms that also engage questions of genre, narrative, spectatorship, and ideology. Looking at these other forms, the multiple melodramas that comprise Waters' sphere of reference as concerns this specific genre or mode, reveals how his use of the melodramatic produces sometimes unexpected correspondences between film forms and production contexts often thought to occupy very different positions within film history and across cultural taste hierarchies.

MELODRAMA'S MOORINGS: A VERY BRIEF DEFINITIONAL HISTORY

Even when confined to the realm of the cinematic, melodrama is a notoriously difficult word to define. One reason for this is that it has an intrinsic impulse to balloon outward, pulling more and more narrative tropes and representational strategies into its orbit. "[E]verybody has some idea of what is meant by 'melodramatic,'" claimed early theorist Thomas Elsaesser.[2] More so than most other genres, these ideas have been shaped by film history and theory itself. John Mercer and Martin Shingler detail how from the consolidation of the U.S. film industry at the outset of the 1910s through 1970 (serendipitously, the year Waters directed *Multiple Maniacs*, his first feature-length, "talkie" film), industry insiders and trade journalists used the term to denote action-oriented films across genres ranging from what we now recognize as westerns, crime/gangster films, and noir. "Ironically," they posit, "what Film Studies has come to regard as 'melodrama' since 1970 are films with more words than action, inactive male protagonists, active and even domineering female characters, and anything but clear-cut and easily identifiable villains," a definition that has in turn "been adopted by Hollywood filmmakers, reviewers and journalists."[3]

Expanding its definitional sweep further are those influential works by Linda Williams, Jackie Byars, and others, who position melodrama "as a mode [that] pervades many genres," recalling this originary industry usage while conditioning it in accordance with developments in Marxist, psychoanalytic, and feminist film theories.[4] Scholar Thomas Schatz, for instance, argues that *all* Hollywood films are in practice melodramas,[5] while Williams goes broader still in her analysis of how melodrama constitutes "a central *mode* of American popular culture," "an evolving mode of storytelling crucial to the establishment of moral good."[6] Even so, the definition that has received the most analytical traction in film studies is that which categorically delineates the "women's" melodramas defined by Schatz as those "popular romances that depicted a virtuous individual (usually a woman) or couple (usually lovers) victimized by repressive and inequitable social circumstances, particularly those involving marriage, occupation, and the nuclear family."[7] These popular works of the 1950s—exemplified for many by Douglas Sirk's late films for Universal International—in Schatz's words, "projected [a] complex and paradoxical . . . view of America, at once celebrating and severely questioning the basic values and attitudes of the mass audience," making them "among the most socially self-conscious and covertly 'anti-American' films ever produced by the Hollywood studios."[8]

WATERS AND MELODRAMA

What Schatz ascribes to melodrama of the '50s is remarkably resonant with Waters' modus operandi throughout the 1970s and into the '80s prior to a seven-year hiatus between *Polyester* (1981) and his first PG-rated film, the mainstream hit *Hairspray* (1988). Waters quickly gained recognition for the way his films reveled in a decidedly tawdry Americana (as reflected in the very titles *Pink Flamingos* [1972] and *Polyester*), while simultaneously reproaching the culture's surplus repressions[9] in correspondingly vulgar terms. In his efforts to *épater la bourgeoisie*, melodrama's own paradoxes and complexities aided Waters' freewheeling incorporation of discordant generic intertexts across forms and iterations that reflect their own industrial histories and culturally stratified taste registers: multiple melodramas, if you will.

Critics and fans alike widely recognize that Waters' films are deliriously overcrowded in their range and layering of filmic citations and influences, a natural outgrowth of his authorial persona as a cinephile who possesses an encyclopedic knowledge that encircles both "high" and "low" film cultures. Even so, he continues to be (not incorrectly) associated most with the midnight movie culture out of which he emerged in the late 1960s, a filmic habitus that certainly contributed to his trash aesthetic and reputation as a cult auteur via perceived affinities with William Castle, Herschell Gordon Lewis, and the like, alongside the queer anarchisms of Kenneth Anger, Jack Smith, and others. Perhaps because of Waters' continued reign as the Pope of Trash (a moniker that has held even in the face of increased industry sanctification as evidenced by, say, his 2023 induction to the Hollywood Walk of Fame), somewhat less discernible are his equally formative inheritances from melodramas of classical Hollywood, including those with which we opened and countless others. When writings on Waters do make such connections, they are at many times fleeting and sometimes unspoken. To take one such implicit example, in their seminal book *Midnight Movies*, J. Hoberman and Jonathan Rosenbaum note Dawn Davenport's "elaborate parodies of distraught motherhood,"[10] a description which immediately calls to mind a character like Mildred Pierce (Joan Crawford) in Michael Curtiz's 1945 film of the same name, or Lora Meredith (Lana Turner) of Douglas Sirk's 1959 film *Imitation of Life*, in which a candid photograph of her taken early in the film is even called "Mother in Distress" by the photographer.

Matthew Tinkcom is one scholar who has explicitly directed attention towards the presence of melodrama in Waters' films, arguing that their "ironic features . . . mark a counterknowledge . . . to the value codings within popular cinema itself" and likening Waters' fascination with "the melodrama or 'women's picture'" to queer auteurs of international arthouse cinema, such as Germany's Rainer Werner Fassbinder and Spain's Pedro Almodóvar.[11] Stating that Waters' "films recognize the history of film melodrama heroines as they have been situated in camp readings for their performative excess of costume, speech, and gesture,"[12] he ultimately maintains a clear *generic* distinction concluding, "Waters directs comedies, not melodramas. Or more to the point, he directs comedies *about* melodramas."[13]

This compact distillation of Waters' complex generic intertextuality—that is, how his films cite both discrete texts in addition to the codes, conventions, and iconographies of entire genre systems—still begs the questions: *What* melodramas are Waters' comedies actually about and *how* are they about them? Here it is helpful to remember Derek Kane-Meddock's argument that, as opposed to "single genre parody," "generic multiplicity allows Waters to mock not just the conventions of [individual subgenres or film cycles] but also the limitations of predictable Hollywood storytelling."[14] While Waters' films are nothing if not melodramatic and comedic, for many spectators they are also shockingly graphic and at times horrific. This recalls melodrama's inclusion as one of Linda Williams' three "body genres," alongside horror and pornography, in her now canonical essay.[15] Waters might fairly be described as the ultimate body genre filmmaker, given how his oeuvre (and many individual films within) bring together all three: pornography (e.g., the unsimulated sex acts and maximum visual display of the body in *Pink Flamingos*, *Female Trouble*, and *Desperate Living* [1977]), horror (e.g., the not infrequent eruptions of gore and severed body parts at least from *Mondo Trasho* [1969] onward, culminating in the slasher-influenced *Serial Mom* [1994]) and, of course, melodrama. All three genres spectacularize the body through representing it "caught in the grip of intense sensation or emotion" and, in turn, see "the body of the spectator . . . caught up in an almost involuntary mimicry of the emotion or sensation of the body on the screen."[16] Distinct from her later analysis of melodrama as an all-pervasive mode, in this earlier piece Williams focuses on the melodramatic form of "'the woman's film' or 'weepie.'"[17] As tearjerkers, these films share in the cultural imaginary what Williams describes as "an apparent lack of proper esthetic distance, a sense of over-involvement in sensation and emotion."[18] Waters in effect launched his entire career by annihilating any such possibility of remove and encouraging a visceral reaction to his films from nonconformist spectators who were often left exhilarated and agog (if not also aghast).

This is concretized in something like the complementary barf bags made to accompany screenings of *Pink Flamingos*, which upon release was called "surely one of the most vile, stupid and repulsive films ever made"[19] (a supposed indictment that Waters quickly snapped up to use in the film's highly successful marketing campaign). Its original theatrical trailer infamously contains no footage from the film itself; instead, it showcases a variety of reactions from individuals who have just exited a screening, many of whom describe their experiences precisely in terms of affect and sensation: "The most disgusting thing I've ever seen in my whole life," "It was a little gross, but I liked it," and "I enjoy dirty things as much as everyone else does, but this isn't even dirty, it's just disgusting."

As Peter Stallybrass and Allon White have theorized, "what is *socially* peripheral is so frequently *symbolically* central."[20] Or, as another *Pink Flamingos* spectator propounded, "I think John Waters has got his finger on the pulse of America. I think he's got his thumb securely up America's ass." As a flash point of uniquely American social ills, discontents, and neuroses in the latter years of the Vietnam War and the representational free-for-all of the sexual revolution, *Pink Flamingos* is the film that marked a pivotal moment in Waters' career. After the bargain-basement, black-and-white aesthetic of his first two features, *Mondo Trasho* and *Multiple Maniacs* (1970), whose plots moved more or less episodically from one appalling set piece to the next, Waters began making (still microbudget) films with more clearly defined character motivations (however outlandish) and narrative arcs (however untamed). Melodrama provided a perfect frame for this more continuity-driven style, as it still allowed and even encouraged the excess—of situation, performance style, and attitude—with which Waters' name was already synonymous.

While classical Hollywood melodrama may seem hoary and naïve by contemporary interpretive codes (qualities that, for decades now, have primed it for camp readings),[21] in the zeitgeist of the sexual revolution Waters restaged and plumbed the depths of a genre that was no stranger to representing filthy behavior. His characters took the worst impulses of their Production Code-bound forebearers and ran amok in Waters' independently financed, less-restrained Dreamland; consider, for instance, the "spiritual" correspondence forged between *Written on the Wind* (Douglas Sirk, 1956)'s Marylee Hadley (Dorothy Malone), who, by her own admission, is "filthy—period" and Babs Johnson (Divine)'s extolment that "Filth are my politics; filth is my life!" in *Pink Flamingos*. If Waters' films were free to build their reputation on their "bad" taste, they did so at least partly through reactivating classical melodrama's own penchant for persistently flirting with the bounds of "good" taste. It may be a shock to see a baby tumble out of the refrigerator in which it was misplaced by its sitter in Waters' *Desperate Living*, but exactly how much more outrageous is this than the neglected baby who sets himself aflame in the late studio era *Susan Slade* (Delmer Daves, 1961)? This particular melodrama—and its "one big shock scene"—was the object of one of Waters' "re-directing" jobs ("Slade 16," 1992), constructed by "photographing a favorite movie the way [he wanted] to remember it, no matter what the original director had in mind" [22] and incarnating for public consumption through a curated series of stills these personal readings, which are at once highly idiosyncratic while firmly situated vis-à-vis traditions of gay male camp.

"Male homosexuals," writes gay critic Paul Roen from the vantage of the 1990s, "have always been devoted fans of the melodrama . . . because of the opportunities it provides for identification with the heroine . . . The camp quality usually lurks in the highly improbable, extravagant dilemmas which comprise the plots of these films, and in the heroine's histrionic response to her various and assorted troubles. Generally speaking, the more turgid, trite, and overwrought her travails, the better."[23] Similarly, queer theorist Alexander Doty notes that melodrama "actually encourage[s] queer positioning as [it] exploit[s] the spectacle of heterosexual romance, straight domesticity, and traditional gender roles gone awry."[24] Such a reading formation no doubt guided Waters' selection of filmic scraps to isolate and aggrandize through photography in these later art projects, which are anticipated by his earlier films' exaggerations of what was always already excessive in the forerunners he clearly reveres. For example, in *Hilda Crane* (Philip Dunne, 1956), the domineering

Mrs. Burns (Evelyn Varden) forces herself into the title character's home minutes before Hilda (Jean Simmons) is to leave for the church where she is due to marry Mrs. Burns' son. Astonishing in its own context is Mrs. Burns' eruption as she begins to pulverize Hilda's bridal bouquet. In Waters' interpretation of the melodramatic form, emotions are already at an eternal fever pitch so that when *Female Trouble*'s Aunt Ida (Edith Massey) bursts in on Dawn (whose marriage to her nephew, Gator, she has likewise forcefully opposed), her action must be magnified accordingly; here her revolt takes the form of a jar of acid flung into Dawn's face, her visage itself bearing the brunt of the fury that in the earlier film was merely visited upon the flowers. I will now consider *Female Trouble* in more depth, as it is likely the most fully realized expression of Waters' use of melodrama at its most multitudinous.

FEMALE TROUBLE (1974)

Upon its release, *Variety* declared, "Regular commercial chances are dubious, but as an offbeat, specialized attraction, 'Female Trouble' has no competition."[25] Melodrama has long proven itself simpatico with exploitation, a mode of production described by Eric Schaefer as a "shadow cinema" to Hollywood's norms.[26] Previously geared towards (and sometimes implementing policies to compel) adult-only audiences, post-World War II exploitation began courting teenage spectatorship. A newly distinct demographic, teens in the 1950s (Waters, on the periphery, turned thirteen in 1959) were "set apart from previous generations of American young people . . . There were more of them, they had more money, and they were more aware of themselves as teenagers."[27] Frequently programmed as double-bills and screened at drive-ins, teen exploitation often rooted adolescent storm and strife in melodrama, with Thomas Doherty noting how, as the decade progressed, films increasingly "mixed two or more exploitation items—rock 'n' roll, drag racing, high school vice—in inventive hybrids."[28] Miles apart aesthetically and in terms of production and exhibition practices while contemporaneous with Sirk's Universal films, such juvenile delinquent melodramas (of which Nicholas Ray's 1955 *Rebel Without a Cause* might be seen as the "upmarket" progenitor) are in fact closer in tone and style to Waters' own via their low budgets, rough-hewn formalism, mannered acting, and ability to skirt the boundaries of '50s "good" taste due to their already-outsider status as exploitation.

Before the family Christmastime scene with which we opened, *Female Trouble* has already established Dawn Davenport as a juvenile delinquent through a series of short scenes set at her Baltimore high school. Here she is part of a clique along with Chicklette (Susan Walsh) and Concetta (Cookie Mueller). Narratively they are defined as "bad girls" through costuming (Chicklette is

Figure 1.1 Dawn (Divine), Chicklette (Susan Walsh), and Concetta (Cookie Mueller) are defined as "bad girls" through costuming, behavior, and attitude in *Female Trouble* (1974).

told by their strict male teacher, "This is a classroom, not a cocktail lounge"), behavior (Concetta threatens to cut up a girl with a knife from her pocket book after the brownnoser calls attention to Dawn's eating of a meatball sandwich during class), and, most of all, attitude: while the three smoke and style their bouffant hairdos in the school bathroom, Dawn grumbles, "I hate this school and all these ignorant teachers who don't know one thing" (Figure 1.1).

Compare this to American International Pictures' *High School Hellcats* (Edward Bernds, 1958), which opens with three young women smoking in a school lavatory (Figure 1.2). A brief argument over how best to initiate a new girl into their pack leads to one throwing the knife with which she has been filing her nails into the door as the title explodes on screen. In the following scene, a disruption caused by students tossing textbooks around the room drives their male substitute home economics teacher to vacate the class, allowing bad girl Connie (Jana Lund) to approach transfer student Joyce (Yvonne Lime) and bluntly inform her, "There's a gang in this class. I'm the boss." The gang, Joyce soon learns, meets in an abandoned cinema and enforces rules that stipulate if members *must* pass their classes to avoid trouble at home, they should do so with grades no higher than a D. Ingénue Joyce becomes the conflicted heroine of this cautionary tale as she is caught up in the police investigation surrounding Connie's death at the hands of a fellow gang member. In its plea for parental attentiveness and renewed understanding between the generations, *High School Hellcats* venerates heterosexual romance and demonizes female friendship (in the film's universe, Joyce's only social alternative to

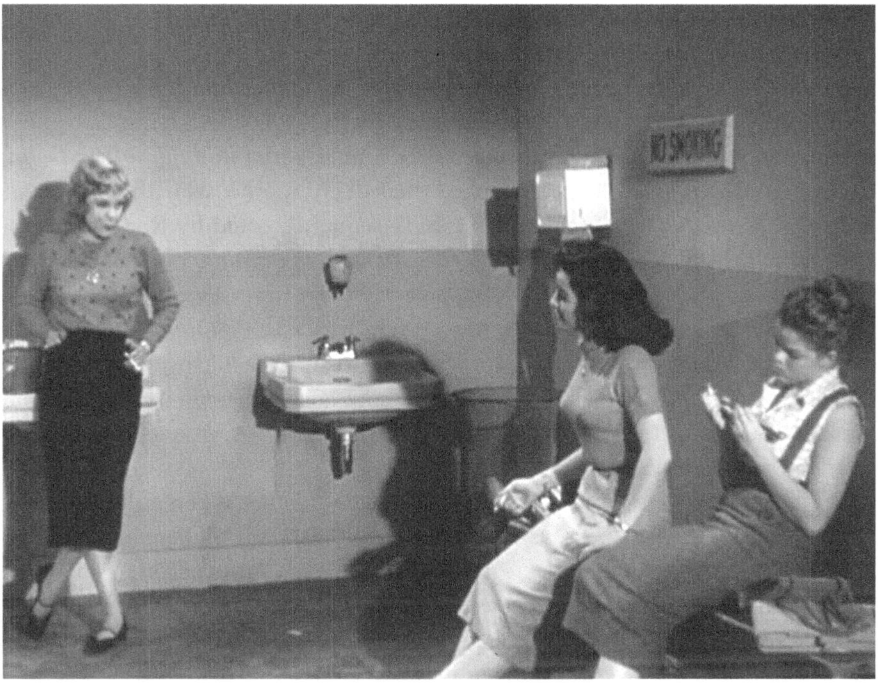

Figure 1.2 Hellcats Connie (Jana Lund), Meg (Heather Ames), and Dolly (Suzanne Sydney) smoke and argue in the school lavatory before class in the teen melodrama *High School Hellcats* (1958).

the aberrant Hellcats is the upstanding young man who works days at the soda fountain and attends night school for electrical engineering). *Female Trouble* trashes (in multiple senses of the word) the normative and didactic impulses found in this and other exploitation melodramas through magnification of their moral codings and the denial of *any* alternate path for Dawn other than to embrace her juvenile depravity with even more vigor as she comes of age, raises a daughter, and achieves public infamy.

As these opening sequences foreshadow, *Female Trouble* luxuriates in the incorporation of multiple melodramatic modes, drawing on more and more as it spins out in deliriously unhinged ways. Its major narrative arc, in which Dawn becomes a "crime model," evokes the confluence of show business and violence as represented in post-classical Hollywood melodramas made during and following the increasingly precipitous decline of the Motion Picture Production Code, such as *Inside Daisy Clover* (Robert Mulligan, 1965) and *The Day of the Locust* (John Schlesinger, 1975), both exposés of 1930s Tinseltown, and the highly influential *Valley of the Dolls* (Mark Robson, 1967), a film that has been read retroactively as "lurch[ing] precariously into John Waters territory."[29] The increasingly graphic, overwrought nature of such films led to melodrama's intensified association with camp and trash aesthetics throughout the '60s, crystalized in images like pink feather-clad Rina Marlowe (Carroll Baker) performing a striptease while literally swinging from a chandelier in *The Carpetbaggers* (Edward Dmytryk, 1964) or Neely O'Hara (Patty Duke) muttering "Boobies, boobies, boobies" as she walks through a red-light district in *Valley of the Dolls*. These "declassed" melodramas reached their likely apotheosis with *Beyond the Valley of the Dolls* (1970), an in-name-only sequel directed by Russ Meyer, a filmmaker held in high esteem by Waters. In many respects, this film reads as a slicker, more highly produced version of a Waters film; several of its motley party guests appear to be cut from the same cloth as Waters' Dreamlanders and, like most of Waters' own, it is a true generic mélange held together within a melodramatic frame. Its blood-soaked climax was also informed by the Manson murders, a personal obsession of Waters, whose early films are littered with references to Manson and his followers.

Violence and showbiz first unite in *Female Trouble* when salon owners Donald and Donna Dasher (David Lochary and Mary Vivian Pearce) convince Dawn to become a crime model, explaining, "You see, our experiment involves beauty and crime. We feel them to be one. We have a theory that crime enhances one's beauty. The worse the crime gets, the more ravishing one becomes. We want you to prove us right." During Dawn's "ascent," Van Smith's costumes and Vincent Peranio's set designs camp the Ross Hunter aesthetic[30] in their gauche "elegance" as Dawn's increasingly outré fashions and styling reflect her progressively monstrous deeds. The Dashers ply her with injections of liquid eyeliner and photograph her as she performs savage acts such as breaking a chair over her trembling daughter and severing her rival's hand. At the film's climax, Dawn performs an avant-garde stage show and cries out, "Who wants to die for art?" After shooting her first eager volunteer, she then begins firing at random into the crowd, who begin to flee the arena in a panic. Waters uses tropes of the showbiz melodrama (for example, the rise to stardom followed by the fall from grace, addiction, the glamorous star persona that masks internal demons, and so on) to lampoon those moralizing discourses of criminality traditionally used to manage political and sexual anarchists like *enfant terrible* Jean Genet, whose own iconoclastic ideas about the relationship between beauty, homosexuality, and criminality resonate with those of the Dashers.[31]

Ultimately, Dawn goes on trial for murder and is sentenced to death in the electric chair. The courtroom is certainly not an uncommon setting for melodrama and often appears near the conclusion (as it does here), at which point the interpersonal tribulations and rash actions of its characters can no longer be contained domestically and rupture outward into the public, legal sphere (see, for instance, *Madame X* [multiple versions, various directors], *Leave Her to Heaven* [John M. Stahl, 1945], *Written on the Wind*, [1956], *Peyton Place*, and *The Other Side of Midnight* [Charles Jarrott, 1977]). The relative realism of Dawn's sojourn on death row and culminating execution

(Waters secured permission to shoot in the Baltimore City Jail) invites comparison with Robert Wise's social issue melodrama *I Want to Live!* (1958), specifically the uncompromising finale with its forensic focus on the mechanics of the gas chamber. The film is based on newspaper articles and personal letters of accused murderer Barbara Graham, nicknamed Bloody Babs and here played by Susan Hayward in an Oscar-winning performance. (In this context, it is hard not to think of Divine's earlier star-making turn as Babs Johnson in *Pink Flamingos*, especially when a psychologist describes Graham as "totally amoral. A compulsive liar with no regard for law and order or the conventions of society." An essential difference between the characters, however, is Graham's "positive aversion" to physical violence.) *I Want to Live!* dramatizes the media circus surrounding Graham's trial and conviction, to which she caustically responds with wit and sarcasm. After her death sentence has been handed down, she snarls at a group of reporters, "I wanna thank the gentlemen of the press. You chewed me up in your headlines and all the jury had to do was spit me out. You're all invited to the execution!" And, as she readies herself in her cell the night before the execution, she insists, "I mustn't disappoint my public" while unpacking her "flaming scarlet" lounging pajamas.

In *Female Trouble*, Dawn takes Graham's irony-seeped defense mechanisms literally.[32] So unbalanced is she that she views her trial and conviction as marking her ascension to the pinnacle of the showbiz ladder: "My fans want me to die in the electric chair. It'll be my final curtain call, the most theatrical moment of my life." Just as Graham takes great care to put on earrings and bucks San Quentin's prohibition of shoes so she can wear her heels to the gas chamber as a final grasp at dignity, Dawn bemoans, "Oh, why won't they let me wear a gown and makeup today? Today of all days! My big moment in the electric chair." When this final moment comes, Dawn embraces her execution (her "big news event") in the form of an awards show acceptance speech as she is strapped into the chair, thanking those whose murders delivered her to this triumphant moment: "Without all of you, my career could never have gotten this far." In an outlandish spectacularization of melodrama's representation of "the oft-times nightmare world of show business,"[33] here the condemned criminal and prizewinning star are collapsed into one. The narrative of *Female Trouble*, then, shows how a high school hellcat becomes a mother in distress and falls so deeply into the valley of the dolls that she loses the common sense to proclaim, "I want to live!" Multiple melodramas, indeed.

POLYESTER (1981)

Julie Sanders has shown how "adaptations and appropriations (or mediations and remediations) can vary in how explicitly they state their intertextual purpose."[34] If *Female Trouble*'s appropriation of melodrama veers between more or less direct citations from sundry instantiations of the form (Technicolor Hollywood, black-and-white exploitation, gritty social commentary, camp spectacle, and more), with *Polyester* Waters offers a more sustained reading of a more circumscribed sphere of the melodramatic, the film conceived as an homage to the melodramas of Douglas Sirk. Even in this, Waters' most explicitly stated engagement with melodrama as a genre, his uses extend to other incarnations beyond the domestic as well as those definitions that reach beyond its formal, textual workings.

Polyester's intertextual rendezvous with the Sirkian melodrama announces itself from its opening shots as the credits run over aerial views of the town that will be the film's setting, mirroring those of Sirk's *All That Heaven Allows* (1955) (Figure 1.3). These picturesque hubs of social life are locations from which the heroines of both films will be societally excluded (in *Polyester* the Fishpaw family's house is revealed to be located at 538 Wyman Way, a nod to *All That Heaven Allows* and *Magnificent Obsession* [Douglas Sirk, 1954] star Jane Wyman). On the soundtrack, Tab Hunter croons the title song (recalling The Four Aces' "Written on the Wind" or Earl Grant's "Imitation of Life," which introduce the respective Sirk films that share their titles). In the manner of a pastiche, the song imitates these predecessors both melodically

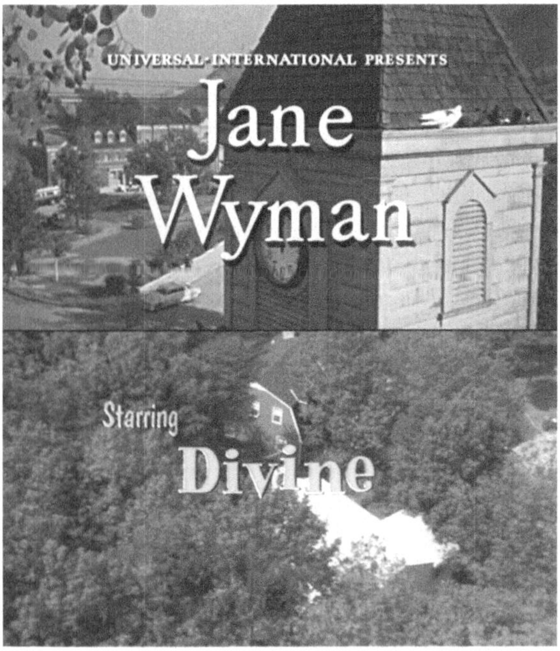

Figure 1.3 *Polyester* (1981) announces its intertextual engagement with Douglas Sirk's *All That Heaven Allows* (1955) from the opening credits.

and lyrically: "See the houses/Look at the trees swaying in the cool breeze/ Oh what a lovely street" narrates what viewers see on the screen, just as in *Written on the Wind*'s credit sequence a metaphoric reference to dying leaves accompanies shots of the same fallen outside the Hadley estate and blown dramatically through its open doorway. "Hey, why don't you come on in?" poses a direct question to *Polyester*'s viewers, just as *Imitation of Life*'s are asked to ponder, "What is love without the giving?" before being told, "Without love, you're only living an imitation." *Polyester*'s direct address and tracking camera continue, inviting us to "Come on upstairs/Meet your polyester queen" as we enter her boudoir and are introduced to heroine Francine Fishpaw in all of "the queered femininity of Divine bodaciousness, one with all the busted-girdle seams showing."[35]

Here and throughout the film references only to reverse the iconographies and attendant ideologies of home and family as represented in the domestic melodrama. Despite being the perfect nuclear family (comprised of dad, mom, son, daughter, and dog), the Fishpaws are a morally debased group, excepting mother Francine who, in a total reversal of Divine's star image hitherto, is a relentlessly put-upon, devoutly Christian housewife. "You bought this house with the profits of porno," she laments to her husband Elmer (David Samson), owner of the town's adult movie theatre, thus indicting the family's surface-level achievement of the American Dream as itself corrupt. Her daughter, Lu-Lu (Mary Garlington), earns pocket money by dancing for boys during the school lunch hour (her frenzied shimmying and gyrating around the house can be read in this generic context as an expansion of Marylee's infamous "Temptation" dance in *Written on the Wind*), fails her classes, and becomes pregnant with the child of her hooligan boyfriend. Her son, Dexter (Ken King), sniffs glue and is a foot fetishist who assails women only to stomp their feet as they go about their errands. The relationship between Francine and her children inverts the antagonisms visited upon widowed Cary Scott (Jane Wyman) in *All That Heaven Allows*, wherein her grown children come to embody the tedious bourgeois conformity from which Cary attempts to break free, while in *Polyester* they are unabashed delinquents who frustrate Francine's desire for a conventional middle-class life.

Later, when Francine's only friend, Cuddles Kovinsky (Edith Massey), visits, Cuddles declares, "This house is just like *Architectural Digest*!" Her observation draws attention to melodrama's emphasis on interior spaces; of course, the house Waters and his crew secured for their location is a far cry from, say, the Frank Lloyd Wright-designed home that features prominently in the second half of *A Summer Place* or even the upper-middle-class environs of *All That Heaven Allows*. Furthering such ironic treatment of spatial symbolism, Cuddles later takes Francine on a picnic and proclaims, "There must be a God! Everything is so beautiful! . . . Happiness is a picnic in the woods!" An association with nature defines gardener Ron Kirby (Rock Hudson)—described as a living embodiment of Thoreau's *Walden*—against the society types in *All That Heaven Allows*, a distinction that animates the film's romantic conflict. In *Written on the Wind*, a bucolic swimming hole symbolizes the characters' lost innocence when incompatible would-be lovers Mitch (Hudson again) and Marylee return to picnic. In *Polyester*, an ant infestation and wandering skunk soon undermine the purity of the natural landscape that provides the site for the picnic, concurrently infesting the purity of the Sirkian generic code as it is evoked herein. Early Sirk scholar Paul Willemen describes how "some of the films have strong parodic elements in them," a strategy most clearly seen in Sirk's "deliberate use of *cliché*."[36] If "Sirk's films distanciate themselves from the bourgeois ideology" through the ironic deployment of clichéd signifiers (the perfectly timed appearance of a gentle deer at the hopeful conclusion of *All That Heaven Allows*, for instance), Waters renders the symbolism literal, trotting out a skunk to declare in no uncertain terms that the use of nature as an overused salve for society's abuses quite plainly *stinks*.

Polyester is replete with narrative complications including social ostracism, juvenile delinquency, maternal abuse, upward mobility through inheritance, adultery, divorce, alcoholism, a nervous breakdown, abortion, attempted suicide, alimony theft, and murder. Any of these alone could sustain the central narrative arc—and requisite emotional excess—of a classical Hollywood melodrama, but are here unreasonably compiled one on top of the other such that the sum total is an excess of excesses. This hyperbolic presentation serves to underscore the constructed nature of all such plots, simultaneously functioning as camp parody and forging yet another direct referential link to Sirk, who "chose to shape his material in such a way that it repeatedly called attention to its own artifice."[37] The film's final moments drive the point home. After Francine's abusive ex-husband, his secretary-turned-paramour, Francine's duplicitous new lover, and her equally treacherous mother have all met violent deaths, she embraces and holds her now-reformed children in front of their home; the family has been purified at last. Having overcome the melodramas that have besieged them, Francine affirms, "Everything smells so much better now," as she sprays an *artificially* scented aerosol air freshener.[38] "The endings of Sirk's melodramas, due in part to the contrivances of the *deus ex machina* resolutions," explain Mercer and Shingler, "often feel rather artificial, and a recurring feature in the films is the 'false happy ending.'"[39] Here Waters seizes the dramatic artifice of Sirk's ironically happy endings as they have been interpreted critically, and again literalizes it through this symbol of American devotion to the synthetic (paralleling the film's title). In this way, Waters not only uses Sirk's films for narrative and symbolic fodder, but also alludes to critical reading strategies that had developed around them at roughly the same time Waters was coming into his own as a filmmaker, thereby dramatizing the interpretive act itself.

Thinking, then, about the discursive construction of melodrama's varied meanings, other non-Sirkian aspects of *Polyester* become legible as emanating from the melodramatic all the same. For instance, Ben Singer's historiographic research examining stage and screen melodramas from around the turn of the last century documents how, in contrast to literally homebound family melodrama, these nail-biters instead offered "an emphasis on action, violence, thrills, awesome sights, and spectacles of physical peril."[40] While certainly not played "straight," filtered as it is through Waters' permeating camp sensibility, under this historical frame of reference even something like *Polyester*'s bus hijacking, accomplished by a minor character with no bearing on the rest of the narrative, becomes as much a part of the film's use of melodrama as its obvious Sirkian influences. So too does the auto accident site at which Francine meets her lover, Todd Tomorrow (Tab Hunter), who calls her over to get a better look at the severed head on the road. Singer cites an 1890 essay in *Harper's Weekly* that avowed, "Melodrama . . . must reek with gore" and a Pennsylvania film censor for whom "the basis of a melodrama" was its "[devotion] to the exploitation of crime."[41] These earlier definitions—having lost their generic purchase under the sign of Sirk and others—also open up an understanding of *Polyester*'s gruesome, action-packed climax (in which Francine's antagonists are variously shot, strangled with macramé, and vehicularly crushed) and the fascination with criminality seen both here and across Waters' filmography writ large as part of melodrama's lineage to the same extent as the Sirkian aerial shots and lilting theme song that opened the film. In this way, *Polyester*'s use of melodrama is rooted in a deeper engagement with Sirkian systems of meaning and the broader melodramatic field of which they are a part than merely its burlesqued suburban nostalgia and general "over-the-topness."

CONCLUSION

Singer's discussion of sensation reminds us how the very earliest cinematic melodramas were predicated on "an attempt to commodify strong stimulus, an attempt to package the sensory and emotional excitement of agitating suspense, startling surprise, [and] rapid action . . . "[42] From the *Pink Flamingo* barf bags to *Polyester*'s release in Odorama, Waters also made the commodification of "strong stimulus" something of a stock-in-trade. What the public devours, the critical establishment has often decried, which also connects Waters to reception histories of certain melodrama forms. As Singer points out, silent film serial melodrama "suffered often vehement critical disdain because of its emphasis on violent action, highly formulaic and disjointed narratives, lack of psychological depth, and appeal to a mass 'lowbrow' audience . . ."[43] While not all of these grievances find direct parallels in early critical dismissals of Waters' films, many of them—disjointed narratives, lack of depth, and appeal to the "wrong" kinds of audiences—definitely echo.

And, as Klinger reminds, "Sirk's films generally fared badly in the press when they were first shown. However, a much different situation arose in the 1970s, when popular critics, after having assimilated auteurism, extolled these films as the work of a bona fide artist."[44] Thus Sirk found critical redemption throughout the decade Waters rose to notoriety. Much as developments in feminist film theory animated early scholarly interest in "women's films" and melodrama, so too has the attention paid to LGBTQ+ film production and audiences along with queer theory provided a series of frameworks for thinking about Waters as a singular artist while also connecting him to histories of gay male cinephilia of an earlier era, that which primed the pump for the uses and abuses of all that Hollywood had to offer independent and outsider filmmakers when at last they grabbed the means of production for themselves.

In *Female Trouble*, as everything unravels at the dinner party Dawn throws for the Dashers, Donna jubilantly exclaims, "Just think of all the little horror stories that go on in other people's lives!" It is easy to imagine a young Waters feeling much the same in his earliest encounters with the trashiest aspects of classical era melodramas, those that would go on to inform his unorthodox sensibility and leave an indelible imprint on his own films as they trashed, celebrated, expanded, and queered the genre's catalog of human aspirations and agonies. Alexander Doty registers the lexical ability of the words *queer/queerness* "to describe those complex circumstances in texts, spectators, and production that resist easy categorization, but that definitely escape or defy the heteronormative."[45] Looked at in this way, Waters' disdain for neat categorization, predilection for genres resistant to the same, and voracious appetite for cinematic influences of all breeds have no doubt contributed to the enduring queer relevance and rebellious impact of his films. As Sirk's Lora Meredith says, "I want more. Everything! Maybe too much."

NOTES

1. A slightly altered version of the above appears in my dissertation *Adapting for a Revolution: Media Adaptation Practices and the Sexual Revolution* (Indiana University, Bloomington, 2021).
2. Thomas Elsaesser, "Tales of Sound and Fury: Observations on the Family Melodrama," in *Home is Where the Heart Is: Studies in Melodrama and the Woman's Film*, edited by Christine Gledhill (London: BFI Publishing, 1987), 43.
3. John Mercer and Martin Shingler, *Melodrama: Genre, Style, Sensibility* (London and New York: Wallflower Press, 2004), 6.
4. Jackie Byars, *All That Hollywood Allows: Re-reading Gender in 1950s Melodrama* (Chapel Hill and London: The University of North Carolina Press, 1991), 11.

5. Thomas Schatz, *Hollywood Genres: Formulas, Filmmaking, and the Studio System* (New York: McGraw-Hill, 1981), 221–222.
6. Linda Williams, *Playing the Race Card: Melodramas of Black and White from Uncle Tom to O. J. Simpson* (Princeton and Oxford: Princeton University Press, 2001), xiv, 12 (emphasis in original).
7. Schatz, *Hollywood Genres*, 222.
8. Ibid., 223, 225.
9. My use of this term comes from Robin Wood's explanation that, whereas basic repression is necessary to co-exist with other humans, "*surplus* repression makes us into monogamous heterosexual bourgeois patriarchal capitalists . . . that is, *if* it works. If it doesn't the result is either a neurotic or a revolutionary (or both) . . ." Robin Wood, *Hollywood from Vietnam to Regan* (New York: Columbia University Press, 1986), 71 (emphases in original).
10. J. Hoberman and Jonathan Rosenbaum, *Midnight Movies* (New York: Da Capo Press, 1983), 160.
11. Matthew Tinkcom, *Working Like a Homosexual: Camp, Capital, Cinema* (Durham and London: Duke University Press, 2002), 156–157.
12. Ibid., 158.
13. Ibid., 177 (emphasis in original).
14. Derek Kane-Meddock, "Trash Comes Home: Gender/Genre Subversion in the Films of John Waters," in *Gender Meets Genre in Postwar Cinemas*, edited by Christine Gledhill (Urbana, Chicago, and Springfield: University of Illinois Press, 2012), 214–215.
15. Linda Williams. "Film Bodies: Gender, Genre, and Excess," *Film Quarterly* 44, no. 4 (Summer 1991): 2–13.
16. Ibid., 4.
17. Ibid.
18. Ibid., 5.
19. "Film Reviews: Pink Flamingos," *Variety*, Wednesday, December 11, 1974, 18.
20. Peter Stallybrass and Allon White, *The Politics and Poetics of Transgression* (Ithaca: Cornell University Press, 1986), 5 (emphases in original).
21. See Barbara Klinger, *Melodrama and Meaning: History, Culture, and the Films of Douglas Sirk* (Bloomington and Indianapolis: Indiana University Press, 1994), 142–156.
22. John Waters, *Director's Cut* (Zurich, Berlin, and New York: Scalo, 1997), 283.
23. Paul Roen, *High Camp: A Gay Guide to Camp and Cult Films Volume 1* (San Francisco: Leyland Publications, 1994), 11.
24. Alexander Doty, *Making Things Perfectly Queer: Interpreting Mass Culture* (Minneapolis and London: University of Minnesota Press, 1993), 15.
25. "Film Reviews: Female Trouble." *Variety*, Wednesday, February 5, 1975, 22.
26. Eric Schaefer, *"Bold! Daring! Shocking! True!" A History of Exploitation Films, 1919–1959* (Durham and London: Duke University Press, 1999), 12.
27. Thomas Doherty, *Teenagers and Teenpics: The Juvenilization of American Movies in the 1950s* (Boston: Unwin Hyman, 1988), 45.
28. Ibid., 115.
29. Paul Roen, *High Camp: A Gay Guide to Camp and Cult Films Volume 2* (San Francisco: Leyland Publications, 1997), 200.
30. In addition to many of Douglas Sirk's most notable films of the 1950s, in the 1960s Hunter produced a number of glossy color melodramas, notable for the glamorous fashions worn by their leading ladies, including *Portrait in Black* (Michael Gordon, 1960), *Back Street* (David Miller, 1961), and *Madame X* (David Lowell Rich, 1966) (the latter two remakes of earlier black-and-white films).

31. For more on Waters and the influence of Genet, as well as that of French Surrealist André Breton, see Hoberman and Rosenbaum, *Midnight Movies*.
32. Even Dawn's tryst with a fellow inmate, Earnestine (Elizabeth Coffey), resurrects a repressed subplot of *I Want to Live!* as the Production Code Administration objected to the inclusion of Graham's lesbian relationship with an inmate who later betrayed her. See "I Want to Live!," *AFI Catalog of Feature Films*, https://catalog.afi.com/Catalog/moviedetails/52606.
33. As stated in the prologue of *Beyond the Valley of the Dolls*.
34. Julie Sanders, *Adaptation and Appropriation*, 2nd edition (London and New York: Routledge, 2016), 3.
35. Elena Gorfinkel, "*Polyester*: The Perils of Francine," *Polyester*, Criterion Collection Blu-Ray edition essay, 2019. Gorfinkel's title, in its play on the Pearl White serial *The Perils of Pauline* (1914), nods to an earlier form of action-oriented melodrama, which is discussed below.
36. Paul Willemen, "Distanciation and Douglas Sirk," *Screen* 12, no.. 2 (Summer 1971): 66 (italics in original).
37. Schatz, *Hollywood Genres*, 248. It should also be noted that Sirk's own "conversancy with theories of representation, such as those of . . . Bertolt Brecht, helped establish him as a serious artist and social critic" for auteurists in the early 1970s. Klinger, *Melodrama and Meaning*, 8.
38. The film was infamously released with Odorama scratch-and-sniff cards that allowed viewers to experience smells—aromatic and foul—alongside the scent-sensitive Francine, cued by flashing numbers in the corner of the screen. The air freshener occupied the tenth and final spot on the card.
39. Mercer and Shingler, *Melodrama*, 59–60.
40. Ben Singer, *Melodrama and Modernity: Early Sensational Cinema and Its Contexts* (New York: Columbia University Press, 2001), 48.
41. Quoted in ibid., 49.
42. Ibid., 11.
43. Ibid., 13.
44. Klinger, *Melodrama and Meaning*, 70.
45. Alexander Doty, *Flaming Classics: Queering the Film Canon* (New York and London: Routledge, 2000), 7.

CHAPTER 2

John Waters in the 1980s: Publication, Performance, and the Redefinition of Authorial Identity

Matt Connolly

In November 1986, John Waters published an essay in *American Film* entitled "Hard Traveling" that promised to educate readers on "how to survive the lean years between films."[1] Waters knew of what he wrote about. It had been over five years since the release of his last feature, *Polyester* (1981), with several follow-up projects failing to come to fruition. An adaptation of John Kennedy Toole's 1980 novel *A Confederacy of Dunces* never went beyond conversation with studio executives.[2] *Hatchet Face*, described by Waters as chronicling "a woman and her multilevel beauty problems," similarly failed to materialize (though the title would resurface as the name of a prominent character in Waters' *Cry-Baby* [1990]).[3] Perhaps the most dispiriting miss of this period was *Flamingos Forever*, the sequel to Waters' 1972 midnight-movie classic, *Pink Flamingos*. Financing difficulties plagued the project throughout. When longtime Waters stalwart Edith Massey, whose performance as an egg-crazed matriarch proved central to *Pink Flamingos*' original appeal, passed away in October 1984, Waters abandoned it as a filmable option and only later published the screenplay.[4] Given this litany of stalled projects and Waters' seeming admission of his own dry spell, it's understandable why critics and scholars have often understood the 1980s as a fallow period in Waters' career. Emanuel Levy offers a typical iteration of this perspective when he observes that, "after enjoying underground notoriety in the 1970s and spending nearly a decade of idleness in the 1980s, Waters experienced the sweet smell of success in 1988 with *Hairspray*."[5]

Only considering Waters' filmic production (or lack thereof) during this period, however, tells an incomplete story. For all its self-deprecating jabs at Waters' "unemployable" status, "Hard Traveling" points to the varied ways in which Waters stayed remarkably productive throughout the 1980s. The article's very presence within the pages of *American Film* (in which he would ultimately publish eight pieces between 1982 and 1986) illustrates Waters' growing cache as a freelance essayist and critic for a range of magazines. Scanning the first page of "Hard Traveling," one finds a textbox noting that the article is actually excerpted from Waters' second book, *Crackpot: The Obsessions of John Waters*, which had been published the previous month by Macmillan.[6] Much of the piece's content recounts Waters' travels to numerous festivals and repertory theaters that showed his earlier films throughout the 1980s—opportunities that Waters took to perform comedic lectures that drew upon his cinematic work but ultimately branched out into broader cultural commentary. Finally, a brief author bio at the end of "Hard Traveling" reveals that "John Waters recently made his acting debut in Jonathan Demme's *Something Wild* [1986]," a notable instance of his flirtations with on-camera appearance across the decade.[7] These forays into publication and performance certainly remain rooted in cinema and express a continued allegiance to the medium that shaped Waters' reputation. At the same time, they reveal not a stalled-out auteur saved by a decade-capping hit but a canny and creative artist finding numerous ways to expand and reimagine his authorial persona.

This chapter argues that an examination of Waters' extra-cinematic output from 1982–1987 not only foregrounds an under-discussed body of work by a modern cultural icon but reconfigures the narrative surrounding Waters' professional trajectory. It does so through a reputation-studies approach, a mode of research and analysis that Barbara Klinger describes as seeking to "grasp the dialogic relation between artistic reputations and history—the dynamic circumstances under which an author's status and the status of her or his works are established, sustained, transformed, unappreciated, or even vilified."[8] Recent scholarship on filmmakers like David Lynch, Steven Soderbergh, and Spike Lee has shown that the specificities of auteurism within American independent cinema—the nature of creative collaboration within and across media industries, the boundary between artistic persona and brand management, the intersections of authorial and minoritized identities—lend themselves particularly well to reputational analysis.[9] Given Waters' longtime engagement with the extratextual as opportunities for personal expression and cultural commentary, a sustained examination of his non-cinematic production throughout the 1980s illuminates the career evolution that would build to (and extend beyond) the success of *Hairspray*. It locates the roots of Waters' contemporary public identity—wry analyst and winking "filth elder"—in creative achievements from decades prior that have allowed him to remain a beloved cultural figure well into the twenty-first century. Finally, it highlights the broader value of extratextual analysis of a director's career, underscoring how seemingly "secondary" materials can prove as foundational to a filmmaker's identity and development as the "primary" filmic texts that so often occupy scholarly study.

WATERS ON THE PAGE

"I consider myself a writer," Waters told *Publishers Weekly*'s Sally Lodge in 1981. "The thing I most enjoy about making films is writing them."[10] Besides his screenplays, though, Waters expressed continual interest in essayistic writing and commentary. As far back as 1969, he published film reviews in *The Red Brick*, a radical student journal out of the University of Maryland, Baltimore County.[11] In the mid-to-late 1970s, Waters wrote pieces for *Oui* magazine (originally a French pornographic publication before it was bought by *Playboy* in the early 1970s) that combined humorous reminiscences on his filmmaking career with sardonic observations about contemporary American society.[12] Some of these articles were eventually incorporated into Waters' first book, 1981's *Shock Value*.[13] Critics largely received the volume with bemused appreciation, noting how Waters' taste for the bizarre and provocative was mixed here with sharp if somewhat cockeyed satire. Even as Waters pursued ultimately unsuccessful filmic projects, then, he began to lean further into his role as a droll and literate chronicler of both his own colorful life and broader cultural mores.

The blossoming success of Waters as a magazine writer can be understood both in terms of quantity and quality. Waters' 80s-era pieces were seen in *Rolling Stone*, *Vogue*, *Film Comment*, *National Lampoon*, and *Baltimore Magazine*, amongst others. The circulation, assumed audience, and level of cultural prestige attached to each of these venues varied, but they collectively constituted a broadening of readership for Waters' essays and reviews. The articles themselves, meanwhile, harken back to established components of Waters' public persona while tempering their outré extremity through the leavening properties of Waters' acerbic-yet-witty prose. His 1985 account of his tour of Los Angeles for *Rolling Stone*, for instance, brings up grisly historical incidents that Waters explicitly evoked in his early films (the suicide of Diane Linkletter, the murders committed by the Manson family) but does so indirectly, ironically recasting the sites associated with these macabre events as chintzy sightseeing destinations.[14] Walking the knife's edge between irreverent humor and insensitive exploitation, these pieces offer the reader a strong taste of Waters' outrageous jocularity, but filtered through his impish prose and without the visual grotesquerie of his films.

As to why so many magazine editors chose to publish Waters' articles across the 1980s, two interconnected factors can be considered. First, the 1981 releases of both *Shock Value* and the comparatively restrained *Polyester* signaled Waters' relative shift towards a more mainstream audience. Second, press coverage of Waters increasingly emphasized his intelligence, style, and roguish humor—acknowledging his idiosyncrasies and midnight-movie past while drawing a noted contrast between what a given reporter expected of an encounter with the filmmaker and the reality of spending time with him. A 1983 profile in the *Wall Street Journal*, for instance, noted that Waters' "ordered life is the antithesis of the chaos confronting his screen characters," further observing (in a description that wove together the disreputable and the mundane) that "he lives in Baltimore, his hometown, in a spacious bachelor apartment that is unremarkable except for the electric chair in the living room."[15] This balance of eccentricity and accessibility helped Waters become a go-to source for reporters looking for snappy quotes on topics that fell within Waters' ambit. Across the decade, Waters was asked for his thoughts on such matters as the changes to the Catholic Church's film-ratings system ("I used to love it when the nuns told you which movies you weren't supposed to see [. . .] It was a great way to find out the names of all the good ones"), the evolving nature of youthful rebellion ("Take whatever you're uptight about with yourself and turn it into a style"), and the film he'd take with him on a desert island (the 15-hour *Berlin Alexanderplatz* [Rainer Werner Fassbinder, 1980], since "it would take longer to get sick of it").[16] These quotes offered bite-sized samples of the type of sharp, puckish observations on cinema and culture that Waters would expand upon in his essays and reviews.

All of these dynamics could be seen in Waters' relationship with the aforementioned *American Film* magazine, the publication of the American Film Institute founded in 1975. The topics of Waters' eight pieces for the magazine—from an appreciation of '50s-era exploitation maestro William Castle to a review of Kenneth Anger's *Hollywood Babylon II* (1984) to an account of his time teaching in a Maryland prison—all connected to his long-standing obsessions with crime, celebrity, cinema, and social disrepute while simultaneously moving those topics out of the lurid camp universe of Waters' movies and into the (for some) more culturally legible modes of criticism and reportage.[17] His presence in the magazine, furthermore, was not limited to his own articles. In June 1985, he joined the masthead as a contributing editor alongside such film cultural luminaries as longtime *Village Voice* critic J. Hoberman and Marcel Ophuls, director of 1969's canonical World War II documentary *The Sorrow and the Pity*. Within that same issue, he was evoked two additional times: excerpted as part of the magazine's tenth anniversary "best of" collection; and quoted in another anniversary piece as one of the "industry insiders and independents [who] examine the past and introduce the future" of film, a list that included Frank Capra, Martin Scorsese, Dan Rather, and Gilda Radner.[18] As with other of Waters' 80s-era forays into more august cultural realms, reactions from the readership of *American Film* spanned the gamut from raucously appreciative to utterly aghast. His first article for the magazine—offering a typically irreverent list of titles he'd like to receive on home video—inspired dueling letters to the editor, with one reader condemning the piece as the "rantings of a sociopathic pornographer" and another praising it as "funny and enlightening" and the inspiration for him to see "every John Waters movie I could find."[19] That these disagreements were occurring within the pages of a respected cinephile publication speaks to the shifting cultural grounds upon which Waters now launched his attacks on social propriety and filmic standards, not to mention revealed a new means by which potential viewers could discover his movies.

Waters had been keen to follow up *Shock Value* with another volume that built upon earlier work and tapped into existing viewer interests, even as it reframed his older accomplishments in a fresh and marketable light. This eventually resulted in *Crackpot*, which packaged together previously published, mildly revised essays that Waters had written across the early-to-mid-1980s along with three original chapters. *Shock Value* had offered a similar mélange of old and new material, but that book focused much of its attention on the individual productions of Waters' films and showcased mainstay Waters acting talents like Divine and Massey. In contrast, *Crackpot* was almost exclusively comprised of Waters' personal reflections, satiric observations, and autobiographical reminiscences. While it undoubtedly connected to the cinematic world that he had developed throughout the 1960s and 1970s, it moved away from his past films and towards broader cultural commentary. This was also reflected in how the two books were marketed. A 1982 advertisement for *Shock Value*, for instance, announced: "Simply Divine! [. . .] by the Creator of *Pink Flamingos* and *Polyester* [. . .] Finally all the classic characters you've come to know and loathe on the screen—the outrageous Divine, Edie the Egg Lady, the infamous Dreamlanders—are immortalized between the covers of Waters' unabashedly entertaining autobiography."[20] The ad splits its focus between Waters as author, promoting his writerly skills through the promise of an "unabashedly entertaining" read that chronicles "classic characters;" and Waters' on-screen creations themselves, tying the book's appeal to a prior era of his career through references to '70s-era figures (Edie the Egg Lady) and imagery (a still of Divine in *Pink Flamingos*). In contrast, a November 1986 advertisement for *Crackpot* focuses solely on Waters—both visually through the use of an arch yet stylish author photo and rhetorically in the simple, winking promise that "John Waters strikes again . . . "[21] Blurbs from such chic literary figures as William Burroughs, Bret Easton Ellis, and Fran Lebowitz (whose praise for *Shock Value* was also highlighted in the earlier volume's ad) underscore the book's cultural positioning as one of eccentric yet fashionable reflection and commentary.

Reviews of *Crackpot* adopted a similar stance, frequently referencing Waters' past penchant for extremity and favorably contrasting it with his purportedly newfound acuity and empathy. Patrick Goldstein of the *Los Angeles Times* observed: "Full of shrewd advice for every occasion, Waters emerges as something of a cross between Evelyn Waugh and Miss Manners," adding that "while his humor is often campy and outrageous, his outlook is more affectionate than mean-spirited."[22] A more middling review by the *New York Times'*

Anthony Schmitz did not pan Waters so much as encourage him to pursue the more observational instincts that select essays within *Crackpot* spotlighted. For Schmitz, Waters' chapters on his time as a prison teacher and "on the 20th reunion of a Baltimore rock-and-roll show [. . .] succeed for the same reason: Mr. Waters puts aside his affections and does some reporting. He keeps his eyes open, listens to what people tell him and writes sensitively about their lives."[23] Indeed, a recurring theme across reviews of *Crackpot* became whether the book's artistic success presaged a broader shift in how Waters would be perceived. As John McClintock of the *Times Tribune* in Palo Alto, California put it, "I think his twisted, off-the-wall essays are even more perversely enjoyable than his films."[24]

Waters himself considered this reputational negotiation when discussing *Crackpot* in the press. On the one hand, he freely admits that a major impetus for *Crackpot* was financial need in the face of floundering film projects. "Every time I've written a book," he told Stephen Hunter of the *Baltimore Sun*, "it's because one of my movies has fallen through."[25] In the same profile, however, Waters extols the virtues of magazine and book writing, including the reduced costs and the encouragement by editors to appeal to a more niche audience. He concludes that "I'd like to do book, movie, book, movie."[26] The sterling critical response to *Crackpot* may have evoked some anxiety within Waters about his eventual return to cinema. He quipped to the *Boston Globe*'s Diane White that "the reason this book's been getting such good reviews is because the critics are relieved I didn't make another movie."[27] Nevertheless, his broader success within journalism and publishing across the decade revealed a larger truth: that Waters' brand of cock-eyed satire and perversely empathetic curiosity was translatable across mediums. Indeed, just as the cult extremity of his earlier movies segued into the devilishly funny cultural observations of his essays, that witty but warmly-reported chapter on "the 20th reunion of a Baltimore rock-and-roll show" that Schmitz admired would soon form the basis for Waters' big-screen return with *Hairspray*.

WATERS ON THE STAGE

If the importance of a writerly identity shaped Waters' self-conception for much of his career, his investment in the film-exhibition space as a site of playful disruption and heightened performance similarly reaches back to his earliest days as a director. Waters would orchestrate guerrilla marketing campaigns and wild publicity stunts to promote his work: the production of crazed stage shows that Waters wrote to accompany the San Francisco release of his 1969 feature *Mondo Trasho*, where star Divine would hurl dead mackerels at the audience; the building of subcultural buzz for *Pink Flamingos* through midnight screenings that promoted active audience engagement and liberal intoxication; the introduction of "Odorama" scratch-and-sniff cards handed out to viewers to accompany screenings of *Polyester*.[28] While Waters' in-person appearances at screenings of his films throughout the 1980s rarely achieved such a level of frenzied bacchanalia, this history is nevertheless key to understanding why Waters continued to conceptualize interactions with filmgoers as sites of creative possibility and public self-definition.

Beginning in the mid-1970s, John Waters film festivals featuring somewhere between three and five of the director's works occurred on college campuses or in repertory houses in Baltimore, Houston, Cleveland, and Provincetown, amongst other cities.[29] Waters would sometimes attend these events and offer comments that went beyond a simple introduction or question-and-answer session tied directly to the films themselves. In the early 1980s, the tenth anniversary of *Pink Flamingos* seemed to prompt a renewed burst of enthusiasm for Waters-centric screening series. Complete or near-complete retrospectives of Waters' features—from *Mondo Trasho* through *Polyester*—occurred in 1982 and 1983 at the Cedar Theater in Minneapolis, the Theatre for the Living Arts in Philadelphia, the Biograph in Washington, D.C., the Charles in Baltimore, and the Channel in Boston.[30] These festivals continued at various venues throughout the mid-1980s, including the Castro in San Francisco, the Uptown in Minneapolis, the Showcase in Sacramento, the Neptune in Seattle, the Baltimore Museum of Art, and the Variety Arts Center in Los Angeles, as well as international events at the Cinema V in Montreal and the Cinémathèque Française in Paris.[31] The consistency of these events speaks to the enduring passion of the director's hardcore fans, their attendance reflecting their devotion to seeing the filmmaker's oeuvre on the big screen and amongst fellow enthusiasts even during a decade when many of Waters' titles became available on home video. At the same time, Waters' growing notoriety as an essayist and author perhaps expanded the potential audience for such events, particularly if those newly engaged with his work via a magazine article or book might have the extremity of his early films reframed via an in-person introduction or discussion with the filmmaker.

Indeed, as the decade progressed, Waters used these continued screenings and celebrations of his movies to both reflect on his past filmic practice and spotlight his present-day observations and musings through live performance. For example, the November 1983 Waters festival at the Channel in Boston offered direct access to some of Waters' most notable performers: a live appearance from Divine ("That's no lady!", the advertisement winkingly promises alongside a stylized drawing of the drag star) with Mink Stole acting as "special guest emcee." Amidst these enticements, the ad also highlighted "a lecture by filmmaker John Waters," a rather staid-sounding prospect for an evening that otherwise guaranteed ribald provocation.[32] This "lecture" format, however, became a frequent go-to mode for Waters, one that he employed whether he attended screenings with cast members or by himself. Waters was "on the stage at the Union Main Lounge speaking to [University of Iowa] students as the third annual Riverfest speaker" in April 1984; headlined "An Evening with John Waters" at the Rhodes Theater in Atlanta in January 1985, noting that he "enjoys the lectures because they allow him free rein to discuss his obsessions;" and paired February 1986 screenings of his cinematic work at Filmmakers at the Fulton in Pittsburgh with "a lecture on 'Shock Value: Obsessions and Anxieties in My Films.'"[33] These lectures offered a free-form space within which Waters could comment on a range of contemporary topics and issues, with many of them dovetailing back to similar concerns in his essays, books, and movies. Previewing the range of planned subjects for his pre-screening talk at Boston's U.S.A. Copley Place Cinemas in September 1986, Waters told the *Boston Globe*'s John Engstrom that the lecture would cover "whatever is my obsession recently. I'd like to talk about parole for some of the Manson girls; about extreme Catholic behavior during the Reformation, which is my hobby; about Japan, where all my films just opened; about Joey Heatherton—you know, just all the normal things that people talk about today."[34] That Waters increasingly incorporated such performances into his public appearances not only points to his shrewd understanding of his fanbase (i.e., that these purported "obsessions" would translate into interesting anecdotes for others) but underscores Waters' talent as a live speaker and storyteller.

Waters' growing confidence in his audience's desires to seek out his lectures as events in-and-of themselves—as opposed to amusing add-ons to a screening of his filmic work—could be seen at the 1987 Telluride Film Festival, held in Telluride, Colorado. The festival was screening *Polyester* "in its original 'Odorama,'" but the more notable event proved to be Waters' "program devoted to outlandish gimmicks employed by moviemakers over the years."[35] As recounted by film critic Roger Ebert, the evening featured Waters, "sporting his trademarks, a pencil-thin moustache and a cardsharp's wardrobe," regaling the crowd with his memories of youthful trips to the movies to see films and experience in-theater stunts by exploitation maestros like William Castle.[36] He then proceeded to show rare footage from outrageous cinematic titles and discuss various forms of filmic ballyhoo, from a "nearly porno movie in which one of the sex scenes was filmed live in a roller coaster" to the "various attempts to involve the noses of theater audiences."[37] The evening stitched together several interconnected pieces of Waters' persona: his actual filmmaking (*Polyester*); his cinematic influences (exploitation movies and their assorted gimmickry); and his writing on said cinematic influences (his essay on Castle, which appeared in both *American Film* and *Crackpot*).[38] Film remained at the center of Waters' event even as he deployed these cinematic references as a means of proving himself as a skilled and engaging performer, one (to quote the *Los Angeles Times*' Sheila Benson) "whose dry wit, pencil-moustache and stand-up introduction to the great old days of movie hucksterism was tons o' fun."[39]

WATERS ON SCREEN

For all his striking sartorial looks, distinctive voice, and familiarity around a film set, Waters did not frequently appear in movies and on television across the 1970s. His "on-screen" roles in his own early cinematic works were audio-only performances (a reporter's voice in *Mondo Trasho*, the narrator "Mr. J" in *Pink Flamingos*), and his TV appearances were often on more niche programs. His on-screen work increased throughout the 1980s but remained scattered across scripted performance, documentary, and publicity material. These nevertheless intersected with Waters' more explicit forays into writing and live performance and laid down templates for self-presentation that he would develop further in the decades to come.

One of Waters' first screen appearances in this period is, in many ways, an extension of his attendance at movie showings discussed in the previous section. The Nuart Theatre in Los Angeles had continuously screened *Pink Flamingos* for almost a decade by the early 1980s. As a token of gratitude to its owners, Waters shot a no-smoking public service announcement for the venue to run before its feature films.[40] In it, Waters stands against a blank wall in medium close-up, wearing a light blue button-up and textured skinny tie. A noted chain-smoker who only quit in the mid-2000s, Waters puffs on a cigarette and addresses the camera, introducing himself and saying that he's been told to inform the presumed moviegoer that there is no smoking in the theater (Figure 2.1). He then

Figure 2.1 Waters takes a luxurious drag off a cigarette while insisting (with a wink) that theatergoers abstain in a PSA shot for the Nuart Theatre in Los Angeles.

immediately dismisses this edict as "one of the most ridiculous things I've ever heard of in my life," bemoaning the amount of time that one would need to forego a cigarette while watching an entire film ("especially a European film!") and extolling the virtues of smoking-related litter as providing "employment for the youth of today" as ushers. He takes increasingly luxurious drags off his cigarette throughout—climaxing in a dramatic French inhale—before reminding filmgoers with a devilish grin to not smoke.[41] At roughly thirty seconds, the PSA is vintage Waters: cheeky and absurd, presenting the filmmaker as both authority figure and impish provocateur in a ludicrous contradiction made even more delightful by Waters' unbroken gaze into the camera. While the short began at a single theater, its eventual spread to other venues (including the Charles Theater in Baltimore) made it a small-but-effective way of circulating Waters' image to the public.[42] When asked in 1985 whether everyday people ever recognize him, Waters responds, "They didn't used to. But I did this no smoking commercial they play in theaters, all over California [. . .] So now when people see me in public, they holler out, 'Hey. Got a cigarette?'"[43]

Waters brought a version of this self-consciously heightened performance of the self to a national audience when he appeared on *Late Night with David Letterman* (NBC, 1982–1993). He was a fairly popular guest on the show throughout this period, coming on the program six times between 1982–1987, once with Divine but otherwise solo.[44] Waters was arguably a bit restrained in his early stints on *Late Night*, offering amusing tales from his life and films but seemingly aware of the audience's at-times tentative responses to his jokes and Letterman's own humorously flabbergasted reactions to Waters' stories. As time went on, though, Waters began to lean further into button-pushing eccentricity. In 1985 and 1986, he brought materials to the set to illustrate his bizarre anecdotes: choice clippings from his favorite tabloids; oddball real-life items mentioned in *Crackpot*, including a miniature toy electric chair and a package of the unfortunately-named candy Dingle Berries which Letterman begs Waters not to show on-camera. While the nature of the program and its audience inevitably shaped how Waters comported himself, the fundamental persona he honed on *Late Night*—knowing, observant, and playfully perverse—only came into sharper focus as the decade progressed.

Finally, Waters experienced the sometimes unsettling, sometimes satisfying feeling of being the subject of another filmmaker's camera in the mid-1980s. While he had been interviewed within non-fiction portraits of his actors such as Robert Maier's 1975 short *Love Letter to Edie*, a more extended iteration of this came in *Divine Waters*, a 1985 documentary on the director himself made by Italian filmmaker Vito Zagarrio. Waters' descriptions of the film's production and distribution reveal some of his ambivalences about the project. He refers to Zagarrio as "an Italian boyfriend of my sister's who wanted to make a documentary about me" and claims that "we had been told the film was being

Figure 2.2 Waters cameos as a sleazy used-car salesman looking for some quick cash in Jonathan Demme's *Something Wild* (1986).

produced only for Italian television and would never be shown in America."[45] Though it never actually aired in Italy, *Divine Waters* would "world premiere" in Philadelphia in March 1985 and subsequently played in Dallas, Houston, Seattle, Denver, Minneapolis, New York, and Baltimore, amongst other cities, frequently as part of Waters film festivals.[46] The movie itself is a largely sympathetic portrait of Waters, with smaller sections focusing on Divine and Massey. A notable element of *Divine Waters*, though, is the extended group interview scenes that Zagarrio conducts with Waters and his parents, which linger on past familial tensions and (according to film critic Steven Rea) finds Zagarrio "fir[ing] a barrage of loaded questions at his subjects."[47] The most unsettling aspect of *Divine Waters* for its principal subject seemed to be the cinematic intrusion of his parents into the space of the movie theater, with Waters observing that "it was too nerve-wracking for me to be waiting backstage and hear my mother's voice booming out into an auditorium."[48] Perhaps instinctually, Waters reframed the experience by jokingly suggesting that they lean into the family drama, exploitation-style: "In each city, we could set up on stage an exact replica of my parents' dining room; Mom and Dad could travel with me and we'd reenact fights we've had over the years."[49]

Seemingly more pleasurable for Waters was the cameo that he had in Jonathan Demme's 1986 romantic comedy/thriller *Something Wild* (Figure 2.2). Playing a shady used-car salesman who sells a vehicle to the film's central couple after taking a bribe to ignore their lack of insurance, Waters dons a garish white-and-orange striped button-down (with matching orange tie) and flashes a slimy grin once he realizes an ill-gotten $100 bill is coming his way. He simply but effectively activates the "sultan of sleaze" connotations surrounding his public persona, offering a moment of comic relief to anyone in the audience who recognizes him. The role was too brief for many critics to comment on it, with Lou Cedrone of the *Baltimore Evening Sun* remarking simply: "I don't know if I would buy a used car from this man."[50] Most reviewers simply noted the presence of Waters alongside that of John Sayles, the director of such acclaimed American independent films as *Return of the Secaucus 7* (1980) and *The Brother from Another Planet* (1984), who appeared in a similarly small part as a police officer. Waters and Sayles form a sort of indie-cinema dyad for those viewers in the know, a nod to two men whose iterations of low-budget filmmaking couldn't be more different but whose respective artistic spirits Demme found worthy of highlighting within his own work. Indeed, the role itself came about after Waters and Demme met at a film festival in Rio de Janeiro where, as Waters recalls, "we did this press conference together and we had a really good time laughing."[51] Demme made his feelings about Waters known when he told the press at that festival: "I am more impressed [. . .] with film-makers like John (Waters) who have their own ideas and can then make a film cheaply that reaches a large audience."[52] Coincidentally, by the time *Something Wild* was released in October 1986, Waters would finally be putting those cinematic impulses to use as he moved towards pre-production on his long-awaited next film.

HAIRSPRAY AND THE FUTURE(S) OF WATERS' PUBLIC IDENTITY

It is inarguable that *Hairspray*'s combination of '60s nostalgia, campy aesthetics, and message of social tolerance revived Waters' fortunes as a director and permanently helped to recast him in the public eye. The film's $2.7 million budget and $8.2 million domestic box-office gross were both career highs for Waters at the time, while its relatively family-friendly content proved that he could work within a more broadly accessible cinematic register. Perhaps more significantly, *Hairspray* has gone through numerous adaptations and remakes throughout the twenty-first century that has kept it ever-present in the public consciousness: a Tony-winning 2002 Broadway musical; a 2007 cinematic adaptation of that musical; a 2016 live television adaptation combining elements of both the 2002 and 2007 iterations; and numerous productions of the stage show across regional, community, and high school theaters.

Waters' 80s-era extratextual output helps to productively illuminate *Hairspray* as an extension of (and not a break from) his non-cinematic work across the previous years. The film's genesis began with the writing of Waters' article "'Ladies and Gentlemen . . . The Nicest Kids in Town!'", which originally ran in the April 1985 issue of *Baltimore Magazine* and was republished the following year as an acclaimed chapter in *Crackpot*.[53] A retrospective account of *The Buddy Deane Show*—the *American Bandstand*-esque teen dance program that ran in Baltimore from 1957–1964 and that is reimagined as *The Corny Collins Show* in the film—"The Nicest Kids in Town" formed the basis for *Hairspray*'s screenplay. In the small-but-memorable role of a crazed, Allen Ginsberg-reciting beatnik, Waters cast Pia Zadora, the oft-maligned young actress that the director praised in the press and interviewed for *American Film* in 1984 (another article that was reprinted in *Crackpot*). Waters himself briefly appears in *Hairspray* as quack psychiatrist Dr. Fredrickson, building off his winking cameo in *Something Wild*. Finally, one might speculate that the cultural goodwill Waters' writings and public appearances built up throughout the decade only helped to inspire well-known performers like Sonny Bono, Ruth Brown, and Jerry Stiller to join *Hairspray*'s cast alongside newcomers such as Ricki Lake and Waters regulars like Divine and Mink Stole. Waters' forays into publication and performance across the 1980s, then, offered crucial building blocks from which to fashion a "comeback" film that both retained and expanded his established directorial brand.

At the same time, Waters' non-cinematic ventures offer as much (if not more) insight into the broader shape of his career than *Hairspray* itself does. While the film's financial and critical success allowed Waters to consistently make feature films throughout the 1990s and into the 2000s, funding eventually became harder to secure as his latter-day titles failed to achieve box-office success. The templates developed in the period between *Polyester* and *Hairspray*, then, took on even more importance and provided numerous pathways for Waters' continued creative expression. Essayistic writing that combines biographical exploration with sharp-eyed social observation has been a major focus for Waters, particularly since the 2000s. Since the release of his first screenplay collection, *Trash Trio*, in 1988, Waters has published a second script compilation; three books that offer extended, humorous reflections both on his life and work and on broader modern culture; a re-purposed commencement address; and a novel. Building off of the "Evening with John Waters" that he developed across the 1980s, Waters has not only continued to give lectures at colleges and festivals but now performs what is essentially a traveling standup act, mixing well-known anecdotes from his career with commentary on contemporary events. And if being in front of the camera was something that Waters approached gingerly in the 1980s, on-screen performance as a means of both deepening and extending his public persona took on greater importance for Waters beginning in the 1990s. He has made numerous appearances in narrative films, documentaries, and television series, bringing his irreverence and intelligence to various parts while continuing to excavate his long-standing fascinations, as when he played William Castle in an episode of *Feud: Bette and Joan* (FX, 2017). (This does not even approach Waters' gallery art, which he began making and exhibiting in the 1990s.)[54] Taken together, this array of artistic and entrepreneurial endeavors helped further hone the persona that Waters has embodied well into the twenty-first century: part obsessive curator of American cinematic and cultural detritus, part bemused anthropologist of contemporary social and sexual mores, part gleeful showman whose very presence connotes queerly tinged mischief and subcultural sagacity. All of these guises undoubtedly link back to his filmmaking, with new generations of fans continuing to discover Waters through his cinematic work. It's perhaps as likely, however, that a newly inaugurated Waters fanatic found him through a book he wrote, a role he performed, even a still image he sat for—a testament to how Waters has maintained his career-long blend of scalding satire and warped affection for society's freaks and misfits while dispersing that indelible energy across an ever-growing range of cultural forms.

Indeed, it briefly seemed as if one of Waters' literary works would be the vehicle that would return him to the screen after a more than twenty-year absence. In 2022, Waters announced that he had adapted his novel *Liarmouth* into a script, with actress Aubrey Plaza expressing interest in the lead role.[55] Sadly, as of November 2024, the film was no longer in development.[56] Should the project ever come to fruition, however, it will be a significant but far from singular example of Waters as a multi-hyphenate artist for whom the image, the word, and the stage form an intricately-connected web within which to explore an enduring set of aesthetic concerns and cultural obsessions. In a contemporary era where filmmakers navigate an increasingly fragmented and persona-driven media landscape, Waters' nimble and inventive navigation of the 1980s looks more prescient than ever.

NOTES

1. John Waters, "Hard Traveling," *American Film*, November 1986, 45.
2. John Waters, "How Not to Make a Movie," *American Film*, July/August 1986, 37.
3. Waters qtd. in Joe Brown, "Baltimore's Master of Bad Taste," *Washington Post*, February 6, 1985, C7.
4. John Waters, *Trash Trio: Three Screenplays* (New York: Vintage Books, 1988).
5. Emanuel Levy, *Gay Directors, Gay Films?: Pedro Almodóvar, Terence Davies, Todd Haynes, Gus Van Sant, John Waters* (New York: Columbia University Press, 2015), 303.
6. John Waters, *Crackpot: The Obsessions of John Waters* (New York: Macmillan, 1986).
7. Waters, "Hard Traveling," 47.
8. Barbara Klinger, *Melodrama and Meaning: History, Culture, and the Films of Douglas Sirk* (Bloomington and Indianapolis: Indiana University Press, 1994), xiii.
9. Antony Todd, *Authorship and the Films of David Lynch: Aesthetic Receptions in Contemporary Hollywood* (London and New York: I.B. Tauris, 2012); Mark Gallagher, *Another Steven Soderbergh Experience: Authorship & Contemporary Hollywood* (Austin: University of Texas Press, 2013); Eleni Palis, "The Economics and Politics of Auteurism: Spike Lee and *Do The Right Thing*," *Cinema Journal* 57, no. 2 (Winter 2018): 1–21.

10. Waters qtd. in Sally A. Lodge, "John Waters," *Publishers Weekly*, July 17, 1981, 7.
11. John Waters, "Water's," *The Red Brick* 1, no. 1 (October 1969): 11; John Waters, "Silver Screen," *The Red Brick* 1, no. 1 (October 1969): 12, 15.
12. John Waters, "All My Trials," *Oui*, May 1978, 56–58, 127–128, 130; John Waters, "Casting for the Heavies," *Oui*, November 1978, 37; John Waters, "Troubled Waters," *Oui*, August 1979, NP.
13. John Waters, *Shock Value: A Tasteful Book About Bad Taste* (New York: Delta, 1981).
14. John Waters, "John Waters' Tour of L.A.," *Rolling Stone*, July 18–August 1, 1985, 55–56, 58, 60, 62.
15. Trish Hall, "John Waters's Films Have Low Budgets, Large Leading Lady," *Wall Street Journal*, March 31, 1983, 1, 20.
16. Waters qtd. in William V. Thomas, "The New Catholic Ratings Look Beyond Sex in Movies," *Baltimore Sun*, February 14, 1982, D9; Waters qtd. in Frank DeCaro, "The Empty 80s," *Detroit Free Press*, December 31, 1986, 2C; Waters qtd. in Robert Osborne, "Rambling Reporter," *Hollywood Reporter*, February 24, 1987, 5.
17. John Waters, "Whatever Happened to Showmanship?" *American Film*, December 1983, 55–58; John Waters, "Look Back with Anger," *American Film*, January/February 1985, 53–55; John Waters, "Blackboard Jungle," *American Film*, April 1985, 42–46, 48. Waters' final three *American Film* pieces not yet mentioned in this chapter are: John Waters, "Mondo Video," *American Film*, June 1982, 17–20, 64; John Waters, "The Pia Zadora Story," *American Film*, July/August 1984, 36–39, 42; John Waters, "Flock Shock," *American Film*, January/February 1986, 38–41.
18. "The Best of *American Film*," *American Film*, June 1985, 9, 11–12, 15–16, 19, 92–93, 95; "The Big Picture," *American Film*, June 1985, 76–77, 79, 81–83, 85, 87–90, 105.
19. Paul D. Mareth, "Muddy Waters," *American Film*, September 1982, 6; James A. Reeves, "Wild About Waters," *American Film*, January 1983, 8.
20. Advertisement, *American Film*, March 1982, 75.
21. Advertisement, *New York Times*, November 16, 1986, BR22.
22. Patrick Goldstein, "Crackpot," *Los Angeles Times Book Review*, November 16, 1986, 4.
23. Anthony Schmitz, "Crackpot: The Obsessions of John Waters," *New York Times*, November 9, 1986, BR33.
24. John McClintock, "How a Crackpot Sees Hollywood," *Times Tribune* [*Calendar*], October 26, 1986, 2.
25. Waters qtd. in Stephen Hunter, "John Waters: Never Quite Gone, He's Back Again," *Baltimore Sun*, October 5, 1986, 7M.
26. Ibid.
27. Waters qtd. in Diane White, "The King of Sleaze," *Boston Globe*, November 6, 1986, 95.
28. Examples of Waters' 60s and 70s-era coopting of the theater space can be found in Waters, *Shock Value*. For more on the development and deployment of Odorama, see John Waters, *Mr. Know-It-All: The Tarnished Wisdom of a Filth Elder* (New York: Farrar, Straus and Giroux, 2019), 13–28.
29. Advertisement, *The Retriever*, March 1, 1976, 9; Advertisement, *Daily Cougar*, February 3, 1977, 9; "Cleveland," *Boxoffice*, April 10, 1978, ME-1; "Waters Films: Tasteless, Vulgar, Campy," *Provincetown Advocate*, August 9, 1979, 5, 25.
30. Advertisement, *Twin Cities Reader*, October 6, 1982, 28; "Waters Retro in Philly," *Variety*, January 5, 1983, 28; Gary Arnold, "Film Notes," *Washington Post* [*Weekend*], July 8, 1983, 18; Charles Paul Freund, "John Waters, Filmdom's Bad Boy, Getting a 'Career Retrospective,'" *Baltimore Sun*, August 5, 1983, C1, C5; Advertisement, *Boston Phoenix*, November 8, 1983, sec. 3, 18.

31. Robert Taylor, "John Waters Film Festival is Not for the Faint of Heart," *Oakland Tribune*, April 6, 1984, D-8; "Landmark Theatres Series of Note," *American Film*, June 1984, 77; "Landmark Theatres Series of Note," *American Film*, July/August 1984, 78; John Hartl, "Sleaze and Sex Get a Showing," *Seattle Times*, January 18, 1985, 19; Lou Cedrone, "Museum Honors John Waters," *Baltimore Evening Sun*, February 7, 1985, D1, D6; "Waters Fest Skedded," *Hollywood Reporter*, October 15, 1987, 8; Thomas Schnurmacher, "Comedy Returns to the Bar Scene," *Montreal Gazette*, July 7, 1984, H-6; "Cinémathèque Française Exhibitions, Homages and Special Events (1937–1986)," *Variety*, October 1, 1986, 40.
32. Advertisement, *Boston Phoenix*, November 8, 1983, sec. 3, 18.
33. Craig Wyrick, "Maker of 'Pink Flamingos' Will Be Riverfest Speaker," *Daily Iowan*, April 12, 1984, 12B; Howard Pousner, "Director Waters' Films Have a New Generation to Offend," *Atlanta Journal*, January 29, 1985, 1B, 11B; Marylynn Uricchio, "Director John Waters Serves Up Humor with Shock Value," *Pittsburgh Post-Gazette*, February 13, 1986, 20.
34. Waters qtd. in John Engstrom, "John Waters: 'Sleaze King of Cinema?'" *Boston Globe*, September 17, 1986, 42.
35. "Soviet Film Is Highlight of Festival," *Daily Sentinel*, September 6, 1987, 3A; Robert Denerstein, "Telluride Film Fest to Tribute Frears, Two Others in '87," *Hollywood Reporter*, September 4, 1987, 22.
36. Roger Ebert, "John Waters, the Father of Odorama," *Daily Sentinel* [*Entertainer*], September 11, 1987, 13.
37. Ibid.
38. For more on the connections between Castle and Waters, see Kate J. Russell, "The Cinematic Pandemonium of William Castle and John Waters," in *ReFocus: The Films of William Castle*, edited by Murray Leeder (Edinburgh: Edinburgh University Press, 2018), 237–254.
39. Sheila Benson, "Telluride Festival Finds Time for Renewal," *Los Angeles Times* [*Calendar*], September 13, 1987, 32–33.
40. Jocelyn Szczepaniak-Gillece, "Smoke and Mirrors: Cigarettes, Cinephilia, and Reverie in the American Movie Theater," *Film History* 28, no. 3 (2016): 109, n. 1.
41. The PSA is available as a special feature on the Criterion release of *Polyester*: "No Smoking in this Theater," Special Features, *Polyester*, directed by John Waters (1981; New York, NY: Criterion Collection, 2019), DVD.
42. Szczepaniak-Gillece, "Smoke and Mirrors," 85.
43. Waters qtd. in Rob Clark, "John Waters," *This Week in Texas*, July 12–18, 1985, 66.
44. These six appearances—March 18, 1982; August 24, 1982; September 19, 1983; June 19, 1985; October 16, 1986; and November 10, 1987—can be viewed across three videos on YouTube: "John Waters (& Divine) on Letterman, Part 1 of 3: 1982," video, February 16, 2018 https://www.youtube.com/watch?v=AIPF8mk1a4Q; "John Waters on Letterman, Part 2 of 3: 1983-86," video, February 20, 2018, https://www.youtube.com/watch?v=Rn96HXDGboo&t=0s; "John Waters on Letterman, Part 3 of 3: 1987-1992," video, February 22, 2018, https://www.youtube.com/watch?v=Ii34WyuAGLg&t=0s
45. Waters, "Hard Traveling," 45–46.
46. Gail Reichstein, "The Bizarre John Waters," *34th Street* [*Daily Pennsylvanian*], March 21, 1985, 5; "Landmark Theatres," *American Film*, May 1985, 71; "Landmark Theatres," *American Film*, July–August 1985, 69; "Film: Revivals," *New York Times*, December 14, 1986, G20; "Openings," *Baltimore Sun* [*Maryland Live*], April 24, 1987, 14.
47. Steven Rea, "A Look at John Waters and His Bizarre Films," *Philadelphia Inquirer*, March 27, 1985, 4G.
48. Waters, "Hard Traveling," 46.

49. Ibid.
50. Lou Cedrone, "'Tai-Pan' is an Old-Style Epic'; 'Something Wild' is New and Strange," *Baltimore Evening Sun*, November 7, 1986, B4.
51. Waters qtd. in Hunter, "John Waters," 7M.
52. Demme qtd. in "300 Films Screened, 300,000 Attend First Rio Film, TV, Video Festival," *Screen International*, December 22, 1984, 14.
53. John Waters, "'Ladies and Gentlemen . . . The Nicest Kids in Town!'", *Baltimore Magazine*, April 1985, 90–95, 140–141.
54. For an overview of Waters' visual art, see Kristen Hileman, *John Waters: Indecent Exposure* (Baltimore: The Baltimore Museum of Art and University of California Press, 2018).
55. John Waters, *Liarmouth: A Feel-Bad Romance* (New York: Farrar, Straus and Giroux, 2022).
56. Joey Guerra, "Filmmaker John Waters Comes to Houston to Discuss the Original 'Hairspray,' His 'Most Devious Movie,'" *Houston Chronicle*, November 12, 2024, accessed February 24, 2025, https://www.houstonchronicle.com/entertainment/movies_tv/article/john-waters-hairspray-houston-q-a-tickets-1988-19905618.php

CHAPTER 3

The Bloodless 1990s: From *Serial Mom* to Wes Craven's *Scream*

Fernando Gabriel Pagnoni Berns and Canela Ailen Rodriguez Fontao

In 1994, John Waters' only horror film opened. *Serial Mom* told of the murderous adventures of Beverly Sutphin, a perfect all-American mother (Kathleen Turner) who is, behind the façade, a serial killer. Beverly brutally kills anyone who may hurt her family. Or anyone who offends her sense of family values. Or just anyone.

It may be argued that Waters' film was a blueprint for Wes Craven's meta-slasher *Scream* (1996). The film, revolving around a serial killer known as Ghostface who is targeting teenagers in the small town of Woodsboro, not only was a smash box-office hit, but single-handedly revived the dormant horror genre.[1] Certainly, the horror genre was basically dead through the first half of the 1990s. Despite Jonathan Demme's *Silence of the Lambs* (1991) winning an Oscar in 1992, the gory slashers of the 1980s had been replaced by sanitized bloodless horror[2] such as *Bram Stoker's Dracula* (Francis Ford Coppola, 1992) and Kenneth Branagh's *Mary Shelley's Frankenstein* (1994), or fantasy-adventure blockbusters like Steven Spielberg's *Jurassic Park* (1993). Horror was dead, at least, until the coming of Craven's slasher.

Just like *Scream*, *Serial Mom* is a meta-film peppered with many references to horror cinema and a more brutal, artistic past (especially B horror). Matthew Lillard's character in *Serial Mom* anticipates his own character in *Scream* (Stu Macher) and that of Jamie Kennedy (Randy, a horror film fanatic). Both films question the decline of horror in the first half of the 1990s and its absorption by Hollywood's safe machine.

This chapter does not argue that Craven used *Serial Mom* as inspiration, but that both films are answers to the decline of brutal horror in the period. While Craven's *Scream* is now part of the horror canon, *Serial Mom* is not even a footnote. This chapter will analyze Waters' *Serial Mom* in the context of the 1990s and how the film engaged with cultural practices of sanitized horror. Many of Waters' films verged on horror, yet *Serial Mom* is the director's only full immersion into the horror genre so far. Waters offers a gross and gory take on horror not so much to satirize middle-class life in America (even if this satire is indeed present throughout the film) but to offer, on the big screen, what the 1990s were not offering: uncompromised red stuff, pushed to the margins not so much by the MPAA but by the rhetoric of good taste offered by Big Budgeted Productions with which Hollywood replaced independent, raw horror. Waters resorts to a double strategy: first, he privileges gory horror, which contrasts sharply with the refined taste of the thriller that would dominate the first half of the 1990s. Second, he uses a meta approach (like *Scream* will do) to discuss the collapse of a certain type of horror during that era.

THE SLOW DECADENCE OF HORROR

The slasher formula dominated the horror landscape throughout the 1980s, giving rise to an over-saturation of masked killers murdering teenagers in increasingly creative, gory ways. The slasher cycle produced the figure of the "Final Girl," meaning, the lone survivor of the massacre who must fight and defeat the killer at the movie's climax. The Final Girl was not born in a vacuum, but was a walking metaphor of Reaganomics and the conservative values dominating America through the years of Ronald Reagan's presidency. The Final Girl "was beautiful but modest in appearance, strong, resourceful, virginal, and friendly, with no vices of any kind. She was the perfect antagonist of both the masked killer and the blonde bitch" and she survived not just because she was smart and emphatic, "but also because she is a good American girl."[3] She was all that Reagan expected from women in the 1980s: smart, funny and with good marks in school, but with a destiny of housewife.

By the first years of the 1990s, the slasher cycle had dried out. On one hand, Second Wave Feminism was replaced by post-feminism and the neoliberal politics of identity as commodity. Post-feminism saw "feminism as a lifestyle choice rather than a political commitment" and "aligned with commodity feminism,"[4] thus weakening the historical goals of First and Second Wave Feminism. The Final Girl, one of the two figures articulating the cycle (the other one being the masked killer), was passé in this new scenario of depoliticization. On the other hand, the production of slashers reached a point of saturation, with audiences increasingly bored with the masked killers, the secluded geographies, and the formula in general. Further, the formula was suited for "sequelization,"[5] benefiting not only new films copying shamelessly the basic formula of a killer stalking teenagers at a secluded location, but also endless series of sequels to the most successful films. Films like *Halloween* (John Carpenter, 1978), *Friday the 13th* (Sean S. Cunningham, 1980), and *Prom Night* (Paul Lynch, 1980) were franchised, offering audiences basic reformulations of the original film and little else. It seemed that every week, a new slasher film opened in 1980s America, offering satisfaction to the compulsion for repetition.

The oscillating tastes of Hollywood swung, leaving the first half of the 1990s virtually devoid of horror films, including the slasher formula. Thomas Schatz cites 1990 as an important turning point for American cinema, with America winning space in foreign theatres in combination with the decline of vernacular cinema in Europe, with some American films actually doing better overseas than in the U.S.[6] By the 1990s, the American blockbuster became stable and profitable, pushing to the margins more risky and/or problematic manifestations such as the horror genre, even if some voices warned about the "blockbuster mentality."[7]

For the studios, making horror, so lucrative in the 1980s, was synonymous with box-office poison. *Silence of the Lambs* promised new heights for horror, but instead the hit proved to be the proverbial last nail in horror's coffin rather than the beginning of a new era of monsters and shivers. Unlike other times such as the 1950s, when American horror was replaced by science-fiction and British scares such as those produced by Hammer Films, or the 1960s, which saw little in terms of American horror hits (at least, until the opening of George Romero's *Night of the Living Dead* in 1968 and Roman Polanski's *Rosemary Baby* in the same year), the decline of horror cinema in the 90s was global in nature. Italian horror was completely dead after burning itself out through its three stages or cycles over the preceding decades (gothic in the 1960s, *giallo* in the 1970s, zombies and cannibalism in the 1980s). As Rui Trindade Oliveira argues, "Italian horror cinema did not totally disappear, in part, thanks to the absorption by video markets, but its once high production levels and diversity decreased dramatically, because the video and TV markets mostly invested in very low-budget horror. This would condition quality and diversity."[8] Further, the ratings were not there, making little money for advertisers.[9] Spain, another European producer of horrors, reached democracy in the late 1970s, and throughout the 1980s and 1990s (and well into the new millennium) focused on denouncing the real horrors of Francisco Franco's dictatorship rather than offering allegorical forms of horror.[10] British horror (and British cinema in general) was slowly fading from transnational presence due to many internal problems, with national film production plummeting.[11] In America, horror was replaced by (erotic and psychological) thrillers and science-fiction blockbusters. The fandom's desire for horror consumption was solely satisfied with the coming of the VHS and films made for that market. But horror cinema opening in theatres was a thing of the past.

The few horror films that opened in the 1990s' first half were luxurious productions made by big studios and, as such, with an eye more on the Academy Awards than gore. *Bram Stoker's Dracula* and *Mary Shelley's Frankenstein* offered good results at the box office, but very little in terms of scares and gore. Meanwhile, slashers were absent from the big screen, now relegated to the direct-to-video market. In the editorial of *Fangoria* 101, dated April 1991, main editor Anthony Timpone says:

> It's hard to believe that I'm feeling nostalgic for the '70s and earlier '80s, with the current decade so fresh. But some recent developments are rekindling memories of these days when you could see an independent horror movie in your hometown theater, heralded by garish ad campaigns and sleazy trailers on late-night television. [. . .]. The independent horror film appears to be an endangered species.[12]

This same issue contains an article on *Silence of the Lambs*, as well as one on the film adaptation of Stephen King's novel *Misery* (Rob Reiner, 1991), an adaptation that excised many of the bloody setpieces King wrote, including a character murdered via a lawnmower and a brutal amputation. The film was a success, with Kathy Bates winning the Oscar for her interpretation of Annie Wilkes. The letters section in *Fangoria* 106, dated September 1991, is revealing. A reader, Jim Turner, asks directors to make more horror films. "For years you've been complaining about the ratings system and now that it has changed, you stop making genre films,"[13] thus indicating that as early as 1991, independent horror films from small studios were disappearing from theatrical releases, with only Hollywood sanitized horror—big names in the cast, little in terms of raw horror, a more family-oriented approach—coming to theatres. Rather than a horror film opening every week, a scarce number of films was released now throughout the year, leaving the impression in the fandom that horror had vanished. Some films made to reach audiences via theatrical release, such as *The Boneyard* (James Cummins, 1991), were bumped to the direct-to-video route to make a profit, as the director tells *Fangoria*.[14] The market was changing and many producers and studios were wary of putting big money into a genre that seemed almost defunct at the time. In an editorial in *Fangoria* 103, Anthony Timpone is troubled about the lack of future big releases in the horror genre and, for the first time, the magazine publishes two articles to analyze this "depressing development."[15] Maitland McDonagh, in her article "State of the Horror Nation," studies the decline of horror cinema after a decade so productive as the 1980s. McDonagh argues that, by the early 1990s, major independents such as "AIP/ Filmways, Avco Embassy and DEG are gone. New World sold off its film feature production division last year. Cannon filed bankruptcy and though it's back in business, the movies aren't out there yet."[16] Major studios were uninterested in the genre, while the major independents were disappearing rapidly in the first years of the 1990s, with no one taking over this market. McDonagh further argues that the fandom was not big enough to justify producers spending much money in a genre that attracted not whole families but just gorehounds missing the slasher years; major studios preferred to put the money into blockbusters such as *Terminator 2* (James Cameron, 1991): "Horror movies aren't a gold mine, and they operate on a relatively narrow profit margin."[17] Horror sequels received increasingly small returns, further shrinking budgets to keep the movies profitable. Lastly, horror was considered, after the excesses of the gory 1980s, a bad name in the industry. "The increasingly graphic depiction of gore turned a lot of people off,"[18] with terms such as "elevated horror" still many decades away.

In "The Market where Evil Dwells," Anthony C. Ferrante argued that the horror genre at the time (the first years of the 1990s) was mostly direct-to-video fare, and even in events such as the LA annual film sales meeting, people were afraid of the genre:

> Suffice to say that "horror" is a very dangerous word. One company *Fangoria* approached was at first quite interested in talking about their product, which consisted of a few horror films. Yet the moment the subject of an article was broached, the representative quickly turned the cold shoulder. Another rep was frightened by the type of publicity and nervously claimed to have no genre titles in their roster. "Oh, we're more into action-animation."[19]

The word "horror" made people (and studios) nervous. In *Fangoria* 112, dated May 1992, Timpone's editorial was titled "It's Not a Horror Film," a phrase that the magazine's editor hated, as directors, producers, stars and studios were eager to distance their films from even touching the genre. A new column was introduced into *Fangoria*, "It Is Not a Horror Film," the title satirizing the proclivity of Hollywood's producers in labeling all horror efforts as thrillers or suspense films to distance the movies from the horror label. By *Fangoria*'s July 1992 issue, Timpone praised the return of horror to the big screen with the opening in the U.S. of *Pet Sematary II* (Mary Lambert), *Innocent Blood* (John Landis), and *Buffy the Vampire Slayer* (Fran Rubel Kuzui), all of which ended up being box-office flops.[20] The magazine's cover, in turn, presented an image of The Penguin, from *Batman Returns* (Tim Burton, 1992), a Gothic film certainly, but not a horror one. The independent horror film, with its unaltered gore and intensity, had gone straight to video, while Hollywood replaced it in theaters with blockbusters and thrillers such as *Cape Fear* (Martin Scorsese, 1991), *Unlawful Entry* (Jonathan Kaplan, 1992), *The Hand That Rocks the Cradle* (Curtis Hanson, 1992), *Single White Female* (Barbet Schroeder, 1992), and *Malice* (Harold Becker, 1993), all films led by A-list actors and actresses, all of which appeared within *Fangoria*'s pages, even if "it's not a horror film."

The Spanish version of *Fangoria*, comprised of a mix of American and vernacular articles, supported this lack of screen horror as a global phenomenon. In the March 1993 editorial of *Fangoria* 17, Luis Vigil prays that the success of Coppola's version of *Dracula* will encourage producers and studios to make more horror films.[21] The editorial of *Fangoria* 26 from February 1994 is titled "Malos tiempos para el terror" ("Bad Times for Horror"),[22] with Vigil arguing that horror is basically dead, to the point that the magazine is at the edge of bankruptcy. Certainly, the Spanish version of *Fangoria* would endure "bad times" up until December 1994, when it folded for good. Horror was dead.

Or, at least, a type of horror was dead, pushed to the margins of direct-to-video, with theaters only accepting sanitized genre efforts such as *Bram Stoker's Dracula*, a film resting on the big, high-class names of Coppola and Stoker, or the *Jurassic Park*-style blockbusters, which were the closest thing to "horror" that many fans could find on the big screen. Thrillers offered some moments of horror, but the undead unstoppable killer was replaced by an all-too-human murderer, with the films remaining mostly bloodless. The Spanish version of *Fangoria* was forced to publish images of *Jurassic Park* on the cover for three months in a row (September–November 1993), basically because there was little else worthy of getting the cover. It may be argued that what took the screens in the early 1990s was a type of bourgeois horror, made to offend no one. Analyzing the slasher cycle of the 1990s (or what was left of it in the first years), Alexandra West argues that academia systematically neglected the consideration of this cycle of horror films to privilege the analysis of the slasher films of the 70s and 80s. This shows not only a complex moment for the production of horror films, but also a certain prejudice in academia regarding films that, taking up old slasher formulas, capitalize on the cultural consumption of adolescence, producing films that seem to respond only to the logic of the market rather than to new aesthetic approaches. West argues that "the main concern around this cycle of films is that they took what was once a powerful force in the independent film scene and commodified sacred elements into something sleek and refined and ready for mass consumption."[23]

Amidst this climate, John Waters turned his attention to the state of horror in America. Waters' cinema always made American suburbia and the hypocrisy of sanitized life and conformity a target.[24] *Cecil B. Demented* (2000) or *A Dirty Shame* (2004) are examples of Waters' attacks on safe art and/or American life in small towns. Yet, *Serial Mom*, Waters' only true horror film (albeit a comedy as well), made a target of the sanitization of horror throughout the 1990s. Gory and dirty, the film does not mock American suburbia so much as how horror was slowly turned "safe" after the 1980s.

TRASHING THE STATE OF HORROR

Serial Mom and Wes Craven's *Scream* are similar films, both speaking about the state of horror in the first half of the 1990s. As noted above, it is not so much that Craven was inspired by Waters' film, but that both directors diagnosed via a meta approach the dire state of independent horror cinema in the first half of the 1990s. Waters' film opens with a title card indicating that the film is based on "a true story" and "on court testimony, sworn declarations and hundreds of interviews." This playful reference to "true" stories closely follows Waters' fascination with trials[25] that began in *Pink Flamingos* (1972). Still, this trial is not just against middle-class hypocrisy (even if this theme is present throughout the film), but, rather, against Hollywood's bland approach to filmmaking during a sanitized era. After the title card, the film cuts to a tracking shot of Beverly's nice home, a two-story house not unlike that where Sidney Prescott (Neve Campbell) lives in Craven's film. Both stories place their horrors amidst suburbia, Craven and Waters distrusting American middle-class conformity.[26]

Serial Mom depicts the stereotypical American family: mother is serving breakfast, father Eugene Sutphin (Sam Waterston) is reading the newspaper—mostly ignoring the family—Misty (Ricki Lake) is the love-struck daughter and her brother Chip (Lillard) is an all-American teenager. Everything seems fine in the household, even when the conversation turns to darker matters: Eugene reads about a serial killer who earned his bachelor's degree in jail. This social rehabilitation, however, falls flat for the father, who thinks the killer should have been executed. Chip applauds the idea, savoring the idea of someone dying in an electric chair, and so he taunts his sister: "you'd probably date him." When a two cops come to the house investigating a series of obscene phone calls made in the neighborhood (Beverly has done the calls), Chip is in ecstasy at the prospect of a serial killer running amok through the suburbs. Later, he is eager to read a letter containing threats and profanity sent to an innocent neighbor. Beverly, in turn, dismisses the killer's murdering spree with "everyone has a bad day," thus sympathizing with him. The scene reveals dark impulses within Americana, a fascination with the morbid lurking beneath the sanitized surface of middle-class suburbia.

The scene finds a mirror in *Scream* in the scene following the killing of Casey (Drew Barrymore). Sidney and her friends, including her boyfriend Billy Loomis (Skeet Ulrich), Tatum (Rose McGowan), Randy (Jamie Kennedy) and Stu (Lillard) meet before their first class of the day begins. After learning about Casey's brutal killing just hours ago, the group seems fascinated, rather than sorry for the loss of a young life. Stu and Randy compare the real murder with horror films, with most of Sidney's friends joking about the case and taunting each other about how to make a perfect crime and how "macho" one needs to be to kill someone. Stu jokes about the killing even if he—as Sidney points out—briefly dated her. The conversation is so dense with black humor that Sidney (whose mother was brutally killed a year ago) leaves the group. Like the Sutphins, there is something slightly askew in these normal teenagers, a dark edge mostly obscured by their middle-class background within white, sunny suburbia. Even the school Principal Himbry (Henry Winkler) comments (after a cruel prank) about "how disgusting" the new generation of teenagers is.

In this scenario, Beverly Sutphin is the epitome of the sanitized first half of the 1990s and family values. First, she dresses as a housewife from the 1950s. This was not just the era of conformity par excellence within American history,[27] framed by "lack of individuality,"[28] but also marked the end of the horror cycle. Certainly, the classic horror cycle began with *Dracula* (Tod Browning, 1931) and ended, exhausted, in the latter years of the 1940s, with classic monsters such as Frankenstein's creature, the Wolfman and Dracula being ridiculed and parodied in Abbot and Costello's films. The horror cycle was replaced by B science-fiction films, albeit, arguably, these films were mixed with the horror genre with the uncanny presence of Big-Eyed Monsters. Beverly evokes a decade which, like the first half of the 1990s, suffered a drought of screen horror. Second, Beverly is the perfect stereotype of the moral values of the 1950s housewives: she is modest and prude to parodic extremes. She asks one of the detectives to spit out his chewing gum, as it is forbidden to eat such sweets in the home. She talks to birds and looks happy all the time. As Eugene states, Beverly is incapable of saying aloud, much less writing, profanity.

Yet, when she is alone, Beverly enjoys her free time calling her neighbor Dottie Hinkle (Mink Stole) to threaten her using a large array of profanity. The dark side of suburbia, however, seems integral to the geographical milieu: Dottie calls her anonymous caller "bitch" and spits profanities with gusto. The next day, Beverly and Dottie exchange greetings, waving their hands to each other with smiles on their faces. When each looks the other way, however, the fake smiles turn into scowls. Both women hide resentments, envy, or grudges lurking behind the plastic and shiny surface of suburbia. Beverly may be the most extreme case, but nobody seems free from a mean streak.

While other characters hide their dark sides, Beverly explores hers via fascination with the macabre. Not only does she empathize with a serial killer's "bad day," she also encourages Chip's passion for horror films. Contrary to what one might think due to her naïve character, Beverly does not see horror films as something negative but simply as an artistic expression like any other. This interest in horror films, especially the gore and trash that Chip loves so much, subverts Beverly's character; in a way, Beverly's fascination with the macabre would "undermine" the character's comic integrity; a woman who rejects out of hand any manifestation that does not exemplify traditional conservative values. However, the focus of Waters' criticism is not so much the conformity of the suburban middle class (which he has criticized in other films) but rather the state of 1990s cinema and how Hollywood purified and softened the savage cinema of the 1970s and 1980s. Beverly may be a housewife lifted right from the 1950s, but she loves her horror uncensored. It may be argued that Beverly is an avatar of Waters' cinema, and *Serial Mom* in particular. *Serial Mom* was Waters' most slick film, made with big names (such as Kathleen Turner), big-budget production values and a coherent plot. Like Beverly herself, the film looks prim and proper. Yet, like Beverly, the good production values hide a dark edge trying to disrupt a filmmaking system that is hostile to independent working methods and any confrontational approach to breaking taboos. In other words, *Serial Mom* has Kathleen Turner in a leading role, but has also Mink Stole, a muse of Waters' trashy cinema. Beverly is a transgressor masquerading as a conformist, which is analogous to Waters himself making *Serial Mom* as a "proper" film that backhandedly disturbs the order with the exhibition of gore and antisocial behavior.

These contradictions are highlighted in the first murder scene, where family values and trashy cinema are combined. Beverly attends a parents' meeting at Chip's school. The school's director, Mr. Stubbins (John Badila), embodies neoliberal traditional values. A sign on the blackboard reads "Determination + Hard Work + Discipline = the Way to Success," a deterministic ethos based on the "sacrosanct valorisation of meritocracy that have enabled neoliberal policies to gain traction."[29] Mr. Stubbins is first shown telling a distressed Black mother that her son is not made for universities; seconds later, with the woman crying, he orders her to leave since there are other parents waiting for their meeting. Mr. Stubbins' conservative values, however, manifest more clearly in his approach to cinema than in his racially prejudiced point of view. Mr. Stubbins is worried about Chip's taste for extreme horror cinema. For the school's director, this taste is symptomatic of repressed frustrations and aggression, both the product of failed upbringing. For Mr. Stubbins, something is wrong in the Sutphins' home; are the parents getting a divorce? Is there a history of alcoholism running in the family? Has been Chip being caught torturing animals? As has been well documented, many serial killers have a history of torturing animals at young age, a pleasure in suffering that they will later extend to humans.[30] Mr. Stubbins insinuates that there is a clear connection between Chip's taste for gore cinema, a dysfunctional family, and disturbing behavior. This simplistic connection between screen violence and real violent behavior was, however, very popular as a moral panic in the 1980s and 1990s.

The concept of moral panic was developed by Stanley Cohen as "a condition, episode, person or group of persons emerges to become defined as a threat to societal values and interests" that later "disappears, submerges or deteriorates."[31] The target of the moral panic will be an identifiable group who will be portrayed as "folk devils," those putting society into danger. A popular moral panic in the U.S. and U.K. was the preoccupation regarding violence on the screen and how it affected youth. Media violence has been shown to make children "more violent than they would naturally become without being exposed to it."[32] For authors such as Dave Grossman and Gloria DeGaetano, the debate about this topic is over: violence on screen and in videogames *do* make children more prone to exert violence on their peers.[33] The neoliberal logic of cultural representation determines heterogeneity in viewers' responses and it is conducive to just one, uncomplicated image of alterity as potentially threatening to moral traditional values.[34] Certainly, horror cinema has come to steal our children's souls.

These studies connecting violence and behavior are mostly based on "reductive assumptions and unjustified stereotypes regarding media content." Further, "this preoccupation with media effects had indeed been criticized for playing in the hands of politicians with conservative agendas"[35] who use alterity to push reactionary agendas. Mr. Stubbins is a reactionary man, using screen violence as a scapegoat. Chip is not even a bad student; the director tells Beverly that her son is attentive and has good grades. Yet, he sees his love for horror films as something that should be carefully policed. Facing Beverly's outrage, he (again) orders her to leave as there are other parents waiting in the school's hall. Mr. Stubbins will be Beverly's first victim, when Beverly drives her car over him after leaving school. It is the mother who is the deranged one, not the horror-fan son. Still, Beverly does not just encourage Chip's love for horror cinema; she seems to be a fan herself, as she asks Chip to rewind a VHS to rewatch a particularly gory scene.

Unlike her neighbors, Beverly's "dark side" is not hidden. Her secret is that she is a serial killer, not that she is a lover of screen violence, treating the latter as an inoffensive activity she shares with her completely healthy, inoffensive son. *Scream*'s Principal Himbry is also disgusted by youth, and he is a reactionary figure like Mr. Stubbins. Principal Himbry furiously talks to students wearing the Ghostface mask about their lack of empathy for two murdered students. For him, youth has lost sensibility; yet it is the Principal who exhibits hostile attitudes bordering on violence in that scene, threatening the students with a sharp pair of scissors. Like Mr. Stubbins, he will meet his end at the hands of the killer. Sheriff Burke (Joseph Whipp) is another adult figure who states he does not understand the youth anymore, even if he seems to forget, like Mr. Stubbins and Principal Himbry, that horror was not a hot property at the moment of the film's opening. It may be argued that *Scream*'s young killers (Stu and Billy) are, indeed, fans of horror films, thus connecting them with prejudices about violence in cinema. Still, as the killers explain, horror cinema does not *make* killers; it only gives them ideas about how to act. Furthermore, Randy is the most passionate lover of horror films within *Scream*, yet he uses his knowledge to try to discern who the killer is. Both films present a nuanced version of the linkage between screen violence and horror in real life. Beverly, Stu, and Billy may be horror lovers, yet they live around other people even more passionate about the horror genre who are not dangerous killers. When the news about the murder of Mr. Stubbins is broadcast on TV, Chip's girlfriend mentions that the killing is "like in a horror movie," undifferentiating real life from screen violence. Yet, Chip is moved. When his sister mentions that he hated Mr. Stubbins, Chip retorts that even so, "he did not deserve to die," thus highlighting that Chip, the fan of extreme horror films, is a sensitive young man.

Scream and *Serial Mom* do not only share topics and actor (Lillard), but also a key scene taking place in a video rental shop. In Waters' film, Misty visits the video rental shop managed by Chip to chat with him about the probability that, maybe, their mother is a serial killer. There, Chip and friends are watching a film about a female serial killer, *Strait-jacket* (William Castle, 1964). Chip and his friends are fans of horror films, and the video rental shop is almost entirely dedicated to horror films: all the posters belong to real horror films, and the only titled section depicted behind Misty is the one labeled "Horror" (see Figure 3.1). In a later scene, Chip attends to Mrs. Jensen (Patsy Grady Abrams), a client who complains about the violence in the films Chip and his friends watch while working at the video rental shop. Grudgingly, Chip turns off the TV so as not to offend this woman, who is a self-proclaimed "fan of Bill Cosby movies." A brief argument ensues when Chip mentions to the woman that she again forgot to rewind the movie; this time he charges her the fine, which the woman complainingly pays. When Mrs. Jensen leaves, Chip comments that her bad mood is due to her fanaticism for "family movies," an ironic comment on the general state of horror cinema in the first years of the 1990s and a twist on the proclivity to link horror cinema to youth criminality and violence. Mrs. Jensen is another figure who links horror films with antisocial instincts and is comically killed by Beverly, who uses a lamb leg as a murder

Figure 3.1 Horror is the most salient genre in Chip's video rental shop.

weapon. Mrs. Jensen dies while watching *Annie* (John Huston, 1982), a meta-commentary used by Waters to destroy commercial cinema through horror cinema. Beverly overheard the discussion between Mrs. Jensen and Chip while hiding in the video store dedicated to the horror genre, thus securing the symbolic relationship between Beverly as the embodiment of a wilder, more independent auteur cinema, and the stultified cinema of Hollywood.

In *Scream*, Stu and Randy talk about the crimes taking place in the suburbs while the former attends the video shop, which is filled with people renting horror movies, now more popular than ever after the murder spree began, thus revealing there is a thirst for horror in sanitized America. Randy tells Stu that their reality is akin to a horror movie, where everyone is a suspect. For Randy, the main suspect, Sidney's father, is just a red herring, with the real culprit being Billy, who is, indeed, the film's killer (together with Stu). There, Randy clashes with Billy, who is also in the shop. Billy turns the tables, mentioning that maybe it is Randy who is the killer. The motive, for Billy, is that Randy's brain has been contaminated by so many horror movies that he is now a serial killer. Both *Scream* and *Serial Mom* engage in dialogue with their *zeitgeist*, dominated in part by a "New Moral Right"[36] with a conservative agenda.

The murders in both films are gory, an artistic decision that not only addresses horror fandom, but also sharply stages what Hollywood wants to keep off-screen. When Beverly kills her daughter's ex-boyfriend with a poker, a piece of the boy's liver is left hanging on the end of the murder weapon. Beverly is forced to touch the piece of flesh to remove it, a scene that forces the audience to confront the gore that has been subtracted from the screens (see Figure 3.2). It should be noted that *Serial Mom* is the only horror film made by John Waters

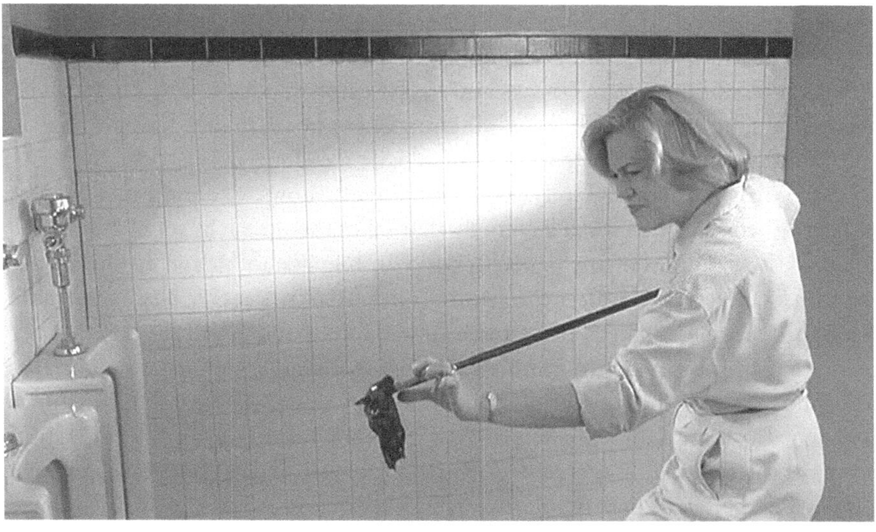

Figure 3.2 Gore and disgust is made prominent by Waters amidst a sanitized era.

to date. It is clear that the director felt he needed to make horror at a time when horror was under attack, to defend its right to be gross and trashy against Hollywood's Oscar-bait horror. Waters makes a slick film to show disgusting moments of absurd gore, declaring that the only way to channel raw horror in theaters is through a pretty package of glossy cinema. Both Waters and Craven made films that commented on horror cinema precisely at a time when horror cinema's presence had been diminishing throughout the first half of the decade.

CONCLUSIONS

The lack of horror cinema in the first years of the 1990s was not due solely to the "conservative agenda" but to the excesses of both the formulaic architecture of the genre and the excessive splatter. The death of horror was global, rather than national (like in the 1960s), with the sanitized thriller replacing horror. Yet, the taste for horror was alive, as the success of *Scream* shows, but this only became clear in the mid-1990s. Before *Scream*, Craven had failed in his attempt to revitalize the genre with his excellent reimagining of *A Nightmare on Elm Street* (1984) in the form of *Wes Craven's New Nightmare* (1994), a film that previewed some of *Scream*'s themes with its meta approach to horror, but flopped at the box office. Maybe the first years of the 1990s saw audiences bored with horror, but the interest was ripe by the coming of *Scream*.

Both *Scream* and *Serial Mom* are graphically violent, but take an ironic view. The films are not against horror, but the current state of the horror market, now pushed to video stores rather than the big screen. Viewers do not see any screen violence taking place in cinemas but, rather, in homes: Chip and friends enjoy horror films in the boy's bedroom, while Stu organizes a party in his house to watch, all friends together, John Carpenter's *Halloween*. Horror has been relegated to video, the world now free from screen violence yet populated by characters hiding mean streaks and deep-seated grudges. The danger, John Waters says, lies rather with those watching *Annie* because they have the law on their side, oppressing any possibility of artistic freedom.

Serial Mom is an anti-Hollywood film, which allows it to exist in a context of horror drought. It is a black comedy that takes the theme of serial killers and some of the formulas of the genre to build an homage to horror. In the end of the film, set five months after the crimes committed by Beverly, she has become a star, her face on T-shirts, pins, and a future film that will tell the story of her life. She is the object of admiration of both young people and other housewives who must repress their anger and envy in order to continue to live and function socially. In *Scream*'s sequel, *Scream 2* (Wes Craven, 1998), Sidney's story becomes the fictional horror saga *Stab*, and reporter Gale Weathers (Courtney Cox) makes her an indispensable character in her books when she deals with her mother's murder. In both cases, the film accounts for the impact of horror cinema on society and the cultural consumption associated with true crimes. This is replicated in the horror cinema of the 1990s, where "films were no longer just films; they were soundtracks, fashions, slang, award shows and identities. The film studios could cross market enough of their products so much so that if an audience member enjoyed a film, they could purchase several other products to go along with it."[37] The interest in horror that both films prefigure (and that would be fully depicted in *Scream 2*) is organized via Beverly and Sidney becoming, in the future, horror icons within their fictional worlds. Certainly, horror cinema would return with a vengeance in the latter part of the 1990s, John Waters and Wes Craven's productions foreshadowing this event.

NOTES

1. John Kenneth Muir, *Horror Films of 2000–2009* (Jefferson, NC: McFarland, 2023), 89.
2. Bryan Turnock, *Studying Horror Cinema* (Liverpool: Liverpool University Press, 2019), 267.
3. Fernando Gabriel Pagnoni Berns, Canela Ailén Rodriguez Fontao and Mariana Zárate, "From Traditional Slasher to Fourth Wave: Fantastical Reconversion in *The Final Girls* and *Happy Death Day*," in *Fourth Wave Feminism in Science Fiction and Fantasy, Volume 1: Essays on Film Representations, 2012–2019*, edited by Valerie Frankel (Jefferson, NC: McFarland, 2019), 79.
4. Lorenza Perini, *Giving Feminism a Bad Name: The Uprising of the Anti-Feminism Instances in Times of Populisms* (Milan: Ledizioni, 2021), 98.
5. William Proctor and Mark McKenna, "Introduction: The Death and Resurrection Show: Horror Franchise Cinema and the Romanticization of Cult," in *Horror Franchise Cinema*, edited by William Proctor and Mark McKenna (New York: Routledge, 2021), 2.
6. Thomas Schatz, "The New Hollywood," in *Movie Blockbusters*, edited by Julian Stringer (New York: Routledge, 2003), 32.
7. Schatz, "The New Hollywood," 34.
8. Rui Trindade Oliveira, *Supranational Horrors: Italian and Spanish Horror Cinema since 1968* (Lanham, MD: Lexington, 2022), 98.
9. Ibid.
10. Javier Pulido, *La década de oro del cine de terror español (1967–1976)* (Madrid: T & B Editores, 2012).
11. Geoffrey Macnab, *J. Arthur Rank and the British Film Industry* (New York: Routledge, 2013), ix–x.
12. Anthony Timpone, "Return of the Indie." *Fangoria* 101 (New York: April 1991).
13. Jim Turner, "Desperately Seeking Scares," *Fangoria* 106 (New York: September 1991), 8.
14. James Cummins, "Bone to Pick," *Fangoria* 108 (New York: September 1991), 8.
15. Timpone, "The Lean Season," *Fangoria* 103, New York, June 1991.
16. Maitland McDonagh, "The State of Horror Nation," *Fangoria* 103 (New York: June 1991), 21.
17. Ibid., 22.
18. Ibid., 23.
19. Anthony C. Ferrante, "The Market where Evil Dwells," *Fangoria* 103 (New York: June 1991), 26.
20. Timpone, "Summer Screams," *Fangoria* 114, New York, July 1992.

21. Luis Vigil, "Reponso", *Fangoria* 17 (Madrid: Zinco Editores, March 1993), 4.
22. Luis Vigil, "Malos tiempos para el terror", (Madrid: Zinco Editores, February 1994), 4.
23. Alexandra West, *The 1990s Teen Horror Cycle: Final Girls and a New Hollywood Formula* (Jefferson: McFarland, 2018), 14.
24. Abigail Waldron, *A History of LGBTQ+ Survival Through the Lens of American Horror Cinema* (Jefferson, NC: McFarland, 2022).
25. Taunya Lovell Banks, "Troubled Waters: Mid-Twentieth Century American Society on Trial in the Films of John Waters," *Stetson L. Rev.* 39 (2009): 153.
26. See Fernando Gabriel Pagnoni Berns and John Darowski (eds.), *A Critical Companion to Wes Craven* (Lanham, MD: Lexington, 2023); James Egan, *John Waters: Interviews* (Jackson: University Press of Mississippi, 2011), 100; David Puglia, *Tradition, Urban Identity, and the Baltimore "Hon": The Folk in the City* (Lanham, MD: Lexington, 2018), 100.
27. Neil Hamilton, *Rebels and Renegades: A Chronology of Social and Political Dissent in the United States* (New York: Routledge, 2002), 231.
28. Nancy Hendricks, *Daily Life in 1950s America* (Santa Barbara: ABC-Clio, 2019), 127.
29. Marissa K. L. E, *Discourses of Neoliberalism in Singapore's Higher Education Context: Individualist and Communitarian Perspectives* (New York: Routledge, 2023), 46.
30. Margo DeMello, *Animals and Society: An Introduction to Human-Animal Studies* (New York: Columbia University Press, 2012), 245.
31. Stanley Cohen, *Folk Devils and Moral Panics* (St. Albans: Paladin, 1973).
32. Dave Grossman and Gloria DeGaetano, *Stop Teaching Our Kids to Kill* (New York, Crown Publishers, 1999), 10.
33. Grossman and DeGaetano, *Stop Teaching Our Kids to Kill*, 22.
34. Clive Nwonka, *Black Boys: The Social Aesthetics of British Urban Film* (New York: Bloomsbury Publishing, 2023), 126.
35. Vera Slavtcheva-Petkova, *Young People, Media and Politics in the Digital Age* (New York: Routledge, 2023), 44.
36. Bill Thompson and Andy Williams, *The Myth of Moral Panics: Sex, Snuff, and Satan* (New York: Routledge, 2013), 130.
37. West, *The 1990s Teen Horror Cycle*, 23.

CHAPTER 4

Artsy Fartsy: *Pecker* and the Guilty Pleasures of John Waters' "Bad" Art Habits

Kristen Galvin

Time certainly flies when you are having fun riding alongside the long and illustrious career of John Waters. *Pecker* (1998), Waters' "independent film" about the art world, just celebrated its twenty-fifth anniversary in 2023, at the height of his recent cultural recognition. The film is congruent with the spirit of his film oeuvre, as Waters reflected in 2024: "All my movies satirized some kind of genre or some kind of world that I liked. That's why I think I've been able to get away with those things. I make fun of things I like, not hate."[1] While Waters consistently champions outsiders in his work, *Pecker* is an outlier in his filmography because it is the only movie to directly address his long-time and competing passion: contemporary art. In *Pecker*, Waters skewers the New York art world in a Cinderella story that is at once personal, critical, and art historical. The film arrives after Waters' shift towards mass-appeal that began with *Hairspray* (1988), followed by *Cry-Baby* (1990) and *Serial Mom* (1994), as a kind of artistic compromise that nods to his earlier work, yet is in the middle of his cinematic spectrum that spans cult to the mainstream.

According to film history, *Pecker* temporally falls within the ascent of 1990s independent film, and the Hollywood turnover that occurred with the new reign of American auteurs such as Quentin Tarantino, Wes Anderson, Spike Lee, Gus Van Sant, Richard Linklater, and Kevin Smith. *Pecker* also cast young, hot actors who were either overhauling their child star image (Edward Furlong and Christina Ricci) or were already ingrained in the 1990s independent film scene (Brandan Sexton III and Lili Taylor). *Pecker* also lies in the wake of independent film's New York art world invasion, when there were multiple cross-over directorial debuts by well-known painters and photographers including *Kids* (Larry Clark, 1995), *Search and Destroy* (David Salle, 1995), *Basquiat* (Julian Schanbel, 1996), and *Office Killer* (Cindy Sherman, 1997).

Not since the New Hollywood period had there been so much acclaim for visionary American filmmaking, and this evolution in the 1990s marked the resurgence of outcasts and dysfunctionality on-screen, but with heightened sex and violence. The movement of New Queer Cinema is also affiliated with this radical expansion of film in the 1990s. Significantly, Waters is credited with paving the way for the movement's new directors such as Gregg Araki, Cheryl Dunye, and Todd Haynes. In the 1990s, Waters was both a patron saint of, and contributor to, the decade's reinvigoration of cinema, placing him once again in a category of his very own. However, by the time of *Pecker*, he was no longer an outsider or scrappy young filmmaker from Baltimore, but a seasoned industry insider across film and contemporary art—first as an avid collector and then as a visual artist.

While prolifically releasing four films between 1990–2000, Waters somehow found the time and creative energy to simultaneously generate enough artwork and gallery buzz to merit a retrospective by the early 2000s: *John Waters: Change of Life* (New Museum, New York, NY, U.S.A., 8 February 2004–15 April 2004). *Pecker* was ironically timed to the rise of Waters' own art star, and functions as his critical response to artmaking within the idiosyncrasies as well as the delimitations of the New York art world. In the 1990s and 2000s, he exhibited at galleries such as Colin De Land/American Fine Arts, Marianne Boesky, and Gagosian Gallery, amongst many other domestic and international spaces, in numerous solo and group shows. Just as the character of Pecker brought the New York art world to Baltimore, albeit by bus, Waters also eventually returned to his hometown in the dual forms of museum retrospective and personal collection display. First, there was *John Waters: Indecent Exposure* (Baltimore Museum of Art, Baltimore, MD, U.S.A., 7 October 2018–6 January 2019), a multimedia extravaganza of over 160 of his own works. Subsequently, he donated his private art collection to the Baltimore Museum of Art (BMA), comprised of approximately 372 works by 125 artists, mostly of the contemporary period. The collection was curated and distilled to ninety works for the BMA exhibition, *Coming Attractions: The John Waters Collection* (20 November 2022–16 April 2023). The show was guest curated by self-identified queer photographers Catherine Opie and Jack Pierson, coincidentally also Waters' friends and 'roommates'—the affectionate name he gives to the artists/artworks who adorn his self-curated homes. Waters' collection was bestowed to the BMA under one distinctive condition: the bathrooms must be renamed and converted to the "John Waters Restrooms/All Gender," which were inaugurated with "a first pee" by transgender artist and activist Elizabeth Coffey.[2]

Like much of Waters' creative work, *Coming Attractions: The John Waters Collection* blends biography, queerness, surprise, imagination, and satire. When the curators/roommates asked Waters if there were any overall themes in his collection, he responded:

> Firstly, I always love art that infuriates people. Sometimes it infuriates me first, and it takes me a minute to realize I love it. And that's when I know I'm going to buy it. Secondly, I would say art that makes me laugh in some way . . . sometimes Mike Kelley's pieces are so rude that they make me chuckle. Confidence, that's the third one . . . The confidence to believe that what you have done is perfectly valued even when no one else agrees. Fourth would be narrative—filmic in a way, even though it doesn't have to be about movies. But narrative—imagined or otherwise—that tells a story that other people might not get. That goes along with confidence too, I think. Catholicism—I guess there's some leftover of that in my damaged psyche. Sexuality, yes, but in a way that's always kind of creepy or funny but not just sexy.[3]

Looking back and across Waters' creative output and collection, these deep throughlines, or consistencies, come into even starker relief when Waters' own standards of exquisite taste becomes a guiding principle, or what this chapter calls his "guilty pleasures." This is a highly productive and personalized queer/nobrow/camp aesthetic that seamlessly fuses creativity with connoisseurship. This framework provides a scholarly opportunity that strays from conceptions of film auteurism alone, to afford a more holistic assessment of Waters' overarching cultural contribution, and in turn, reevaluate the often-overlooked film, *Pecker*. Waters' interwoven themes of infuriation, humor, confidence, storytelling, Catholicism, and sexuality that determine his collection and connoisseurship also drive the narrative of *Pecker*, and what this chapter advances as Waters' signature of "guilty pleasure."

For decades, Waters has been tapdancing across the edges of camp, cult, trash, independent, and mainstream cinema via guilty pleasure. Simultaneously, he writes beyond just screenplays and is a best-selling author who pens fiction, memoir, cultural criticism, and journalism; collects and creates art; performs one-man shows (such as his popular Christmas tour); and even directs an adult summer sleepaway camp. Waters' promiscuous creativity and connoisseurship demonstrate a fannish love of cultures beyond the purely cinematic. As a prolific polymath, Waters' activities form his complex yet highly identifiable taste, or personal aesthetic of guilty pleasure.

Through the text of *Pecker*, this chapter examines how Waters stretches across cultural industries, from Baltimore to Los Angeles to New York, and bouncing back and forth again. Waters' adherence to personal taste and aesthetic, which include playful distinctions between good/bad and love/hate, are deeply rooted in guilty pleasure as defining structure, no matter the medium. Therefore, Waters' nuances and loops of life imitating art and art imitating life—and even art imitating art or other artists' lives—are examined via *Pecker*. Through tactics of camp humor, Waters' own "life as art/art as life" strategy is closely aligned with his reworkings of refined and reviled cultures as guilty pleasure. Together, they merge into his own queer and "nobrow" aesthetic that merrily skips through the muddied postmodern terrain of high and low cultural recombinations. Adopting John Seabrook's term as theoretical springboard, "nobrow" names the ambiguous spaces that lie between traditional categories of high versus lowbrow cultures, which manufacture systems and assumptions of good versus bad taste.[4]

However innovative, shocking, or surprising, Waters is not the first to establish this pattern of queer and nobrow postmodern inquiry as practice. Andy Warhol, who Waters was both an acquaintance of and collects, moved from advertising to fine art to underground film to popular culture, via queer tastes. By the end of Warhol's career and life, he was dabbling in cable television with a show on MTV (*Andy Warhol's Fifteen Minutes*, 1985–1987), and with *Interview Magazine* (1969–present) at the height of its circulation. Warhol's most surprising performance of guilty pleasure, a televisual guest appearance that was five years in the making, occurred in 1985 when he finally boarded the *Love Boat* (ABC 1977–1986).[5] Taking notes from Warhol, but starting in do-it-yourself filmmaking as opposed to commercial illustration, Waters' proclivities are more excessive and humanizing than Warhol's most "underground" artistic gestures, whether outrageous, beyond banal, or shamefully naughty or trashy. Primarily, guilty pleasure is self-pleasing and self-amusing and is not conducted for others, and certainly not for audiences, film distributors, or museum/gallery directors. Following one's guilty pleasure certainly takes "confidence." Furthermore, without his upper-middle-class, white, and Catholic upbringing, the fun factor of Watersesque guilty pleasure loses currency if there is no higher stake of guilt, no matter the number of Hail Marys required to absolve the "sin," with obsessive, addictive, and "crackpot" behaviors closely in tow. From the character of Little Chrissie's love of sugar in *Pecker* to the parade of sex addictions and fetishes in *A Dirty Shame* (2004), Waters indulges himself first, and audiences secondarily and vicariously. He enacts such visual cultural mischief and misbehaves despite knowing all the boundaries and taboos—and does so no matter how major or minor the transgression—in the direct face of shame itself as guilty pleasure. Thus, guilty pleasure is a useful framework for interrogating the very binary opposition of shame versus pride, affects that politically contextualize understandings of queer history and movements.

Importantly, overcoming shame and celebrating failure can be extremely empowering and are central to the politics of LGBTQIA+ communities and history, as well as queer theory. Waters self-identifies as gay and as a long-time queer advocate since the pivotal wave of Gay Liberation followed by AIDS/HIV activism, and has lived experience as a gay man from the decriminalization of homosexuality in the 1960s to the legalization of same-sex marriage in 2015 in the U.S.A. Shock, shame, and stigmatization, in opposition to social acceptance, assimilation, and pride, are crucial to how negative affects can be mobilized and reclaimed to advance the cultures, rights, and livelihoods of LGBTQIA+ identified people.[6] Queer theorist Jack Halberstam dismisses such easy conceptions of positive/negative binarism and recuperates negative affect by embracing the potentialities of 'the queer art of failure.' Advancing what is aptly termed 'low theory,' Halberstam perceives failure as challenging both hetero- and homonormative capitalist institutions which determine and dictate success and happiness to offer actionable alternatives: 'there is something powerful in being wrong, in losing, in failing, and that all our failures combined might just be enough, if we practice them well, to bring down the winner.'[7] Waters' "queer art of failure," in the shape of his relentless celebration of losers and underdogs, which doubles as guilty pleasure, extends his initial cinematic impulse to subvert social and sexual taboos. Film scholar Elena Gorfinkel also advances failure as key to the potency of cult film in the context of Waters' early work, asserting:

> the cult film could reconstruct the oppositions between high- and low-brow tastes with the exceeding forcefulness of its outré images, its messy bodies, and its unruly fans . . . taking the principle of failure—on visual, cultural and political grounds—as its guiding logic.[8]

For Gorfinkel, Waters' nobrow cult film strategy is directly connected to the cult film's politics of failure, and thereby its agency. The playful queer imagination and visual cultural fluidity of Waters, accomplished through his astute intellectual fluency in what constitutes good versus bad taste, and high versus low cultures, cuts across systems of legitimizations and media types under the maxim of guilty pleasure.

Unlike his other films, Waters' critical eye on the contemporary art world, and the history of photography, also constitute the guilty pleasures of *Pecker*. This chapter analyzes how Waters combines his obsessive artistic and cinematic habits via the film text, which correspond to his larger operations in the art world, and ultimately facilitate a more rigorous and full understanding of Waters' queer and nobrow camp aesthetic. To effectively reexamine Waters' transmedial production/consumption with 2020s hindsight, the framework of guilty pleasure overrides any separation between contemporary art and film, or subculture and mainstream. To my point, when Waters was invited by *Film Comment* in the early 1980s to write a feature on his own guilty pleasures, he made the shocking confession to readers about his own film snobbery: "but what really shames me is that I'm also secretly a fan of what is dreadedly known as the 'art film.'"[9] For all his hybridity, experimentation, curiosity, and boundary wreckage, Waters consistently follows the guiding light of his own guilty pleasure, as extraordinary John-of-all-trades. The satirical *Pecker* illuminates

Waters' deep take on art, artists, creativity, and the confines of the New York art world, as dual criticism and love letter to the very absurdity of contemporary art itself.

THE DIRTY SHAM OF CONTEMPORARY ART

Before discussing *Pecker*, a few points on Waters' love-hate relationship with contemporary art. In the spirit of the queer art of failure, Waters adores flipping failure and turning losers into winners. He is deeply attuned to the power of art's deceptions, whether in the gimmicks of modernist innovations in art history, art market overvaluations and speculations, or screen gags. Most of all, he appreciates the beauty in art's transformative power. He harnesses its capacity to elevate others/failures/outsiders into lovable characters of mainstream film and musicals, and to repurpose objects and cultures as "capital-A-Artist." Echoing Halberstam, Waters has commented on several occasions, but significantly at his inspiring and hilarious commencement speech for the School of Visual Arts (2022), that he has "failed upwards" and encourages freshly minted graduates to get out there and to do so too.[10] Waters' fascination with contemporary art, extremely broad in its definitions of what is or can be art, is also what maintains his curiosity and drive in this arena. He is enchanted by the outrage of art, even after the shocks of avant-garde movements over a century ago.

While there is a fine line between distinctions of art versus non-art, Waters is well versed in modern and contemporary art's deft navigation of these poles, that overlap but can snap at will. Furthermore, contemporary art is as much outside of everyday mass culture as cult film is outside of Hollywood, and arguably even more niche as subculture. As previously quoted, Waters cherishes art that he hates at first or, before its time, was considered a failure upon initial display. But then phoenix-like, such art has the power to rise and challenge and change his mind as well as that of art history. This is the space where art and Waters' fascination meet: the "magic" of art is in its capacity to deceive and infuriate. He demystifies the innerworkings of this illusion in *Pecker*, but also revels in the glorious lies and trickery of it all, as guilty pleasure. Through the power of art, one can flip and sign a urinal under a fake name (Marcel Duchamp, *Fountain*, 1917) or defecate in a can (Piero Manzoni, *Artist's Shit*, 1961), and create precious, highly valued objects. And what is more Watersesque than these abject, "greatest hits" of art history?

However, by comparison, Pecker's photography is quite tame, especially when contextualized within the 1980s–1990s culture war controversies over queer and religious content in the work of photographers such as Robert Mapplethorpe (e.g., *X Portfolio*, 1978; *Man in a Polyester Suit*, 1980) or Andreas Serrano (e.g., *Piss Christ*, 1987). Instead, *Pecker* celebrates the naïve yet "so bad it's good" eye of a teenage photographer as outsider artist, even if the character and very name of "Pecker" uphold the norms of art market worth as white, male, and straight. Waters gleefully exposes the ridiculousness of contemporary art as industry and is especially attentive to its eagerness to exploit for profit, with its gate keepers, insiders, and taste and canon makers, which are all lovingly deflated in *Pecker*.

THE "BAD" PHOTOGRAPHY OF *PECKER*

Distributed by New Line Cinema with a modest six-million-dollar budget, *Pecker*'s R-rated rags-to-riches story is a triumph of the Baltimorean white underclass, which is certainly not new territory for Waters. In the opening credit sequence to the tune of the uplifting "Happy Go Lucky Me" (Paul Evans, 1960), Pecker (Edward Furlong) documents his fellow bus riders, friends, family, residents, and the humping rats of the Hampden neighborhood with his trusty camera, a gift from his mother's thrift shop that fashionably clothes the homeless. Nicknamed Pecker for pecking at his food as a child, Waters indulges in the film's running "dick joke" that he gets away with by desexualizing the antiquated schoolyard slang term. Defending his title choice of *Pecker* in a meeting with the Motion Pictures Association of America, he quipped that if *Free Willy* (Simon Wincer, 1993) and *Shaft* (Gordon Parks, 1971) were not censored, why should *Pecker* be?[11] More of Waters' savvy wordplay in the film includes the constant double use of "Mary," referring to Pecker's grandmother, or Memama's (Jean Schertler) ventriloquist dummy of the Virgin Mary, or his sister Tina's (Martha Plimpton) constant use of "Mary" to affectionately address gay men in queer allyship.

By pure chance, Pecker is unexpectedly discovered by an ambitious New York City gallerist, Rorey Wheeler (Lili Taylor), who drops in on Pecker's pop-up photography exhibition at his workplace, a local hole-in-the-wall sandwich shop called The Sub Pit. While Rory appreciates his eye, and buys a photograph for $30, Pecker's boss does not, and promptly fires him after a near riot breaks out after a close-up abstract photograph is revealed to be the lesbian stripper T-Bone's (Maureen Fischer/drag king performer Mo B. Dick) "full bush." Pecker is offered a solo show on site and quickly infiltrates the upper echelons of the art world. He experiences instant and meteoric success as casual photography's latest sensation and chronicler of Baltimore's most "culturally challenged."

As second act antagonism, Pecker and his family quickly learn of celebrity's downsides and the eagerness of the worlds of contemporary art and fashion to exploit them. The calamities include Memama's talking Mary losing her miraculous ability to speak, and Tina getting fired from her emcee job at the local gay go-go bar, The Fudge Palace. Further, Pecker's family's house gets robbed. The people of Baltimore have turned on Pecker because they themselves do not want to be turned into art. When they are photographed and become art, they suffer, and in the case of his family members, they lose what is most important or sacred to them. Pecker, staying true to his roots and putting his family and loved ones first, seeks to regain his lower-class cultural capital, which was lost when his photography graced the cover of *ARTFORUM*. As emblazoned on the front of *New York Magazine*, the gutsy Pecker becomes an inconceivable figure to the art world: 'The Boy Who Said No To The Whitney [Museum of American Art]' (Figure 4.1). In this act of institutional defiance, Pecker forces New York to come to Baltimore for a photography show that reverses his camera's lens to expose the frailties of the art world's elite, in a revamped version of his father's bar called Pecker's Place, also a hybridized gallery/thrift store/chapel space.

The film commences with an exuberant dance party and witty reflexive toast to "the end of irony." In a wink to Waters himself, when asked what is next for the art wunderkind, Pecker declares he wants to make a film. In a happy ending of autobiographical fantasy, Pecker is set to follow in Waters' footsteps—no longer naïve—but armed with the knowledge that New York and Los Angeles are artists' fool's gold, and that truly inspirational art is to

Figure 4.1 Film still of Pecker on the cover of *New York Magazine*, *Pecker* (1998, Waters).

be found and made in Baltimore. Waters' fondness for the *The Wizard of Oz* (Victor Flemming, 1939) is well known, and its influence is threaded throughout his work, including *Pecker*'s art morality tale: when it comes to art and authenticity, "there's no place like home."

At the time of *Pecker*, the 1990s art world was also in transition, and a totally different landscape from today as it predated the rise and prominence of art fairs and biennales, as well as globalization's impacts on the market. In the mid-1990s New York was still the center of the art world, but on the cusp of a major art neighborhood turnover when galleries began to migrate from Soho to Chelsea and explode in number. By 2007, 350 storefronts were located there.[12] However, *Pecker* captures a space and time in art history that is much closer to the 1980s than the 1990s, with the fawning over marketable young male art stars, and the desire to create them in order to exploit them. Historically, the standout examples are Keith Haring and Jean-Michel Basquiat, who shaped the booming art market and the emergent Downtown Scene. The pump and dump economy of the 1980s art market, jet fueled by Wall Street and the rising class of billionaires, crashed by the end of the decade, with both Haring and Basquiat succumbing to tragic early deaths by 1990. Waters has directly acknowledged this historical correlation on the plausibility of *Pecker*, reflecting, "That could have happened, especially in the '80s."[13] The 1980s art scene's cruel and predatory nature is ridiculed even further by Waters as a punchline in the film's final scene, when it is revealed that Pecker's art dealer has quickly moved on to a new art sensation to promote: a blind male photographer.

In assessing the inspiration for *Pecker*, and parsing what is autobiographically inspired and not, there are multiple and competing accounts. While every work of art can generally be considered a "self-portrait," even if not explicit, Pecker the character and *Pecker* the film both serve as avatars of Waters, partially inspired by his own life experiences. According to Waters, *Pecker* did not originate from his own adventures in the art world as artist/collector/scenester. By the late 1990s, Waters was not only exhibiting his own artwork, but was a longtime friend of Larry Gagosian, who, by consensus, is considered the most formidable figure (and richest dealer) in the art world, and who Waters is often seated next to at power dinners. In part, the idea for *Pecker* came from an article in *Newsweek* that humorously claimed, "If a modern photographer is taking your picture, run for your life."[14] That creative impetus later becomes a gag in the film when Pecker's girlfriend, Shelley (Christina Ricci), sobs, "I hate modern photography!" after she catches Pecker in a kiss with his art dealer.

Waters also commented in another interview on the film's origin: "But in some ways, the idea came from [wondering], 'What did the little kid with the hand grenade [in] Diane Arbus' pictures think when years later that photograph sold for $300,000?' So how do people react to sudden fame?"[15] Yet, in an earlier interview in 1983 with *High Times*, that sentiment gets complicated as Waters reflects on his own childhood via *Child with a Toy Hand Grenade in Central Park, N.Y.C.* (Diane Arbus, 1962):

> You know that picture in the Diane Arbus book of a kid holding a hand grenade? That's what I felt like as a kid. Not that I was an especially angry child. But I was never interested in what I was supposed to be interested in. I would make my own scrapbooks, draw imaginary characters, make up horror stories.[16]

While we see similarities, overlaps, and influences between filmmaker and subject, Waters also claims that *Pecker* "was not based on any particular photographer or me at all. Some things that happened to Pecker happened to me, but I was never like Pecker."[17] But what can be concluded is that *Pecker* is an amalgam of Waters' knowledge of photography and identification with Arbus' history of capturing marginalized and disenfranchised people, which he was personally impacted by. Again, art historical knowledge becomes fodder for humorous one-liners as critics praise Pecker as "a teenage Weegee [Arthur Fellig]" and "a humane Diane Arbus." Elisa Padilla has written one of the few scholarly essays on *Pecker*, dedicated to analyzing the relationships between the film's own branding of Pecker's photography as derivative of two iconic female American photographers, Diane Arbus and Nan Goldin (both in Waters' art collection). Further, Padilla examines how the choice of Arbus and Goldin as models, who collectively are best known for photographing queer subcultures, circus performers, and persons with substance use disorders and/or mental health conditions, underscore distinctions between class, taste, and geography in the film.[18] While *Pecker* holds a mirror to the contemporary art world, the history of photography, and Waters' past, it also demonstrates art's queer failures as empowering: when outsiders or "others" challenge or take over institutions, or gain visibility, such representational "wins" for diversity and inclusivity create meaningful and poignant art.

Indicative of Waters' constant twists and play with distinctions between art and life, Pecker's photographs were shot by a young male photographer in his late twenties, Chuck Shacochis, who worked at a camera shop in Baltimore that Waters frequented.[19] Waters even referred to him as his own Pecker-like photo-star discovery, or the "Lana Turner" of the film. What is truly unusual in *Pecker* is the process of this stand-in "real" photographer. First, Shacochis deliberately took technically "bad" photographs. He experimented with different "bad techniques," using glass, dirt, and tea, to diminish and dirty the photographic quality, and to signify unprofessionalism with graininess and lack of focus. Second, Shacochis shot on the set, and the daily prints were used immediately after in subsequent scenes, becoming part of the film, as an embedded meta-documentation process of the developing narrative. Thereby, narrative moments of the recent past are quickly re-viewed, recollecting Pecker's experience through the satisfying surprise of seeing the "actual" photographs, as viewers re-witness the quirkiness of Baltimore through Pecker's lens.

THE NICEST FILM IN TOWN

Despite the film's references and incorporations of badness in photography, in a recent interview, Waters commented on *Pecker*'s goodness, even if not entirely wholesome with its R-rating:

> *Pecker* is kind of my nice film—even though it has in it, you know, teabagging and singing Virgin Mary statues and all sorts of stuff. . . .There's also anti-pubic hair campaigns, characters risking felony charges to have public sex in a voting booth and rats humping in an alley trash can.[20]

Because of its PG-rating and popular adaptations, *Hairspray* is often thought to be Waters' "nice" film given its box-office appeal and cultural staying power. Like the way that *Hairspray* momentarily "resolves racism" in the civil rights era with a happy ending, through a modern fairytale of an overweight white teenage girl dancing on local television—so too does *Pecker* provide such fantastical "good will," but strictly in terms of class and assumptions of low culture in regional cities. Both are American dream narratives as feel-good integration comedies, which follow the unlikely success-stories of its optimistic and sincere adolescent characters (Tracy Turnblad in *Hairspray* and Pecker). They are plucky good-natured underdogs from loving but disadvantaged and struggling households, which embrace Waters' valorization of failure: "My films are about people who would never win in real life. They always win in my movies."[21] While the characters are cis-straight in their on-screen representations and romances, Pecker is a queer ally and Tracy's struggles for plus-size weight acceptance can be read as LGBTQIA+ metaphors for gender and sexuality equality.

Both *Pecker* and *Hairspray* share happily-ever-after endings, where the good guy or gal wins, and both culminate in joyous democratizing dance parties. In the two films, dancing is the medium of integration across differences, allowing opposites to mingle by gyrating on the dancefloor. Waters' depictions of insiders/outsiders, black/white, fat/thin, queer/heterosexual, rich/poor, Baltimore/New York City, play upon assumptions of good versus bad taste, to tell stories that propose alternative and better modes of living and being, on-screen. Waters' epic dance party in *Pecker* is the queer art of failure's utopian

Figure 4.2 Film still of the final queer dance party scene, *Pecker* (1998, Waters).

silver screen climax (Figure 4.2). Waters describes the final dance party scene in *Pecker* as a kind of queer paradise:

> That last part is my dream, my ultimate bar. I would go there every night—the New York art world, male and female strippers, blue collar Baltimore, all together with their families, and everyone on drugs and liquor. That's my idea of a perfect night. I think that scene contains the two things that make for happiness: one, people make fun of themselves and learn to have a sense of humor; and two, they are turned on by people outside of their own class.[22]

For queer theorist José Muñoz, utopia signifies queerness and potentiality, and likewise, queer worldmaking manifests through performances of utopia or collective futurity. According to this line of thinking and Waters' own sentiment, *Pecker*'s finale is the ultimate "Watersville," created via his cinematic fever dream—a euphoric party at a mixed dive bar in Baltimore.[23]

THE ART OF WATERS

Yet, at the time of *Pecker*, Waters' own photographic art practice is vastly different from Pecker's. Waters' technique is rephotography, mostly of appropriated entertainment media and specifically film. He does not shoot original photographic images of gritty daily life like Pecker, but interestingly, he did produce a *Mark* series (*Mark #1–Mark #15*, 1998) of the floors of the film sets. To Waters, the taped marks to aid actors looked like abstract drawings and were ripe for conceptual photography. However, Waters' signature foray into fine art was a project he called "little movies." Rephotographed film and television stills were displayed up to twenty-four at a time, in series as short narrative storyboards, to deliver a punchline. Shooting CRT screens mostly playing films, he initially rephotographed out of practical need. In 1992, Waters was asked for a specific still of his muse, the great camp queen Divine (Harris Glenn Milstead), from his film *Multiple Maniacs* (1970). Unfortunately, such a still did not exist. To solve the problem, Waters set out to capture the exact moment for himself, setting up a television, VCR, VCR tape of *Multiple Maniacs*, and a 35mm camera. The process ignited his career as a visual artist, mixing the mediums of film, television, and photography.

However, rephotographing existing media has its undeniable roots in the 1970s in the practices of Richard Prince and Sherrie Levine, and more generally, artists affiliated with the late 1970s Pictures Generation. Including other major forces in American contemporary art such as Cindy Sherman and Barbara Kruger, this group of loosely affiliated artists is recognized for manipulating photography in an experimental and conceptual way; re-contextualizing media images; and questioning the roles of the gaze, authorship, desire, and consumerism. Waters is well aware of this art history, as Sherman has a cameo in *Pecker*, and is even captured in one of Pecker's photographs as homage. Moreover, iconic rephotographed works are now highly valued, as Prince's *Spiritual America* (1983) and *Untitled (Cowboy)* (1989) are some of the most expensive photographs on record by auction house sales to date. Prince's bankable work already skyrocketed the rephotography of low visual cultural images into the realms of critical acclaim and art market value. Waters' photographic sensibility is naturally inclined towards the Pictures Generation as he shares their visual interest in investigating cinema, the politics of the gaze, low-tech photography, and consumer culture; and subverting high versus low categorical distinctions. Waters appropriates the appropriators and turns the highly commodifiable practice of rephotography into cultural camp.

Because he repurposes rephotography's past, John Waters, "visual artist," has been problematic for some art critics: he not only has to compete with his own celebrity and infamous shock value, but also must top a "bad boy of art," Prince. Holland Cotter, longtime and venerable art critic for the *New York Times*, commented on the show, *John Waters: Change of Life*:

> There is nothing either egregiously edifying or particularly shocking about the photographic pieces that he began to create around 1995, which make up the bulk of the New Museum show. Maybe for that reason, they feel a bit distant and thin in the aggregate, and their debt to Andy Warhol and Richard Prince is a shade too apparent. At the same time they are distinctly Watersesque in character and are probably best taken as extensions of his films rather than as stand-alone gallery art.[24]

Forever pressured by expectations to shock, Waters' derivation of Prince and Warhol is negatively noted as redundant, despite being openly acknowledged by Waters himself. However, Waters' humor and taste, and the guilty pleasures that drive his image selection and sequencing towards punchline, are entirely his own (or Watersesque). While subject matter and his roles as director/photographer cross lines, his practices as filmmaker and photographer are different. Furthermore, Waters' remix style of rephotography has absolutely nothing to do with the contemporary trend of cinematic photography of the time. Simulating stills from blockbuster films, this high-tech, expensive, and complex re-staging style of photography employs crews, elaborate sets, special effects, and even A-list stars, as exemplified in the work of Gregory Crewdson, Jeff Wall, and Charlie White.

By contrast, Waters eschews this overwrought and high budget technical excellence in 1990s photography: his rephotographic works are small, precious, obsessive, and DIY as independent and individually controlled images. Like his early films, and in contrast to cinematic photography, his "little movies" are low-tech and low-budget, with Waters wearing all hats in writing, directing, editing, and producing. Waters even refers to his method of rephotography as "re-directing" and has stated that the work is all about editing. Waters comments on this process in conjunction with the recuperation of failure in the catalogue for *Change of Life*: "By defacing, removing and severely editing the failed moments of my own work and the under-praised work of others, maybe we can look at films that were initially dismissed or despised in a more optimistic way."[25] In Waters' pursuit of optimism, or of editing failure into pleasure (even if for purely his own self-amusement), he reconstructs his own "little movie," as visual joke and revalorization. Aligning with Waters' rephotography practice, *Pecker* is also a "little movie," with its smaller budget and intimacy harkening back to the methods of his earlier trash cinema, immediately after his "biggest" and most expensive film, *Serial Mom* (1994).

The art of Waters also extends to the work he owns, and just donated from his personal collection. As previously mentioned, the artists/works that he likes enough to hang on the walls of his multiple homes are amusingly called his roommates—as if Waters is creating his very own imaginary MTV *Real World* doll house. His cohabitors are lovingly addressed in Waters' book, *Role Models* (2010), in his "Roommates" chapter, where he describes the artists and their representative artworks. Importantly, there is no room for the merely decorative here. Beauty is truly in the eye of the beholder, as Waters is interested in outrage and the outré, whether inherent in the subject matter, execution of the piece, or in the magic trick of calling something art that in any other context would be passed over as boring, deemed total crap, or accidentally stepped on. Waters takes immense pleasure in the contempt that can be so easily generated in skeptical viewers of contemporary art, through its inaccessibility, unapproachability, exclusion, elitism, and indignation: "I love the seriousness and elitism of the art world. I think art for the people is a terrible idea."[26] Moreover, the capacity

Figure 4.3 John Waters, . . . *And Your Family Too*, 2009, c-print (edition of 5), 11 x 14 inches, © John Waters, courtesy of the artist and Marianne Boesky Gallery, New York and Aspen.

of contemporary art to anger viewers is directly addressed and literally spelled out in one of Waters' text-based works, which reads, "Contemporary Art Hates You," and the joke continues in the work's title . . . *And Your Family Too* (2009) (Figure 4.3). This sentiment, humorously inscribed across four rephotographed screens, is peppered throughout *Pecker* in the film's representations of art world exploitation. The line also ironically structures the final scene's moment of table-turn as resolution and restitution (that also toasts "the end of irony"), when Pecker's final photographs reveal the disgraceful, yet simultaneously levelling, characteristics of the film's powerful art players.

The intimate relationship of both living with and personifying art is also lampooned in Waters' curatorial strategy in the exhibition, *Absentee Landlord* (Walker Art Center, Minneapolis, Minnesota, U.S.A., June 11, 2011–March 7, 2012). As guest curator he selects some of his own "roommates" from the Walker's permanent collection, and mixes in some new ones to shake things up and make things interesting, and even includes a few works of his very own. As explained in *ARTFORUM*'s review, "The conceit of the show is that Waters is the landlord, the galleries are rental apartments, and the eighty or so artworks are the tenants."[27] Walker chief curator Darsie Alexander is quoted in the show's press release, stating "John's approach to the collection is classic Waters: a mix of brilliance and complete irreverence about intuitional 'rules.' . . . As an artist himself, he is keyed into the subtle personalities and foibles of artworks as if they were people. Its effect is both hilarious and remarkably humanizing."[28] Of course, Waters could not help himself and could not stop at the role of curator alone. Waters' audio tour of the show was also a work of art: he recorded his descriptions of the works in Pig Latin to parody the ridiculousness of pretentious jargon in art criticism, which he flattens into gibberish. To further extend the art experience for museum visitors, he created 1) a sound art piece in the parking garage composed of audio of car wrecks and shrieking tires; and 2) a limited-edition photograph of an unpalatable meal, eponymously titled *Blue Plate Special*, which was sold as a menu item in the Walker Garden Café. While Waters indulges in the art of infuriation and "hate," Waters loves contemporary art's potentiality to surprise and catch people off-guard. Thus, he kept museumgoers on their tippy toes by activating the spaces of the museum where art is usually not found, nor necessarily appreciated, as a call to pay closer attention to what is happening in your local Sub Pit.

DENOUEMENT: "I'M SO RESPECTABLE, I COULD PUKE"[29]

In hindsight, this chapter returns to the text of *Pecker* at the time of its twenty-fifth anniversary to more completely review Waters' uncanny ability to straddle the worlds of contemporary art and film via guilty pleasure. Yet, this moment of reexamination is also composed of multiple types of celebratory retrospections. The above quip is John Waters' self-reflective zinger to the promotional trailer for his monumental exhibition, *John Waters: Pope of Trash* (Academy Museum of Motion Pictures, Los Angeles, U.S.A., September 17, 2023–August 4, 2024). The slogan is prominently stenciled across the pink walls of the exhibition's "Filth Shop," where visitors can buy Waters-inspired merchandise, including a *Pink Flamingos* car air freshener in the iconic silhouette of Divine. Waters' playfully incongruous sentiment, "I'm so respectable, I could puke," makes fun of his own distinctive talent for mucking about in the permeable boundaries that separate good and bad taste. Crowned as nobrow national treasure, Waters is now commemorated by the commissars of legitimization in Hollywood: The Academy of Motion Picture Arts and Sciences—and moreover, in their newly anointed museum space (2021). This exhibition even inspired, or required, the Academy Museum to produce a secondary supporting show, or broader means to historicize and contextualize Waters' expansive film career, titled *Outside the Mainstream*. With films by Andy Warhol, Kenneth Anger, and Gregg Araki, Waters is firmly placed within the historical trajectories of the American avant-garde, underground film, and New Queer Cinema.

However, this is not a standalone incident of lifetime achievement recognition for Waters, as there were other significant awards celebrating his filmmaking in the 2020s. In 2023, Waters' star status was literally concretized in The Hollywood Walk of Fame in the category of Motion Pictures. He absolutely delighted in receiving his sidewalk star, exclaiming, "God, here I am, closer to the gutter than ever!"[30] Moreover, just two years before, in 2021, *Pink Flamingos* (1972) entered the Library of Congress' National Film Registry. The once dangerous, banned, and inflammatory film of cult cinema's golden age of lurid midnight screenings is now officially recognized for its unique cultural contributions to American cinema.

Waters, as cherished cultural figure, demands a comprehensive and interdisciplinary perspective to fully understand his tremendous artistic achievements that ironically take great pleasure in the potentialities of failure. From being censored to lauded, and reviled to revered, Waters has freely moved between the worlds of art and film, and this fluidity and fluency are starkly articulated in *Pecker*. Waters' subversions and systemic inversions of cultural value through guilty pleasure are as dizzying and disorienting as they are imaginative and fabulous. Furthermore, in the age of ascending censorship, sensitivities, and cancel culture in the U.S.A., the revaluation of Waters' career is truly extraordinary in the divisive sociopolitical climate of the 2020s. In looking back at *Pecker*, the film is charming, feel-good and good-natured, despite its Watersesque naughtiness and brazenly queer displays of genitalia from teabagging to fighting for "full bush" rights. But in the end, it is all in the name of good fun under the unifying principle of guilty pleasure.

Waters is now entering a zone of timelessness in his cultural appreciation, with individual works that would be difficult (if not impossible) to create now. But somehow, Waters still feels exciting, fresh, irreverent, and delightfully shocking, especially for first-time viewers, against the backdrop of American art and entertainment today. According to the lingo of drag culture, Waters' newfound respect is indeed "sickening."

NOTES

1. Adelosa Thomas, "Bad Influence: John Waters Reflects on His Unabashedly Filthy Filmography," *Letterboxd*, May 10, 2024, https://letterboxd.com/journal/john-waters-retrospective-interview/
2. Ed Gunts, 'John Waters Introduces the World to His "Roommates,"' *Washington Blade*, May 8, 2022, https://www.washingtonblade.com/2022/12/08/john-waters-introduces-the-world-to-his-roommates/
3. Staff/BMA Stories, "Coming Attractions: John Waters in Conversation with Catherine Opie and Jack Pierson," *BMA/Stories*, January 27, 2023, https://stories.artbma.org/coming-attractions-john-waters-in-conversation-with-catherine-opie-and-jack-pierson/
4. John Seabrook, *NoBrow: The Culture of Marketing, the Marketing of Culture*, 1st ed. (New York: A.A. Knopf, 2000).
5. Richard Kinon, 'Hidden Treasure/Picture from the Past/Ace's Salary,' *Love Boat*, Season 9, Episode 3, ABC, October 12, 1985.
6. David M. Halperin, and Valerie Traub, eds., *Gay Shame* (Chicago: University of Chicago Press, 2009).
7. Jack Halberstam, *The Queer Art of Failure* (Durham: Duke University Press, 2011), 120.
8. Elena Gorfinkel, "Cult Film or Cinephilia by Any Other Name," *Cinéaste* 34, no. 1 (2008): 35.
9. John Waters, "John Waters: Guilty Pleasures," *Film Comment* 19, no. 4 (July/August 1983): 20.
10. School of Visual Arts, "John Waters Keynote Address: Make-up Commencement for Classes of '20 and '21," *YouTube*, August 2, 2022, https://www.youtube.com/watch?v=YGLvzIhKthg&t=1s
11. Film at Lincoln Center, "John Waters on 'Pecker,' Retrospective Trailer," *YouTube*, August 28, 2014, https://www.youtube.com/watch?v=JTrDtoBpwXE
12. Zoë Lescaze, 'How Chelsea Became the Unlikely Center of the Art World,' *The New York Times*, September 28, 2023, https://www.nytimes.com/2023/09/28/t-magazine/chelsea-new-york-art.html
13. Thomas, "Bad Influence."
14. Peter Bowen, "Flash in the Pan," *Filmmaker Magazine*, 1998, Access date May 5, 2024, https://filmmakermagazine.com/archives/issues/fall1998/flash_pan.php#:~:text=And%20Pecker%20was%20based%20on,I%20was%20never%20like%20Pecker
15. Thomas, "Bad Influence."

16. Larry "Ratso" Sloman, "High Times Greats: Interview With John Waters," originally published in *1983, High Times*, April 22, 2020, https://hightimes.com/culture/high-times-greats-john-waters/
17. Peter Bowen, "Flash in the Pan."
18. Elisa, Padilla, "The Baltimore Artist: Taste, Class, and Distinction in John Waters' *Pecker*," *Quarterly Review of Film and Video* 39, no. 2 (2022): 341–359.
19. Lou Stoppard, "The Photographer Behind John Waters' Cult Classic 'Pecker,'" *Aperture*, March 27, 2019, https://aperture.org/editorial/john-waters-chuck-shacochis/
20. Thomas, "Bad Influence."
21. Dennis Cooper, "Interview: John Waters," *Bomb Magazine*, April 1, 2004, https://bombmagazine.org/articles/2004/04/01/john-waters/
22. Bowen, "Flash in the Pan."
23. José Muñoz, *Cruising Utopia: The Then and There of Queer Futurity* (New York: New York University Press, 2009).
24. Holland Cotter, "Art Review: In Photos as Well as Films, John Waters Blithely Puts His Worst Foot Forward," *New York Times*, February 6, 2004, https://www.nytimes.com/2004/02/06/arts/art-review-photos-well-films-john-waters-blithely-puts-his-worst-foot-forward.html
25. New Museum, "John Waters Change of Life," *New Museum*, access date May 13, 2024, https://archive.newmuseum.org/exhibitions/412.
26. Drew Daniel, "Experience & Innocence," *FREIZE*, June 1, 2012, https://www.frieze.com/article/experience-innocence.
27. Jonathan Thomas, "Absentee Landlord," *ARTFORUM*, December 6, 2011, https://www.artforum.com/events/absentee-landlord-191473/
28. Walker Art Center, "John Waters to Take Over Walker Galleries as Absentee Landlord," April 1, 2011, https://walkerart.org/press-releases/2011/john-waters-to-take-over-walker-galleries-as
29. *John Waters: Pope of Trash*, Exhibition Trailer, *Academy Museum of Motion Picture/YouTube*, September 28, 2023, https://www.academymuseum.org/en/exhibitions/john-waters-pope-of-trash
30. Chris Garder, "John Waters Salutes 'Desperate Showbiz Rejects' at Hollywood Walk of Fame Ceremony: 'Here I Am, Closer to the Gutter Than Ever,'" *Hollywood Reporter*, September 18, 2023, https://www.hollywoodreporter.com/news/general-news/john-waters-salutes-desperate-showbiz-rejects-hollywood-walk-of-fame-ceremony-1235593112/.

CHAPTER 5

"Full of Grace": John Waters as Auteur with the Semiautobiographical Film *Pecker*

John P. Bray

John Waters' film *Pecker* (1998) is part of a trend that emerged during the late 1990s in which directors created films that were inspired by their own youth: Franco Zeffirelli's *Tea with Mussolini* (1999), which featured characters inspired by Zeffirelli's childhood; Cameron Crowe's *Almost Famous* (2000), based on Crowe's adventures as a rock 'n' roll journalist with *Creem* and *Rolling Stone Magazine*; and Greg Mottola's *Adventureland* (2009), based on Mottola's experiences working in a family-owned amusement park. With each of these films, there is a protagonist who is a surrogate for the filmmaker: we see these characters wrestle with their desires, but the existence of the film itself promises that everything will work out in the end. The surrogate protagonist can closely emulate the filmmaker (such is the case with rock journalist Will in Cameron Crowe's *Almost Famous*), or, in the case of John Waters' titular character in *Pecker*, the character can be quite different while retaining the wonder and joy the filmmaker experienced living with Baltimore's subculture. While Crowe's *Almost Famous* interrogates the notion of "cool," featuring a fifteen-year-old rock journalist who vies for band approval, *Pecker* stands between the then-and-now for Waters: the yesteryear life of a young man who has not yet experienced fame, and Waters as the celebrated icon he has become. In a way, Waters seeks to let his "trash cinema" audience know that he has not forgotten them while venturing into more commercial fare.

The film serves as a "what if?": What if Waters had been born to a working-, rather than a middle-class family? What if he had been naïve? What would his trajectory be? Would he be able to reconcile the sensibilities of high art and the working class? When asked about his thoughts about the two worlds of art and film, Waters said he tries to keep them separate, because "The film world has to play in Peoria; in the art world, if it plays in Peoria, it's probably bad. No one in the art world ever tells you to dumb it up. It is a great relief to me to work in a medium that only has to appeal to a very small, intelligent group that respects wit."[1]

Although these terms would suggest Waters must have a sense of disdain for one or the other, Waters asserts: "The thing is, all the stuff that people hate about the art world, I love. I embrace all the elitism. I think it's hilarious. I love impenetrable art writing. I make fun of it, but I make fun of things I love. I don't hate the art world at all. I find it fascinating. It's a secret club; you have to learn the rules."[2] The notion that Waters makes fun of what he loves is key for so many of his films, which can be easily identified by their sincere-to-the-point-of-exaggeration characters, who wear wild and colorful outfits in a world without judgment. The characters in *Pecker* are just as exaggerated as his characters in his more shocking films: we are told, for example, that the title character Pecker has been given this nickname as he used to "peck away at his food" as a small child. Although this explanation is mundane, the name itself is of course provocative in Waters fashion, as the title is undoubtedly a wink to his devoted fans.[3] What makes *Pecker* unique, however, is that even with this exaggeration the actors perform the characters with much more sincerity and sweetness, a departure from Waters' previous works.

Waters had already defined himself as a leading auteur, the venerable Pope of Trash, starting with the underground success of *Pink Flamingos* (1972). The closing shot, the infamous "dog shit eating sequence," would forever cement Waters' place as provocateur, and, as Elisa Padilla suggests,

> [propel] the career of John Waters, the director, and Divine, the performer, into Midnight Movie cult stardom. Indeed, the celebration of such an epic act of filth could never be disassociated with their perpetrators: the closing scene of *Pink Flamingos* casts such a large shadow that Waters, by his own admission, "could never live up to it."[4]

Nonetheless, Waters would continue to create films celebrating the degenerate with follow-up works *Female Trouble* (1974) and *Desperate Living* (1977). From here, we establish what has become the comfortable narrative for John Waters: early underground films staged in church basements in Baltimore, followed by several exploitative gross-out features, with a turn towards more commercial fare reaching a zenith with *Hairspray* (1988), which would be adapted into a Broadway play, which itself would be adapted into a popular film directed by Adam Shankman in 2007. *Cry-Baby* (1990), featuring hot, young Hollywood actor Johnny Depp, would follow.[5] The narrative continues with Waters creeping back into trash territory with *Cecil B. Demented* (2000), until finally directing what would be (at the time of this writing) his last film, *A Dirty Shame* (2004), which received an NC-17 rating.

Waters clearly wanted to let yesterday's audiences know he had not abandoned them in spite of receiving commercial acclaim. In short, *Pecker* stands as a lynchpin between his commercial ventures—arguably reaching a zenith with the Kathleen Turner vehicle, *Serial Mom* (1994)—and his return to his more ironic, trash fare with *Cecil B. Demented*. With *Pecker*, the worlds of art, film, and class are celebrated and lightly satirized, with each side of the economic divide having their snobbery or prejudices towards the other interrogated to the point of absurdity.

John Waters has long been considered a leading auteur, first in amateur and then mainstream cinema. Timothy Corrigan has argued that the notion of auteurship would change from an applied label to something that could be commodified post-New Hollywood, with directors themselves becoming in charge of their own branding. Nathan Koob takes this stance when considering John Waters, writing:

> To suggest that John Waters' name has such influence is, arguably, to refer to him as an auteur. When discussing John Waters' auteur image, it is worth noting that it is certainly not fair to saddle him with the full responsibility of how his name is used, though we also cannot ignore the fact that Waters has a hand in building his own auteur image and continues to use it himself.[6]

Borrowing from Janet Staiger's *Authorship Approaches*, Koob argues that film authorship comes from repeated "performative statements" that "[open] up the possibility of an author's own adoption of the culturally recognized auteur category which must then be recognized in their work by the culture and accepted as auteurist."[7] Koob's sentiments on auteurship read as complicated, and at times negative; however, the notion that auteurship is something that can be the result of both how one crafts a film (the mise-en-scene, repeated visual motifs, and so on) and how one chooses to craft their persona certainly speaks to Waters as a filmmaker and personality. His films and his image (the pencil-thin mustache, wet hair, and his disdain for khaki and things "men should wear") create the sense that Waters is an Oscar Wilde-esque aesthete, that the only time his art mirrors nature is when the mirror belongs in a funhouse.[8]

From his very beginning as a director, Waters' works can easily be identified thanks to his exploration (if not creation) of the trash cinema oeuvre (William S. Burroughs gave Waters the moniker "Pope of Trash" in 1986).[9] Furthermore, whether making a film intended to make an audience feel ill or entertained or both, Waters explores ideas, themes, and characters he himself truly enjoys. As Waters states:

> I don't make films about things I hate [. . .] What always make me laugh are people who have very extreme taste but think they're very normal. That to me is the funniest. I don't look down on it. I'm in awe of people who have on the most hideous outfit and think they really look good. Who am I to say that they don't really?[10]

In this regard, *Pecker* is an extension of Waters' life-long project, to laugh with (or at) those who have extreme taste that they themselves believe to be normal. We see this taste reflected in the pictures Pecker captures (quick, grainy, out-of-focus), in Pecker's mother Joyce's desire to help the homeless be more fashionable, in Pecker's older sister Tina's desire to be popular with the Fudge Palace's gay clientele, and in Pecker's father Jimmy's distaste for pubic hair, particularly in strip clubs where alcohol is served ("pubic hair causes crime").[11] Pecker's girlfriend Shelley's need for control at the laundromat where she works also speaks to her taste for order, and similarly, a line is drawn at the male review club The Fudge Palace, where teabagging is prohibited, demonstrating that this go-go bar has good taste.

Pecker is a surrogate for a young John Waters, and most (if not all) of the characters and places in the film are drawn from Waters' autobiography. Pecker himself is also an auteur, who paints with his camera the world as he sees it, becoming, in the words of one art critic later in the film, a "humane Diane Arbus."[12] Elisa Padilla further explores the notion of Pecker being a hybrid of Arbus and Nan Goldin, as Padilla successfully argues Arbus (borrowing from an argument made by Halberstam) brings together "queerness and freakery" via photographs of strangers and different locales, while Goldin "brings together queerness and intimacy," as Goldin's photographs were of lovers and those closest to her.[13] Although elsewhere Waters indicated that *Pecker* was not truly based on any photographer, he does say in *Mr. Know-It-All* that Diane Arbus and Nan Goldin inspired the film:

> *Pecker* was really inspired by the lives of Diane Arbus and Nan Goldin. How did that little kid holding the hand grenade in the Arbus photo feel when he saw the six-figure auction price of that fleeting moment in his young life that day in Washington Square Park? Proud, it turns out.[14]

Waters also offers sympathy to Goldin, whose subjects felt exploited by her intimate photographs. Waters argues, "Nan picked up the tab of their restaurant dinners for years, gave many of them prints of their portraits that would today be worth a fortune, and received little back in return."[15] In this way, Waters is ready to defend both Arbus and Goldin through a naïve Pecker.

Padilla unpacks Pecker's art, which "consists in spontaneous snapshots of the city and its people":

> two teen black girls with outlandish beehives, a scary-looking blonde shaving her legs on the bus, the theft of a bystander's toupee wig, a pregnant young woman giving the finger to the camera, two rats having intercourse in a rubbish bin, a graffiti that tells everyone to "Eat One". They seem to capture the streetscape and personality of the city, which makes it weird and outlandish: its denizens, their costumes, backstreets and alleys, and trash.[16]

For Padilla, "Pecker's Baltimore is immediately revealed as an artistic enclave for those who are able to see it." Furthermore, this is Waters *writing* his remembered Baltimore, as a world of trash art awaiting a utopian ideal where highbrow and lowdown can mingle peaceably. In Waters' words, "I would never want to live anywhere but Baltimore. You can look far and wide, but you'll never discover a stranger city with such extreme style. It's as if every eccentric in the South decided to move north, ran out of gas in Baltimore, and decided to stay."[17] To balance the eccentricities, Waters cast Furlong to play the titular *Pecker*. In his words:

> For Pecker to be Pecker, he had to be handsome but nerdish, so cute he didn't even know it, which to me is [the] best look that anyone could possibly have. Lili Taylor says in the film, "We don't have boys that cute in New York." That's not true. It is just that everyone who is great looking in New York knows it. In Baltimore, there are a lot of people who could knock 'em dead here [in New York], but in their own neighborhoods people think they are ugly because of that thin gray line between ugly and beauty.[18]

Furlong has a charming, pleasant, and likeable demeanor and plays naiveté well. Waters also cast Furlong for the very practical reason that he found funding with Japanese markets as "Japanese girls loved Edward Furlong."[19]

There are other characters and places that are based on Waters' friends, acquaintances, and places that Waters frequented. In his 2006 Special, *This Filthy World*, Waters recounts seeing the dying embers of vaudeville with Divine, with whom he'd ditch school to visit The Gayety Burlesque, an obvious inspiration for The Pelt Club. He tells the story of Zorro, a performer who was "really butch. She looked like Johnny Cash, and she just came out nude, she didn't strip. And she'd look at the men in the audience and say, 'what the fuck are you looking at?' And they loved her. We loved Zorro. I'm here today because of Zorro's example."[20] Lady Zorro was raised by her grandparents, was out in high school, and, after a customer grabbed her behind, threw a drink in his face, telling him to "fuck off," thereby ending her life as an airline attendant. She became a drag king, donning a "Zorro" mask to hide her large nose (she was not considered conventionally attractive). In Waters' words:

> "Z" (as she was known right up to the end by people in her life) had a real rage she brought to the stage, which added a demented hostile sex appeal. An angry stripper with a history of physical and sexual abuse with a great body and the face of a man. Now *there's* a lethal combination.[21]

In *Pecker*, Zorro is represented by T-Bone, a drag king who was played by real life drag king Mo Fischer (drag name: "Mo. B Dick"). T-Bone is joined by a second drag king, who appears in Pecker's Place at the end of the film, dancing and grinding on one of the art critics. The second drag king is based on Zorro's friend and fellow stripper Ray (short for "Rachel"), who made Zorro's costume for her.[22]

The Fudge Palace, where Tina works, is Waters' homage to Atlantis, "a male strip club located next to the Maryland Penitentiary."[23] Of Atlantis, Waters remembers,

> I always took out of town guests there, everybody from Gus Van Sant to many of the New York art dealers (both gay and straight) who were participating in the Print Fair at the Baltimore Museum of Art. Even my friend Judge Elsbeth Bothe went with me one night after a long day on the bench. When I told her that "sometimes you get teabagged by the naked dancers if you sit too close," she didn't chicken out; she just wore a hat for protection. God, how I miss that place.[24]

Waters' sense of longing is palpable, both in terms of his autobiography and in *Pecker*. The audience is left wanting to believe this place exists, and yet it feels delightfully uncanny.

Upon its initial release, critics were surprised that Waters did not push the envelope as he had with his previous films. Indeed, during their review of *Pecker* on *Siskel and Ebert*, Roger Ebert laments the film is "too kind and too gentle," and Gene Siskel reminds audiences "John Waters used to be the 'shock master.' Movies have passed him by."[25] Critics such as Michael Dequina of *The Movie Report* quip: "In short, the film doesn't have much of a pecker."[26] Perhaps the most controversial aspect of this film is its title, *Pecker*, which was rejected by the MPAA for appearing "obscene, profane, or salacious."[27] However, Waters argued before a hearing at MPAA Headquarters that there were far more salacious titles that got a pass (Waters lists *Shaft* [Gordon Parks, 1971], *Octopussy* [John Glen, 1983], *In & Out* [Frank Oz, 1997], *Spaceballs* [Mel Brooks, 1987], and the Barbara Streisand vehicle *Nuts* [Martin Ritt, 1987]).[28] He argued and won in a unanimous decision, and thus the title remained.

Perhaps Waters wasn't shocking enough with *Pecker*; perhaps he could have pushed boundaries harder as in his earlier provocative works. However, what he did give audiences was a charming and soulful film about learning to love the art in the mundane, to love the art in our own exaggerated idiosyncrasies, and to live with each other with grace.

Pecker is about a teenage amateur photographer whose overnight success becomes first a cause for celebration amongst his Baltimore community, then a source of suspicion and pain. In the concluding moments, both the New York Art World and the Baltimore working class find a common ground, whereby object-of-study and those-who-gaze become like two mirrors, reflecting each other endlessly, but played with a nostalgic and wistful touch. The film opens with Paul Evans' ironic song, "Happy Go Lucky Me" (1961), a blend of joyful hopeful lyrics and maniacal laughter to a bouncy beat. We have our first look at Baltimore, with a shaky title card that reads "a film by john waters."[29] Pecker snaps photos while waiting at a bus stop. On the bus, he takes pictures of two young women, who are all too happy to pose for him. There is no dialogue, just laughter.

Furlong's expression is one of quiet contentment, a sort of Elwood P. Dowd for the later twentieth century.[30] He looks at all of Baltimore and its citizens with the same sense of wonder with which Dowd and his imaginary rabbit friend Harvey regard their midwestern hometown.[31] Pecker snaps a picture of a man having his toupee stolen, a woman shaving her legs on the bus, and another woman on a bench reading a book called *Fat and Furious*, who growls at Pecker in the photo. Finally, Pecker takes a picture of two rats having sex in a tipped-over garbage can, with the title card "written and directed by john waters."[32] We linger on the image, and while it is a far cry from the dogshit-eating scene of *Pink Flamingos* in terms of shock value, this moment alerts the audience that Waters, while making a more joyful film, will also embrace his literal trash aesthetic. Waters negotiates two very different directions in which he is being pulled: the one being towards his profane and earlier works, and the other towards his more commercial tendencies, with an added layer of personal nostalgia for his earlier days.

Waters has stated that the central character in *Pecker* is not based on himself: for example, Waters is from an upper-middle-class family and enjoyed a degree of economic privilege. In Waters' words:

> I wasn't naïve. Pecker was. I wanted New York to discover my early works; they just never did until later. I wasn't blue-collar either, even though I wish I were. True, there once was rumbling from my core acting troupe that I was getting rich from my movies and they weren't (the way Pecker was from his photographs), so the main eight people who were the most involved in those first productions banded together and decided who should benefit, and I agreed to give them 25 percent of the profits to split.[33]

When discussing the genesis of the film, Waters has said: "If a modern photographer is taking your picture, run for your life. That gave me the idea for the movie. It was not based on any particular photographer or me at all. Some things that happened to Pecker happened to me, but I was never like Pecker. I was never naive; I was in on it from the start."[34] Pecker might be naïve, but his naiveté is also his strength. He does not judge what he sees, but rather takes it all in and experiences artfulness in the mundane as well as the grotesque. When

Figure 5.1 Pecker (Edward Furlong) photographs a cockroach in a plate of French Fries in *Pecker* (1998).

he serves an order to a customer, he notices a cockroach hiding amongst the fries. Rather than taking the plate away, he snaps a photo. He does not interfere; he is just there to shoot a picture. Pecker's exaggerated characteristic is that he can never not take photographs if something of interest catches his eye. Waters is very much the same vis-à-vis capturing moments that feel simultaneously mundane and exaggerated. Therefore, despite the key differences, he is still a surrogate for Waters, as both follow Formalist Viktor Shklovsky's notion that "art is a way of experiencing the artfulness of an object."[35] For both Waters and Pecker, that object is Baltimore.

Pecker lives with his family, and each family member has their own exaggerated feature: his mother, Joyce (Mary Kay Place), helps homeless populations find a love for fashion; his father, Jimmy (Mark Joy), runs The Crab Shack and has very strong opinions about pubic hair; his older sister, Tina (Martha Plimpton), is a DJ at a go-go bar called The Fudge Palace where she calls everyone "Mary," believing it to be affectionate term for a gay man; his Memama (Jean Schertler) has a miraculous Virgin Mary ventriloquist puppet/statue that caws "Full of Grace;" and his younger sister Little Chrissy (Lauren Hulsey) is a sugar-addict, spending most of the film ingesting confections (including straight sugar) in a zombie-like state. His girlfriend is Shelley (Christina Ricci), a laundromat authoritarian who runs people out if they break the rules. Pecker's best friend is a local thief, Matthew (Brendan Sexton III), whom Pecker never judges, even claiming that though he's a thief, "he's a really nice guy."[36] The performers play their characters with absolute sincerity, a contrast to the more ironic performances in his other commercial works: for example, when the titular character in *Cry-Baby* shouts

"I'm the happiest juvenile delinquent in all of Baltimore!," it's played for a laugh.[37] As a contrast, when Pecker catches his younger sister, Little Chrissy, late at night standing on a chair near a cupboard eating directly out of a bag of sugar and tells her, "I love you, Little Chrissy, no matter what," during which she looks at him, drooling thick white sugar down her shirt, Furlong plays it sincerely. We see his love. We see the same level of sincerity throughout the film with both the performances and Waters' overall direction, in which there are no exaggerated angles or close-ups (outside of the photos Pecker snaps). *Pecker* is mostly played straight.

Pecker's life is status quo until an art dealer, Rorey Wheeler (Lili Taylor), discovers his works hanging on the wall at the burger place where Pecker is employed and brings Pecker and his family to New York for his first show. At the gallery in NYC,[38] Pecker takes pictures of the critics and members of the elite, who drink champagne and admire his work.[39] Pecker and his photographs are a hit in New York City and become the talk of the art world. However, the art world mocks the subjects of Pecker's photos and declares his family "culturally challenged," leading his community to feel exploited and thus shy away from Pecker and his camera. As Pecker weighs his personal life against his artistic life, the world around him seems to crumble. Matt can no longer shoplift without getting caught, and ends up working at The Fudge Palace as a stripper; Tina is fired from The Fudge Palace as throngs of fans line up to be teabagged (which is not allowed—causing the manager to ask everyone for "gay ID") and child protection services take an interest in Chrissy, who is diagnosed with ADHD and is forced off sugar in favor of Ritalin.[40] Most upsetting is what becomes of poor Memama: just moments after hugging her

Figure 5.2 Jean Schertler as Memama in *Pecker* (1998).

statue, declaring "you're a mother, you're a virgin, and you're all mine," two self-described "Friends of Mary" arrive to "come to see Our Lady."[41] When Memama introduces them to her statue, they note that Memama herself is making the statue speak. They label her a "heretic," with the ladies promising to tell Monsignor. Meanwhile, T-Bone, a drag king who performs fully nude at The Pelt Room (and whom Pecker has secretly photographed) is arrested for displaying her pubic hair. In short, Pecker's fame is at the cost of everyone in his life.[42] Pecker sees the results of these devastating moments firsthand. He is clearly racked with guilt, recognizing that it is his fault and his pictures that have caused his corner of the world to crumble. And yet, he remains steadfast in his love for photography. He does not want his Baltimore to change or to feel exploited. That his pictures have caused so much pain is heartbreaking and creates a sense of loss.

While in this state of loss, he becomes open to Rorey's advances, and they end up sharing a kiss witnessed by Shelley. Rorey's behavior is predatory in this scene, and yet Lili Taylor (as with the other performers in the film) plays her role truthfully: there is no exaggeration. We don't see someone who is lecherous for a younger man (boy), but rather Rorey demonstrates an uncomfortable vulnerability which the young, naïve Pecker is open to, just for a moment (this will, of course, be a part of her predatory nature, which we learn later in the film). This beat in the film mirrors a relationship from Furlong's own life: when Furlong was sixteen, he and his twenty-nine-year-old tutor, Jacqueline Domanc, became involved in a romantic relationship that lasted five years.[43] Vernon Scott once interviewed Furlong when Domac was present, writing: "To the casual observer, Furlong and Domac would seem to be stuck on each

Figure 5.3 Shelley (Christina Ricci) and Pecker (Edward Furlong) in *Pecker* (1998).

other romantically. It might be a case of puppy love, but then one of them really isn't a puppy."[44] To what extent Furlong brought his personal material into this beat would be conjecture, but it cannot be ignored that Pecker and Furlong himself were both faced with the advances of an older woman, with ultimately devastating results for Furlong.[45] Unlike the Furlong and Domac affair, Pecker's relationship with Rorey lasts only for one kiss, and it has been witnessed by Shelley, who flees, declaring, "I hate modern photography!"[46]

Like Waters, Pecker finds the art in everything he sees, and wants everyone in his various circles to see art, not necessarily how he sees it, but rather just to be open to anything visual as a possible source for artistic engagement. Pecker chases Shelley into a voting booth and explains to her that she, too, can see her world through an artistic lens:

> Shelley: I don't understand any of that art crap.
> Pecker: You could if you just opened your eyes.
> Shelley: Pecker, I work in a laundromat.
> Pecker: Art is everywhere.
> Shelley: Yeah, in my endless bags of dirty laundry.
> Pecker: Yeah, it is if you think about it.
> Shelley: What, the brilliant green of a grass stain?

Waters underscores "brilliant green of a grass stain" with a harp and an animated spark of green dancing around the screen. As Shelley describes each stain, a harp underscores her realization that art is all around, with animated colors sparkling across the screen. The music underscoring this sequence feels ethereal, holy, and pure:

> Pecker: Yes! Yes! Let your mind go and you'll be free forever!
> Shelley: Oh, Pecker, I think I finally see it!
> Pecker: Art, Shelley! Art![47]

The harp plays, a rainbow of animated sparkles dances across the scene, and Shelley and Pecker have make-up sex, rocking the booth, while a rule-abiding Precinct Captain (Mink Stole) watches on. She interrupts them with a scream. Waters has crafted a very touching scene while retaining his own particular style: after all, it concludes with two characters having sex in a voting booth, which is outlandish. Yet somehow Waters, Furlong, and Ricci are all able to play it sincerely. Even with the scene ending with a joke (the Precinct Captain screaming because someone has broken the rules, not to mention two laws: sex in public and no more than one person in a voting booth), there is something entirely wholesome about Pecker and Shelley. Pecker is the living embodiment of good faith. Shelley, despite being betrayed, understands him. He has opened her world. This moment also encapsulates Waters' views on our ability to see art in everything, and our stubbornness to accept that truly basic concept:

> That scene is really against the contempt for investigation, which almost all regular people have about contemporary art. You show them something, and they start sputtering, "Jeez, my kid could have done that." Of course! That's the kind of art I like, where you have to learn to look at it in a different way. If there is one, that's the message of every movie that I've ever made.[48]

Here, Waters is lovingly satirizing the "regular" person's contempt for high art: why can't a stain be beautiful? This notion is evocative of Marcel Duchamp's *Fountain* (1917), a urinal which Duchamp signed "R. Mutt" and placed in a gallery. Waters himself even requested that the Baltimore Museum of Art's bathroom be named after him.[49] Art can have form, it can have function, or it can have none of the above. The key insight Waters is offering via Pecker is to demonstrate how we in the audience can learn how to look differently at what we encounter, and to find the artfulness in everything, from rats, to roaches, to stains, to people—particularly, people who are not posing for a picture.

Pecker pulls his show from The Whitney and instead hosts his own exhibit at The Crab Shack, now renamed "Pecker's Place." He invites members of the New York Art World to visit him there. Like his previous work, the pictures are slice-of-life fare; however, his subjects are now the members of the NY art scene themselves, whom Pecker snapped at his show in New York. The critics and fashionistas must reconcile with their own status as objects of study, as the playing field occupied by artist, critic, art object, the working class, and the high class becomes level. The blurring of these boundaries becomes a moment of celebration for all in attendance. For example, Dr. Klompus (Bess Armstrong), one of the elites who had previously not allowed any homeless persons to sit at her table in New York, steps into a room where Joyce has helped homeless lady Ms. Betty find the perfect outfit: a dark coat with a feaux-fur collar. Joyce tells her it looks wonderful, to which Ms. Betty responds, "I don't know, will it wrinkle if I sleep in it?" Joyce assures her that it looks good, with Pecker offering, "You know, that's flameproof too, in case someone sets you on fire." Betty is sold. Dr. Klompus, standing next to Betty, is wearing almost the exact same outfit. They both immediately recognize a kindred spirit, smile, and Dr. Klomps brings Betty into an embrace. "Isn't fashion something?" Joyce asks, beaming to both.[50] Fashion, as with any other art, is for everybody.

Each character has found what they are looking for. Even Rorey, no longer able to manipulate Pecker, has discovered a photographer who is blind, and therefore must rely on her. Here, Waters is demonstrating that Rorey is indeed a predator, and their kiss earlier was not just out of a moment of transference.

Rorey wants someone she can control. Rorey needs someone to need *her*. This is not something Waters spends time with, for in this moment Rorey is letting Pecker know that she is letting him go, and Pecker's reaction demonstrates that he is fine to not have to deal with her again (he isn't rude, but his demeanor suggests he is truly done). However, Waters is also letting the audience know that he is aware Rorey's behavior is beyond reproach. A speculation could be that Waters may have been alerting Furlong to his own situation with Dormac, who allegedly once quipped, "I know how much power I have over Eddie."[51] Dormac and Furlong ended their relationship in 1998, the same year *Pecker* was released.

This is also not the first time Waters brought in a performer who had been exploited as a teen. *Cry-Baby* co-star Traci Lords starred in pornographic films from the time she was fifteen (allegedly lying about her age), which would lead to scandals and lawsuits. Lords moved away from pornography into mainstream Hollywood. *Cry-Baby* was her second non-pornographic film, and she maintains a close friendship with Waters.[52] Patricia Hearst, who appears in several of John Waters' films including *Pecker*, is another example of an exploited celebrity who found a second life with Waters.[53] In short, John Waters has found a way of giving people who have seen the worst side of being a child celebrity if not a second childhood, then at least a second chance. Waters creates a safe space for both performers and characters to be who they are, without judgment.

The utopian bar Waters presents at the end of *Pecker* is how he must imagine Heaven (if there is one), with one of the patrons shouting, "to the end of irony!"[54] Even the Virgin Mary puppet starts talking again, but this time, without the help of Memama. "Full of Grace, Holy Mary Mother of God!" the statue declares. Pecker says: "Our prayers have been answered!" as the statue continues, "Grace Holy Grace," and so on.[55] The bar is blessed, the patrons have all found grace. In the closing moments, Pecker is asked what he wants to do next. He looks around the room, and lines up his fingers as if looking at everyone through a camera lens, and says "You know what? I'm thinking of directing a movie." Here, Pecker finally becomes Waters. Furthermore, despite Waters trying to separate himself from Pecker (as mentioned earlier), he is clearly making the audience aware of their similarities, giving an at last ironic wink in an otherwise unironic film.

Waters uses the titular Pecker as a means of looking back to where he had been before his commercial acceptance without disparaging his success. Waters is successful in bridging the divide, despite the early negative reactions. Although the film did not satisfy those who wished for a more shocking Waters, it has in recent years found its champions. In 2019, John Waters was given a Star on the Baltimore Walk of Fame, where tourists can acquire a map to the locations that inspired the film. Furthermore, there is even talk of a *Pecker* musical being penned for the Instagram age.[56] With *Pecker*, Waters uses his own autobiography to create a wistful pastiche of a utopian community, comprised of members of various walks of his who exist in a bar with high-art and teabaggers, a picaresque Heaven, where thief, photographer, critic, and stripper exist in a state of perpetual harmony, enjoying the artfulness in everything.

Pecker marks the end of Waters' flirtations with commercial cinema as director, and is also his most personal film, as he captures not just the Baltimore that he knows and loves, but the utopian hope for bizarre and outlandish people that populate both his real world and his worlds of story. It furthermore is Waters' own satire of the very different worlds of fine art and commercial cinema. The resulting film allows Waters to shine as auteur while making a picture that is more approachable, or in his word, "nice."[57] It also allows him to bridge together the worlds of high-art and low, trash cinema and commercialism, with a lead that is a charming, wide-eyed surrogate for Waters himself.

NOTES

1. "Flash in the Pan," *FilmmakerMagazine* (online), fall 1998, accessed April 30, 2024. https://filmmakermagazine.com/archives/issues/fall1998/flash_pan.php
2. Taylor Dafoe, "'Contemporary Art Hates You': John Waters, the Prince of Puke, on His New Retrospective," *art net* (dot com), October 31, 2018, https://news.artnet.com/art-world/contemporary-art-hates-you-john-waters-the-prince-of-puke-on-his-new-retrospective-1383673
3. *Pecker*, directed by John Waters (1998), Fine Line Features, 1hr. 26mins., https://www.amazon.com/Pecker-Edward-Furlong/dp/B007HZD71A
4. Elisa Padilla (2022), "The Baltimore Artist: Taste, Class, and Distinction in John Waters' *Pecker*," *Quarterly Review of Film and Video* 39, no. 2: 341. DOI: 10.1080/10509208.2020.1842093
5. *Cry-Baby* would also be adapted into a Broadway play in 2008, though it was far less critically and commercially successful than *Hairspray*.
6. Nathan Koob, "The Gentrification of John Waters," *Film Criticism* 43, no. 1 (March 2019). DOI: https://doi.org/10.3998/fc.13761232.0043.104.
7. Nathan Koob, "The Gentrification of John Waters."
8. For a longer discussion on Mr. Waters' style, see Lauren Cochrane's "One Memorable Look: Mr John Waters' Rule-Breaking Tailoring," *Mr. Porter*, August 23, 2023: https://www.mrporter.com/en-us/journal/fashion/john-waters-director-style-menswear-exhibition-film-suit-24476782
9. "John Waters: Pope of Trash," *Academy Museum*, https://www.academymuseum.org/en/programs/series/john-waters-pope-of-trash
10. Emanuel Levy, *Gay Directors, Gay Films?: Pedro Almodóvar, Terence Davies, Todd Haynes, Gus Van Sant, John Waters* (New York: Columbia University Press, 2015), 268.
11. *Pecker*, directed by John Waters (1998, Burbank, CA: Warner Brothers), Amazon Prime.
12. *Pecker*, directed by John Waters.
13. Elisa Padilla (2022), "The Baltimore Artist: Taste, Class, and Distinction in John Waters' *Pecker*," *Quarterly Review of Film and Video* 39, no. 2: 346. DOI: 10.1080/10509208.2020.1842093

14. John Waters, *Mr. Know-It-All*, 84.
15. John Waters, *Mr. Know-It-All*, 84.
16. Elisa Padilla, "The Baltimore Artist: Taste, Class, and Distinction in John Waters' *Pecker*, 343.
17. John Waters, *Shock Value: A Tasteful Book About Bad Taste* (New York: Thunder's Mouth Press, 2005), 76.
18. "Flash in the Pan," *FilmmakerMagazine* (online), fall 1998, https://filmmakermagazine.com/archives/issues/fall1998/flash_pan.php
19. John Waters, *Mr. Know It All*, 81–82.
20. *This Filthy World*, directed by John Garlin (2006, Los Angeles: Red Envelope Entertainment/Netflix), *YouTube*, https://www.youtube.com/watch?v=epA-cj5utuM
21. John Waters, *Role Models* (New York: Farrar, Straus, and Giroux, 2010), 134.
22. John Waters, *Role Models*, 134–136.
23. John Waters, *Role Models*, 146.
24. John Waters, *Role Models*, 146–147.
25. *Siskel and Ebert*, "*Pecker* review," 1998, *YouTube*,https://www.youtube.com/watch?v=zgCsCYSJ6T8
26. Qtd. "Pecker Reviews," *Rotten Tomatoes*, https://www.rottentomatoes.com/m/pecker/reviews
27. John Waters, *Mr. Know-It-All*, 82.
28. John Waters, *Mr. Know-It-All*, 82.
29. *Pecker*, John Waters.
30. Elwood P. Dowd is the affable and "oh so pleasant" protagonist from Mary Chase's 1944 play *Harvey*, which was adapted into a 1950 film featuring Jimmy Stewart.
31. Although Waters has not directly mentioned Mary Chase's *Harvey*, Waters himself has a deep love for old Hollywood and even earned a Gold Star on the Hollywood Walk of Fame in 2023. See: Madalit del Barco, "'Here I am, Closer to the Gutter Than Ever': John Waters Gets His Hollywood Star," *NPR Weekend Edition*, https://www.npr.org/2023/09/24/1200624382/here-i-am-closer-to-the-gutter-than-ever-john-waters-gets-his-hollywood-star
32. *Pecker*, John Waters.
33. John Waters, *Mr. Know-It-All*, 84.
34. "Flash in the Pan," *Filmmaker* (online), nd, https://filmmakermagazine.com/archives/issues/fall1998/flash_pan.php
35. Viktor Shklovsky, "Art as Technique (1917)" *Modern Criticism and Theory: A Reader* (London: Langham, 1988), 17.
36. *Pecker*, John Waters.
37. *Cry-Baby* DVD, directed by John Waters (1990), Universal Pictures, 1 hr. 25 minutes.
38. See Jim, "Art in the Movies," *WordPress*, November 12, 2013, https://artinthemovies.wordpress.com/2013/11/12/pecker-1998/#:~:text=Pecker's%20big%20opening%20is%20the,Marks%20flash%20on%20the%20screen
39. *Pecker*, John Waters.
40. *Pecker*, John Waters.
41. *Pecker*, John Waters.
42. *Pecker*, John Waters.
43. "Edward Furlong & Jacqueline Domac Affair is the Scandal Hollywood Forgot," *Eighties Kids*, https://www.eightieskids.com/edward-furlong-jacqueline-domac-romance/
44. Vernon Scott, "Reporters Who Would Interview 16-Year-Old Edward Furlong, the Charismatic Young Costar of 'Terminator 2' and Other Hit Films, Are Asked to Sign an Agreement," *UPI Archives*, https://www.upi.com/Archives/1994/04/20/Reporters-who-would-interview-16-year-old-Edward-Furlong-the-charismatic/5404766814400/

45. "Edward Furlong & Jacqueline Domac Affair Is the Scandal Hollywood Forgot," https://www.eightieskids.com/edward-furlong-jacqueline-domac-romance/
46. *Pecker*, John Waters.
47. *Pecker*, John Waters.
48. "Flash in the Pan," https://filmmakermagazine.com/archives/issues/fall1998/flash_pan.php
49. "John Waters Says It's 'fitting' to Have an Art Museum's Bathrooms Named after Him," *As It Happens*, CBC Radio, November 13, 2020, https://www.cbc.ca/radio/asithappens/as-it-happens-friday-edition-1.5800938/john-waters-says-it-s-fitting-to-have-an-art-museum-s-bathrooms-named-after-him-1.5800944
50. *Pecker*, John Waters.
51. "Edward Furlong & Jacqueline Domac Affair is the Scandal Hollywood Forgot," https://www.eightieskids.com/edward-furlong-jacqueline-domac-romance/
52. Winston Gieseke, "Getting Steamy with Traci Lords," *Palm Springs Life*, September 9, 2019, https://www.palmspringslife.com/traci-lords/
53. Erik Maza, "John Waters and Patricia Hearst on Covid, the Met Gala, and 30 Years of Friendship," *Town and Country*, October 29, 2020, https://www.townandcountrymag.com/society/tradition/a34395567/john-waters-patricia-hearst-conversation/
54. *Pecker*, John Waters.
55. *Pecker*, John Waters.
56. Ed Gunts, "Baltimore Gets Very Own Walk of Fame: Hampden's Newest Attraction Is a John Waters Star Walk," *Baltimore Magazine*, May 29, 2019, https://www.baltimoremagazine.com/section/artsentertainment/baltimore-john-waters-hampden-star-walk-of-fame/
    See also: Jason Adams, "Looking Back on John Waters' 'Pecker' on Its 25th Anniversary," *Mashable*, September 22, 2023, https://mashable.com/article/pecker-john-waters-25-anniversary
57. John Waters, *Mr. Know-It-All: The Tarnished Wisdom of a Filth Elder* (New York: Picador, 2019), 81.

CHAPTER 6

"Technique Is Failed Style": John Waters, Style, and *Cecil B. Demented*

Brian Brems

In John Waters' *Cecil B. Demented* (2000), the radical filmmaker of the title played by Stephen Dorff kidnaps Hollywood movie star Honey Whitlock (Melanie Griffith) and forces her to play a role in his *verité*-style guerilla film in which a group of cinematic terrorists try to foment a revolution. As a way of introducing his own philosophical dedication to the art of cinema to the movie star he has taken as a hostage, Cecil and his crew of revolutionaries, The Sprocket Holes, show off tattoos of their favorite filmmakers' names: Rainer Werner Fassbinder, David Lynch, Herschell Gordon Lewis, Andy Warhol, Sam Peckinpah, Spike Lee, Kenneth Anger, William Castle, Pedro Almodovar, and Sam Fuller. Cecil's own tattoo is dedicated to Otto Preminger, which he bears on his forearm. This list of directors reflects Waters' competing artistic impulses (many his personal favorites): some are Hollywood filmmakers of the 1950s and 1960s who made their livings inside the system (albeit while developing reputations as mavericks); others are outsiders working in profoundly radical traditions that deconstruct cinema itself; still others attempted to reconcile two seemingly irreconcilable demands: making money and making personal statements through the cinema. *Cecil B. Demented*'s collision of opposing forces—art vs. commerce, independence vs. mainstream, unpolished style vs. polished technique—offers Waters' most substantive discourse on the art form of cinema itself.

As a filmmaker who worked far outside the system like Cecil, and also inside the studio system like Whitlock, Waters knows the demands of both spaces, which he smirkingly describes in a chapter titled "How *Not* To Make a Movie" in his book of essays, *Crackpot*.[1] Waters jokingly offers this piece of advice: "Kidnapping a major star and forcing him to do your film is a surefire way to generate excitement about your project,"[2] an aside that lays the groundwork for this film's plot nearly twenty years ahead of schedule. *Cecil B. Demented* is a philosophical anchor point revealing Waters' own cinematic values and principles—its ideas had clearly been on his mind for some time. As a film made late in Waters' career (and as of publication, at least, what may prove to be his penultimate movie), *Cecil B. Demented* offers evidence of a filmmaker working through his own understanding of his personal style. In its self-conscious deployment of *verité* style, *Cecil B. Demented* finds Waters returning to the guerrilla roots of his early films, which featured handheld camerawork (in many cases operated by Waters himself). However, arming the lunatic cinematic insurrectionist Cecil with the *verité* approach of a radical independent filmmaker calls attention to the ways in which cinematic style serves as a label of a director's ideological commitments, be they political or artistic. *Cecil B. Demented* tracks the inevitable lurch of those commitments towards compromise brought about both by an artist's innate desire to make work that reaches an audience and a degree of professionalization in craft that materializes through repetition. This trajectory is embodied in the character arcs of both Honey and Cecil, but also in the film's visual style.

Waters' own visual style shows signs of increasing professionalization as his career progresses. Working with an extremely small crew in his native Baltimore on early films like *Mondo Trasho* (1969), which featured no spoken dialogue and used unlicensed pop music as the soundtrack, and the sound film *Multiple Maniacs* (1970), Waters' approach is unsurprisingly rough around the edges. He stages many scenes in wide shots, with actors speaking to one another across the playing space of the image. In *Pink Flamingos* (1972), his breakthrough midnight movie hit, the general style remains handheld, but he shows an increasing awareness of the ways in which that style can be used to stage scenes of gross-out spectacle, the long unbroken takes refusing to let the audience look away from taboo-busting imagery, like Babs Johnson (Divine) fellating her son Crackers (Danny Mills), a performance artist opening and closing his own anus for the camera outside of a trailer, and in the film's final moment, Babs eating dog feces. According to Howard Hampton, "by *Pink Flamingos* Waters had developed a viable aesthetic: rattling, spasmodic, and expressively incongruous."[3] Waters' use of *verité* camerawork in these early films has a deliberately grimy quality, matching the aesthetic of "filth" espoused by his characters. In general, this stylistic identity continues through his next two features, *Female Trouble* (1974) and *Desperate Living* (1977). Ed Halter says the use of locations throughout Waters' *Female Trouble* marks the filmmaker's "clever aestheticization of budgetary necessity [that] has its roots in the sixties underground movies of Andy Warhol and brothers George and Mike Kuchar, all of whose work inspired Waters to take up filmmaking."[4] In the early part of his career, Waters, a filmmaking autodidact who learned by watching films and imitating them, tried to turn those budgetary limitations into strengths.

The pivot film for Waters stylistically is *Polyester* (1981), made on a higher budget; it minimizes handheld style, and directly imitates the Hollywood melodramas of Douglas Sirk in an affectionate send-up of the genre's trappings and soft look. A German émigré influenced by theorist and playwright Bertolt Brecht, Sirk came to Hollywood and found a home in the melodrama, which he ironized through an infusion of existential dread into otherwise comfortable spaces of domesticity with a surprisingly menacing and unsettling use of mise-en-scene. As a self-conscious artist working inside a commercial system where the demands of industry usually won out, Sirk labored under conditions that forced "an ongoing exchange between his creativity and the sometimes stifling realities of studio filmmaking in the 1950s."[5] *Polyester* mimics Sirk throughout in Waters' careful attention to style, and in so doing, "wryly and reflexively narrates Waters' own place in the film industry, at once huckster, shrink, and soothsayer."[6] Waters is undoubtedly an effective mimic who is highly attuned to filmmaking style even in the smallest details, extending to the paratextual materials beyond his films: the DVD menu of the Artisan release of *Cecil B. Demented* begins with a sunny-looking image of Honey Whitlock's latest film *Some Kind of Happiness*; then, Cecil's voice roars over the soundtrack and bullets riddle the screen; the backdrop falls away, with a hand-scrawled navigation menu replacing it. Amongst the lines chosen for the dialogue sample are the declaration by Sprocket Hole Chardonnay (Zenzele Uzoma), "fuck the studio system" and, of course, Cecil's credo: "We believe technique to be nothing more than failed style."

If *Cecil B. Demented* has a mission statement, it is that declaration. Cecil and The Sprocket Holes, after kidnapping Honey from the Baltimore premiere of her film *Some Kind of Happiness*—Waters' parodic title of a Hollywood "screwball romantic comedy," as Honey calls it in a phone interview—hide out at the Hippodrome, an abandoned Charm City movie house which they have turned into their own outlaw cinema paradise. Cecil gives himself a dramatic introduction, lowering himself down to her level on a director's crane he has adorned with a feather bed. He wants her to star in his new film, *Raving Beauty*, a raw, visceral, guerrilla attack on mainstream Hollywood films. Held at gunpoint, Honey has little choice but to go along with the charade, and after a costume fitting, the makeup chair, and an aggressive bleaching that gives her a shock of Hitchcockian blonde hair, the director is ready to shoot the first scene. Taking place outside of a mocked-up façade of a movie theatre, Honey is tasked with playing the matriarch of a gang of revolutionaries not unlike The Sprocket Holes themselves. This expositional scene is performed self-consciously in the style of Waters' earlier films: Demented (and Waters, working with director of photography Robert Stevens) uses wide shots, fairly minimal blocking, bracingly direct dialogue, and performers who never really seem to lose a sense that the camera is watching them, recalling the approach of Waters' Dreamlanders cast members. As the stars of *Raving Beauty*, ex-porn star Cherish (Alicia Witt) and drug-addled Lyle (Adrian Grenier) adopt a particularly Watersian approach to their acting in the movie within the movie. Howard Hampton describes the performances of Mink Stole and David Lochary in *Pink Flamingos* like this: "Neither actor is good in an accepted sense, and both are utterly great: epitomes of a performance style pitched to the sweet spot between actual-inmates-take-over-the-*Marat/Sade*-asylum and talent night at the *Untamed Youth* reformatory."[7] In *Cecil B. Demented*, the Dreamlanders-style line deliveries by Witt and Grenier are slightly stilted and deliberate, carrying the earnestness of non-professional actors without formal training. After they've finished the master shot, and Cecil says to print the take, Honey is incredulous: "No coverage?" Her insider knowledge of the mainstream system demands they shoot more angles, but Cecil is unconvinced: "There are no rules in outlaw cinema." For Demented, the simple process of professionalized craft is a fig leaf masking a cinematic work's artistic bankruptcy. Waters, however, shoots plenty of coverage—by this point in his career, he shows plenty of technique.

This sequence in *Cecil B. Demented* and *Raving Beauty* is the only deliberate echo of Waters' early work and visual style. Cecil, imbued with a messianic sense of artistic purpose, announces his intention to take the film out of the confines of the makeshift soundstage and into the streets. To the crew, he declares: "You see, I've had a vision. And that vision is called 'ultimate reality.' The rest of our film is shot in real life, with real people, and yes, with real terror." Following the tradition of American independent cinema throughout the 1960s and beyond, the primary way that *Cecil B. Demented* communicates the realism Cecil desires is through its adoption of *verité* style; as a visual shorthand, it expresses authenticity in its reactive handheld camerawork that follows the action rather than working in harmony with it. As a tool of documentary cinema, *verité* had lofty ideological ambitions that were supposed to be unlocked by the apparently unmediated style. According to Betsy McLane, *verité* "seemed to offer the possibility of an objective observer [. . .] It was felt that the presence of the camera was soon taken for granted by the subjects—ignored mostly, sometimes forgotten altogether."[8] Waters' use of *verité* never intended to allow the camera to disappear into the background, but instead reversed the purpose entirely. Shaky, handheld camerawork was the delivery method for images of grotesqueries of sexuality, violence, and general disgust that drew the spectator's attention to the construction of an undesirable image built for their viewing displeasure.

In *Cecil B. Demented*, some initial uses of *verité* style occur in the kidnapping melee at the Senator Theatre; as the revolutionary filmmakers spirit Honey out of the auditorium and fight their way through panicked filmgoers, the handheld camera captures the chaos of the moment. The kidnapping of Honey Whitlock, initially a hostage who transforms into a radical herself, is Waters' reimagining of the real-life story of heiress Patty Hearst, who was herself abducted by a group of radicals calling themselves the Symbionese Liberation Army in 1974. In the late 1980s, Waters developed a personal friendship with Hearst herself, and she has appeared in a number of his films in a variety of roles; in *Cecil B. Demented*, she is the straight-laced mother of the twitchy Fidget (Rodney Barry), one of Cecil's Sprocket Holes. *Verité* style has been associated on screen with Hearst before—in the satirical *Network* (1976), screenwriter Paddy Chayefsky's lacerating attack on the corrosive effects of television, director Sidney Lumet stages the film's Patty Hearst-like Mary Ann Gifford (Kathy Cronkite) in grainy footage that the gang of radicals shoots of themselves during a bank robbery. It is the footage's raw, unfinished quality that attracts craven executive Diana Christiansen (Faye Dunaway), and she commissions a show to be developed around the gang's activities following its inspiration. One of *Network*'s most incisive critiques is the way in which the radical impulses of revolutionaries are easily co-opted by forces of capital. The Communists later spend significant time haggling with Diana's lawyers about subsidiary rights and residuals.

Waters follows a similar thread, as the *verité* style that Cecil strives to achieve with *Raving Beauty* slowly merges with a more polished, professionalized approach to filmmaking that increasingly characterizes *Cecil B. Demented*, especially as the action scenes get more complicated and feature more gunplay and special effects. While the stage-bound scenes in the gang's lair at the Hippodrome have been anchored, with smooth tracking shots and stable framing, the scene immediately following Cecil's declaration of his vision is shot handheld inside the back of the van the revolutionaries use to get around, as they travel to their first location inside a small strip mall theatre that is playing *Patch Adams: The Director's Cut*. Inside, a collection of Baltimoreans are blubbering at the overwrought film in stable, locked-down images. Steadicam shots follow the crew through the parking lot, but *Raving Beauty*'s director of photography Pam (Erika Auchterlonie) is shooting on a shoulder-mounted camera that she swings wildly to follow the increasingly unpredictable action, as the gang waves guns around and terrorizes the girl behind the ticket counter. Waters' camera adopts this same *verité* approach, following the revolutionaries as Cecil fires his gun into the air and Cherish takes violent issue with the quality of the popcorn. A handheld shot of Cecil standing next to Pam, who is shooting in the direction of the lens, is a perfect mirrored microcosm of the radicals' style infiltrating and consuming the larger film itself. That *verité* style extends further into the auditorium as the gang crashes the *Patch Adams* screening, sending the patrons into vomiting and screaming paroxysms. *Cecil B. Demented*'s director of photography Robert Stevens' camera swings to the right to catch an older woman hurling into the aisle, a simulacrum of documentary realism that was no doubt perfectly planned.

Figure 6.1 Mirror images in *Cecil B. Demented*; the film camera watches the film camera.

The gang's next attack follows a similar pattern: handheld in the van, Steadicam as the revolutionaries get into position, and stable, locked-down images at the Inner Harbor banquet celebrating location shooting in Baltimore. After Honey crashes the dinner by leaping from the second story of the building above, the camera goes back to handheld, following the action as it spins out of control: Honey tosses what turns out to be a live grenade, and the police arrive, killing hairstylist Rodney (Jack Noseworthy), with the other crew members shooting back. In this sequence, however, Waters oscillates back and forth between *verité* style and a more controlled approach. Narratively, this sequence is critical—initially Honey tries to use the opportunity to escape her captivity, but the cops apprehend her, treating her like one of the revolutionaries, and she converts to their cause. Visually, Waters merges the *verité* style espoused by the radicals and the glossier Hollywood style Honey represents. In this second attack sequence, the balance between the two traditions is roughly equal, but used to illustrate an opposition between The Sprocket Holes' disruptive terrorism and the police's efforts to stop them. Handheld shots take Honey's point of view as she first looks over the edge of the roof, and a slow tilt up after she sticks the landing, then follow through the subsequent three shots as she says her first line, menacing the Film Commission hoi polloi, culminating in her tossing the grenade, which explodes over the side of the balcony, the camera responding with a surprised, pronounced shake. The camera is locked down on shots of the police, guns drawn, moving into position to aim and fire at the revolutionaries. Once the gunplay kicks off, the pace of cutting increases, but so too does the chaotic shake of the handheld camera in medium close-ups of The Sprocket Holes, while the reverse shots on the cops firing from cover are stable. A Steadicam shot tracks to the right as Honey surrenders to the police, as she tries to retreat to the stability of law enforcement and mainstream filmmaking, fleeing her captivity with the radicals. When the cops treat her like any other perpetrator, she calls out for Cecil in a mounted wide shot; she is no longer a prisoner of the radicals and their *verité* style, but of Hollywood's predictable stability.

The third major attack comes when Cecil and the gang infiltrate the Baltimore soundstage where a Hollywood crew is shooting *Gump Again*, a sequel to *Forrest Gump* (Robert Zemeckis, 1994). Unlike the previous action sequences, the *verité* style is kept to a minimum; the revolutionaries' seizing of the soundstage is much more surgical and professionalized. A Steadicam shot follows driver Petey (Michael Shannon) as he leads a Teamster to the back of The Sprocket Holes' truck, where he is subdued by a taser and hauled inside. The subsequent overhead wide shot of the *Gump* soundstage, with the director of photography high above on a crane, acts like a sanitized version of the gang's Hippodrome lair, communicated in a traditional establishing shot. In the next shot, a group of Teamsters plays cards in the foreground, while Petey enters in depth, with Waters' camera drifting left on a track, moving against Petey's screen right heading. Back on the set, the *Gump* crew and actor Kevin Nealon (stepping into the role of Forrest—presumably Tom Hanks was unavailable) ready to shoot a take; Waters cuts back to The Sprocket Holes slowly taking over the soundstage, but again, resists the *verité* style. A stable medium shot sees Lyle and Cherish snatch a pair of production assistants; a fluid, Classic Hollywood-style shot, in which a scene begins on a close-up of a Teamster with duct tape on his mouth, then smoothly pulls back to a medium as Lewis (Lawrence Gilliard Jr.) and Fidget leave two men strapped to their chairs; a floating Steadicam shot follows the script supervisor to Video Village, where Dinah (Harry Dodge) chokes her out from behind and drags her quietly behind a curtain; a brief vertiginous crane shot sees Cecil and Pam climb a scaffold; yet another Steadicam shot shows Lyle and Raven (Maggie Gyllenhaal) grab a makeup artist in the foreground, dragging her off at gunpoint screen left, before the camera pushes forward to reveal Honey and Cherish sitting in the makeup chairs, self-applying touchups with assistance from Fidget; the crane shot of Cecil is back next, as he ascends the scaffold, reaching parity with the *Gump* director of photography and camera operator on their own crane; a crash into Lawrence bracing a crew member's throat with a pipe is accomplished with a Steadicam that shifts the focus once again to Fidget grabbing another man with a gun in his face. A quick montage shows Cecil licking the Panaflex logo on the camera he has commandeered; Dinah calling "roll sound!;" Chardonnay taking over the sound board; Cecil adopting an accent to shout "camera rolling" and Pam responding "mark it!" The *Gump* director calls action, without a clue that his

Figure 6.2 Radical filmmaker Cecil B. Demented (Stephen Dorff) leads a hostile takeover of a soundstage, assuming the commanding heights of the crane.

entire crew has been replaced by the radicals. Their filmmaking practice cannot help but be co-opted by the slick, glossy Hollywood machine; on the soundstage, they are at their most polished, and *Cecil B. Demented* follows suit.

In fleeing from their terrorist attacks, the gang takes refuge in disreputably coded theatrical spaces, which extends Waters' understanding of style beyond the space of the frame and into the domain of exhibition; after the Inner Harbor dustup, they pass through a theatre playing an action movie, and the audience immediately rallies to them, standing in the way of a pursuing mob of angry family film fans; after the violence of the assault on *Gump Again* that leaves several of the gang dead, the survivors hide out in a porn theater playing one of Cherish's films, *Rear Entry*; a crowd of zombie-like masturbators pushes back a justice-seeking group of Teamsters from the *Gump* set. As is typical of Waters' work, *Cecil B. Demented* elevates "low" genres and film traditions, legitimating them and their audiences as authentic, at the very least, and in their willingness to both rescue and fight on the radicals' behalf, their heroism. Waters' well-documented admiration for the marketing-gimmick cinema of horror maestro William Castle comes to narrative life in his celebration of the nobility of the denizens of movie houses playing kung fu movies and stag films. For Waters, the best cinematic experiences are the ones that leap off the screen and into the audience; in his description of his love of the buzzing-seat trick that accompanied Castle's *The Tingler* (1959), Waters says: "As I sat there experiencing the miracle of Percepto, I realized that there could be such a thing as Art in the cinema."[9] He sees the direct impact of cinema on the audience as an extension of the filmmaker's style; it does not end at the edges of the frame. From the beginning of his career, he has been concerned with the visceral, physical response of his audiences, especially to his parade of grotesque, shocking images (see the woman vomiting in The Sprocket Holes' attack on *Patch Adams* in the film's first act). In her analysis of the relationship between Waters and Castle, Kate J. Russell argues that "Waters' cinema privileges the communal space of the theatre as a social environment and an outlet for pleasure where anticipation explodes into riotous screams, laughter, and retches."[10] Both as a site of terror attacks staged by The Sprocket Holes and as refuges from persecution from moralizing antagonists, the physical space of the cinema in *Cecil B. Demented* is a reflection of Waters' own attitudes about the shared value of the act of collective viewing, and the impact of his stylistic choices on his audience. Russell argues that both Castle and Waters "cultivated the cinema as a space in which spectators respond viscerally to moments of spectacle."[11] This impulse would return in the final image of *A Dirty Shame* (2004), to this point Waters' final film: a splash of CGI-generated semen, years before the resurgence of 3D, covers the screen.

While Castle's fondness for gimmickry always looms large in Waters' cinema, another filmmaker hangs over *Cecil B. Demented*; the title is an obvious play on the name of one of Hollywood's most famous directors, Cecil B. DeMille. Like so much about Waters' character Cecil, the name is adopted (his real name is Sinclair), a performative gesture designed to illustrate his character's radicalism. Cecil B. DeMille, the director of grandiose Biblical epics like *The Ten Commandments* (1959), might seem like an odd inspirational choice for a cinematic insurrectionist like Demented, but DeMille's visual style was similarly infused with a desire to titillate and provoke audiences with salacious narrative material. DeMille's "biblical epics were highly recommended for children by priests and parishioners, but they were also accused of having thrown more sex-and-sin into the audience's faces for longer than anyone else dared to."[12] For Thomas Doherty, DeMille was "the preeminent auteur of the biblical disaster film" whose films *The Sign of The Cross* (1932) and *Cleopatra* (1934) both "wallowed in an orgy of paganism before the Judeo-Christian deity broke up the Greco-Roman shenanigans in a way that is only His."[13] *The Sign of The Cross*, set in ancient Rome during the reign of Nero, is particularly notable for a daring scene where Empress Poppaea (Claudette Colbert) bathes nude in a tub full of milk. Foster Hirsch calls DeMille "Hollywood's premier wrangler of ancient-world orgies," but also acknowledges that by 1959, with the release of *The Ten Commandments*, he "has been restrained." In that film, the stylistic contrasts between the competing impulses of DeMille have been balanced, as "he cuts furiously between scenes of reverence and revelry, saintliness and sensuality."[14] Like Castle and Waters, for Hirsch, DeMille was "a shrewd showman."[15]

Unlike Castle, DeMille largely saved the spectacle for the screen itself. Waters admires Castle as a cigar-chomping madman who cooked up anything and everything to get anyone and everyone to come see his cheaply made horror movies; DeMille, by contrast, is often perceived to be the kind of self-serious, moralizing scold that Waters routinely makes fun of throughout his work. Whatever DeMille's personal politics and religious beliefs, his work has routinely carried an anarchic streak; not only do his films revel in a certain kind of sinful display of collective sensuality, but they also show an equal interest in chaotic violence, destruction, and terror. The constraints of the Hollywood studio system (and, in the 1930s, the weight of the cameras) would have prevented him from using *verité* style to photograph one of these catastrophes, but the pace and energy of the climactic zeppelin disaster in *Madam Satan* (1930) is a close stylistic cousin. As a wind-tossed, distressed blimp wobbles high above New York City, wealthy costumed partygoers leap from the decks using the many built-in parachutes. The tone of the sequence oscillates between terror and farce, as the high society caricatures who had, just minutes before, been enjoying their wealth, are suddenly thrust into a life-or-death situation. In some shots, DeMille's camera tips to the right or left as the blimp lists to one side or the other, walking up to the line of *verité* identification with the surroundings; a series of canted angles and bobs of the frame accompany the increasing mania. A piece of the blimp's metal structure falls into the foreground in one image, and the camera shakes slightly as though it were suffering the impact, a forerunner of the *verité* approach in *Cecil B. Demented* when the camera rattles in reaction to the grenade explosion. A restless movement of the camera continues throughout the remainder of the sequence, escalating in its instability as the zeppelin breaks apart completely. As early as 1930, DeMille found a way to merge the spectacle of Hollywood destruction with a simulacrum of *verité* style that was attuned to the way it would feel to be on the decks of a blimp smashing itself to pieces. Cecil B. DeMille was himself more than a little demented.

The irony of director Cecil B. Demented's reliance on *verité* style is that by the year 2000, handheld, improvised camera movements had codified into a signifier of authenticity rather than authenticity itself. It was the hallmark of grit as the dominant visual style of the Baltimore-set NBC show *Homicide: Life on the Street* (1993–1999), which would in turn be shared by police procedurals like ABC's *NYPD Blue* (1993–2005) and FX's *The Shield* (2002–2008), all of which reached large audiences. NBC's primetime sitcom *The Office* (2005–2013) was soon to follow, showing how safe and mainstream *verité* style had come to be. Action films like *The Bourne Supremacy* (Paul Greengrass, 2002) likewise used a hyper-kinetic *verité* style to place the viewer alongside action hero Jason Bourne (Matt Damon). This mainstream studio system co-optation of a previously subversive technique reflects the inevitable absorption of innovations in style into the classical storytelling language of Hollywood cinema. According to David Bordwell and Kristin Thompson, "Directors nowadays tell us that they are in search of energy, a moment-by-moment spiking of audience interest. You can get it through fast cutting, arcing camera movements, sudden frame-entrances, the nervousness of the handheld shot, or all of the above."[16] Whatever Cecil is looking to expose with his on-the-ground, in-your-face realistic style, his audiences would likely have no trouble understanding it. They could see it on NBC, Thursdays at 10PM. This mainstreaming of once radical stylistic traditions undermines the cause that Cecil is fighting for; "Death to mainstream cinema!", he shouts, but his film's visual style has already been swallowed by it. He's shooting blanks.

Waters undoubtedly knows this, which sets up the entire stylistic negotiation that defines *Cecil B. Demented*, as *verité* realism is locked in a tug of war with a more professionalized, finely-tuned craft. As early as 1983's "How *Not* to Make a Movie," where so many of the ideas of *Cecil B. Demented* seem to have been born, he says, "Hollywood has co-opted the slash-and-trash formula, and these days even garbage needs a big budget."[17] In the latter portion of Waters' *Female Trouble*, protagonist Dawn Davenport (Divine), on the teenager-to-murderer express, takes the stage at a club and bellows, "Who wants to die for art?," then pulls a gun and starts shooting into the crowd, a flagrant act of public criminality bound up in performance that ultimately leads to her arrest, trial, and sentence to die in the electric chair, where she ends up addressing the camera as though winning an Oscar. In *Cecil B. Demented*, Cecil takes a similar stand, announcing both his and The Sprocket Holes' willingness to die for the film they are making. Over the course of the film, many of them do, shot to death by police or gun-toting Teamsters. But it's Cecil himself who gets the most grandiose exit. Seriously wounded from a gunshot, he hops into a wheelchair on the roof of a drive-in theater projection booth. The wheelchair, of course, is a signifier of his independent cinema roots—it is the poor man's way to achieve a relatively smooth tracking shot. A crew member douses him in gasoline and lights him ablaze. He rockets the wheelchair towards a gun-toting police officer, knocking him off the roof and saving Honey's life. In his act of sacrifice, he surrenders his radicalism to Honey, whose high-profile movie stardom has fused with Cecil's revolutionary cinematic deconstructionism. Cecil's act of self-immolation is a manifestation of the closing paragraph of Waters' book *Role Models*, in which he, playing the role of a cult leader, advocates for the group's preferred method of dying: spontaneous combustion. With winking romanticism, Waters muses: "It's a beautiful death, dramatic, scary, internally cleansing, and all you leave for the rest of the world to see is a really good pair of shoes."[18] But Cecil's death is also an acknowledgment that dying for art is the idealized conviction of youth. Young filmmakers have to believe in what they do almost totally, and the style of the films they make reflects their complete commitment to their work.

The final paragraph of Waters' *Mr. Know-It-All* offers a counterpoint to his dreams of spontaneous combustion: "I'm fully content, loved and protected, and if there's such a thing as happiness, well, this is it. I will sit here for eternity not wanting a thing."[19] Older filmmakers, like Waters at the time of *Cecil B. Demented*, are more open to compromise, and in many cases, happy they didn't die for art, because, in continuing to live, they got to keep making it. The inclusion of several of Waters' early films in The Criterion Collection in recent years led to an inevitable series of restorations, a process that Waters himself is ambivalent about. In the interview that appends this volume, he describes the restoration process as marked by compromises: "When Criterion redid a lot of them, restored them, it was a thin line. I don't want that scratch there; it was an accident. But don't make it look like something it isn't. Don't leave the dirt in if there's one shot, but still don't make it look too good."[20] One of the mastering supervisors for The Criterion Collection, Lee Kline, offers a slight counterpoint: "He's a guy who wants to make the movies look as good as they can [. . .] He wants them to look like Bergman films."[21] This tension is an acknowledgment that Waters would not have fallen back on *verité* style as a hallmark of his own brand of "outlaw cinema." He would much have preferred a more polished product: "Always, I want it to look like a '50s Hollywood movie. I always wanted to look slick. I never could."[22]

For all of Cecil's bluster about the stale, uninteresting films cranked out by Hollywood, there is a degree of resentment in his exclusion from it. He is happy to make grand proclamations like "Power to the people who punish bad cinema!," but ultimately, he wants an audience. In an essay on *Multiple Maniacs* by Linda Yablonsky, she argues that "[i]ndignation grounds this and every one of [Waters'] films, whether they're taking on religion, gay icons, bigotry, homelessness, the dictates of beauty, the desire for fame, or middle-class complacency."[23] That indignation is certainly there in Cecil, and his stylistic outlet to express his distaste for contemporary cinema is the raw, handheld, authentic shake of *verité*. But there is also more than a little echo in Cecil of Waters' own admission that he "always wanted to sell out. The problem is nobody wanted to buy me. Ever since I was a toddler I longed to be a film director (or a mad bomber), so I was lucky not to waste time floundering around in youth looking for a vocation."[24] Waters' equating of a film director and a terrorist reveals a link in his mind between acts of creation and destruction; through the harnessing of these competing, contradictory ideas, he uses *Cecil B. Demented*, his most overt examination of the state of the cinema and his own place in it, to negotiate the trajectory from the *verité* style of the outsider to the slick polish of the Hollywood insider.

NOTES

1. John Waters, "How *Not* to Make a Movie," in *Crackpot: The Obsessions of John Waters* (New York: Scribner, Trade Paperback Edition, 2003), 138–149.
2. Ibid., 148.
3. Howard Hampton, "*Pink Flamingos*: The Battle of Filth," *The Criterion Collection*, June 28, 2022, https://www.criterion.com/current/posts/7845-pink-flamingos-the-battle-of-filth
4. Ed Halter, "*Female Trouble*: Spare Me Your Morals," *The Criterion Collection*, June 26, 2018, https://www.criterion.com/current/posts/5767-female-trouble-spare-me-your-morals
5. Tom Ryan, "Sirk, Hollywood, and Genre," *Senses of Cinema*, Issue 66, March 2013, https://www.sensesofcinema.com/2013/feature-articles/sirk-hollywood-and-genre/
6. Elena Gorfinkel, "*Polyester*: The Perils of Francine," *The Criterion Collection*, September 17, 2019, https://www.criterion.com/current/posts/6590-polyester-the-perils-of-francine
7. Hampton.
8. Betsy McLane, *A New History of Documentary Film*, 2nd Edition (New York: Bloomsbury, 2012), 229.
9. John Waters, "Whatever Happened to Showmanship?", in *Crackpot*, 17.
10. Kate J. Russell, "The Cinematic Pandemonium of William Castle and John Waters," in *ReFocus: The Films of William Castle*, edited by Murray Leeder (Edinburgh: Edinburgh University Press, 2018), 238.
11. Ibid.
12. Anton Karl Kozlovic, "DeMille, Cecil B.," *Senses of Cinema*, Issue 66, March 2013, https://www.sensesofcinema.com/2013/great-directors/cecil-b-demille/
13. Thomas Doherty, *Pre-Code Hollywood: Sex, Immorality, and Insurrection in American Cinema 1930–1934* (New York: Columbia University Press, 1999), 65.
14. Foster Hirsch, *Hollywood and the Movies of the Fifties* (New York: Alfred A. Knopf, 2023), 512.
15. Ibid.
16. David Bordwell & Kristin Thompson, *Minding Movies: Observations on the Art, Craft, and Business of Filmmaking* (Chicago: University of Chicago Press, 2011), 168.
17. Waters, "How *Not* to Make a Movie," 138.
18. John Waters, *Role Models* (New York: Farrar, Straus, and Giroux, 2011), 294.
19. John Waters, *Mr. Know-It-All* (New York: Picador, 2019), 364.
20. John Waters, Interview by Michelle E. Moore and Brian Brems, November 2, 2023.
21. Qtd. in Joshua Hunt, "Sure, It Won an Oscar. But Is It Criterion?", *The New York Times*, February 29, 2024, https://www.nytimes.com/2024/02/29/magazine/criterion-collection.html
22. John Waters, Interview by Michelle E. Moore and Brian Brems.
23. Linda Yablonsky, "*Multiple Maniacs*: Genuine Trash," *The Criterion Collection*, March 21, 2017, https://www.criterion.com/current/posts/4467-multiple-maniacs-genuine-trash
24. Waters, "How *Not* to Make a Movie," in *Crackpot*, 138.

CHAPTER 7

Little Movies: John Waters and the Visual Arts

Nicholas Morgan

In *Art: A Sex Book* (2003, co-authored with the art critic Bruce Hainley), John Waters remarks that "Hollywood is an entire industry based on voyeurism," but that the "smoke and mirrors" of "music and sound" disguise or suppress this base dimension of the medium. Grindhouse cinema, pornography, and other lowbrow genres are closer, Waters argues, to the visual arts than they are to Hollywood film because painting, photography, and sculpture lack such polite appurtenances and alibis: "There isn't much smoke and mirrors, except intellectually, in art work. All the smoke and mirrors in art is based on what you can see and how far you are willing to go to see it."[1] In the years after this conversation was published, as funding for large-scale film productions from mainstream sources dwindled, Waters increasingly turned to making visual art.[2] Within Waters' oeuvre, such works thus function as what Pavle Levi calls "cinema by other means," or "the practice of positing cinema as a system of relations directly inspired by the workings of the film apparatus, but evoked through the material and technological properties of the originally nonfilmic media."[3] Waters' evocation of cinema within static media links contemporary art and the studio film system in terms of their shared lowbrow dimensions, examining the bass note of prurience thrumming beneath the surface of Hollywood narratives and rendered explicitly as pure surface in much of the visual art he admires and produces. Both Waters' films and his visual art examine subterranean or repressed currents within film history, and considering Waters' visual art practice in relation to his films shows how both the films and the artwork constitute a reformulation of dominant Western conceptions of the aesthetic. Waters' aesthetic trades values like disinterest, beauty, and complexity for humor, abjection, eroticism, and—a term that arguably encompasses all of these qualities—gimmickry.

Waters has often narrated how he came to make his first artwork: in 1992, in need of a still of Divine from *Multiple Maniacs* (1970) and unable to find an image of the particular moment he had in mind, he resorted to the same quasi-amateur toolkit that had fuelled his earliest collaborations with the actor. Using a consumer-grade "automatic, point-and-shoot 35mm camera," he photographed a television monitor playing a VHS tape of *Multiple Maniacs*.[4] The shot comes midway through the film, depicting Lady Divine (played by Divine) writhing on a sidewalk after being assaulted by two glue-sniffing hoodlums. Moments later, Mink Stole's character finds Lady Divine and takes her to a church, where they engage in a rapturous, sacred-yet-profane bout of pew-bound queer lovemaking. Viewers need not be aware of this narrative context to appreciate the 1992 photograph, entitled *Divine in Ecstasy* (Figure 7.1). Seen in isolation, the rephotographed Divine radiates outwards against an abstract background, exuding charisma in a yelp of bliss or pain. The title hammers home the immediate visual resonances with Bernini's *Ecstasy of St. Theresa* and other scenes of eroticized yet violent encounters in Baroque art. Video artefacting and high contrast infuse the image with ambiguity, overtly displaying the low-budget means of its production (much like Waters' earliest films). As Waters later recounted, the print "didn't look like the movie. It looked better.

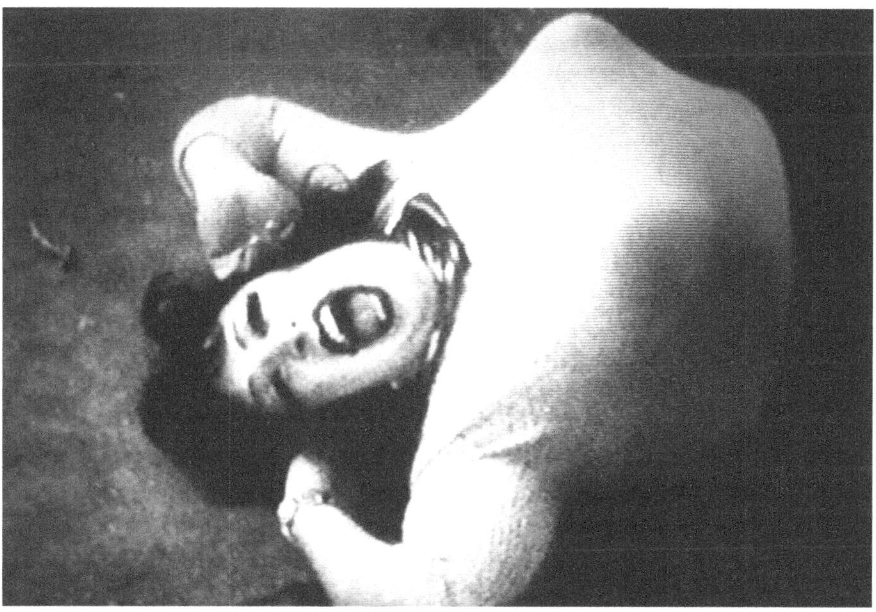

Figure 7.1 In his first work of visual art, Waters returns to his own archive, using an amateur point-and-shoot camera to re-present a moment from *Multiple Maniacs*. John Waters, *Divine in Ecstasy*, 1992 , 10 × 13 inches. © John Waters. Courtesy of the artist and Marianne Boesky Gallery, New York and Aspen.

The films that I made that had the worst technical qualities work much better for art than well-lit Hollywood movies. So it's all in reverse."[5]

The relationship between Waters' filmic oeuvre and his visual art can be productively understood in terms of this idea of the "reverse," since reversal suggests both repetition with a change and a kind of sameness paradoxically not far from utter opposition.

Colin de Land, proprietor of the prestigious yet bohemian New York gallery American Fine Arts, Co., saw *Divine in Ecstasy*, liked it, and offered Waters a solo show. One critic framed the 1995 exhibition as self-consciously toying with the notion of celebrities making art, who "usually aren't taken very seriously" not so much because the quality of the work is lacking but because "the celebrity already *is* a cultural artifact—a conundrum certain to spark cognitive dissonance."[6] *Village Voice* photography critic Vince Aletti also understood the show as self-referential: "Film is both subject and raw material here. . . . it's the filmmaker's shrewd, obsessive take on the medium itself that's the main attraction."[7] Hainley, with whom Waters would go on to collaborate on *Art: A Sex Book*, gave an especially incisive account of the role of the cinematic in Waters' visual art: "Waters learned it at the movies: silence, severity, surface, smarts, glamour, style, perversion, language, menace, rhythm, awe. . . . His photos are memos: while watching movies, think about their strangeness and your own, the strangeness of visuality itself."[8] Hainley has in mind what Waters called his "little movies," sequences of carefully arranged photographs, framed and displayed as single works, all shot—starting with *Divine in Ecstasy*—with a handheld camera aimed at a television screen.[9]

Some of the little movies continue the first photograph's focus on Waters' own oeuvre: *Sullen Cookie* (1998) consists of six stills of Cookie Mueller, shot in quick succession as she turns her eye towards the camera, lips pouting. Others cull from both the Waters oeuvre and other televisual material. *Manson Copies Divine's Hairdo* (1993) hilariously juxtaposes a shot of Divine with a shot of Charles Manson (himself often referenced in Waters' work) in which the murderous cult leader's coiffure indeed resembles the actor's with astonishing closeness. Some utilize only work from films by other directors, either a single film or multiple films. *Illusion-O* (2014), for example, consists of six prints shot from William Castle's melodramatic *13 Ghosts* (1960). The first few stills capture the ghost-detecting glasses characters in the film wear to be able to see the dead, while the last cuts to one of the horrifying figures themselves. Castle's trash cinema contributed to Waters' aesthetic formation, as he confesses in a 1983 essay: "King of the Gimmicks, William Castle was my idol. His films made me want to make films."[10] But *Illusion-O* is more than an homage: it recalls and reactivates a little-remembered moment in film history, when Castle developed a gimmicky apparatus for watching his film. Tinted glasses included with admission could be taken on or off at a viewer's will, since without the glasses the tinted ghosts were not visible (especially handy if a viewer was too scared by the ghosts). The gesture linked spectators' movements to those of the characters in the film, a cinematic footnote *Illusion-O* honours. The little movies comprise acts of editing or re-editing, turning movies Waters loathes into ones he could like and turning films he does like into revised versions even closer to the anarchic revaluation of trash aesthetics promulgated in his own films. Although *Illusion-O* cites *13 Ghosts*, more than the film itself the artwork celebrates the ostentatious publicity apparatus surrounding it.

As an interpretation of cinema history and meta-commentary upon film post-production and distribution, the little movies emphasize the centrality of editing, working largely through montage and juxtaposition. They also claim a participatory and personal relationship with the mass-produced artifacts of the culture industry, which become stranger when they age, are discarded, and become defamiliarized. In *Santa Molester* (2009), Waters rephotographs and stitches together moments from *Santa Claus vs. the Devil* (René Cardona, 1959), modifying the original narrative such that Santa appears to voyeuristically gaze at a young boy through a window before invading his home and forcing him to worship at his feet. In the original film, Santa returns presents stolen by other children to the boy and earns his thanks. Waters exacerbates the original film's weirdness, rather than impose weirdness on an originally normative filmic artifact: flouting conventional Christmas narratives, Cardona's Santa works in outer space and is antagonized by the Christian devil. With the evocation of child sex abuse, though, Waters undeniably transforms the cult film into something even eerier. The artwork both de-idealizes one of America's cheeriest, family-centered rituals (Christmas) by associating it with perversion and presents the specter of the child molester as a dark counterpoint to benevolent Santa's place in American culture insofar as he takes the discursive position of an unseen yet present force of evil. *Santa Molester* recalls dual parental adages: if you are a good child you will get presents, but also, don't take candy from strangers.

Thematic resonances between Waters' little movies and his big-screen movies are easy enough to come by: *Movie Star Jesus* (1996) consists of a number of photographs of Jesus as played by actors in a range of different films, organized within a cruciform frame that evokes medieval reliquaries. Lightly sacrilegious, it raises the question of what it means to turn the Biblical figure into a mass cultural product, while also emphasizing the eroticism with which depictions of his crucified body are often endowed. In both of these senses, it chimes with the representation of Jesus-as-hunk in *Multiple Maniacs*. To take another example, in *Cecil B. Demented* (2000) Dinah uses a book about the director David Lean as a shooting target, an idea actually enacted by Waters himself in the slightly earlier sculptural work *Awful David Lean* (1996), which consists of a crumpled c-print of a rephotographed title card for the director, whose successful yet "pompous and boring" work sparks Waters' ire.[11] Also in *Cecil B. Demented*, Cherish describes a nightmarish recovered memory of a Christmas when she was gang raped by her extended family, exclaiming "My father sat on my face as he opened his Christmas presents!" The transgressive or "trash" notion of perverting Christmas here anticipates *Santa Molester*, and is part and parcel of Waters' general strategy of dismantling the sentimentalized myths of normative American society. Throughout these works, Waters engages in a complex process of both self-archiving and experimentation: in *Illusion-O* producing hilarious and alluring diagrams of the lowbrow inspirations for his earlier films, in *Movie Star Jesus* reflecting on and drawing freely from his own film oeuvre, and in *Awful David Lean* trying out an idea that later was introduced into new filmic work.

The direct citation of that which is literally placed off-screen by cinema history sets *Santa Molester* and the other little movies apart from their thematic correlates in Waters' films, however. Waters is interested in films that occupy little to no place in canonical narratives of film's evolution, but also in the detritus of industrial film production, including Castle's glasses (most of which would have been discarded post-screening). Consider *Leader* (1995), which consists of eight prints, first of luminous, almost hypnotic or phantasmagoric numbers counting from three to eight, then announcing "picture start," and culminating in a creepy shot of a child actor clutching a doll and grinning maniacally. Recalling the prominent position Andy Warhol afforded leader in his screen tests and other films, cinema is reduced to its degree zero. The majority of several little movie works, such as *Eat Your Makeup* and *Portrait of Pat Moran* (both 1996), consist of title cards. *Despair* (1995) comprises shots of five title cards crediting Alan Smithee, a pseudonym used by directors wishing to disown a finished film. The little movies celebrate detritus, whether in the form of movies that are occasionally screened on late night film channels but are almost certainly not destined to be recuperated as forgotten classics or even camp or cult hits, or the literal scraps more likely to end up in a studio's trash bin than in an official archive. It is the base materiality and physical address of the medium, that which both upholds narrative film and is extraneous to it, that Waters centers. His films regularly engage a similar project: In *Cecil B. Demented*, catty corner to the Baltimore film studio where a middlebrow *Forrest Gump* sequel is being shot stands a pornographic movie theater screening one of Cherish's erotic films. The hope or fantasy underlying this image is of a space—such as the grindhouse or porno theater—in which the morass of culture industry fodder can be interrupted or remade such that antinormativity, camp, and anarchism are able to poke through the official aesthetic and cultural forms they subtend but from which they are, despite intimate proximity, banned.

The little movies rewrite film history by looking into the studio's trash cans, collating discards, and letting abjected erotic, horrific, and queer content run wild. Since this project is shared by Waters' films, a closer look at *Divine in Ecstasy* will shed some light on what is specifically accomplished by carrying it out through visual art, rather than filmic means. Though not a film, the photograph points back to a pre-existing film. It foregrounds the life of one of those who participated in the making of that film, emphasizing the personality that infuses *Multiple Maniacs* with energy more than its plot. Divine died unexpectedly in 1988, the same year *Hairspray* was released. Made four years later, *Divine in Ecstasy* has an elegiac quality that honours the actor's magnetic intensity while embalming what had been an animated performance within the stillness of the photographic medium. The image functions as a death mask as much as a substitute publicity still: stillness, here, is a deathliness opposed to the animacy of an unspooling film reel, even as both photograph and screen performance offer the possibility of celebrity's semi-eternal renown. In Waters' photograph, overt remediation (here, the "representation" of the filmic medium in a photographic medium) intensifies this tension.[12] Visible scan lines resulting from interpolation reveal the source material to be a video rather than a film projection. These scan lines align with the weave of Divine's sweater, making the video medium even more apparent while also introducing a degree of self-reflexivity common in the art of the period.[13] In the original scene from *Multiple Maniacs*, Divine is lying down, so the sweater's vertical weave is rotated to a horizontal pattern that matches the scan lines. But Waters has sometimes allowed the photograph to be reproduced in a portrait orientation that renders it more like a headshot than a screen grab, and turns the scan lines into vertical stripes closer to the abstract painter Morris Louis than to VHS.[14]

Chromatic instability augments this spatial ambiguity. The photograph is of a black-and-white film being displayed on an analogue television set with color capabilities. The photograph itself is a chromogenic print (the most common form of color photography in the art world between the 1970s and the early 1990s), rather than a gelatin silver (or black-and-white) print. In other little movie artworks, Waters printed his photographs as gelatin silvers: this is the case for *Sullen Cookie*, for example, and suggests a measure of intentionality underlying the material support of *Divine in Ecstasy*. These factors admit into consideration the hue of the photograph, which in some reproductions is more monochromatic, in others tinted dusky blue. The image's tone likely results from poor scan quality and/or shoddy color correction when the film elements of *Multiple Maniacs* were transferred to video for the VHS release he used. The quality gap between this transfer and the Criterion Collection's recent, painstaking edition of the film is striking.[15] The blue may instead or additionally be a by-product of the television's settings, since color televisions can be modified by the user to adjust for brightness and the like, and NTSC, the standard for analogue television in the United

States, inadequately represents filmic depth. In either case, this chromatic dimension reminds the photograph's viewer of the remediation entailed in its production.

Such matters informed Waters' thinking about cinematography in the period. In an extended 1992 interview with John G. Ives, Waters discussed the rising price of black-and-white film stock, by then equivalent to color stock. Waters notes that he finds it absurd when people object to colorizing black-and-white movies because an individual viewer could simply adjust their television's settings to black-and-white. "I always said I wished somebody would colorize *Mondo Trasho* and *Multiple Maniacs*—all in green," he says. "You know, that puke green."[16] Colorization comprises another variety of the gimmickry to which Waters' work gravitates, one that tries to render the old and outmoded newly desirable.

The cycle of remediation *Divine in Ecstasy* materializes forms a closed loop. Chromogenic prints are produced from celluloid negatives, and the final, framed print is thus a film print, returning Divine to the medium of his original performance. *Divine in Ecstasy*'s essence thus cannot be isolated within one particular instantiation or sphere. The work does not so much live between the film world and the art world as point to the differences between these poles, sharpening one's attentiveness to them. A deeper layer of self-reflexivity is introduced when one considers the photograph in relation to transformations in the art world at the time. Video, rather than 16mm or 35mm, was the material support most closely linked with experimental artistic engagement with the moving image in the 1990s. Video was prominent in, for example, Matthew Barney's first solo show in 1991 at the Barbara Gladstone Gallery in New York.[17] In translating Waters' back catalogue from film into video and then into photography, *Divine in Ecstasy* and many of the other little movie works map the arc of his career onto a transition into a new sphere of production, the contemporary art world.

A structurally analogous transfer occurs in *Kiddie Flamingos* (2015), for which Waters videotaped a table read of his cult classic *Pink Flamingos* (1972). A table read is an event marking the conclusion of preproduction and the beginning of production, at which actors and crew gather for a live read-through of the entire script. *Kiddie Flamingos* is firmly an example of video art, and not a contribution to Waters' filmic oeuvre: as with many examples of video art and other moving image-based work by visual artists, *Kiddie Flamingos* can only be exhibited in a museum, art gallery, or collector's home, and does not circulate as a publicly accessible work online or otherwise, except in the form of a brief teaser trailer.[18] Like other video artworks by, say, Barney, *Kiddie Flamingos* exists in a limited edition (a means of artificially limiting the theoretically infinitely reproducible nature of technical media to subtend its market value that has an earlier history in printmaking, and, in the twentieth century, in both sculpture and photography). Alexandra Keller and Frazer Ward note that Barney's moving-image artworks are distributed in limited editions of ten as luxury objects: while the actual work would reside on a simple DVD, the packaging for those works is a "vitrine/sculpture that includes an elaborate case for special silk-screened and signed DVDs."[19] For Keller and Ward, the customary ways moving-image work circulates as a commodity within the art market signals the utter complicity of Barney's work with capitalism, and thus its critical bankruptcy. More simply, this is a sales tactic, and thus a kind of gimmick.

Even as *Kiddie Flamingos* participates in the recherché conventions of editioning and art collecting, Waters elsewhere satirizes it. Another work, *Faux Video Room* (2006), consists of a curtain hung against a wall, behind which an iPod attached to speakers emits noise (Figure 7.2). The gag is that a viewer expects to part the curtains and enter a gallery screening room, the customary environs for viewing video artworks—but one is met only with impassable wall. A work made for an imagined ambitious collector who wants to acquire video artwork but lacks the necessary domestic space in which to display it, *Faux*

Figure 7.2 This installation, comprised of speakers, painted wood, synthetic velour, and an iPod, pokes fun at the strange conventions for collecting and exhibiting moving-image-based work in the art world, which are utterly distinct from cinematic modes of distribution. John Waters, *Faux Video Room*, 2006, 110 3/4 × 96 × 6 inches. © John Waters. Courtesy of the artist and Marianne Boesky Gallery, New York and Aspen.

Video Room underlines the odd conditions of exhibition of moving-image-based artworks. The piece suggests a class hierarchy within the already elite tier of art collectors. *Secret Movie* (2000) also hinges on contrasting cinematic and art world conditions of display: atop a minimalistic plinth too high for a spectator to gaze upon, a monitor plays an unknown film whose title Waters will never release. The tease here recalls conceptual artist Louise Lawler's 1979 *A Movie Will Be Shown Without the Picture*, for which the artist rented out movie theaters and presented only the soundtrack, not the accompanying images, of various films selected by her, in what amounts to a critique of the dominance of hypermediated images in late capitalism. Yet in Waters the conceptual gesture is tempered by the teasing humorousness of the work's central mystery, and whatever the film really is (*if* it is), it is surely marginal within mainstream cinema histories.

At the same time as Waters contrasts art world and mainstream moviegoing spectatorial infrastructure, his practice inevitably points to the porousness between film and art. Like other works discussed above such as *Divine in Ecstasy*, in *Kiddie Flamingos* the transfer is again from film to video, and also from the world of film to the world of fine art as marked by its editioning. The content of this new media artwork is literally that of an earlier medium: a film, and its script. However, these are dramatically recontextualized, rather than straightforwardly re-presented. The performers gathered at the table read are all children. Waters revised the original *Pink Flamingos* script so that it would be suitable for performance by his young actors; the notorious substance Divine ingests towards the end is changed from dog faeces to dog food. The resulting work is charming, especially when the children occasionally break into giggles. While the art world appears permissive in its embrace of avant-garde culture, it is, ironically, the zone in which the once X-rated becomes G-rated. In this sense, *Kiddie Flamingos* sends up the idea of the art world as a space of radicality or subversion. Another subtext is the normalization of Waters: *Pink Flamingos*, despite the dog dung, has become so acceptable within, even celebrated by, mainstream American society that even children can re-perform it. It is a short leap from the Criterion Collection to the Disney Channel, the work seems to suggest. If Waters had by 2015 been sanctified precisely for his transgressive aesthetic, especially that of his 1970s work, then the G-rated quality of *Kiddie Flamingos* becomes a new form—perhaps the only possible form—of transgression, sanitizing the by-then canonized trashiness of *Pink Flamingos*.

Yet despite the tactful redactions to the script, it is startling to see children rehearse the original film. And given the preponderance of false right-wing associations between gender nonconformity and child abuse, Waters' choice is a bold affront. Though it antedates the swell of reactionary protests against drag performances in secondary schools and similar events, with its irresistible charm *Kiddie Flamingos* is almost purpose-built to puncture such violent responses. The performers in *Kiddie Flamingos* are queer children in the sense Kathryn Bond Stockton employs: figures unencumbered by the restraint of adult customs, open to strangeness in the face of normativity, and aligned with an anarchic, anti-teleological temporality.[20] Watching *Kiddie Flamingos*, one thinks of the how the protestors in *Polyester* (1981) would respond, with their chant "What do we love? Disney! What do we hate? Filth!" In a typically dialectical move, Waters' acknowledgment of his own canonization in the amusing register of *Kiddie Flamingos* is at the same time a re-radicalization of the sharply subversive edge of the now-accepted work.

Table reads are a mainstay of Hollywood film production, to a degree that they have sometimes been dramatized in industry fare about the industry.[21] In the years since Waters made *Kiddie Flamingos*, it has become not uncommon for networks to post video recordings of the table reads of landmark episodes (say, series finales) to YouTube, and in this sense *Kiddie Flamingos* presciently anticipated the gimmicky use of this normally off-screen facet of studio production as a promotional tool.[22]

But aside from its occasional use as a special feature, fan service, or publicity tool, the table read is meant to prepare the cast and director for the arduous process of shooting itself. Like leader, it is outside the finished aesthetic product. In this sense, although *Kiddie Flamingos* postdates *Pink Flamingos*, it returns to an earlier moment in the production schedule. Moreover, a table read reduces film to its literary dimension, and is thus antithetical to theories of pure cinema in which dialogue pollutes the essential qualities of duration and movement. (This ethos was influential during Waters' development, as in the work of his exact contemporary Anthony McCall, also born in 1946.[23]) Rather than positing cinema's essence in its formal qualities, Waters directs the spectator towards an understanding of off-screen Hollywood rituals and quotidian elements of production as the cinematic dimension which his artistic cinema by other means explores. In his *Screen Tests* of the 1960s, Warhol similarly foregrounded a facet of studio film production which is meant to be discarded and unavailable to general audiences. A table read, though, strips away all *mise-en-scène* even more forcefully than a screen test's measuring of *photogénie*. Insofar as *Kiddie Flamingos* remediates Waters' filmic oeuvre into visual art, it is this lack of *mise-en-scène* that differentiates the two spheres. In re-presenting *Pink Flamingos* in the form of video art, and updating the work's casting conceit in ways that intervene into recent phobic discourses, Waters stages a kind of inversion—another "reverse."

The fact that Waters stringently defines *Kiddie Flamingos* as a work of video art and *Pink Flamingos* as a film demonstrates his attentiveness to the institutional borders cordoning off the art world and the film world respectively. While many art historians define "contemporary art" by its conceptual rather than visual nature, Waters frames it as a style.[24] Reflecting back on *Divine in Ecstasy* in 2018 he noted: "I saw it and thought, oh God—this looks even artier than I could ever imagine."[25] He explained this arty look to novelist Dennis Cooper: "the bad technical aspects of the early work lend themselves very well to contemporary art. . . . if you primitively photograph badly photographed movies, it becomes a new kind of rawness that I believe can work in the contemporary art world."[26] Defining contemporary art on primarily aesthetic grounds desublimates the lofty philosophical ambitions embedded in theories of contemporary art's conceptualism. By identifying its visual codes as recognizable or stereotypical, Waters engages with contemporary art as a system in itself, as when a work like *Kiddie Flamingos* is made available at home only to those who actually can afford the kind of display space parodied in *Faux Video Room*.[27] Waters even spatializes this understanding of the art world as a discrete system, noting that he purposefully works on his artworks in a separate studio from that used for film work.[28]

Pecker (1998) examines this understanding of the art world as a coherent, morphologically identifiable sphere on the level of narrative. The title character, an amateur photographer, delights in documenting his Baltimorean friends and family, who become alienated when the New York art world suddenly takes Pecker's work up and begins marketing and exhibiting it.[29] Do the images more properly belong to their sitters, ideally exhibited in the local sandwich shop where Pecker works, or in a white cube gallery? It is snobby, yet ultimately redeemed, cosmopolitan figures who recontextualize Pecker's output as a valuable commodity. Ultimately, his work is appreciated by both the SoHo elite and the local subjects, who reconcile in a climactic party. *Pecker* analyzes the institutions of art in a way coextensive with Waters' art practice. That a particular object's status as art is socially constructed, and not ontological, is demonstrated by the ambiguous status of the aesthetically striking photographs produced within the film's diegesis by Pecker. Never exhibited in real-world art institutions or offered on the art market, they were taken by a Baltimore-based photographer, Chuck Shacochis, who has sometimes lamented the fact that his contribution to the film cannot form part of his artistic oeuvre because it belongs to the production.[30] Just as *Divine in Ecstasy* looked like contemporary art to Waters when he first saw it, Shacochis' shots "look like" the fine art photography of Bill Dane or Diane Arbus (whose image *A Young Brooklyn Family Going for a Sunday Outing, N.Y.C., 1966* inspired Divine's appearance in *Female Trouble* [1974]). This emphasis on resemblance, even when resemblance includes a reversal or a difference, undermines conceptual definitions of contemporary art in favor of morphological affinities—suggesting, as literary theorist Sianne Ngai has, that conceptual and/or immaterial art itself may share, despite its avant-gardism, the logic of the gimmick.[31]

The respected painter Peter Halley once commented to Waters that "Looking at these photo works of yours, even though they're in an art format, I think they read really differently than art."[32] The point is that Waters' works do look like art, even if their status as art is complicated by their always already compromised status as works by a celebrity and by their jokiness. Comedy's central place distinguishes this work from the work of morphologically similar artists such as Cindy Sherman, because neither the institution of art nor Western aesthetics in general since the Enlightenment make much place for puns.[33] Art historian Benjamin Buchloh describes "the critic's inability to laugh, to respond to a joke, and by implication his inability to respond to any artistic intervention that aims to offer a moment of sudden relief from the continuous and collective conditions of repression."[34] Critics have indeed expressed confusion or dismay over Waters' art's status as what one calls "one-note jokes that defy you to interpret them."[35] Another writes that *Faux Video Room* is "a good trick, but it works only once," flagging "the tepidness of such gags."[36] Waters himself has published elucidations of the puns in many works, as has Brenda Richardson—texts that have the anti-humorous quality of explaining a joke.[37] With these explanations, Waters himself leans into the one-liner quality the critics describe. Although he clarifies that "I've done it before, been a human Acoustiguide . . . but that doesn't mean that's how I think they, or you, should see it," the status of these works as explicable jokes nevertheless comprises a sustained attack on the aesthetic values of complexity and depth.[38] Many traditional approaches to art, film, and literature assume that a work of art comprises impenetrable depths that reward continuous exploration and endless cycles of new interpretation. Deflating this myth, Waters shows how despite its dense conceptual trappings and institutional infrastructure, contemporary art functions as a gimmick. Gimmickry may be the theme or content of some of Waters' visual art (as in the references to Castle's tinted viewing glasses in *Illusion-O*), but it is also the underlying nature of contemporary art in general. Since film and art both comprise arms of the culture industry, Waters engages the same interest in the gimmick in his film work: with the stunt casting of Tab Hunter in *Polyester*, for example, and its evocations of the over-the-top melodrama of Douglas Sirk.

For Ngai, the gimmick tends to be flashy yet to fail quickly, and is "our society's distinctively aesthetic way of processing the fundamentals of capitalist accumulation: the production of wealth as value, the binding of value to labor's abstraction, the determination of abstract labor by socially necessary labor time. Yet protected by its own slickness," the gimmick is "a thing whose sheer stupidity cleverly neutralizes the critical feeling it incites."[39] *Faux Video Room* is, as art critics have complained, a "good trick," that is, a gimmick. But it is a gimmick that parodies the essential gimmickry of the commodification of video art itself. Barney's DVD work in a fancy case presented as sculpture is the ultimate gimmick in the sense Ngai discusses, a shiny sales tactic that also ages poorly. By converting conceptual art into comedic one-liners in ways that violate orthodox conceptions of artistic autonomy and complexity, Waters spotlights the logic of the gimmick as that which both expresses and conceals capitalism's failures and ambitions.

One prominent contemporary form of capitalist gimmickry is the film remake, and the remake with splashy recasting is especially gimmicky. Despite its distinct sphere of circulation and circumscribed audience limited to museumgoers, *Kiddie Flamingos* can be understood as a remake of *Pink Flamingos*. As in a professional table read, folded placards along the table identify each character, and the director (Waters) reads the stage directions aloud. Diverging from this typical approach, though, the performers are already in costume—albeit charmingly slipshod costumes that evoke the original characters without trying to trick the viewer. A boy playing Divine, for example, wears a wig cap to evoke the actor's high hairline. A sketchy backdrop of crayon on paper hangs behind the table, lending a sense of landscape to the video without aiming at illusionism. The video is at once closer to the film than a genuine table read recording would be, and emphatically not circulated or presented as a part of Waters' cinematic corpus.

Resting somewhere between remake and remediation, it is no coincidence Waters conceived the artwork in the very moment when the Hollywood logic of remakes and franchises seemed to utterly eliminate the possibility of new visions or novel characters flourishing within the industry. *Kiddie Flamingos* enacts a parodic Marvel-style approach to creative property, like the ongoing chain of Spiderman remakes featuring increasingly youthful casts. Waters himself has witnessed a bout of accidental "remakes" of the stage version of *Hairspray*, when local populations and regulations around discrimination force casting decisions that render the plot of the original fundamentally illegible (for example, when a thin actor plays Tracy Turnblad, or the entire cast is white). Waters revels in this surreal warping: he once said, "I guess I could do 'Female Trouble' in an old-age home. I could do 'Desperate Living' with deaf people. You can do each one of them rewritten for a new niche audience, which again is satirizing the movie business."[40] As a conceptual artwork, the idea of producing niche versions of cult classics sends up the commercial incentives motivating most remakes, and yet the satire here also opens onto the notion of the niche in general. Like the niche desires, fetishes and passions expressed by the characters in many Waters films, a *Female Trouble* set in an old-age home might appeal to only a few spectators, but such an audience would pay through the teeth for such a pleasure. The same can be said for Waters' hypothetical acid-hued colorized versions of his earlier films. Such forms of cultish film hyper-specialization, like visual art or movies espousing a particular fetish, necessarily circumscribe the distribution and reception of the work, but they do so in a profitable way. In this they are not unlike the fine art world's practice of editioning. It is important to note that Waters mimes and mimics, but does not critique from without or above. In his essay on Castle's gimmicks, he praises "the drive-ins that routinely cause car crashes by unveiling hard-core porno in full view of speeding, merging traffic," and the grindhouses, "where waiting in line is always scarier than the film itself."[41] With joy rather than condescension, he celebrates the peculiar mores of the art world, including its sales tactics, much as he celebrates the outré protocols attending forms of cinephilia that hinge more on extra-filmic dimensions of a screening than on plot or drama.

If *Kiddie Flamingos* and the self-citational little movie works parodically engage the logic of the blockbuster remake, taken as a sign of creative fatigue within studio filmmaking or capitulation to the needs of increasingly globalized distribution networks, a similar procedure addresses the art world. Many of Waters' visual works "remake" the work of established artists, adopting their aesthetic in a way that again aligns with Waters' institutional conception of art. Before the little movies, both Larry Clark and Lee Friedlander took a number of snapshot photographs of television screens that emphasize scan lines. *Melissa* (2006) draws directly from Larry Johnson's *Untitled (Movie Stars on Clouds)* (1983). *Unwatchable* (2006) adopts Jack Pierson's signature technique of spelling single words or short phrases out of bits of found vintage signage, and *Playdate* (2006) is eerily similar to Maurizio Cattelan's *Him* (2001). The point is not that in these appropriations Waters is being unoriginal; it is rather that he has experimentally applied the Hollywood logic of the remake within the utterly distinct sphere of the art world to see what will happen. Engaging the logic of one mode of production within another in which even the critique of originality is usually immediately recuperated as a unique intervention, these artistic "remakes" crosspollinate between the two distinct systems or institutions in the most perverse way possible.

Waters incorporates gimmicks into his films both by referencing them within his narratives and by incorporating them into the structure of his work. In *Hairspray*, Tracy Turnblad's father Wilbur owns the Har-de Har Hut, source of the weaponized pranks—such as fake snakes and itching powder—used to torture racist antagonist Velma Von Tussle. In *Polyester*, as critic Alex Weintraub notes, "pornography has replaced family friendly entertainment; the nightly news sensationalizes fetishistic violence; even art cinema relies on gimmicks to attract its cinephile audience, offering trays of truly heinous-looking oysters on the half-shell at its concession stand."[42] An equivalent structural gimmick in *Polyester* is the use in its original release of "Odorama." Ticket buyers received a scratch-and-sniff card with ten separate scents to be released at moments signaled throughout the film. The scents are distinctly abject or trashy, such as the smell of the glue sniffed by the protagonist's violent son Dexter. This interest in the cinemagoing gimmick extends to artworks, especially Waters' sculpture *Fellini's 8 ½* (2014). The basis for this sculpture is a ruler in Waters' personal collection of cinema memorabilia. Eight and a half inches in length and bearing the title of Fellini's film, the ruler was the ultimate public relations ploy. A disposable gift produced to promote an arthouse film, it did so by literalizing its title. Waters' sculpture enlarges the original ruler to eight and a half feet long. The exaggerated scale of the resulting work emphasizes the humor and transparency of the gimmick it appropriates, both a gross commercialization and funny in its crassness. At the same time, the scale shift reflects on the outsize influence of Fellini's film. As cinema by other means, the sculpture suggests that publicity and promotion are as central an aspect of the cinematic as screen projection itself. (Another Waters sculpture, *Looser Gift Basket* [2006], mimics the lavish gift baskets distributed at awards ceremonies, themselves promotional bonanzas.) *Fellini's 8 ½* may also remind the viewer of the use of rulers to measure penis size: eight and a half inches would be a perfectly respectable, even enviable, length on a gay hook-up app. But eight and a half feet defies anatomical possibility—like, say, Caprice's breasts in *A Dirty Shame*. *Fellini's 8 ½* remakes the arthouse film canon for size queens.

Waters uses the gimmick to engage with nonvisual aspects of the sensorium, such as smell and touch. In this warping of both the cinema and gallery apparatuses, film and art aim to reach multiple parts of the body: to measure genitalia, to make one flinch at the smell of glue, or, in *Hardy Har* (2006), to spit upon the viewer. This striking work consists of a framed photograph of flowers and a hidden element that, when a viewer approaches to inspect the image up-close, sprays them with a spurt of water. The work parodies the way in which museumgoers are chided by security guards for coming too close to artworks they seek to admire more closely. But it conducts this parody through a gimmick inspired by the film world, especially the buzzers Castle installed below movie theater seats to shock viewers at the climax of *The Tingler* (1959). Waters fondly conveys tales of Castle's gimmick gone awry: a "beefy truck driver . . . so incensed" by the buzzer that he "ripped his entire seat from the floor," and an impertinent projectionist who allowed the devices to run during a sombre screening of *The Nun's Story* (1959).[43]

Although no such violent reactions or visceral misuses have so far characterized the reception of *Hardy Har*, it encodes their possibility insofar as the work's viewer finds themselves in a situation not unlike Velma Von Tussle: targeted by a gimmick, and perhaps wondering why the title had not earlier set off alarm bells. Contrary to the idea that Waters' artwork fails to sustain repeat viewings, when I encountered this work and was at first shocked by the spray as it hit me, I was nevertheless delighted to repeat the experience several times—although the repetition was of the same original surprised pleasure rooted in the transgression of orthodox art appreciation codes, rather than the pleasure of discovering ever-profounder insights in a long-inspected painting. Such embodied experiences are only found in previous spectatorial experiences of either the cinema theater or the museum when those institutions present content that breaches the normative and rubs at the edges of the canon (the same terrain Waters explores in his little movies). The gimmick, here, yields good fruit, making connections between Waters' films and visual art that defy, yet are tied into, his institutional analysis of the separate spheres.

Waters' visual art, his cinema by other means, presents an idiosyncratic vision of the cinematic in which extraneous elements from title cards to promotional tools are foregrounded and masterpiece status is bestowed upon the baser and physicalized dimensions of spectatorship. Recall Waters' insight about how both visual art and Hollywood film are rooted in "voyeurism," but that mainstream film uses "music and sound" as "smoke and mirrors" to deny this baseness, whereas "there isn't much smoke and mirrors, except intellectually, in art work."[44]

Liz Taylor's Hair and Feet (1996), a baroque extension of the little movies, powerfully visualizes this idea (Figure 7.3). It consists of a large rectangle of snapshots of Elizabeth Taylor in a wide range of film roles, each cropped so that only her hair is visible. Tiled, these surround an empty, blank center. This is a screen upon which nothing is projected: no face, no normative copulation or full body, only sex's fetishized part object or art's framing detritus. In this, it

Figure 7.3 Waters strips away the smoke and mirrors of Hollywood film, reducing Taylor to the part objects of primary interest to a small body of fetishistic spectators. John Waters, *Liz Taylor's Hair and Feet*, 1996, Each image: 5 × 7 inches. © John Waters. Courtesy of the artist and Marianne Boesky Gallery, New York and Aspen.

recalls *Leader*, since the frame is ostensibly meaningless and supplementary to visual art in the same way leader is supplemental to a film reel. Below the rectangle, separated by a small gap that calls attention to the margin of blank space on the wall separating the two elements of the work, is a sequence of similar snapshots, this time isolating Taylor's feet as recorded in various movies. If film is inherently fetishistic, and especially tied to the particular fetish of voyeurism, as Waters claims, this artwork distils the medium to that which is most basic to its success and yet which it often denies. *Liz Taylor's Hair and Feet*, in other words, offers a manifesto celebrating those aspects—embodiment, deviance, shock, titillation—that for Waters comprise the radical aesthetic potential of cinema. As an artwork, it is funny, and a little bit silly, a glamorous take on deconstructive accounts of contemporary art that celebrate its attention to framing strategies. Yet in the end the work is all about teasing, and looking—and about the pleasures of these twin activities. It places its finger on the undercurrents thrumming beneath so many narratives.

Though made by Waters, and emblematic of the way his visual art incorporates cinematic effects in order to suggest an underlying gimmickry common to film and art alike, one wonders if *Liz Taylor's Hair and Feet* work resembles what Dexter, the anarchic son in *Polyester* who delights in fetishistic foot stomping, would have produced as his career developed and his oeuvre advanced. Dexter declares at the end of the film: "I am rehabilitated. I am an artist now!" Far from rehabilitation, though, Waters' visual art and the many references to visual art in his films reveal art as a space of unreconstructed pleasure and trash aesthetics. In this, his visual art continues to access that which is ever rarer in the realm of narrative film writ large. Waters reconnects viewers with riotousness, corporeality, and gimmickry though deep dives into the archives of cult and forgotten film, and through self-made encounters with more mainstream Hollywood archives that in turn reshape and reimagine those archives as reservoirs of queer intensity, anarchy, and trash.

NOTES

1. John Waters and Bruce Hainley, *Art: A Sex Book* (London: Thames and Hudson, 2003), 13.
2. See Barend de Voogd, "Things That Should Be Illegal," *The Flashback Files*, September 2009, https://www.flashbackfiles.com/john-waters-interview
3. Pavle Levi, *Cinema by Other Means* (Oxford: Oxford University Press, 2012), 27.
4. Marvin Heiferman, "Everything Always Looks Good Through Here! John Waters and Photography," in *John Waters: Change of Life* (New York: New Museum of Contemporary Art, 2004), 20–41: 24.
5. "Wolfgang Tillmans in Conversation with John Waters," in *John Waters: Indecent Exposure*, edited by Kristen Hileman (Berkeley, CA: University of California Press, 2018), 154–167, 157.
6. Howard Halle, "John Waters, "Director's Cut,"" *Time Out New York*, November 28, 1996.

7. Vince Aletti, "Photo: John Waters," *The Village Voice*, May 9, 1995.
8. Bruce Hainley, "John Waters," *Artforum*, September 1995.
9. These are collected in John Waters, *Director's Cut* (Zurich: Scalo, 1997).
10. John Waters, 'Whatever Happened to Showmanship?,' *American Film* 9 (December 1983), 55–58.
11. Peter Halley and Bob Nickas, "John Waters," *Index* (1997), http://www.indexmagazine.com/interviews/john_waters.shtml
12. Jay David Bolter and Richard Grusin, *Remediation: Understanding New Media* (Cambridge, MA: MIT Press, 1999), 45.
13. See Rosalind Krauss, *Under Blue Cup* (Cambridge, MA: MIT Press, 2011), 24–26.
14. For example, advertisements and didactic materials produced around the 2018 Baltimore Museum of Art exhibition *John Waters: Indecent Exposure* feature the image in a horizontal rotation.
15. *Multiple Maniacs* was released on VHS by Cinema Group Home Video (which became Palisades Home Video in 1988) in 1987.
16. John G. Ives, *American Originals: John Waters* (New York: Thunder's Mouth Press, 1992), 59.
17. See Erika Balsom, *Exhibiting Cinema in Contemporary Art* (Amsterdam: Amsterdam University Press, 2013), Chapter 1.
18. "Teaser: John Waters' *Kiddie Flamingos*," *New York Times*, January 7, 2015, https://www.nytimes.com/video/t-magazine/100000003435098/teaser-john-waters-kiddie-flamingos.html
19. Alexandra Keller and Frazer Ward, "Matthew Barney and the Paradox of the Neo-Avant-Garde Blockbuster," *Cinema Journal* 45, no. 2 (Winter 2006): 3–16: 10.
20. Kathryn Bond Stockton, *The Queer Child, or Growing Sideways in the Twentieth Century* (Durham, NC: Duke University Press, 2009).
21. For example: *Curb Your Enthusiasm* (HBO, 2009), S7E9, *Episodes* (Showtime, 2011), S1E3, and *Reboot* (Hulu, 2022), S1E2.
22. NBC's YouTube account posted a recording of *The Good Place* finale in August 2020, for example, which now boasts more than one million views.
23. See Jonathan Walley, "The Material of Film and the Idea of Cinema: Contrasting Practices in Sixties and Seventies Avant-Garde Film," *October* 103 (Winter 2003): 15–30.
24. Peter Osborne, *Anywhere or Not at All: Philosophy of Contemporary Art* (Brooklyn, NY: Verso Books, 2013), 48.
25. Lauren LaRocca, "Cult Classic," *Baltimore Magazine*, October 2018, https://www.baltimoremagazine.com/section/artsentertainment/john-waters-shares-highlights-from-upcoming-bma-retrospective/
26. Dennis Cooper, "John Waters," *Bomb*, April 2004.
27. In this, Waters echoes Arthur Danto, "The Artworld," *The Journal of Philosophy* 61, no. 19 (October 1964): 571–584.
28. Cooper, "John Waters."
29. See Heiferman, "Everything."
30. Lou Stoppard, 'The Photographer Behind John Waters' Cult Classic "Pecker",' *Aperture* 234 (March 2019).
31. Sianne Ngai, *Theory of the Gimmick: Aesthetic Judgment and Capitalist Form* (Cambridge, MA: Harvard University Press, 2020), Chapter 3.
32. Halley and Nickas, "John Waters."
33. See Kristen Hileman, "Inappropriation," in *John Waters: Indecent Exposure*, 16–27.
34. Benjamin H.D. Buchloh and Hal Foster, *Exit Interview* (New York: no place press, 2024), 162–3.

35. Linda DeLibero, "John Waters: Indecent Exposure," *ASAP/Journal*, February 5, 2019, https://asapjournal.com/review/john-waters-indecent-exposure-linda-delibero/
36. Jennifer King, "John Waters," *Artforum* 50, no. 10 (Summer 2012).
37. Brenda Richardson, "John Waters: Stop, Look, and Listen," in *Unwatchable* (New York and Zürich: Marianne Boesky Gallery and de Pury & Luxembourg, 2006), 77–84.
38. Todd Solondz, "Interview with John Waters" in *John Waters: Change of Life*, 107.
39. Ngai, *Theory of the Gimmick*, 9.
40. Jordan Riefe, "Bieber, Pimples, Lassie with a Facelift: John Waters on His L.A. Art Exhibition," *Los Angeles Times*, February 16, 2021.
41. Waters, "Whatever Happened to Showmanship?"
42. Alex Weintraub, "Divine Wisdom: Polyester and the Return of Trash Cinema," *Los Angeles Review of Books*, December 21, 2015, https://lareviewofbooks.org/article/divine-wisdom-polyester-and-the-return-of-trash-cinema/
43. Waters, "Whatever Happened to Showmanship?"
44. Waters and Hainley, *Art: A Sex Book*, 13.

PART II

Collaboration, Subversion, and Queering the Family

CHAPTER 8

Once Upon a Time in Dreamland: 2015 Recollections and Reflections

Chris Holmlund

Waters often referred to himself and his 1960s pals as part of a "gang." His friends contributed vastly to the early films: indeed, they functioned both as crew *and* as cast. As captain of the Dreamland ship—one of his childhood idols was James Hook—he has always credited and acknowledged them, even as he developed what would become his own distinctively cross-product, cross-medium, cross-market brand.

To add to the first-person historical records Chloé Griffin, Jack Stevenson, Matthew Hays, and Gerald Peary have compiled, I excerpt four interviews that I conducted with *Female Trouble*'s cast and crew in 2015. I included some of their responses in my little book on that film, but much here is new: Mink Stole, George Figgs, Pat Moran, Vincent Peranio and Delores Deluxe, and Mary Vivian Pearce all talked about other early films as well as *Female Trouble*. All shed light on what the late 1960s–early 1970s period was like. All were card-carrying members of the original Dreamland "gang." Mink was often the "heavy," Bonnie (Mary Vivian) the ingenue. Jack-of-all-trades George had small but memorable roles. Artist/production designer Vincent contributed cheap special effects, bold colors, trashy style. Pat was always at John's side as his firecracker trouble-shooter *cum* producer.

All are now in their late seventies; I am slightly younger. As left-leaning hippies based in Baltimore and just outside DC, respectively, we shared experiences and held similar opinions. Mink, George, Vincent, and Delores welcomed me into their book-, art-, and memento-filled homes. I met Pat Moran in her casting office. I reached Bonnie by phone in Nicaragua. We had fun; there was lots and lots of laughter. "You would have been part of this group!" Bob Adams told me. "It's a magnet. Waters seeks its own level. It always happens." I was honored.

John has no problem admitting that he does not and never did have all the answers. From film to film, he and his friends were a DIY indie team; everyone learned as they went along. Rereading these recollections, I hear everyone's voices once more, complete with "Balti-moron" inflections. I hope my transcriptions convey something of Pat's staccato energy, Vincent's laidback enthusiasm, and George's Renaissance-like reflections. Mink's and Bonnie's voices ring distinctly for me as well; I find it harder to convey in print how they speak. Each adds pieces to the Dreamland puzzle. Together their camaraderie, dedication, inventiveness, artistry, generosity, and commitment were essential to the "for-real" film fairytale that was "once upon in Dreamland."

INTERVIEWS

1. Vincent Peranio and Delores Deluxe

Chris: Let's start with how you met John.
Vincent: I met him at a party we were having where I lived, in Fells Point on Broadway. About six of us had just graduated from the Maryland Institute of Art. We came for a party for Halloween and visited some Maryland Institute friends. As we were going home we saw a building for rent. Turned out it was $100 per month for twenty-two rooms—two buildings for $100 per month—because they were going to tear down the neighborhood of Fells Point and build a highway.

Chris: They were asking for a hippie collective to move in!
Vincent: You had free rein of the neighborhood, 'cause half of it was boarded up. We would have a lot of parties with Maryland Institute students and Hopkins students. It became a little Grand Central Station. At one of our parties John and his whole group of Dreamlanders came all at once: John and Mink and David Lochary, Marian Vivian [Pearce], Van [Smith], and Pat [Moran]—all at the same time. They had just finished doing *Mondo Trasho*, and they made *Multiple Maniacs* soon, within a year. John said, "Well, Vince, *you're* an artist, can you make me a giant lobster?"

Chris: And so Lobstora was born.
Vincent: That's the first thing I ever did for film. My brother and I made it at the Fell's Point Gate Company where we worked. It cost $35. It was aluminum and chicken wire and papier mâché. I painted it bright red because it was a lobster, but I forgot that a red lobster would have been a dead lobster. Luckily it was a black-and-white film!

Then I made the little furniture that rejects the characters, and all the little special effects. Of course, we all played maniacs. We would do this on weekends, for maybe five months or so. Some people still worked. Some of us were hippies, and some of us were young artists, so we didn't work [laughs]. We were just having fun. John would call up Friday night and say, "Hey, meet me at Mill Race Road at 6 o'clock in the morning, and bring some blankets and sheets. We're going to do Stations of the Cross." And that's what we did. We all got up. We all had blankets and sheets. I think he rented two Roman gladiator costumes and those were the only costumes. We'd spend the day doing the Stations of the Cross.

I always thought of myself as an anti-art director, because, you know, with the characters that I was working with, I didn't have to play straight. For *Female Trouble* I tried to make my interiors as nutty as the characters; it's their environment and their world. We had no money whatsoever; I can't imagine I had more than $100 for any of those films. Glitter and paint and cheap fabric help.

Chris: Did you coordinate at all with Van?
Vincent: We never coordinated, we never sat down and systematically said "my walls are going to be orange with deep black spots, then I'll do such and such . . ." We just always were interested in what the other was doing. We would always stop in and talk to each other. I would see his pictures and he would see my pictures.

Female Trouble was the first real decorated sets that I did for John. In *Pink Flamingos*, basically, the main thing was the trailer. I set that all up. The rest of it was either John's apartment or somebody else's apartment. We might move things around a little bit, but it wasn't like a dressed set.

Chris: In *Female Trouble*, where Divine is chasing Little Taffy with a car aerial, there's a little table with a lamp. You had found that lamp, found that table?
Vincent (chuckles): Um hum. Got those car parts! And the car accident, that's all shot on Pat's second floor. And when it came time to change for Edith, I took all that stuff out, painted everything red, and threw glitter all over it.

Chris: How much time did you have to change the sets?
Vincent: Well, you know, it wasn't rushed, because some of us still had jobs so it was still done on weekends, on certain days when people were off. It wasn't a full-time thing. I was still working, building gates and fire escapes and that kind of stuff. Eventually I quit Fells Point Gate Company. I was an artist, and I didn't get into metal work to build fire escapes. That was boring to me. After *Female Trouble* I quit, because I decided film work was what I would like to do, and that was really thanks to John. I'd never ever really thought of working in film. It was important for me to do other people's films, to prove to myself I could do it, because I never took a film course or production or theatrical courses, I was fine arts. I wanted to make it on my own and not just with John.

Back then I was pretty much a one-person art department. My brother Ed helped some, but I gave myself top billing and called myself the Art Director [laughs]. I was *also* the person under the Art Director . . .

Anyway, those were tough times, but really fun. We were young, we didn't have much money, but could we ever get a lot done! Everybody had a lot of passion. We loved John. He was the dearest friend, even before his filmmaking. He's got a lot of energy. He's totally driven. When I'm working on TV shows and then maybe a small film, I'm exhausted from the 14-hour days, which saddens me. But with John it was always doing art!

Chris: It was also the era: budding feminist, radical hippie, early gay movement, anti-war.
Vincent: We all went to the demonstrations in DC. We know tear gas [laughs], running from the cops, but in large groups. It wasn't like we were brave or anything, but honestly, that era, and the Vietnam War demonstrations, the civil rights, the gay, and all that, is stuff that we believed in. And yet John could make you laugh at stuff! It wasn't just straight man against hippie. He could make people laugh by criticizing anybody, first of all the hippies.

Chris: Were you there every day on *Female Trouble*?
Vincent: Most days.

Chris: Was that true of the other principal actors?
Vincent: No. They'd be downstairs, while the crew was inside, because those little row houses are small. On the other films we were just the Dreamlanders. *Female Trouble* was the first time we had a crew. I worked on every one of John's films.

For *Polyester* Delores and I went to a country club community and posed as a married couple looking for a home and rented that house in the cul-de-sac. We weren't married at the time. And then an entire film crew moved in, and the basement was the production office and catering and the rest of the house was filming and the first day Dave Insley was doing the shot flying over the country club and the house when the helicopter crashed on the ninth green. We did not make a good impression.

Chris: I read online that you helped revive the pink flamingo.
Vincent: I think I helped revive it. I don't know if it ever really went out of style. It was the era of good junk stores and good used clothing stores. The reason thrift stores and junk shops got so popular was everybody just hated the designs of that era. Everything was polyester, so we got into vintage clothing. And antiques were cheaper. For me it was really interesting seeing stuff that had carvings on it or had an aesthetic to it, compared with the orange and avocado, mushroom of my childhood. Baltimore was always about ten years behind anyway in style and stuff. We just did what we wanted on the films.

Chris: The *Village Voice* wrote that "the production values of *Female Trouble* are certainly a lot different and classier than *Pink Flamingos*. The sets have a kitsch superconciousness [sic] as does the costuming, which inhabits a state of imagination somewhere between Fredericks of Hollywood and Buck Rogers."
Vincent [laughs]: That's about right. It was so wonderful to get bad reviews because we were getting *reviews*! At least we were pissing somebody off, we were

being noticed, and isn't that what this whole shock business is about anyway? Wanting to be noticed? We loved bad reviews. John did a great job marketing them. "Worse than the *Emperor Worm*!"

Vincent: Delores was my art director on *Polyester* and *Cry Baby*.

Chris: What was your background Delores?
Delores: I started living with Vince, living with Alan Rose, and he was doing the credits; Vince and Alan and Patty Burgee did most of the graphics on John's films. Later he came to me and said, "I want you to be Nurse Nancy in the sex change clinic scene [in *Desperate Living*]. All you have to do is be mean to Susan Lowe when she comes in and then scream the rest of the scene. You'd be perfect for it." Then he made me come over every week to rehearse the scene and he wanted me to do it exactly like he did, it wasn't like I was perfect for it. It wasn't about me, really. It was funny because I was perfect to be mean and then scream on my own.

Vincent: We all knew John started in puppetry.
Delores: We've had the last forty years to analyze the guy!

Vincent: He still surprises me sometimes.

Chris: When did you see the script for a film?
Vincent: When John told us the script was done, on a yellow legal pad, the way he wanted. It was merely up to our interpretation. John was always ready; his homework was always done; he seldom changed his mind; and he really went by the script. With *Pink Flamingos* you read the script, everything is there, word for word. Not only word for word, but John would take the actors and have them meet weeks in advance, practising exactly how he wanted them to say it, in his voice. We didn't get paid on *Female Trouble*. The first three we did for free. Then we went to the opening in NY for *Female Trouble* and Andy Warhol gave us a party, and that was great. We met David Bowie. When we got back we realized this is really going to be a big commercial thing.

Delores: We were entering into a new realm, and we were doing this for nothing, and at expense to ourselves.
Vincent: Pat and I talked this out a little bit. He gave each one of us a point, so we got paid. Forty years later I'm still getting $5 for *Pink Flamingos* every quarter.

Delores: And he was never mean about it. He acquiesced totally. In those days, overhead, rent, gas, and all cost so much less, and if you got a check for $200, man, that was a big help! Every once in a while we still get one for over $300 and I am shocked. But we have gotten many for $1.51 and John gets so frustrated because I save all the checks because he signs his own checks. Anything under $10 I can get that for the autograph, and he knows that. He's like, "Can I balance my checkbook?" I'm like, "Never. I'd rather have the check!"

2. George Figgs

Chris: You probably have done a zillion interviews.
George: Well, I've done a lot of interviews about a lot of different things. I'm a Poe scholar, a music person, a movie person, a painter, an actor, a writer. I've been many different things. I make characters up. I like to be different things. I pretend a lot. I've been with John since 1964. I met him downtown when he was a 16–17-year-old looking for beatniks. We're the same age.

Chris: You were looking for beatniks?
George: And booze. Because we weren't of age yet, we weren't 21. We were looking for people to buy us Chianti and little matchboxes full of marijuana. Back in those days that was a nickel, a nickel bag. A matchbox full of twigs and seeds and a little pot.

I remember Mink in second grade. St. Thomas Aquinas. Cathlickers. She switched to public school I guess in fifth grade, but I'll never forget her marching in, in her Brownie uniform, like a little Nazi, marching up the aisle of church. She looked like the real Taffy. Taffy is Mink.

Chris: On *Female Trouble* you were just in the Lipstick Beauty Salon scenes, right?
George: No. A lot depends on what was needed for that day. If more crew was needed then we went out. But usually John wouldn't want extra people on the set that were just hanging out.

Chris: Did you have any special costume or makeup as Dribbles? They definitely did something to your hair!
George: No, my hair was just long. My hair was hippie length, and I had a little scruff of a beard. We didn't do anything special to my hair, just put it in a ponytail I think. I had a pretty outrageous costume: a pair of silver lamé coveralls, overalls. I have the stills on my computer. And a puffy sleeved shirt, sort of like a mambo outfit. That, actually, was part of my wardrobe.

Chris: I'm glad I'm doing these interviews because it gives me much more of a sense of the creativity of the people involved.
George: Oh, we were all artists! We all had our own ideas. But there wasn't much spontaneity happening, per se, because John wrote that script and you remembered every line and every word and said it exactly the way that he said it, because, you know, he would act the whole thing out. He would show you exactly what he wanted you to do and how he wanted you to do it. It was easy to follow. You knew what he meant because we all laughed at the same things in the bar together. We all hung out. We were a gang. We were all crazy hippies, on drugs, and artists, and we were all participating in like a free-for-all-theatrical experience of some kind, channeling our energies in to do whatever needed to be done.

Chris: And sometimes for really long days.
George: Oh yeah. If you noticed in *Multiple Maniacs*, a lot of those lines are delivered with breaths very visible in the cold. And even in *Desperate Living*

those nudist camp scenes were shot in 30 degrees. We were all generating that kind of chaotic aggressive demonstrator type of energy.

Divine's voice was a strange and wonderful thing, kind of gender-less. *Polyester* is a real fairytale, like a fractured fairytale. *Hairspray* is our message movie, and then there's *Cry Baby*. The early ones are the ones where John lives. A lot of people pick *Female Trouble* as John's peak. For me, it's *Multiple Maniacs*, just because it's the last really funky one. And *Pink Flamingos*. *Multiple Maniacs*, *Pink Flamingos*, and *Female Trouble* are the three great films! They're the three that remain, that stand against the horizon. The early films have an energy that held them up. The enthusiasm that we put into them, just living and doing them, is in the films.

When I started with John, I was the Grass Man in the *Wizard of OD*. [John's 1968 short, usually called *Dorothy, the Kansas City Pothead*.] I was also the Prince in *Eat Your Makeup*. We/I arranged for the first public showing of a John Waters' film at the coffee house that I worked at. That was before the church basement, the very first public showing of *Hag in a Black Leather Jacket*, *Roman Candles*, and *Eat Your Makeup*.

Saint Edith. She was our mother. Bonnie [Mary Vivian Pearce] and I and Eddie Peranio found Edith. She was tending bar across the street from Pete's Hotel, in the Lone Star, which later became Bertha's. We said, "god Edith, what are you doing over here?" Nobody ever came in there. She never made any tips. We talked to Uncle Pete, the guy who owned Pete's Hotel, and said, "Man, you've got to get this barmaid, she's amazing!" Her voice was just. . . . So, he got her, and we brought her over to Pete's Hotel, and she became the barmaid over there, and the rest is history. She had Edith's Shopping Bag even then I think, but it was uptown, on Preston Street.

Chris: Chan told me, very affectionately, "We all hated Mink, because she always remembered her lines!"
George: Well, Mink's a pro. She was always the pro. She was always the best actor besides Divine and David Lochary. David—he was a phenomenon.

Chris: I asked John and others about craft service on set.
George [guffaws]: Well, on one of the swankiest shoots we ever did, I ran dailies for *Pecker*, and our craft service was pretzel sticks and beer.

Chris: John just looked at me funny when I asked and said, "But they were all on speed!"
George: Right, so we didn't eat. We couldn't afford food. We just took our speed.

I left Baltimore in '66. I'd come back whenever John was shooting. I was in New York because I was playing music for a living. I had an album out on the Vanguard label in '68.

Chris: What kind of music?
George: Billboard called it acid hillbilly music. We were among the first folk rock people. We were less psychedelic and more bluegrass-y and blues. We made

a living playing music, two-lane-blacktop gigs and up in the ski resorts and up to Amherst and Smith and Bennington and Marlboro and Harvard. Lots of mixers.

Chris: Did you have much to do behind the scenes before *Female Trouble*?
George: Everybody did everything, whatever needed to be done. The most appropriate person to do it would do it. We were always there, I mean in *Mondo Trasho* and *Multiple Maniacs* the crew was also the actors. The whole thing was an evolutionary process, like with every film.

Chris: I asked Vincent if he coordinated with Van on the colors, the art design.
George: No, they didn't, things just happened, almost like a mosaic. Each frame is a tile; and you can't see the whole thing until the whole thing is edited, and then you stand back from it, and it makes the picture. It was a happenstancial [sic], wonderful thing, the creative process at its most obvious and ebullient. I'm sure they had meetings with John. . . . They were like the engine room of the film. And Divine, and Pat, of course. Pat did everything: she planned things out and figured out who was going to do what; she was the production coordinator. Back in those days we all did as much as we could do as possible, as much as we were good at. Pat handled the details. Later, when there were permits, she would get in touch with the business owner and let them know we were going to be there, just making sure everything ran right and as on time as possible. She's the one that watched the clock and watched the money. She and John have always worked together. When we all first got together, she was young, and really beautiful and glamorous and really, really hot.

Chris: What was the plot of the *Wizard of OD*?
George: It kind of followed the plot of *Wizard of Oz*, but it's something about Dorothy getting busted. I can't remember exactly; but Toto was a duck on a string, a mechanical duck. The Wicked Witch was Maelcum Soul. Maelcum was the first Divine. Maelcum was the bartender, the first godmother, almost a little bit like Vampira. She was just an arch beatnik. She'd been in the West Village in the early '60s, '60 and '61. I got there in '64 or '65. She would tend bar in a nun's habit at Martick's on Mulberry Street.

Chris: Say more about your role in the *Wizard of OD*.
George: I was the Grass Man, the Scarecrow, and I was made out of marijuana.

Chris: You were probably smoking as you were going.
George: Oh yeah, it was fun. I can't remember too much of it. It was attempted in color.

Chris: What about *Multiple Maniacs*?
George: My kids wanted to see me as Jesus. But I didn't let them see the bead scene. I had to edit it because they were quite young at the time, 8 or 10. Of course, our parents have never seen it, John's parents or my parents. My mother won't watch any John Waters movies. I don't think she's met him. She would love him if she met him but she's too afraid of him because she's so Catholic.

Figure 8.1 Art designer Vincent Peranio ("Freak" in the Cavalcade of Perversions; here, a sleeping disciple) and George Figgs (a junkie in the Cavalcade; here, "Jesus Christ") reenact Jesus' prayers in the Garden of Gethsemane. (*Multiple Maniacs* DVD © Criterion Collection, 2017).

Chris [laughing]: Where'd she go wrong with you, George?
George: I'm a changeling, actually I was going to be a priest, I attended seminary for three years.

Chris: Oh well, no wonder you were chosen to be Jesus.
George: I am Jesus, I mean I was Jesus, I really thought I was Jesus at the time. I was taking a lot of LSD. I probably was pretty well convinced that I was the Christ. I took LSD in 1963, Sandoz from Switzerland.

Chris: Do you think of *Female Trouble* as a camp film?
George: I think of it as a multi-faceted piece of work. John's work is very complicated, very complex. What John and Mink and Divine are trying to do is tell a story that happens to be fantastical and out of proportion to reality. It was counter-cultural for sure, but . . . "camp" is a funny word.

3. Pat Moran

Chris: I'm so excited to interview you, Pat! I know you're really important to John's early films, and that you're an old, old friend of his. When did you meet him?
Pat: In 1964, in Baltimore. We were both out of high school. Chan [Wilroy] was a couple of years older than us.

Chris: I asked Chan how *he* met John. He told me how John would wait outside the bar where you all went because he was underage. . . .
Pat: Oh yeah, John would be in the alley. He would wait until the owner left and then he would come in. The drinking age was 21.

Chris: Chan remembers John wearing white go-go boots and carrying a gun and a holster.
Pat: I don't remember that. Here's what I remember: those shoes were silver, spray silver. I don't remember his shoes being white, ever. Believe me, I would of. They were probably silver, a Warholian influence.

Chris: You ended up meeting John downtown.
Pat: Because we had the same boyfriend.

Chris [laughing]: Now there's a sign of the times!
Pat: How did I get downtown? Being a girl from that area at that time, you tried to get married. But is that all there is? . . . I used to have my hair done where David Lochary was working as an apprentice. Divine was in hairdresser school, too. My gay friends taught me everything I wanted to know about, taste, style, writing, painters. . . . I was more in the gay life than John was. A lot of these guys, they were teachers, they would lose their jobs. I loved them. We suffered by losing so many people to AIDS.

Chris: For me John's early films are a cross between exploitation and underground.
Pat: Yeah, you needed the exploitation, because you needed to get noticed, with no money, and the underground was the place to go.

Chris: Did you have a hand in marketing the films?
Pat: We used to go out and do wild postings. We would post everywhere. We would go to campuses. We would put leaflets down on tables; we called that plate jobs. And we would go all over town; we called that wild posting. We did it all the way up to . . . I can't remember to what film. . . . Somebody always, within our little tribe, would drive. Two of us would jump out, boom! boom! When you wild post bring thumbtacks, push pins, scotch tape, scissors, and never post over top of anybody else!

Chris: You were kind! *We* used flour and water to stick political posters up *forever*.
Pat: Oh yeah, that was what pros did in New York. But the thing is you couldn't piss off people any more than they would be over the content of the films. . . . We had a driver who was careful, and we would . . . . boom! boom! boom! boom! boom!

It was a different world, a different world. You could tell who was who and what side they were on, just by looking at people.

Chris: Was anybody in the Army, did anybody get drafted and go to Vietnam?
Pat: N. O. Anything you could do you did to avoid that! Some people went to Canada. Chuck [Yeaton; Pat's husband] had a ton of money in his pocket ready

to go to Canada. John got out for being gay. Bob Adams said he got out because he was gay, and his hearing is so bad.

Chris: I was talking with Dave Insley, he's just a year older than me, and I said, "you remember these were the days when you hitchhiked?" I hitchhiked to school. Any VW bus that went by, they would pick you up, they were automatically your friends, and they would get you high.
Pat: Exactly. You'd smoke pot.

Chris: I got to school later and later.
Pat [agrees encouragingly]: Right, right, forgot I was going to school. . . .

Chris: I could no longer take 8 o'clock classes by the end.
Pat: It's amazing that anybody got through. I was an English major.

Chris: I was a French lit major. For me *Pink Flamingos* was very much Jean Genet's *The Maids*, especially those scenes with Chan.
Pat: As you know, John is an avid reader. There's not much you can pull out of the hat that he's not aware of. Though sometimes you don't know what influences you. I don't think he ever sat down and said, let me do this like Genet, let me do this like Tennessee Williams.

Chris: Were you involved with casting for *Female Trouble*?
Pat: We did everything. I was his production manager. We were a non-union shop. I didn't even know what that meant, none of us did. I had my finger in everything except the technical. I didn't pretend to do that. Nor did John. In the beginning he shot and edited, in the early days with scotch tape. We didn't even know what we didn't know. We just knew he had a story to tell, and I was going to help him tell it. Mostly, any shit that was going to start, I was there. Anything that I'd need to turn away from him, that he didn't need to know. . . .

Chris: Did you interact with the crew a lot?
Pat: Oh yeah, and the crew still loves John. *Female Trouble* is my favorite film. The genius of Van Smith is overwhelming. Even if you went back to *Pink Flamingos*.

Chris: Vincent's work, combined with Van's.
Pat: And they didn't even have to speak to each other.

Chris: On a Hollywood film you would talk about color scheme, and it would all be carefully planned out, but I love the way the colors pop in *Female Trouble*, from the orange dress to the silvery purple wallpaper and so much is going on that your eye is just going. . . .
Pat [interrupts me]: Thank God there's no mono-chromatic. There's another thing today in filmmaking that I hate. Take your beige somewhere else! If you can't make me feel something by looking at this, if you got to do this with the gloom doom, go back to film school! Perpetrated out of home filmmaking. . . . Please help!

Chris: And the scripts are so funny.
Pat: Everybody's screaming. We still quote those early lines.

Chris: Like the one from *Pink Flamingos*: "You've been convicted of assholism!"
Pat: I think we said that last week. And we aren't the only ones! Other people do it, too!

Chris: There was *no* improvisation.
Pat: Not the word "the," not even. Nothing.

Chris: I asked Elizabeth [Coffey] about her love scene in prison with Divine in *Female Trouble*. Was she showing off her new vagina? [She had had the first bottom surgery paid for by Maryland taxpayer money.] Elizabeth said, "Oh no, honey, nothing like that, nothing was up to me." She said it was John's idea, not hers. It was a call back to *Pink Flamingos* and the scene in the park where, playing a hooker, she flashes the penis she then had.
Pat: That's a great scene. People lose their minds with that scene. I'm in the prison scene in *Female Trouble*, screaming. [Her voice lowers confidentially.] Let me tell you what was great about *that* scene. When you hear them shut those doors behind you, you never forget that sound. It makes you want to never do anything wrong. You knew, this was it, man, and don't do anything that's going to put you in here! Other than civil disobedience.

Chris: So, you went to demonstrations?
Pat: Oh yeah, of course, all the demonstrations. We were against the Vietnam War, and we wanted civil rights, we wanted equal rights. . . . We all *collectively* felt that way. . . . Our gang was gay, straight, crazy. We were just like the times! We took drugs. But nobody took drugs when we were making movies. Nobody smoked pot. Nobody did anything. You don't have time for that. You know hard it is to convince some asshole to get off a quarter so you can make a movie with maniacs? Think about that! John's father gave him the seed money for *Pink Flamingos*. Which he paid back. We were serious about that, just like we were serious about everything else. But we were never humorless. We were always flip and edgy. And that was why that whole gang stayed together because everybody had the same politics. ABSOLUTELY! We all supported the Weathermen! We wanted Patty Hearst to get away! We were left-wing radicals if you had to say what we were. Radical filmmakers, absolutely, and with me, and I think most of us, it's always been like "gimme the downtrodden! come over! if people don't like you, good, we do!" But we never lost our sense of humor.

Chris: No one had the whole script, right, except for you?
Pat: I still have the yellow legal pad.

Chris: Bob Adams said his lines were much longer.
Pat: Yeah, right. They would go on and on and on. But in the end John truly believed, and I think still believes, you should tell a story in about ninety minutes.

[Heatedly] If you can't tell a story in 90 minutes, then get out! Go back to film school!!!

Chris: I heard that John would say the lines with people and sometimes his voice would come out on the soundtrack, so they would have to retake, or they couldn't use that footage. Or Edith [Massey] would blow her lines.
Pat: Oh my God, yeah. Edith in the bird cage in *Female Trouble* was something! We were up there for a thousand hours!

Chris: There's a certain style of performance. Divine's the center piece, obviously. There's more modulation in his delivery. His character is so different toward the end: you get the manic Divine, the scream Divine.
Pat: He was so not like any of that, though. He was really sweet. Now remember, he was gay, overtly, he was heavy, what the fuck do you think that bully situation was? We were his family, and he was truly a part of my family. He was a real pro.

Chris: Did you get paid at all?
Pat: Maybe like 2 cents. That's not why anybody did it. I don't remember on which one you first got a check. I think it was on *Polyester*. Chuck and John handled the money – they were the only ones to sign checks. Nobody was ever paid much. And Chuck and I had to close the store at Christmas time, so it *cost* us money! You didn't dare knock on that door at Christmas time: people were upstairs filming! Not to mention half the wardrobe, half the shit's in the house. . . .

Chris: What's John like as a director?
Pat: He's intense. He's never mean to people but let me tell you there ain't no playing around. Be on your mark!

Chris: Were you on set every day?
Pat: Every day, every minute, every time. There wasn't any 9 to 5. There were days we would work twelve hours. The Lipstick Beauty Salon [in *Female Trouble*] was a day of hell. We were shooting all night long. The pipes in the cellar broke. I went home that night and laid down and cried, with exhaustion, and you know what, I never thought of not going in the next day. If he was standing, I was standing, and if we were standing, they were standing. It was hard, but it was fun.

4. Mink Stole

Mink: We dressed out of thrift shops, but we were not hippies, and we were too young to be beatniks. Most of us did not start getting high until we were out of high school. I took my first acid trip before it was illegal, in 1965, *after* I graduated from high school. I have never made any secret about my fondness for LSD. It always made me happy.

I voted three times for McGovern. They didn't ask for an ID; you didn't have to give an address. I lived in San Francisco in 1972 but I registered three times and voted three times.

Chris: I remember from reading old clippings that John says somewhere he voted three times for Gerald Ford.
Mink: Well, he may have done that. But Gerald Ford was later, way after McGovern, in the '80s. So, John copied me!

Chris [laughing]: The muse. . . .
Mink: Oh, I never think of myself as John's muse. Divine was John's muse. I think he thought of me when he was writing these parts. He had my voice and face in his head, especially when he was writing Taffy.

Chris [cracks up]: That's telling!
Mink: I grew up in this neighborhood. This neighborhood can tell you I was a little bit of a Taffy. I was an unhappy kid. I think of Taffy as an unhappy kid. I don't think of her as bad. I think of her as *desperately* unhappy. And she had reason to be. She was unloved, she was basically tolerated. And that's how I felt as a child, though I was loved more than I thought I was. I was the fifth child in a family of ten. My father died when I was 8. I had a month-old brother and a 15-year-old sister. My mother was completely unprepared for my father's death. We all turned out fine but there was not a great deal of parental attention or affection. I related very strongly to Taffy, to her unhappiness, and to her need to find her father. There was *tons* of stuff about Taffy that really spoke to me. I found her less interesting after she joined the Hare Krishnas. Then she was at peace, and it was a fake peace. As Taffy I kill my father and my mother kills me; there's all this convolution going on.

Chris: It's classic Greek tragedy.
Mink (with conviction). *Yes!* It's a very funny movie; those lines. I think it's a better film than *Pink Flamingos*. The script is tighter, the acting is more consistent. No words were ever improvised. As far as physicality, I don't remember John ever giving me a note on physicality.

Chris: Did you watch rushes of Hilary Drew as Taffy?
Mink: I don't remember ever seeing what she did, and I certainly wouldn't have copied her. I was much too attached to the role as my own to have copied her. And the way they made me up: they smeared my lipstick; they smeared my eye makeup and my eyebrows. In *Pink Flamingos* my hair was a great red, redder than Pat Moran's red, and Pat has gotten redder and redder over the years. She's been a strong redhead since I met her in 1966. Which is when I met John as well, though he will tell you that we met in '64, but we didn't, we met in '66.

But John's life is fuller than mine, so I have more room for stuff like math than he does in my brain. And if he says something once he will say it until the day he dies, which is fine. We met in Provincetown during the summer of '66 because I graduated from high school in '65 and it was not that summer; it was the summer afterward.

Chris: Did John shoot in sequence?
Mink: I honestly don't remember. I only knew which days to show up. If your scene was that day, then you were on the set from the beginning to the end. I can remember on *Desperate Living*, even though I lived down the street, I had to be on set at 8 o'clock even though I wasn't shooting until 4 o'clock. The only set that was ever closed was the singing asshole in *Pink Flamingos*. That was done with nobody there.

Chris: Did you see the entire script?
Mink: I very specifically remember that we did not in *Pink Flamingos*. I knew I was going to die and that I wasn't going to win, that Divine would win, and David and I would be killed, but I didn't know exactly how. I never won. I was a perpetual foil. The first time I actually got to be on the side of "good" and didn't have to die was in *Hairspray*. Otherwise, I was always the one who would have a come-uppance. We filmed a certain amount of *Pink Flamingos* in sequence because of the physical set. Once the trailer was torched, it was gone, *burned*! It's funny because people have asked me if I still live in the trailer. First of all, I never did live in the trailer. Second of all, the trailer wasn't livable. Thirdly, we *burnt . . . it . . . down . . . to the ground*, on film. What do you not understand about this?

Figure 8.2 Mink Stole's "Connie Marble" scathingly dismisses a job applicant: "I guess there's just two kinds of people, Miss Sandstone. My kind of people, and assholes. It's rather obvious which category you fit into. Have a nice day." (*Pink Flamingos/Female Trouble* 25th anniversary edition DVD © New Line Home Entertainment, 2001.)

Chris: If you'd seen the entire script would that have made a difference to how you played the character?
Mink: Oh, I started big and stayed big. . . . As Taffy, I felt very, *very* free. It was wonderfully liberating to be snarky.

Chris: And all your dresses were too small. . . .
Mink: Well, they were short, but they fitted on top. I got in them, there was no adjustment. They were bought right out of the children's department. Van chose them; and one of them had been Pat Moran's.

I remember that my hair was lightened. Chris Mason didn't tell me she put peroxide into the shampoo. It was always open season on my hair! What everybody wanted I gave them, particularly the corn rows in *Polyester*. They ruined my hair. My hair is not corn-row hair, and the beads were heavy. That hair never grew back. I did my own hair in *Pink Flamingos*. David bleached it white for me, then I put red ink on it. David always did his own hair. He was way ahead of his time. He used magic markers.

Somewhere I have a couple of pages of *Multiple Maniacs*, handwritten, both sides of the page, in ink. John would write everything out by hand, longhand, for everyone. I remember the rehearsal process from *Pink Flamingos*. We'd get together on a Tuesday or Wednesday night to prepare for next weekend's filming. John would read everybody's lines as he wanted them delivered, which was basically the same for everybody, heavy italics, very heavy italics. Everything was highly dramatic. No throw away lines. Then by the weekend we had to have it all memorized. I know that I've done blocking rehearsals with him, but I can't remember how often.

Chris: Did you retake a lot of scenes?
Mink: NO! John kept on going. If everybody remembered his lines, it was on to the next scene. There were very few retakes. Though some scenes had multiple retakes. One of Edith's scenes he did shoot twenty-nine times, the one with Edith [Massey] in the cage. She says, "You'd be a great little baby butch." She blew this line over and over and over and over again. Every time she goofed John would get angrier, which would make her just a little more nervous, which would make her blow it again. He would give her difficult lines and then he would get frustrated with her when she didn't do them. Otherwise, unless something was flubbed you just went on. I know in *Pink Flamingos* whole story lines were cut. We shot hours of film that didn't get used.

John would stand behind the camera and mouth the dialogue, which is why we never altered it by so much as a comma. It was delivered as written. There was none of this "she's lonely," "here's what the character feels." Our job was not to do that. If you heard a strong Baltimore accent, it was real.

Chris: In film you ended up getting . . . type cast is too strong . . . but personally I don't think you have gotten the roles that would do justice to your talent.

Mink: I'm a better actor than I'm given credit for. I've gotten much more subtle in my later years.

Chris: You've done a lot of theater.
Mink: I was with the Ridiculous Theatrical Company, among others.

Chris: Is that style closer to these films?
Mink: Well, yes and no. There are things that were similar about Charles Ludlam and John. They were both the central moving force of a creative group of people without whom there wouldn't have been what was going on. The difference was when we were with John it was work, work, work. When we were with Charles, he would start without a completed script, and just be hanging out on stage, just wanting to chat. That never happened with John. Yet with both of them there was an absolute commitment to absurdity as reality. There was no winking at the audience. That's what makes John's movies work, and that's also why Charles' plays worked.

In film, the minute I put on an outfit I change into the character. My outfits always came from thrift stores. I got my first store clothing in *Desperate Living*. I actually got a beautiful dress in the beginning when I'm a housewife that cost a lot of money, $100 back then, which was a lot.

Chris: Someone remembers that John did not direct actors much other than to say "louder, louder, louder!"
Mink: Oh yeah, "louder, faster, funnier," though he didn't ever say those words. Although I have to say in later years, my direction now from John is "take it down." He has developed. My early training with John was "Know your lines. Come prepared."

Chris: Chan [Wilroy] said affectionately that you were hell on set, and everybody hated you because you always knew your lines.
Mink [chortles]: I never knew that! There was one scene with Chan in *Pink Flamingos* where he's got the wig and the suit on and I slap him and pull his ear, and he would always forget a line right after I did that so we would have to retake that scene. . . . Because at that time I didn't really understand the subtlety of *not* really pulling his ear. I mean, the scene was twenty minutes long. But if you blew a line nineteen minutes in you had to start back at 1.

Chris: Did you actually spit in Gator's face in *Female Trouble*? Was that in the script?
Mink: I'm sure it was in the script. That's not something I would have improvised. John is very specific about his scripts. He was specific about hair. He was specific about costumes. He was extremely lucky that he had so many amazingly talented people to call on. It would have been very different without Van Smith, without Vincent [Peranio]. But whatever it would have been it would probably have worked for John because John is one of those people that things work for.

Chris: Divine is wonderful in *Polyester*. It's so tragic, it's high melodrama. The scenes with Tab Hunter are really fun.
Mink: It wasn't camp. When he would come out to do his musical numbers with the maracas, now that was camp. But not his acting performances. I always say Divine was a much better actor than he was given credit for, because he played women, and played them so convincingly. And he was a nice guy. I always think of Divine as a "he." The character may be a "she." Divine wasn't Glenn off-screen, Divine was always Divine. We called him "Divine" or "Divvy." He did not refer to himself as "she" except every now and then, especially in drag. He didn't live as a woman. And I never thought of them as gay films. I mean John was gay. But I didn't know he was gay for six months when I lived with him. I didn't care when I found out, but this was something we never discussed.

Chris: John seems really concerned with keeping up with old friends.
Mink: Yes, and he's better at it than most people I know. He's better at it than I am.

Chris: And once you became Mink . . .?
Mink: I was pretty much Mink. Even my family calls me Mink.

5. Mary Vivian Pearce

Mary Vivian: The Dreamland Studio was when John was making movies in his bedroom, in his parents' house in Lutherville. We did *Hag in a Black Leather Jacket*, and I wore one of his mother's evening gowns. We filmed that. That's when we started calling it Dreamland. Some of *Roman Candles* was filmed there.
Chris: Mink remembers always having some job or other. She said she worked in a drug store for a while. She always had crap jobs. Others don't remember working. Does that mean you shot on the weekends and rehearsed on the weekends or evenings?

Mary Vivian: Why do you think that scene is so long with the wait for the bus in *Mondo Trasho*? Well, it's a Sunday, and the buses run every fifty minutes!
Chris: How did you get the script for *Female Trouble*? Did you see the whole thing or just your scenes?

Mary Vivian: I didn't see the whole thing, just my scenes. We had rehearsals a couple of times a week. I never saw the entire script.
Chris: Bob Adams said, "John would never have shown us the whole script. He knew that some of us were real gossips." But surely Pat must have seen the whole thing and Vincent I would think had to know how to design the sets.

Mary Vivian: I don't think a whole script existed until afterwards.
Chris: It's forty-some years ago.

Mary Vivian: You know, "if you remember the '60s you weren't there."
Chris: You couldn't change your lines, everybody says. John would read the lines, give you the intonation.
Mary Vivian: He acted out all the parts.

Figure 8.3 In simple black suit and rakish black hat, the elegant Mary Vivian Pearce ("Donna Dasher") testifies against the grotesque and increasingly insane "Dawn Davenport" (Divine) in *Female Trouble*. (*Female Trouble* DVD © Alliance Atlantis, 2004).

Chris: You've got just wonderful costumes in *Female Trouble*, and in *Pink Flamingos*, too. It was so cold! Thank God you had that fur there! You were the only lucky one.
Mary Vivian: How ridiculous does that look, Divine's out there having a barbecue and there are no leaves are on the trees and I'm in a mink?!

Chris: Pretty ridiculous. But this is why everybody loves these movies! They're so over the top! You always had the sort of glamour parts in these films. Mink was always the villain. Mink said, "I didn't see the whole script, but I knew something bad was going to happen to me because it always did." Poor Divine also. He was always a trooper, but something bad always happened to him.
Mary Vivian: He was one game actor! There's the famous scene with dog poop, and he crawls through pig shit, too, in *Pink Flamingos*. We didn't ask for permission to use the farm. We just went out there and shot. And then we had to wrap Divine up in blankets and put him in the heated car and oh did that car stink!

Chris: So many people who worked on the early films have died. . . . What was it like working with Edie?
Mary Vivian: Now *she* had trouble with her lines. John would yell and scream, and she'd be writing them all down, trying to memorize them that way, and then she would read the stage directions as part of her dialogue. John would yell, "Don't say that!"

Chris: You were often paired with David Lochary.
Mary Vivian: He was my favorite screen husband. He was wonderful to work with.

I got along really well with David.

Chris: Do you remember doing multiple takes on any of your scenes?
Mary Vivian: I don't remember doing anything like that on any of John's old movies. I would do take after take in the later movies. There had to be all the master shots and then the same thing over and over.

Chris: Did you participate in what Pat called wild postings?
Mary Vivian: I remember doing wild posting for a lot of the movies but not for *Female Trouble*. For *Eat Your Makeup* we had this drawing of a person looking like they were going down on a lipstick tube and I'd say, "Eat it, read it, and come!"

Chris: My sense every time I talk to any of you or the other Dreamlanders is that I would have had a lot of fun with you, and you would have taught me a lot. . . .

CHAPTER 9

Family Values: Charles Manson and John Waters' Cult Cinema

Kate J. Russell

In a 2018 interview, John Waters suggests that "every serious subject I think you can have fun with," with one personal exception: the Manson Family.[1] The Manson Family has preoccupied Waters in many guises over the course of his career, appearing in his scrapbooks, films, writings, and fine art practice, but the tenor of this preoccupation shifts significantly throughout the decades, from glib provocations to a remorseful sensitivity towards those whose lives were shattered by two fateful nights in 1969. Misguided provocations are the purview of youth; propelled by a heady mix of naivety and the impulse to test boundaries, it is, as Waters advises soon-to-be-graduates in his RISD commencement speech, the time to "make trouble."[2] For Waters, however, one particular juvenile transgression haunts him, which is his flippant attitude towards the Manson Family, who appear as a gauche punchline in *Multiple Maniacs* when protagonist Lady Divine taunts her partner that he is Sharon Tate's killer; the murders were initially unsolved during filming, and the later arrest of the suspects was incorporated into the plot. Lapses in judgment are the privilege of the adolescent mind, and most of us are fortunate that we have not committed our most egregious and regretful offenses to celluloid, since preserved for posterity by the esteemed Criterion Collection. Nor do we later become close friends with the (in)famous targets of those infractions, as Waters has done with Leslie Van Houten, opening a chasm of guilt for careless acts that cannot be undone. Waters reflects on his earlier instrumentalization of the Manson Family as a punchline, confessing that, "I am guilty, too. Guilty of using the Manson murders in a jokey, smart-ass way in my earlier films without the slightest feeling for the victims' families or the lives of the brainwashed Manson killer kids who were also victims in this sad and terrible case."[3] The benefit of hindsight and his subsequent friendship with a remorseful and thoroughly reformed Leslie Van Houten prompts contemplation about his initial perception of the horrific events and subsequent trial. While history cannot be rewritten, just as regretful actions cannot be reversed, it can be contextualized. This chapter revisits John Waters' engagement with the Manson Family, not to open old wounds, but to read it through Waters' evolving attitude and preoccupations, and to situate his work within the wider sociohistorical contexts in which it was produced.

Charles Manson and "The Family" rocketed to infamy in December 1969 when Manson along with Susan Atkins, Linda Kasabian, Patricia Krenwinkel, Leslie Van Houten, and Charles "Tex" Watkins were apprehended for the atrocious murders of pregnant actress Sharon Tate, wife of director Roman Polanski, along with her friends, the Folger coffee heiress Abigail Folger, Folger's boyfriend Wojciech Frykowski, celebrity hairstylist Jay Sebring, and Steven Parent, the teenage friend of the residence caretaker at 10050 Cielo Drive on August 9, 1969. The following night, on August 10, 1969, supermarket chain owner Leno LaBianca and his wife Rosemary were also brutally murdered, and as more details emerged about the crimes and the perpetrators, the Family wormed their way into the national consciousness as America's boogeymen. In Jeffrey Melnick's scintillating study of Charles Manson's influence on American popular culture, he asks, "How has this small-time con man and his ragtag minions creepy crawled through our social, political, and cultural life for close to fifty years now?"[4] This chapter takes up Melnick's question with a granular focus on John Waters, interrogating how the Manson Family has creepy-crawled into Waters' work and life.

This creepy-crawl traces the evolution of Waters' engagement with the Manson Family as juvenile shock humor morphs into empathy with Charles Manson's victims, which includes, for Waters, those who lost themselves under Manson's influences and were compelled to commit sickening acts on his behalf. Criminology scholar Karlene Faith taught the Manson girls in prison, helping to sever Manson's hold over them through education and feminist consciousness-raising, and her biography of Leslie Van Houten, born also from a close friendship, is a testament to Van Houten's remorse and reformation. It follows a woman slowly coming to terms with the heinous acts she committed while under Manson's thrall and learning to live with the crushing guilt of the pain she has caused by dedicating herself to rehabilitation through therapy, education, and supporting others.[5] Van Houten is, in many ways, the litmus test for abolitionist convictions and whether one believes that incarceration should have the goal of punishment or rehabilitation. Jeffrey Melnick's comprehensive book on the cultural impact of the Manson Family notes Faith and Waters as exceptional in their investment in the inner lives of the girls in a cultural landscape determined to paint them as nothing more than villainous, irredeemable murderers.[6] Waters' essay, "Leslie," echoes the portrait painted by Faith, and likewise draws attention to a "justice" system predicated on retribution rather than reformation, unveiling an underexplored aspect of Waters as a public figure, as someone who advocates on behalf of the incarcerated and who sympathizes with criminals without condoning their actions. Waters has also written about his work teaching in Maryland's Patuxent Institution, a correctional facility that employed extensive psychiatric treatment rather than merciless punishment. He acknowledges the impact of violent crime on victims and their families, but also demonstrates a sensitivity to the "total lack of community sympathy" and "unwanted notoriety" faced by families of perpetrators.[7] Cognizant of how he uses crime and its potential glorification in his films, as well as his lampooning of judicial processes and carceral institutions, Waters' work with prisoners and his refusal to judge his incarcerated pupils reveals a dedication to advocating on behalf of the socially abject beyond the frames of his films.

Examining Waters through the Manson Family, and vice versa, does not absolve the real-life atrocities committed by the Manson Family, nor does it dismiss the regret that Waters feels for his previously irreverent deployment of the Manson Family, but instead looks askance at how Manson's crimes and Waters' work present two divergent responses to repressive postwar America and its hypocrisies. In radically different ways and to different ends, both disrupt normative American values and institutions such as the church and the "family," bringing to the surface the implicit violence undergirding the polite civility demanded by such institutions. The Manson Family exploded into the national imaginary via sensationalized news reports and came to figure as a lightning rod that absorbs and reflects deeply held fears about the fragility of the normative social order, and likewise acts as a cipher that gestures towards Waters' own antipathy towards structures of normativity as well as his engagement with questions of cultism, community, crime, and celebrity. While the Manson Family occupied the front pages and induced a collective terror felt most acutely around Los Angeles, Waters was making independent films that similarly took aim at unsettling the dominant social order, pulling at the threads the Manson Family opened in the American social fabric and refashioning their social destruction into queer visions of comedic antisociality. This chapter interrogates how both direct references to and indirect resonances with the Manson Family in Waters' work do more than just work as shock humor; explicitly, the Manson references destabilize the valences of traditional institutions, such as the church and the family, and implicitly, the murderous cult is reworked to stage a queer community of antisociality.

From his childhood until around 1972, Waters created scrapbooks that include: reproductions of contemporary artworks; newspaper clippings about serial killers, scandals, and riots; photographs of friends; film reviews; religious pamphlets; promotional materials; personal invitations; advertisements; celebrity profiles, and so on. A distinct sensibility emerges from the assorted scraps that aligns with Waters' public artistic output and its investment in comedic detournements of organized religion, fringe sects, idolatry, and unusual forms of community, which are collaged together in the scrapbooks. The items often seem haphazardly stuck into place with tape that has mostly since perished, but some arrangements on pages suggest the creation of deliberate correlations between items. In particular, a number of pages position material on the Manson Family alongside Catholic imagery, offering a lens through which to interrogate how Waters puts orthodox religious practices into conversation with cultic collective derangement. The scrapbooks cull materials from various sources and assemble them into imaginative configurations that illuminate the interests and processes behind his singular visions. Scrapbooks, as Ellen Gruber Garvey points out, are often created by those who lack political or social capital, offering a means for marginalized subjects to assert "their own cultural authority" by creating new narratives from recontextualized source material.[8] Diana W. Anselmo reads the scrapbook interventions of movie fan Florence Kidwell in which she scrawled notes of stars' divorce details, health issues, and untimely demises over their studio portraits as embodying her disillusionment with Hollywood's impossible promise of heteronormative happiness. Anselmo reads her recontextualization of movie-related ephemera through "queer negativity" expressed via collage's "propensity for disobedience and fluidity," arguing that the scrapbooks produce "a queer embrace of the aberrant, the uninvited, the death driven—the perverse appeal of life failure."[9]

But where Kidwell's scrapbooks evince a perverse and melancholic attachment to the failures of romance and celebrity, Waters' scrapbooks instead create an ecstatic confluence of social transgressions, religious absurdity, celebrity scandal, and bizarre crimes as forms of antisociality that, paradoxically, form of the basis of a cult community. For example, a single page draws together photographs of Dreamlander (Dreamlanders is the collective name for Waters' cohort of recurring collaborators, such as Mink Stole, David Lochary, Divine, Edith Massey, George Figgs, Cookie Mueller, Vincent Peranio, and Van Smith, amongst others) Mary Vivian Pearce, Charles Manson, and a barefoot hippie on a single page, constructing an imagined heterogeneous community that encompasses the peace and love generation, a notorious cult leader, and Waters' own close friends. Another page juxtaposes James Dean in his trademark leather jacket with Patricia Krenwinkel and Susan Atkins smiling vacantly and dressed demurely for court, leveling hierarchies between the teen heartthrob and the young killers, drawing them into a community of rebels despite the drastic differences between their respective rebellions. Waters is drawn to outsider figures, and on the scrapbook's pages, the distinctions between various subcultures and antisocial modes are erased and instead mingle as new communities created through the collaged ephemera.

The scrapbooks also suggest that Waters' interest lay more in the antics of the Family as a spectacle of collective delusion than in the murders' macabre details; there are no clippings about the slayings, and the Manson material begins with the arrest of the suspects. This material pertains to the more bizarre events surrounding the trial and attests to their shared lunacy, such as newspaper clippings on: the congregation of followers with newly shaved heads outside the courthouse, who "vowed to set themselves afire in the event their leader was sentenced to death;" the assassination attempt on jailhouse informant Ronnie Howard; and the cockamamie plan to hijack a plane and kill passengers until Manson and the others were released from jail.[10] A short paragraph excerpted from a longer newspaper article reporting on the verdict focuses on the disruptive courtroom behavior as the girls entered to learn their fate "giggling and smirking," while another newspaper article reports on the woman who accosted Tex Watson at trial, declaring her love because, as she informed the judge, "she knew Watson 'through the Holy Spirit.'"[11] The scraps of articles and images culled from newspapers speak more to the intensity of the Family's collective obsession to reunite, and to the peculiar behaviors they perpetuated and drew from others, than to the slaughter of unsuspecting victims.

Waters is often cited as a cult filmmaker, but his work also evinces expression of a cultic ethos that uses comedy to construct a world of orthodox religion gone awry through its associations with filth and sexual depravity. In the scrapbooks, this ethos appears on pages that pull the Manson Family and the Catholic Church into constellations with one another, or, as in the copy of a Christmas card made by Waters, merge them together. Waters assembled an image of Mary and Joseph holding their newborn son from a traditional Christmas card, except instead of the angelic Christ child, a crudely cut picture of Charles Manson is pasted in his place. When Waters sent it to friends, it retained the interior greeting of "He is born."[12] This image of the Holy Family reconfigured to include the notorious cult leader reads as a condensation of themes that will preoccupy Waters throughout his career: travestying orthodox religious practices, bastardizing the family, and building non-normative communal relations predicated on a theatrical fascination with transgression. The scrapbooks also create montages of religious figures and the Manson Family, such as one page that positions Charles Manson's face beside three of the Manson girls laughing and above Pope Paul VI kissing a foot with a caption explaining that instead of the usual practice washing and kissing the feet of seminarians, the Pope performed this act on "112 poor, old Italian men from a nursing home."[13] The laughter of women bonded through murder and the abjection of the head of the Catholic Church presents a contrast between the giddy and carefree demeanors of the accused murderers and the subdued, almost fetishistic, reverence with which the Pope approaches his subject's foot. As a form of montage, this page embodies the perverse dialectic of transgressive laughter and holy abjection as cult phenomena that also appears in his films; in films such as *Mondo Trasho* (1969) and *Multiple Maniacs* (1970), Catholic imagery and rites are debased in comedic detournements that find pleasure in this blasphemy alongside other transgressions. *Mondo Trasho* sees the Virgin Mary miraculously appear in a laundromat, a psychiatric ward, and a pigsty, bringing the Holy Mother down to the profane earth in camp spectacles, while *Multiple Maniacs* sees its protagonist pleasured anally with rosary beads while she visualizes Christ's Passion.

On this scrapbook page, then, the open-mouthed laughter of the accused murderers disregards their horrific crimes, while the downcast eyes of Susan Atkins and Charles Manson, separate but beside her, seem to mock the Pope below them. This laughter undermines the sanctity of institutional proceedings and is a provocation against taking seriously the means through which punishment will be determined. Such laughter resonates with the final frames of *Female Trouble* (1974) when protagonist Dawn Davenport (Divine), driven mad by her criminal pursuit of fame, cackles maniacally as she fries in the electric chair. In the scrapbook, this transgressive laughter is repurposed to seemingly ridicule the Pope, with the arrangement on the page presenting a carnivalesque world-turned-upside-down in which hierarchies between fringe cult menaces and orthodox religious leaders are inverted, but it also points to a reconfiguration of the sacred through laughter beyond hierarchical inversion. In Waters' work, humor is crucial in travestying orthodox religious practices and organizing alternative communal relations around non-normativity, filth, and transgression, up to and including murder, which here might be read as a perverse comedy that emerges between these fragments.

Other parallels between Manson and Catholicism around questions of repentance are created on a page that collects an image of a priest marking a young boy's head with ash alongside newspaper article excerpts detailing Lynette Fromme and Nancy Pitman's trial testimony, which included Manson's alleged abilities to bring dead birds back to life and to subdue venomous snakes, and an argument between Family members and Linda Kasabian about Kasabian's culpability during her testimony as star witness for the prosecution.[14] The Ash Wednesday ritual of marking a cross on the forehead serves as a reminder that our bodies will return to the dust from which they came and the necessity of repentance in the face of such mortality, an image of which sits above an newspaper article fragment reporting on a courtroom exchange in which Family members demand Kasabian accept fault in the crimes (Kasabian drove to the scenes, but did not participate). Interestingly, the longer article from which Fromme and Pitman's testimony is excerpted also includes Fromme's explanation that the crosses carved into the Manson Family's foreheads would symbolically "show that the family members were 'clearly marked,'" clarifying that it was "a fallen cross [that] means the system as it now stands has fallen."[15] This missing text provides a structuring absence between the cross marked on congregation members on a day for penance with the cross etched and burned into the Manson Family, a symbol of their unity in unrepentant defiance.

Waters has incorporated references to the Manson Family into his films since the moment the news broke, beginning with *Multiple Maniacs* (1970), which uses the evolving status of the Tate-LaBianca murders as a plot device, and traces a line from the Manson murders to an orgasmic climax facilitated by a meditation on the Passion of Christ. At the time of filming, the Tate-LaBianca murders remained unsolved, giving travelling sideshow star Lady Divine (Divine) the opportunity to taunt her partner, Mr. David (David Lochary), that he was involved. Lady Divine's accusations feed Mr. David's paranoia, and he seeks comfort in the arms of Bonnie (Mary Vivian Pearce); when Lady Divine finds out about their affair, she is guided to a church by the Infant of Prague where she meets Mink (Mink Stole), the "Religious Whore." Mink sodomizes her with rosary beads while reciting the Stations of the Cross, with cross-cutting between anal eroticism and Christ's final moments cleaving together sexual and religious ecstasies. Since the supposed murderers were caught during filming, the climactic scene sees Mr. David find the *Daily News*' front cover headline from December 2, 1969, which declares "Arrest Weirdo in Tate Murder," prompting him to realize that he has no connection to "Charles Watson" and "Patricia Kernwinkel [sic]."[16] This realization occurs in the midst of a succession of bloody murders that culminates in Lady Divine cannibalizing Mr. David's internal organs.

Attention to the mise-en-scène of the house in which this ghastly charade unfolds ensconces the Manson narrative device in religious paraphernalia, with miniature statues of Jesus on the cross, the Infant of Prague, and the Virgin Mary reworking the associations between Manson and Catholicism that are rehearsed in the scrapbooks. Some of these religious trinkets reappear in *Pink Flamingos*, with the Infant of Prague and the Virgin Mary now joined by a framed portrait of Susan Atkins in the villains' home, shown briefly in close-up (Figure 9.1).

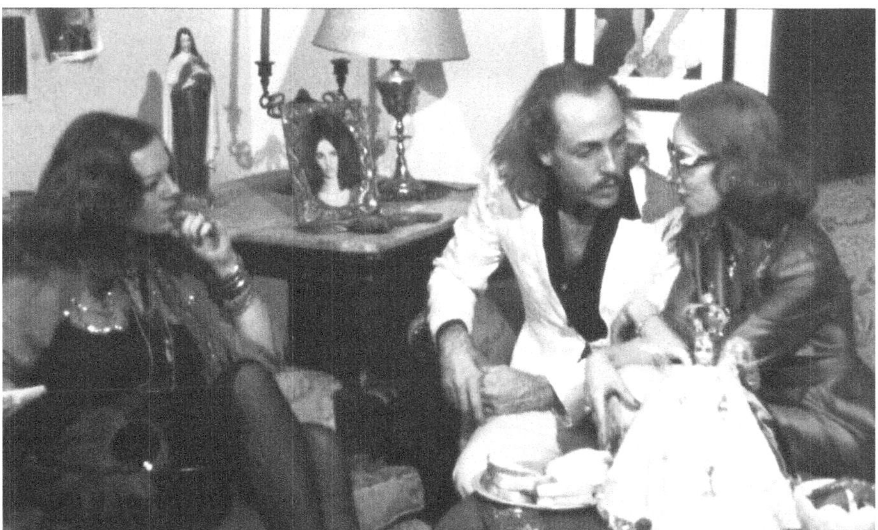

Figure 9.1 The Marbles' residence in *Pink Flamingos* (1972).

On one of Divine's crime sprees in *Pink Flamingos*, during which she shoplifts a steak via her crotch and defecates in public, she struts past a wall graffitied with the words "free Tex Watson." In close reading a text, Kartik Nair demonstrates how paying attention to the seemingly insignificant allows one to feel "the text's many contexts unbracketing themselves," as we perceive "histories of production and reception pressing on the film."[17] Following Nair, cult references in the mise-en-scène both situate the film in its historical moment as well as gesturing towards Waters' changing views on Manson; by *Desperate Living* (1977), a painting of Charles Manson sits next to paintings of Adolf Hitler and Ugandan dictator Idi Amin in the villain's castle (Figure 9.2). This signals a shift from implicitly drawing parallels between Manson and religious icons as both an indictment of organized religion's false idols and an elevation of Manson (symbolized by Susan Atkins) to a sacred status, to associating Manson with evil as personified by genocidal dictators instead, as well as an indication of Waters' differing attitudes towards Manson's followers, for whom he later evinces sympathy, and to Manson himself.

Tellingly, it is not Manson that Waters dedicates *Pink Flamingos* and *Female Trouble* to; *Pink Flamingos* is dedicated to "Sadie, Katie, and Les," while *Female Trouble* is dedicated to "Charles Watson" (Figure 9.3), since Waters credits attending the Manson trial and visiting Watson in prison for inspiring

Figure 9.2 Queen Carlotta's castle in *Desperate Living* (1977).

Figure 9.3 The opening credits to *Female Trouble* (1974).

Female Trouble's theme of "crime is beauty."[18] Although Watson disagreed with Waters' concept, he made him a wooden helicopter that appears in the credits to the film, with Waters noting that the words "Game is Blame," "Tweak," and "Fear" written on it signal that he was "still coming out of his Manson indoctrination."[19] *Female Trouble* follows the trials and tribulations of Dawn Davenport (Divine) as she graduates from teenage delinquent to petty criminal before modelling for salon owners Donna and Donald Dasher (Mary Vivian Pearce and David Lochary), who use her to prove their thesis that "crime is beauty." The climax of this experiment sees Dawn perform onstage in a skin-tight sequined two-piece, bouncing erratically on a trampoline and bathing in a playpen while hurling dead fish into the delirious crowd. The final act makes the connections between criminal activities and perverse glamour explicit when Dawn describes herself as "crime personified" in an impassioned tirade before listing her exploits ranging from framing left-wing antiwar activists to sexual dalliances with infamous murderers. She ends with the affirmation "and I'm so fucking beautiful I can't stand it myself!" then demands to know, "Who wants to be famous? Who wants to die for art?" A man yells, "I do!" and she promptly shoots him dead.

Dawn is soon apprehended and tried for murder, where she takes the witness stand and orders that her trial be moved "downtown," to a "large, large theatre," before whispering to her attorney that he is a "terrible press agent" for booking her a gig where no cameras are permitted. This approach to judicial proceedings as a fashion spectacle draws from Waters' hobby as a "trial buff," detailed in *Shock Value*, where he argues that "all people look better under arrest. The ugliest sex criminal and the motliest junkie take on a special glamour as they are handcuffed and dragged before the crime-hungry American public."[20] He describes the Manson girls as "starlets" who "were out to grab headlines" and "were the most style-conscious defendants," while Manson himself behaved "as a true star should, he would flash his *Life* magazine eyes and strut to his seat" as "old women would gasp, teenage girls would squeal, and the sickies would quiver in ecstasy."[21] Waters further explores the glamorization of crime and the spectacle of judiciary processes in *Serial Mom* (1994), a film that satirizes white suburban mores through the perceived normality of a serial killer. It follows Beverly Sutphin (Kathleen Turner), a housewife who responds to minor social infractions with untrammeled violence: a teacher admonishes her son, so she runs him over; a boy spurns her daughter, so she stabs him with a poker; a man complains about her husband's dental practice, so she knocks an air conditioner on top of him. Her husband's fear that there's a psychopathic rage bubbling beneath her respectable façade is confirmed when he finds her scrapbook of murderers and cult leaders, including items on Charles Manson, the Jonestown massacre, and Richard Speck, as well as a personalized tape from Ted Bundy. If he'd paid closer attention to his wife's reading materials, he would have noticed that her book about birds conceals *Helter Skelter*, the Manson prosecutor's true crime account, opened to full page portraits of Manson and Tex Watson; the police will later cite finding *Helter Skelter* in her garbage as evidence of her psychopathy (but of course, as Waters knows, keeping scrapbooks on murderers and reading true crime are not necessarily portents of a homicidal pathology).

After her arrest, Beverly's daughter capitalizes on the attention by selling "serial mom" merchandise and her son orchestrates an adaptation of the events for television. Perhaps spurred by his almost decade-long friendship with Van Houten, Waters self-reflexively critiques the fascination with real-life horror through satire that targets the perverse romanticism that often accompanies true crime fanaticism. This satirization of true crime media and the tabloid glamorization of abominable figures also recurs in Waters' fine art practice in a series of diptychs that juxtapose photographs of Brad Pitt, Dorothy Malone, and Richard Gere with photographs of Manson sporting similar hairstyles and fashion to each of them.[22] This commentary on the correlations between crime and celebrity are most pointed, however, in "Manson Copies Divine's Hairdo," which sees Divine in *Pink Flamingos* positioned below Manson with his hair similarly shaved back to his temples, implicating Waters and his fans in the satire.[23] *Serial Mom*'s satire targets those fooled by the respectable veneer presented by white, upper-middle class homemakers, as the jurors, won over by Beverly's wit and charm, find her not guilty. However, during the trial, unbeknownst to them, Beverly becomes increasingly incensed at Juror #8 (played by Patricia Hearst, fittingly herself a victim of a trial-turned-media-circus) for wearing white after Labor Day. Immediately after her acquittal, she accosts the offending juror and uses a courthouse payphone to bash her over the head until a final blow knocks her unconscious. Amidst a frenzy of reporters and fans, Beverly coolly rejoins her family and meets Suzanne Somers, who is set to play Sutphin in an upcoming biopic, when a shriek cuts through the commotion, alerting the crowd to the body's discovery. Suzanne Somers stares at Beverly in horror as she realizes that she has just been associating with a cold-blooded killer; Beverly returns her gaze with a defiant smirk, the film's final image conjuring a freeze-framed soccer mom parody of the Manson girls' demure smiles and giddy laughter as they were shepherded along the Los Angeles County Courthouse corridors.

Waters constructs forms of non-normative community in his early films that assemble motley assortments of characters bonded through anti-social proclivities, and in his scrapbooks that collate various subcultural and outsider figures into social configurations that meld political dissidents, Hollywood icons, cult members, and his own coterie, the Dreamlanders. However, many critics noted a shift in Waters' sensibilities and visions of non-normative social relations with the release of *Polyester* (1981), which saw his overtly transgressive comedy largely replaced by a satirical approach to white suburbia.[24] But as noted from the resonances between trials as spectacle in *Female Trouble* and *Serial Mom*, there are threads that run throughout Waters' oeuvre, suggesting that this alleged break with transgressive subjects and aesthetics perhaps overdetermines his evolution as a director. There are thematic continuities, if not stylistic ones, as Derek Kane-Meddock and Walter Metz both note, in the continual lampooning of traditional American values, particularly as embodied by the institution of the nuclear family. Kane-Meddock examines how Waters parodies gender and genre in ways that "cast a critical eye on that evocative symbol of normalcy and repository of morality, the family," noting that what unites Waters' independent and Hollywood films is an "ambivalence about all forms of social categorization" that "denaturalizes the familiar."[25] Similarly, Metz reads how "Waters' films produce a queering of the American family that is consistent across the eleven features," observing the continued motif of biological families constructed negatively and replaced by new formations of familial relations in which "an aberrant family" is "preferable to the seemingly normal bourgeois one."[26]

Importantly, Metz briefly notes Waters' fascination with the Manson Family, arguing that they present an example of the "psychologically unstable families" that is reinterpreted in Waters' films to question so-called "normal" family dynamics.[27] When Waters came of age during the sixties, the family as an institution saw its cultural stranglehold challenged by communes, as disillusionment with the capitalist rat race impelled many to "drop out," abandon their biological families and start new group living arrangements. Manson and his followers represent the most extreme example of the post-World War II nuclear family's reconfiguration, and, as Melnick argues, one of their legacy's most enduring facets is that they "posed a remarkably robust challenge to what a family should look like and how it should operate."[28] The Manson Family became the locus point for a number of overlapping discourses on perceived social crises and alleged moral degeneration incited by the unsettling of the family's institutional authority. David E. Smith, the Haight Ashbury Free Clinic's medical director in the late 1960s and early 1970s, and Alan Rose, the clinic's former administrator, studied the dynamics of "group marriage," including its polygamous sexual practices and communal child care, which were "a direct affront to the dominant culture's expressed moral code," using the Manson Family at Spahn Ranch prior to the murders as their case study.[29] But although communal life promised utopia outside stultifying norms, Smith and Rose observed that it replicated the traditional family's patriarchal structure and division of labor, with women relegated to domestic work and sexually subordinated to men.[30]

The Family's women, however, disavowed these oppressive conditions in favor of a dedicated communal vision as created by their leader and savior, Charles Manson. This dedication appears in a scrapbook article that details Family member Cathy Gillies' threat that "People who put people in gas chambers or behind bars are going to get what they put out," and her claim that the murders were intended as "copycat" murders to free Bobby Beausoleil, who was in jail for the prior murder of Manson associate Gary Hinman.[31] This latter point was often repeated by Family members, and it runs counter to prosecutor Vincent Bugliosi's theory—put forward at trial and since cemented as fact—that the murders were intended to trigger "Helter Skelter," a race war that would end with Manson as leader.[32] Bugliosi's sensational idea took up Manson's more fringe beliefs, racist ideology, and harebrained schemes, and blew them up into the official narrative, ignoring the much more plausible motive of "love of brother," which was continually affirmed by the members themselves.[33] This fierce bonding through wicked acts gets reworked in Waters' "trash trilogy" of *Pink Flamingos*, *Female Trouble*, and *Desperate Living* (1977), where social relations are formed through shared abjection and criminal pursuits in the absence of a dangerous manipulator and abusive patriarch.

In the "trash trilogy," Waters creates community through the singularity of his characters' proclivities, assembling communal relations predicated partially on the antisocial acts of non-reproductive sexuality, but also on criminal undertakings ranging from petty theft to murder. In *Female Trouble*, Dawn Davenport's best friends are also her partners-in-crime, and like the teenage runaway Manson girls, Dawn absconds from her safe, suburban family. She then becomes an antagonistic mother to Taffy (Mink Stole), who endures incestuous come-ons from both her stepfather (Michael Potter) and father (Divine), joins a religious sect, and is eventually murdered by Dawn. Suffice to say that in *Female Trouble*, family by blood or marriage is an obstacle to be overcome, while companions found through crime and perversion present a welcome alternative, an antisocial community for the socially marginalized. *Desperate Living* continues the theme of a found family, as hysterical housewife Peggy Gravel (Mink Stole) and her maid Grizelda Brown (Jean Hill) flee to Mortville, a filthy makeshift slum for social exiles, after accidentally smothering Peggy's husband to death. A lesbian couple takes them in, but Peggy, unable to let go of her hang-ups, joins forces with the town's despotic ruler Queen Carlotta (Edith Massey), while Grizelda helps the town's inhabitants gain freedom through massacring and cannibalizing the Queen. Such narratives take the disturbing and manipulative elements of Manson's familial inversions and rework them as convivial support.

This reworking of both the nuclear family and the Manson Family's social bonds is most pronounced in *Pink Flamingos*, which follows Divine (Divine) as she competes with Connie and Raymond Marble (Mink Stole and David Lochary) to maintain the title of "the filthiest people alive," a narrative that functions as a framework for escalating vignettes of grotesque acts, lewd behavior, and violent crimes. The Manson Family's possible "love of brother" motive is refashioned into a carnivalesque attack during Divine's birthday party when policemen arrive to break up the festivities. The revelers swarm the police, using makeshift weapons to hack at them with abandon, wrenching their limbs and cackling as they gnaw on the bloody meat. This violent intervention, culminating in the antisocial acts of murder and cannibalism, paradoxically guarantees the continuation of the non-normative community gathered around Divine. Rather than presenting community as either a homogenizing identity-based project or as a politically-motivated imperative, *Pink Flamingos* adopts the Family's bonds based in transgression, up to and including murder, and reworks it as a queer fantasy of a radically non-normative community established through crime, filth, and abjection, with the utopian overtures promised by Manson come true.

Pink Flamingos also dismantles and reconfigures the traditional family unit, inverting biological family roles as matriarch Divine cares for her playpen-bound mother and shares a home with her "traveling companion" Cotton, who is also sexually involved with Divine's son and gets off on voyeuristically watching him decapitate chickens during sex. Deviant sexuality challenges the family as an institution, threatening the social order and its privileging of monogamous practices and reproductive capacities. Writing in 1974, gay liberationist Dennis Altman wrote that "modern Western societies are based on the institution of the family," with the nuclear family's cultural hegemony bolstered by state and religious institutions that offer financial advantages to the married and child-bearing and secure heterosexual monogamy as righteous and moral.[34] Altman notes that while the "homosexual represents the most clear-cut rejection of the nuclear family that exists," anyone living outside the norms proscribed by familial institutions is rendered "deviant" to a degree.[35] Part of what made communes so threatening to American society in the 1960s was that their inhabitants engaged in non-monogamous sexual practices, and post-mortems of the Manson case often focused on their deviant sexuality as a determining factor in the events that unfolded. For instance, a *Los Angeles Free Press* article details how cult initiation involved testing new recruits' sexual inhibitions to gauge their potential willingness to follow Manson.[36]

Jeffrey Sconce also interrogates how Manson's position as "the consummate icon of evil incarnate" is inextricably bound up with how his perverse sexual prowess exposes "the American family's usually occluded drama of oedipalization."[37] Since the inhabitants of Spahn Ranch generally viewed conventional marriages as "psychologically destructive," Manson harnessed pathologies endemic to the nuclear family to sever followers' biological connections, weaponizing "daddy issues" and familial traumas, real or imagined, until Manson himself became a replacement paternal figure.[38] The spectre of incest then lurked in the blurred roles of father, brother, and husband embodied by Manson, a conflation that is made explicit in *Pink Flamingos* when Divine and her son succumb to an overwhelming desire for one another during a frenzied defilement of the Marbles' home.[39] After maniacally licking furniture, the pair begin to grasp one another as Divine repeats that Crackers is her "flesh and blood," her "genes," before taking his flaccid penis in her mouth, unsimulated.

The trash trilogy's antisocial forms of community work as a feminist queering of the Family's patriarchal dynamics, as deviant women find support in the social abjection that results from abandoning or being excluded by normative family structures. The "antisocial" turn in queer theory wrestles with disillusionment towards communal life through advocating the refusal to assimilate to a social order predicated on heteronormative ideals. Scholars such as Lee Edelman and Leo Bersani recuperate the homophobic insistence on queerness as a threat to social cohesion, civil morality, and a better future as a viable political stance, adopting "queer negativity" as a strategic denial to acquiesce to a social order that privileges monogamous heterosexual reproductivity as propped up by both the liberal left and the reactionary right.[40] But even as Bersani seeks out where "gay desire" redefines social relations as a "withdrawal from relationality itself" and is drawn to writers who "discover in homosexual desire . . . *anticommunitarian* impulses," he also aims for an "anticommunal mode of connectedness," which resonates with how Waters takes the antisocial and transforms it into the basis for communal relationality.[41]

To return to Waters' first mediated encounter with the Manson Family, what struck him upon beholding their photographs was that the "Manson Family looked just like my friends at the time!"[42] There is a spark of recognition that prompts Waters to ask, "How had these kids, from backgrounds so similar to mine, committed in real life the awful crimes against peace and love that we were acting out for comedy in our films?"[43] In his writing, there is the hint of alternative histories in which if the Manson Girls met the Dreamlanders, they could have been underground movie stars, making use of Spahn Ranch's former purpose as a set for Westerns, or, perhaps, if Waters and the Dreamlanders had not sublimated their socially transgressive tendencies into film, they could have ended up in prison. While the media furore around the Manson Family dehumanized them as monsters and mythologized them as evil incarnate, Waters instead saw their eerie similarities to his own cohort of social misfits and acid heads. Leslie Van Houten, for instance, "pretty, out of her mind, rebellious, with fashion-daring, a good haircut, and a taste for LSD," shared these attributes with the women involved in Waters' social circle and early films, prompting Waters to ask, "If Leslie had met me instead of Charlie, could she have gone to the Cannes Film Festival instead of the California Institute for Women?"[44] Such a question cannot be answered, of course, but in Waters' films there are traces of the Manson Family's lessons in non-normative community and violent antisociality, albeit transformed into queer utopian potential and visions of lives lived otherwise. Waters has long campaigned for Van Houten's parole and in 2023, after fifty-three years behind bars, it was finally granted. If there is a better way to atone for a transgression than helping someone get their life back, I am not sure what it is.

ACKNOWLEDGMENTS

I would like to thank the editors, Michelle Moore and Brian Brems, for their generous and thoughtful feedback; Jeffrey Melnick for his sharp insights as a respondent to an earlier version of this paper presented at the Society for Cinema and Media Studies conference in Boston, 2024, as well as my co-panelists Timothy Holland and Juan Carlos Kase; Joan Miller at the Reid Cinema Archives for facilitating my work with the scrapbooks; and James Cahill and Meghan Romano for their helpful feedback.

NOTES

1. John Waters in Ben Walters, "John Waters: Why the Auteur of Outrage Won't Joke about the Manson Murders," *The Guardian*, November 8, 2018, https://www.theguardian.com/film/2018/nov/08/john-waters-homotopia-festival-liverpool-manson-murders.
2. John Waters, commencement speech, Rhode Island School of Design, May 30, 2015, *YouTube*, https://www.youtube.com/watch?v=Hl05XGifKb4; the speech is reprinted in John Waters, *Make Trouble* (New York: Algonquin Books of Chapel Hill, 2017).
3. John Waters, *Role Models* (New York: Farrar, Straus and Giroux, 2010), 45.

4. Jeffrey Melnick, *Creepy Crawling: Charles Manson and the Many Lives of America's Most Infamous Family* (New York: Arcade Publishing, 2018), x.
5. Karlene Faith, *The Long Prison Journey of Leslie Van Houten: Life Beyond the Cult* (Boston: Northeastern University Press: 2001).
6. Melnick, *Creepy Crawling*, 83.
7. John Waters, "Going to Jail," in *Crackpot: The Obsessions of John Waters* (New York: Scribner, 2003), 48.
8. Ellen Gruber Garvey, *Writing with Scissors: American Scrapbooks from the Civil War to the Harlem Renaissance* (Oxford: Oxford University Press, 2013), 209.
9. Diana W. Anselmo, "Picture Pain: Anti-Heteronormative Female Fandom in Early Hollywood," *JCMS: Journal of Cinema and Media Studies* 62, no. 1 (Fall 2022): 20, 8, 13.
10. Newspaper clippings, "5 Women Followers Shave Heads," and "Second Attempt to Kill Tate Trial Star Witness," in *Scrapbooks 5 by John Waters, 1968–1972*, collection 19 series I, box 4, folder 3, John Waters Collection, Reid Cinema Archives, Wesleyan University, Middletown, CT; newspaper clipping, "Manson 'Family' Robbery Case," in *Scrapbooks 5 by John Waters, 1968–1972*, collection 19 series I, box 4, folder 4, John Waters Collection.
11. Newspaper clipping, "Watson Gets Hug in Court," in *Scrapbooks 5 by John Waters, 1968–1972*, collection 19, series I, box 4, folder 2, John Waters Collection.
12. Waters, *Crackpot*, 132–133.
13. Newspaper clippings, in *Scrapbooks 5 by John Waters, 1968–1972*, collection 19, series I, box 4, folder 3, John Waters Collection.
14. Newspaper clippings, in *Scrapbooks 5 by John Waters, 1968–1972*, collection 19 series I, box 4, folder 2, John Waters Collection.
15. John Kendall, "'Family' Member Says Life Was a Game with Manson," February 4, 1971, https://www.cielodrive.com/archive/family-member-says-life-with-manson-was-a-game/.
16. "Arrest Weirdo in Tate Murder," *Daily News*, December 2, 1969, 1.
17. Kartik Nair, *Seeing Things: Spectral Materialities of Bombay Horror* (Oakland, CA: University of California Press, 2024), 19.
18. John Waters, *Shock Value: A Tasteful Book About Bad Taste* (Philadelphia: Running Press, 2005), 94.
19. Waters, *Role Models*, 50.
20. Waters, *Shock Value*, 114.
21. Ibid., 117.
22. See "Manson Copies Brad Pitt" (2003), "Manson Copies Richard Gere" (2000), "Manson Copies Dorothy Malone's Collar" (1998), in Kristen Hileman, *John Waters: Indecent Exposure* (Baltimore: Baltimore Museum of Art in association with University of California Press, 2018).
23. "Manson Copies Divine's Hairdo" (1993) in Hileman, *John Waters: Indecent Exposures*, 91.
24. For instance, see Janet Maslin, "The Screen: 'Polyester,' An Offbeat Comedy," *New York Times*, May 29, 1981, C6.
25. Derek Kane-Meddock, "Trash Comes Home: Gender/Genre Subversion in the Films of John Waters," in *Gender Meets Genre in Postwar Cinemas*, edited by Christine Gledhill (Urbana: University of Illinois Press, 2012), 206.
26. Walter Metz, "John Waters Goes to Hollywood," in *Authorship and Film*, edited by David A. Gerstner and Janet Staiger (New York: Routledge, 2003), 163, 166.
27. Ibid., 166.
28. Melnick, *Creepy Crawling*, 5.
29. David E. Smith and Alan J. Rose, "The Group Marriage Commune: A Case Study," *Journal of Psychedelic Drugs* 3, no. 1 (September 1970): 115.
30. Ibid., 117.

31. Newspaper clipping, "Manson Follower Warns the Jury," in *Scrapbooks 5 by John Waters, 1968–1972*, collection 19 series I, box 4, folder 3, John Waters Collection.
32. Vincent Bugliosi, *Helter Skelter: The True Story of the Manson Murders* (London: Arrow Books, 2018).
33. Melnick, *Creepy Crawling*, 11.
34. Dennis Altman, "The Homosexual and the Family," in *Coming Out in the Seventies* (Boston: Alyson Publications, Inc., 1981), 42.
35. Ibid., 42–43.
36. "M.D. on Manson's Sex Life," *Los Angeles Free Press* 7, no. 4, issue 288, January 23–29, 1970, 1, 8.
37. Jeffrey Sconce, "XXX: Love and Kisses from Charlie," in *Swinging Single: Representing Sexuality in the 1960s*, edited by Hilary Radner and Moya Luckett (Minneapolis; London: University of Minnesota Press, 1999), 219.
38. Smith and Rose, "The Group Marriage Commune," 117.
39. Melnick, *Creepy Crawling*, 6–7.
40. See Lee Edelman, *No Future: Queer Theory and the Death Drive* (Durham, NC: Duke University Press, 2004) and Leo Bersani, *Homos* (Cambridge, MA: Harvard University Press, 2009).
41. Bersani, *Homos*, 7, 10.
42. Waters, *Role Models*, 46.
43. Ibid., 48.
44. Ibid., 48.

CHAPTER 10

Queer Moms, Trash Aesthetics, and Suburban Filth: The Portrayal of Maternal Abject in John Waters' Cinema

Sony Jalarajan Raj and Adith K. Suresh

John Waters' mothers are frequently depicted as larger-than-life characters, embodying both the grotesque and the absurd. For instance, in *Pink Flamingos* (1972), the character of Divine, who plays the role of an unconventional mother, subverts traditional maternal expectations through her outrageous behavior and defiance of societal norms. Similarly, in *Serial Mom* (1994), Kathleen Turner's character Beverly Sutphin presents a satirical take on the archetypal suburban mother, whose obsessive commitment to maintaining her family's image leads to homicidal extremes. Waters uses these hyperbolic portrayals to critique and parody the idealized notions of motherhood and female sexuality, revealing the complexities and often hypocritical standards imposed on women in society. His films thus transform the mother figure into a site of rebellion and critique, highlighting the absurdity and constraints of conventional maternal roles.

This chapter explores how Waters transforms the maternal figure into an abject entity that embodies the tension between societal norms and individual identity. By analyzing films such as *Pink Flamingos* and *Female Trouble* (1974), it examines how these maternal characters negotiate their complex gender identities and sexual preferences in a suburban setting. Waters' mothers subvert aesthetic, social, cultural, and political norms, challenging the conservative ideologies that underpin popular representations of motherhood. The significance of this study lies in its exploration of how trash cinema, with its celebration of the grotesque and the obscene, offers a powerful medium for critiquing societal norms and embracing marginalized identities. Waters' deliberate use of the abject mother figure disrupts the dominant heteronormative narratives and opens up a space for alternative expressions of identity. This chapter will contribute to a deeper understanding of Waters' impact on queer cinema and cultural studies, highlighting the radical potential of trash aesthetics to challenge and redefine conventional perceptions of identity and motherhood.

Julia Kristeva describes the abject as that which "disturbs identity, system, and order,"[1] provoking both repulsion and fascination. Abjection represents the boundaries between what is considered acceptable and what is not.[2] Ambiguous because it exists on the threshold, neither fully inside nor outside the norms, it challenges clear distinctions and definitions, and resides in a state of in-between. Kristeva says: "when one is in a state of abjection, the borders between the object and the subject cannot be maintained."[3]

Kristeva's concept of abjection considers that what we reject or find disgusting remains a part of our psychological landscape, constantly challenging our sense of order and self. It is about the constant interplay between the subject and the abject, where the abject is never fully excluded but instead always lingering at the borders, threatening to disrupt the stability of the self. In John Waters' cinema, the representation of motherhood often aligns with the concept of the "maternal abject," which imagines and represents motherhood as a source of abjection, challenging normative boundaries and societal taboos. Waters' mothers are symbolic monsters, transgressing conventional roles and evoking a sense of the grotesque. They embody excess and deviance, contrasting starkly with traditional images of nurturing and purity. Waters utilizes these abject maternal figures to critique and subvert the idealized American family, exposing the underlying dysfunctions and moral decay.

In *Pink Flamingos*, Divine's character, Babs Johnson, epitomizes the maternal abject. She is not only the head of her family but also a notorious criminal, proudly flaunting her title as the "filthiest person alive," which is represented by moments such as the notorious scene of Babs fellating her own son. This scene, along with her criminal activities and expressions of "filth," highlights Waters' critique of conventional maternal roles and the superficiality of societal morality. Divine's maternal role is far removed from conventional ideals; she revels in perversion and immorality, embodying a monstrous maternity that defies societal expectations. Similarly, in *Polyester* (1981), the character of Francine Fishpaw, also portrayed by Divine, is a suburban housewife whose life unravels in a series of grotesque events, including infidelity, addiction, and familial betrayal. A key moment occurs when Francine discovers her husband's infidelity, exposing the dysfunction beneath the veneer of suburban respectability. Waters uses Francine's exaggerated suffering to reveal the hypocrisy and hidden corruption of suburban life, subverting the image of the content and capable suburban mother.

In *Female Trouble*, Divine takes on the role of Dawn Davenport, a delinquent teenager who becomes a notorious criminal and, eventually, a mother. Dawn's journey from a rebellious youth to a grotesque parody of motherhood is marked by violence, crime, and perversion. Her character's transformation rejects traditional female and maternal roles. The film shows Dawn's abusive and neglectful behavior towards her daughter, Taffy, rejecting the notion that motherhood brings inherent fulfilment and virtue. As Dawn, Divine constructs a drag mother queen identity that is both outrageous and subversive. Dawn's flamboyant appearance and criminal behavior starkly contrast with her pregnancy and subsequent motherhood, which are marked by neglect and abuse, rather than transformation or fulfilment. This depiction mocks conventional expectations by presenting motherhood as part of Dawn's larger narrative of deviance and rebellion, thereby challenging and critiquing the traditional, nurturing role typically associated with maternal figures. Through these films, Waters uses Divine's characters to challenge and subvert conventional maternal roles, exposing the hypocrisy and superficiality of traditional expectations and exploring themes of deviance and abjection.

During the 1960s and 1970s, artists like Andy Warhol and John Waters popularized the white trash aesthetic. Waters' many images such as the "Pope of Trash,"[4] the "Prince of Puke,"[5] the "Duke of Dirt,"[6] and the "godfather of gross-out,"[7] are based on his ideology of "choosing bad taste over socially approved taste."[8] However, in Waters' own words, "to understand bad taste one must have very good taste" because "good bad taste can be creatively nauseating but must, at the same time, appeal to the especially twisted sense of humor, which is anything but universal."[9] Waters' transgressive cult films are notorious for incorporating extravagant camp elements, often highlighting the tragic trash queen narrative through actor and drag queen icon Divine.[10] He says that his films are deliberate attempts to provoke strong reactions in the audience; because it is "impossible to not to tell somebody about it."[11] His films are a vibrant exploration of filth and rebellion set against the backdrop of suburban America. His early films of the 1970s "challenged taste, morals and values through shock tactics that parodied the paranoia and fear that America harboured towards subcultures at the time."[12] Suburbia in Waters' films, as seen in works like *Pink Flamingos* and *Polyester*, is a veneer of respectability that barely conceals the depravity and dysfunction beneath. His use of suburban settings underscores the hypocrisy and hidden decay of middle-class American life, turning the mundane into the bizarre and highlighting the artificiality of societal norms.

The performative nature of 1970s midnight movies transformed cult film viewings into spectacles of post-countercultural protest.[13] During this period, films like *Pink Flamingos* were attempting to defy traditional morals, with marketing promoting its shocking content as a unique form of alternative cinema.[14] At the filmmaker's request, *Pink Flamingos* was moved to a midnight slot at New York's Elgin Theatre, where it began its rise to cult fame and arthouse popularity.[15] Waters soon became "one of the most revered auteurs in American independent cinema."[16]

Waters' characters are emblematic of sexual rebellion and countercultural defiance. They reject conventional morality and embrace anarchic freedom, which is both shocking and liberating. Divine, a recurring figure in Waters' work, epitomizes this rebellion with her unapologetic embrace of outrageous sexuality and grotesque glamour. Characters in *Pink Flamingos*, *Female Trouble*, and *Desperate Living* (1977) defy societal expectations, engaging in behavior that is not just unconventional but deliberately transgressive. By celebrating these characters, Waters critiques the repression and conformity of mainstream culture, instead presenting a world where the marginalized and the freakish take center stage. He says that:

> [T]he reason for making those movies was to make me and my friends laugh. With *Pink Flamingos* I basically made a movie that would make fun of "political correctness". Obviously that phrase didn't exist then, but this was the early 1970s and there was still all that 1960s peace and love stuff around. So to make a movie for hippies that praised violence was very politically incorrect. What I was trying to do was to make all the liberals realise that *they* have limits even though they always think they don't. *I'm* a liberal, my audience is liberal, and what I'm always trying to do is to make humor about that grey line of how far you can go.[17]

Nick Salvato notes that "the trash spectacle is an exhibition of bad taste; it flouts a community's standards by flaunting whatever that community considers crude, vulgar, or obscene."[18] The sociopolitical landscape of America in the early 1970s profoundly influenced Waters' films. This era, marked by the aftermath of the 1960s counterculture movements and the rise of conservatism, was a time of significant social upheaval and shifting norms. The hippie culture, with its emphasis on free love, anti-establishment sentiments, and experimental lifestyles, finds a distorted reflection in Waters' films. He captures the energy and perversion of this period, transforming the idealism of the '60s into a more cynical, satirical vision. The sexual liberation and questioning of authority that characterized the hippie movement are exaggerated to the point of absurdity, serving both as a critique and a celebration of countercultural impulses. Therefore, "Waters' films do not merely 'disgust,' but rather provide a 'twisted' and self-aware meditation on what it means, at our historical moment, to be disgusted or disgusting."[19]

Waters' depiction of filth is symbolic, representing the dirt lurking beneath the polished surface of American society. His films expose the contradictions and hypocrisies of the era, particularly the disjunction between public virtue and private vice. The characters' extreme behaviors and the film's embrace of "trash" aesthetics are acts of defiance against a culture that often equates worth with cleanliness and conformity. By reveling in what society deems obscene or worthless, Waters challenges viewers to reconsider their values and the true nature of decency. His films, through their vivid and unapologetic embrace of filth, offer a powerful commentary on the social and moral landscape of

America in the early 1970s, questioning who determines what is considered respectable or deviant.

Waters is a central figure in the White trash studies, which became popular in the 1980s and 1990s as a way to critique representations and misrepresentations of lower-class white culture.[20] His films are noted for their "unequivocal celebrations of white trash culture" where "[w]hite trash figures are always represented as heroes, as underdogs who overcome adversity and middle-class repression through the strangest and most unlikely means."[21] Baltimore, Waters' hometown and the setting for many of his films, provides a rich sociopolitical context for these narratives. His films repeatedly "celebrate the offbeat quality" of the city.[22] As a Baltimore native who has consistently filmed in his hometown, Waters' work exemplifies image-making that crosses both space and place.[23] The city's working-class roots and its own struggles with crime, poverty, and social change mirror the themes of disintegration and rebellion in his films. These films depict Baltimore as a haven for delinquents and miscreants, highlighting sociospatial exclusion through encounters with abject individuals and events.[24] In *Pink Flamingos*, he exemplifies the contemptible behavior often stereotyped in urban areas. Waters uses these portrayals to celebrate the lurid, salacious, and dissident elements of society, suggesting they should be cherished rather than feared or suppressed.[25] Trash aesthetics takes inspiration from working-class fashion and brings together a range of practices and cultural products that are

Figure 10.1 Babs Johnson's trailer, located on the outskirts of Phoenix, Maryland, is seen with a gazing ball and a pair of plastic pink flamingos in front of it, capturing the kitsch aesthetic central to John Waters' *Pink Flamingos*.

characterized by their low value and widespread media presence.[26] Baltimore becomes a character in itself, reflecting the raw, unvarnished reality that contrasts with the sanitized version of America portrayed in mainstream media. In *Pink Flamingos*, the urban decay and industrial backdrops underscore the film's themes of filth and abjection. The city's gritty authenticity amplifies the shock value of the characters' transgressions, grounding their outrageousness in a recognizable, albeit extreme, reality.

The concept of abjection is "the impossible desire to transcend corporeality."[27] *Pink Flamingos* is notorious for its deliberate embrace of the abject. The film's exploration of filth, bodily functions, and extreme behaviors pushes the boundaries of societal norms and highlights the tension between the desire to transcend physical limitations and the inescapable reality of the body. The character of Divine, who competes to be the "filthiest person alive," engages in acts that are viscerally repulsive and shocking. These acts include everything from cannibalism to eating dog faeces. The disgust and horror associated with the abject are reflected in such filthy acts. The abject is about "representing unmentionable elements of the self that are vigorously to be kept subliminal."[28] Through these extreme representations of bodily excess and degradation, Waters forces the audience to confront the abject directly. The film's relentless focus on the physical and the base aspects of human existence underscores the impossibility of escaping corporeality. Divine's character, with her exaggerated drag persona, embodies a form of abjection that challenges normative ideas of beauty, gender, and identity. The drag performance itself is an act of transcending ordinary physical limits and societal expectations, creating a new, flamboyant identity that defies conventional gender roles. However, by engaging in abject acts, Divine also reminds us of the inescapable reality of the body and its functions. The desire to transcend corporeality through the creation of a larger-than-life persona is always brought back to the grotesque realities of the physical body. In *Pink Flamingos*, the abject is not just about filth and degradation; it is also about the struggle and failure to maintain a clean, distinct identity separate from the bodily and the impure. The film's celebration of filth and the abject reflects a rebellion against the sanitized, repressive norms of suburban America, exposing the hypocrisy and artificiality of its moral standards.

Waters uses the characters and settings in *Pink Flamingos* to critique the impossibility of escaping the physical and the abject, regardless of one's environment. In the film, the veneer of societal decency and order is symbolized by the contrasting lifestyles of Babs Johnson and the Marbles. Babs and her family live in a dilapidated trailer in the woods, embracing filth and perversion openly, while the Marbles, who reside in a relatively conventional home, maintain an outward appearance of propriety. However, the Marbles' own grotesque behavior and criminal activities reveal the underlying abjection and corruption that exists beneath their façade of respectability. By juxtaposing these two settings, Waters shatters the illusion that any environment, suburban or otherwise, can fully repress the abject. The film brings repressed elements into the open, showing that societal norms and cleanliness are mere surfaces over inherent human filth and immorality. This critique extends beyond the physical settings to challenge the broader societal attempt to hide and suppress the abject aspects of human existence. The film's infamous scenes are a confrontation with the parts of human existence that society tries to hide or deny, illustrating the persistent, unavoidable presence of the abject. Ultimately, *Pink Flamingos* demonstrates that the desire to transcend corporeality is impossible because the abject is an inherent part of human existence. By embracing the abject, the film reveals the continuous, underlying presence of bodily realities that cannot be fully transcended or ignored. This confrontation with the abject disrupts conventional social and aesthetic boundaries, forcing the audience to acknowledge and grapple with the corporeal aspects of their own existence.

Shock remains an integral aspect of this abjection. Waters deliberately employs shocking imagery and scenarios to jolt viewers out of complacency and force a visceral reaction, making the abject impossible to dismiss. This combination of abjection and shock not only critiques societal norms but also aligns Waters' work with the tradition of shock cinema, which seeks to provoke and unsettle audiences to encourage deeper reflection on societal taboos and personal discomforts. Through this dual approach, Waters effectively uses shock to enhance the impact of abjection, ensuring that the challenge to conventional perceptions is both immediate and profound.

The maternal abject is described as a result of the separation of an infant from its mother and the subsequent construction and development of the child's identity.[29] Following this separation, the child's body and identity are "mapped" through language acquisition and the internalization of societal norms and taboos.[30] This process integrates the individual into a specific social structure and further solidifies their identity within that context.[31] The suburban setting in Waters' films plays a crucial role in accentuating this moral decay. The early 1970s in America was a period marked by a façade of suburban bliss that often concealed profound social and familial dysfunction. The pristine lawns and cookie-cutter homes of suburbia become a backdrop against which the abject and the monstrous stand out starkly. Waters' mothers, with their perverse behaviors and grotesque excesses, reveal the cracks in this façade, suggesting that the real perversion lies not in their actions but in the hypocrisy and repression of suburban life itself. These characters serve as a critique of the societal norms that seek to suppress deviance and maintain a veneer of order and decency, only to perpetuate a deeper, more insidious form of decay.

John Waters films the maternal abject in a way that refuses to allow the spectator to look away, using both close-ups and long takes to confront the viewer with the grotesque and the obscene. In scenes with Divine, Waters often employs extreme close-ups that emphasize the exaggerated makeup, expressions, and actions, forcing the audience to confront the abject up close and personal. For example, the infamous dog feces-eating scene in *Pink Flamingos* is filmed in a tight close-up, making it impossible for viewers to escape the visceral impact of the moment. Additionally, Waters uses long takes that linger on grotesque actions and situations without cutting away, such as the prolonged scenes of chaos and depravity in *Female Trouble*. This technique compels the audience to endure the discomfort and abjection, breaking down any distance between the spectator and the abject. By refusing to provide an easy escape or reprieve, Waters ensures that the viewer must grapple with the abject realities he presents, thereby intensifying the critique of societal norms and the superficiality of conventional maternal ideals.

Waters' depiction of abject motherhood thus serves as both a symbol and a critique. The monstrous maternal figures challenge viewers to confront their own perceptions of normalcy and deviance, forcing a re-evaluation of what constitutes moral and social integrity. By situating these figures in the decaying suburbs of Baltimore, Waters draws a direct line between the personal and the political, suggesting that the rot in American society is as much a product of its own contradictions and hypocrisies as it is of the individual transgressions of his characters. His films become a lens through which the dysfunctions of the 1970s—the clash between conservative values and burgeoning countercultures, the economic struggles, and the shifting social mores—are examined and satirized. The monstrous mothers in his films are not merely figures of shock and repulsion but are also agents of critique, exposing the underlying tensions and hypocrisies of their suburban environments. Through his use of Baltimore's sociopolitical landscape, Waters roots these critiques in a specific cultural and historical context, making his films not just grotesque spectacles but also pointed social commentaries.

An important aspect of Waters' cinema is that it is "an intersection of cult and queer cinema" which "plays with comedy, transgression and shock value."[32] His treatment of sexuality, violence, queer politics, dark humor, social taboos, and cultural norms in his films shows the extent to which cinema as a creative medium and aesthetic practice can be pushed to its extreme limits. The representation of abject motherhood in his films intertwines with themes of queer identity, most notably through the central character of Divine. Divine's drag queen body embodies a white trash identity,[33] which in the context of queerness and motherhood challenges and subverts traditional notions of family, gender, and sexuality. Waters' use of Divine as a grotesque "drag queen" figure reflects the "gender slippage" and queer politics that challenge traditional notions of femininity by exaggerating and distorting them.[34] In *Pink Flamingos* and *Female Trouble*, Divine's portrayal of maternal figures not only underscores the grotesque and abject but also positions the character as a queer mother, embodying the intersection of drag and motherhood. In *Pink Flamingos*, Babs, with exaggerated makeup and costumes, distorts traditional femininity. Her role as a mother mocks conventional nurturing, creating a family dynamic that perversely inverts the idealized nuclear family. Similarly, in *Female Trouble*, Dawn Davenport transforms from a rebellious teenager to a notorious criminal and abusive mother, with her exaggerated femininity and violent behavior critiquing traditional maternal roles. Waters' portrayal of Divine as a maternal figure in drag highlights the fluidity of gender and the performative aspects of both motherhood and femininity. By using Divine's drag persona, Waters exposes the constructed nature of these roles, queering motherhood to challenge normative gender expectations and celebrate alternative forms of family and care. This portrayal disrupts conventional moral parameters and critiques the heteronormative structures of suburban America.

Mike Kelley observes that "Waters celebrates 'queerness' for its abject nature relative to dominant American society. One need not search for an outside aesthetic in his films, because 'you,' the supposedly empathic film viewer, already represent the other."[35] In *Pink Flamingos*, Babs is introduced as the "filthiest person alive," living with her family in a trailer outside Baltimore. The family unit here is anything but conventional; Babs' mother, Edie, is infantilized and addicted to eggs, while Babs herself engages in criminal activities to maintain her filthy reputation. Divine's maternal role is inherently queer, not just because of her drag identity but also because of how she subverts traditional

Figure 10.2 Babs Johnson (Divine) sits next to her mother, Edie (Edith Massey), in a playpen, sharing a moment over a basket of hard-boiled eggs in John Waters' *Pink Flamingos*.

Figure 10.3 Babs Johnson (Divine) and her son Crackers (Danny Mills) break into the home of their rivals, Connie and Raymond Marble. In an act of revenge, Babs begins licking objects to spread their "filth," showcasing the film's outrageous and rebellious spirit in *Pink Flamingos*.

motherhood. Instead of nurturing, Babs revels in perversion and deviance, embodying an abject form of motherhood that defies societal norms. In one scene, Divine and her delinquent son Crackers trespass into the home of their jealous rivals Connie and Raymond Marble, a couple who try to surpass Divine in terms of "filthiness." In the Marbles' house, Divine and Crackers engage in unconventional behavior by licking and rubbing the furniture to transfer their filth, an act that arouses them to the point where Divine performs oral sex on Crackers. The incestual sexual act between Divine and her son gives a transgressive image of the mother figure that Divine represents. However, in the context of the film, which celebrates "filthiness" and abjection, this devours the moral boundaries of relationships, identity, and aesthetic representation of desire. Waters, when asked about this infamous scene, emphasized the satirical aspect of its relevance in the "porno chic" era where films like *Deep Throat* were sensational and hard-core pornography was becoming mainstream.[36]

In the film, the setting of the Marbles house, a typically domestic and private space, becomes a site of radical queer action. The unconventional behavior within this space challenges the notion of the home as a sanctuary of traditional values and normative family structures. In the house's basement, the Marbles run a black-market baby ring by kidnapping young women, having them impregnated by their manservant Channing, and selling the babies to lesbian couples. The profits from this operation are used to fund pornography shops and support a network of heroin dealers targeting inner-city elementary schools. Divine and Crackers find Channing and come across two pregnant women imprisoned in the basement. Using a large knife, they free the women, who then castrate Channing with the knife. The discovery and subsequent liberation of the pregnant woman in the basement can be seen as a metaphor for challenging and breaking free from societal oppression. The use of a knife to free the women symbolizes an active, rebellious stance against patriarchal control, embodied by Channing's character. The emasculation of Channing by the women represents a powerful reversal of traditional gender roles and power dynamics. In a heteronormative context, masculinity is often associated with power and control. By castrating Channing, the women (aided by Divine and Crackers) symbolically dismantle these patriarchal structures, asserting a form of queer empowerment and resistance. Michael Moon and Eve Kosofsky Sedgwick observe that *Pink Flamingos* has a subversive portrayal of food and the body. The film blurs the boundaries between consumption, body, and waste.[37] For example, the scene where Divine inserts a raw steak into her crotch, recontextualizes the food item into a symbol laden with complex meanings—panty substitute, sanitary napkin, genital stimulation, and a critique of fatphobia. This act challenges the conventional lifecycle of food from animal to waste, instead imbuing it with alternative, provocative significances.[38] Through these scenes, queerness is portrayed not just as a matter of sexual orientation, but as a broader challenge to societal norms and an assertion of freedom and resistance against oppressive structures.

The perversions of Raymond are also subverted in the film. Raymond engages in exhibitionism, often using shock value to scare women and steal their money. He ties a large kielbasa sausage and a turkey neck to his penis and exposes himself to women. The shock and horror of this exposure typically cause the women to flee, at which point Raymond steals their purses. However, later in the film, Raymond's scheme backfires when he attempts to target a trans woman. Instead of reacting with fear and fleeing, the trans woman responds by exposing her own body, revealing her breast, penis, and scrotum. This unexpected and bold reaction catches Raymond off guard, reversing the power dynamic and causing him to flee in shock. Similarly, in another scene, where Channing dresses in Connie's clothes and mimics her, there is a subtle reference to queer politics by highlighting themes of subversion, visibility, and marginalization. Channing's cross-dressing and mockery can be seen as a form of resistance against the oppressive and controlling Marbles, who represent societal norms and power structures. His imitation and ridicule challenge the authority and superiority of the Marbles, exposing the performative nature of their own roles and the fragility of their power. However, the Marbles themselves are complex figures that complicate this interpretation. As Babs' primary competition for the title of "filthiest person alive," they also embody elements of queerness and subversion. The Marbles' queered sexuality is evident in their explicit sex scenes, and their baby farm for queer women, despite being exploitative, shows a twisted form of support for marginalized identities. Their unconventional physical appearance, with red and blue hair, further marks them as outsiders to traditional norms. These details suggest that the Marbles, while representing certain power structures, also challenge conventional boundaries and embody a form of subversive counterculture.

Acknowledging these complexities, Channing's mockery can still be seen as resistance, but it is resistance within a world where all characters, including the Marbles, participate in the transgression of societal norms. This layered depiction highlights the performative nature of all identities and power structures in the film, suggesting that authority and subversion are not clear-cut opposites but are instead intertwined in a continuous struggle for dominance and recognition. Thus, while Channing's actions undermine the Marbles' power, they also reflect the broader theme of performative identity that pervades *Pink Flamingos*, reinforcing the film's critique of societal norms through its embrace of the grotesque and the abject. The Marbles' reaction—firing Channing and confining him to a closet—serves as a metaphor for the historical and ongoing oppression of queer individuals, who have often been forced into hiding or "closeted" due to societal rejection. This punishment underscores the punitive measures faced by those who dare to transgress or mock normative boundaries, reflecting the harsh realities of queer existence in a heteronormative world. The scene encapsulates the struggle for visibility and autonomy within a system that seeks to silence and marginalize non-conforming identities.

Queer dress emphasizes gender performativity, affirming that gender identity is not fixed or biologically determined, but shaped by power relations and discourse. In such power structures, "dress might function as a disruptive political strategy when it is manipulated, or ridiculed, by the ones who use it as such, against actors who just use style as an individualistic aestheticized way of existing."[39] Isabelle Held observes that Waters' deliberately provocative films challenged beauty standards in American cinema, attracting a cult following of self-identified outsiders.[40] For example, the diamond-studded cat-eye glasses worn by Mink Stole as Connie Marble in *Pink Flamingos*, and the Frederick's of Hollywood "Zingy Zip-up" black patent heels worn by Edith Massey as Aunt Ida in *Female Trouble*, challenged conventional views on sexual orientation.[41] Massey's character notably lamented her nephew "coming out" as straight, declaring that "queers are just better [. . .] the world of heterosexual is a sick and boring life."

Elizabeth Grosz interprets Kristeva's abject in the context of motherhood: "Like the abject, maternity is the splitting, fusing, merging, fragmenting of a series of bodily processes outside the will or control of the subject."[42] The maternal body here is not a site of purity or sanctity but one of transgression and excess, aligning with Barbara Creed's concept of the "monstrous-feminine" in horror.[43] This suggests that the maternal figure often embodies abjection, disrupting social and symbolic boundaries through a mix of fascination and disgust. The scenes involving bodily processes—such as the infamous act of eating dog feces—highlight the uncontrollable, fragmenting nature of the body. This controversial scene suggests that the concept of the abject, which encompasses things that are socially or psychologically repulsive and threatening, can be made more understandable and controllable by associating it with tangible and familiar objects that evoke fear or disgust (like blood, germs, guts, feces, and vomit). These concrete objects act as symbolic representations of deeper, unsettling experiences or traumas that individuals may encounter in life.[44] By relating these abject objects to specific fears or anxieties, individuals can then attempt to cope with or manage these unsettling experiences within their own mental framework.

The combination of filth and motherhood in Waters' films destabilizes normative structures. This portrayal not only questions the binaries of good and bad, clean and dirty but also subverts the idea that motherhood is inherently pure or virtuous. By presenting motherhood through a lens of filth and abjection, Waters confronts the viewer with the uncomfortable reality that these categories are socially constructed and inherently unstable. In *Pink Flamingos*, Babs' actions can be seen as a form of reclaiming power or control over her identity and circumstances. In embracing the abject, she defies conventional notions of femininity and motherhood, asserting her own agency and autonomy outside societal expectations. This defiance is central to the film's critique of suburban morality and the hypocrisy underlying middle-class values. By portraying Babs as a character who not only engages with but revels in the abject, Waters challenges viewers to reconsider their own perceptions of what is acceptable or normal, pushing boundaries and confronting the discomforts associated with the abject in a confrontational and provocative manner.

Through these cinematic techniques, Waters invites the audience to reconsider the rigid boundaries that define acceptable behavior and identity. Divine's drag queen mother identity becomes a powerful symbol of resistance against these boundaries. The exaggerated performances, grotesque scenarios, and overt sexuality of Waters' films force viewers to confront their own discomfort with the abject and the queer. This confrontation is not merely for shock value but serves as a critical examination of the societal forces that marginalize and oppress those who do not conform to dominant norms. In this way, Waters' films are deeply political, using the aesthetics of filth and the concept of abject motherhood to challenge and destabilize the status quo. Divine's characters, with their exaggerated femininity and deviant behaviors, embody a form of motherhood that defies traditional gender roles and highlights the fluidity of identity. The drag performance itself is an act of transcending and subverting gender norms, creating a space for queer identities to challenge and resist societal expectations. By presenting the queer mom as a monstrous feminine figure, Waters not only critiques the limitations imposed by patriarchal society but also celebrates the radical potential of queer identities to disrupt and transform these norms.

John Waters' cinema, particularly *Pink Flamingos*, represents queerness and motherhood, as a combination of radical critique of societal norms and suburban morality. Waters' films portray the concept of the "maternal abject" through the central character of Divine, whose grotesque and deviant behaviors starkly contrast with traditional maternal ideals. Divine's iconic characters such as Babs Johnson and Dawn Davenport embody a queer form of motherhood that challenges and subverts heteronormative family structures, positioning filth and abjection as central themes. This juxtaposition of filth and motherhood not only highlights the moral decay in suburban environments but also celebrates the resilience and defiance of marginalized identities. Waters uses the suburban setting of Baltimore to reinforce these themes, providing a backdrop that mirrors the dysfunction and hypocrisy of middle-class American life. The portrayal of abject queer motherhood in Waters' films serves as a critique of the artificiality and repression inherent in suburban ideals, using the aesthetics of trash and the grotesque to expose the contradictions within societal norms. Through Divine's drag mother queen identity, Waters constructs a powerful symbol of resistance against conventional gender and family roles, challenging viewers to reconsider their own perceptions of morality and decency. By embracing filth and abjection, Waters' characters reclaim agency and identity in defiance of societal constraints. This approach not only entertains but provokes critical thought about the social structures that marginalize those who do not conform. Waters' films, with their unique blend of shock, humor, and social commentary, invite audiences to confront their discomfort with the abject and the queer, making a profound statement about the fluidity and instability of cultural categories.

NOTES

1. Julia Kristeva, *Powers of Horror* (New York: Columbia University Press, 1982), 4.
2. Ibid.
3. Charles Penwarden, "Of Word and Flesh: An Interview with Julia Kristeva," in *Rites of Passage: Art for the End of the Century* (London: Tate Gallery Publications, 1995), 22.
4. Emanuel Levy, *Gay Directors, Gay Films?: Pedro Almodóvar, Terence Davies, Todd Haynes, Gus Van Sant, John Waters* (New York: Columbia University Press, 2015).
5. Mary Carole McCauley, "Baltimore Museum of Art Opens Its John Waters Exhibit Sunday—And It Is as Weird as You Might Expect," *The Baltimore Sun*, October 5, 2018.
6. John Waters and Hilton Als, "The Duke of Dirt," *Grand Street* 53 (1995): 10–23.
7. Dennis Harvey, "The Godfather of Gross-Out," *Film Comment* 36, no. 4 (2000): 34.
8. Hazel Cills, "Teenage Girls Assaulted by Wild Animals! An Interview with John Waters," *Rookie*, February 17, 2012.

9. John Waters, *Shock Value: A Tasteful Book about Bad Taste* (New York: Thunder's Mouth Press, 2005), 2.
10. Konstantinos Eleftheriadis, "'Not Yet Queer Enough': Constructing Identity through Culture," in *Queer Festivals* (Amsterdam: Amsterdam University Press, 2018).
11. John Waters, "Out on the Edge," *Index on Censorship* 24, no. 6 (1995): 10.
12. Ingrid Lyons, "Unapologetic Protagonist," *Irish Arts Review* 36, no. 3 (2019): 83.
13. Elena Gorfinkel, "Cult Film or Cinephilia by Any Other Name," *Cinéaste* 34, no. 1 (2008): 33–38.
14. Daniel Herbert, *Maverick Movies: New Line Cinema and the Transformation of American Film* (Oakland, CA: University of California Press, 2024).
15. Jack Stevenson, "From the Bedroom to the Bijou: A Secret History of American Gay Sex Cinema," *Film Quarterly* 51, no. 1 (1997): 24–31.
16. Jenny He, "John Waters: Pope of Trash an Introduction," in *John Waters: Pope of Trash*, edited by Jenny He and Darra Jaffe (New York: DelMonico Books, 2023), 18.
17. John Waters, "Out on the Edge," *Index on Censorship* 24, no. 6 (1995): 9–19.
18. Nick Salvato, "Tramp Sensibility and the Afterlife of 'Showgirls'," *Theatre Journal* 58, no. 4 (2006): 638.
19. Ibid., 639.
20. Tammie M. Kennedy, Joyce Irene Middleton, and Krista Ratcliffe, "The Matter of Whiteness: Or, Why Whiteness Studies Is Important to Rhetoric and Composition Studies," *Rhetoric Review* 24, no. 4 (2005): 359–373.
21. Daniel Mudie Cunningham, "The 'Film' on Whiteness: Depicting White Trash in U.S. Film, 1972–2002" (Ph.D. diss., University of Western Sydney, 2004), 151–152.
22. Chris Kaltenbach, "Divine Fans Want to Build a Monument to Late Actor," *The Baltimore Sun*, January 18, 2016.
23. Nathan Koob, "The Gentrification of John Waters," *Film Criticism* 43, no. 1 (2019).
24. Dennis Wayne Everette, "The Filthiest People Alive: Productions of Urban Spaces and Populations in the Films of John Waters" (MA thesis, Miami University, 2011).
25. Ibid.
26. Konstantinos Eleftheriadis, "'Not Yet Queer Enough': Constructing Identity through Culture," in *Queer Festivals* (Amsterdam: Amsterdam University Press, 2018).
27. Elizabeth Grosz, *Sexual Subversions* (Sydney: Allen & Unwin, 1989), 79.
28. Rosemary H. Balsam, "The Embodied Mother: Commentary on Kristeva," *Journal of the American Psychoanalytic Association* 62 (2014): 94.
29. Ibid., 87–100; Mireille Astore, "The Maternal Abject" (Dissertation, Sydney College of the Arts, The University of Sydney, 2002).
30. Julia Kristeva, *Powers of Horror* (New York: Columbia University Press, 1982), 72.
31. Kelly Oliver, ed., *The Portable Kristeva* (New York: Columbia University Press, 1997).
32. Elisa Padilla, "The Baltimore Artist: Taste, Class, and Distinction in John Waters' *Pecker*," *Quarterly Review of Film and Video* 39, no. 2 (2022): 341–359.
33. Daniel Mudie Cunningham, "The 'Film' on Whiteness: Depicting White Trash in U.S. Film, 1972–2002" (Ph.D. diss., University of Western Sydney, 2004).
34. Mike Kelley, "Cross-Gender/Cross-Genre," in *Foul Perfection: Essays and Criticism*, edited by John C. Welchman (Cambridge, MA: The MIT Press, 2003), 106.
35. Ibid., 106.
36. John Waters, "Out on the Edge," *Index on Censorship* 24, no. 6 (1995): 11–12.
37. Michael Moon and Eve Kosofsky Sedgwick, "Divinity: A Dossier, A Performance Piece, A Little-Understood Emotion," *Discourse* 13, no. 1 (1990): 12–39.
38. Ibid., 33.

39. Konstantinos Eleftheriadis, "'Not Yet Queer Enough': Constructing Identity through Culture," in *Queer Festivals* (Amsterdam: Amsterdam University Press, 2018), 134.
40. Isabelle Held, "John Waters: Pope of Trash," *Fashion Theory* (2024).
41. Ibid.
42. Elizabeth Grosz, *Sexual Subversions* (Sydney: Allen & Unwin, 1989), 79.
43. Barbara Creed, "Horror and the Monstrous-Feminine: An Imaginary Abjection," *Screen* 27, no. 1 (1986): 44–71.
44. Andrea Celenza, "Maternal Erotic Transferences and the Work of the Abject," *Journal of the American Psychoanalytic Association* 70, no. 1 (2022): 9–38.

CHAPTER 11

Fame! Fortune! Glamour!: John Waters Remembers Midcentury TV

Hollis Griffin

When Tracy Turnblad (Ricki Lake), the working-class teen girl protagonist in *Hairspray* (1988), realizes some of the perks that will attend her selection for a role on a locally-produced television variety program for teens in Baltimore, Maryland, she exclaims: "Oh my God! Fame, fortune, glamour!" In keeping with the movie's ironic sensibility, this line operates as a joke insofar as any celebrity resulting from a role on a local television program in a largely working-class city in the early 1960s is well below the scale and plenitude to which terms like "fame," "fortune," and "glamour" might refer. But the fantasies of transcendence that the overweight teen ascribes to her new role on the fictive *The Corny Collins Show* are meaningful to her, her friends, and the teen audience that the program courts in the movie's diegesis. More importantly, though, the hopefulness and optimism that characterize Tracy's dialogue in this scene point to the fantasies of transcendence that *Hairspray* attributes to postwar television. The movie's play with the signs and signifiers of postwar fashion, music, and popular culture in the United States (U.S.) is not a depoliticized hagiography of the power of television at midcentury. Rather, the movie uses a television variety program to narrate struggles around race, class, and space/place that characterized the era in which it is set.

Hairspray is one of several Waters movies that construct viewing positions for audiences that draw on modes of address associated with television, especially midcentury television, for the purposes of humor, pleasure, and commentary on bourgeois social norms. When considering *Hairspray* alongside *Pink Flamingos* (1972), *Female Trouble* (1974), *Polyester* (1981), and *Serial Mom* (1994), Waters' attention to television unites seemingly disparate objects in his filmography. What do the films of John Waters tell us about television and what does television tell us about the films of John Waters? Waters' engagement with film history and culture, as well as his affection for cultural forms typically relegated to the bottom of conventional aesthetic hierarchies (e.g. tabloids, melodramas), are oft-discussed elements of his oeuvre. The director's fondness for television is typically only implicit in this commentary. Using historically-embedded close readings, the chapter demonstrates how Waters invokes genres associated with the medium during its earliest decades, especially variety shows, soap operas, and tabloid news. These television genres are the means by which Waters centers class, race, gender, and sexuality diversity in his movies to rejoice in deviance; they are the vehicles through which he champions the odd and aberrant and celebrates scenarios that run afoul of conventional tastes and social norms. As such, the chapter builds on the large body of work that examines the aesthetics and politics of Waters' movies to argue that midcentury television provides a useful lens for understanding the director's stylistic and ideological investments. Using formalist and narrative elements of three television genres—variety shows, soap operas, and tabloid news—the chapter illustrates how Waters' movies feature familiar stock characters and plots, well-established syntactic arrangements in shot sequences, and strategic use of sound and music to provide metacommentary on midcentury television and the social mores associated with the medium during that era. In bringing television to the fore in this way, the chapter complicates common understandings of Waters' work and his influences.

The verb of the title—"remember"—is a strategic choice because of its open-endedness in terms of subject, object, and valence. Given that Waters' references to midcentury television are used for different ends and are sometimes more explicit than others, it would be imprecise to say that he or the movies themselves "remember" television in any consistent way. Furthermore, metonyms for remembering like "nostalgia" and "parody" are also inaccurate given that the former is often associated with a desire to return to some simpler time and the latter points to a critical remove that Waters, in the affection he expresses for his source material, disavows. His movies do not condescend to or express a desire to return to prior moments, nor do they mock or disparage the cultural forms to which they refer. To that end, "pastiche" is probably the term that best characterizes how Waters' movies remember midcentury television—though not in the most widespread use of that concept. Critics often use "pastiche" to point to an ideologically empty imitation of cultural texts from prior eras. For instance, Frederic Jameson famously cast pastiche as being "amputated" from any political project—"devoid of laughter and of any conviction," equating it to "a statue with blind eyeballs."[1] In contrast, critics more firmly situated in cultural studies use pastiche more loosely, to signify the processes by which works of art combine ideas drawn from other works of art for a range of different ideological ends. For instance, Richard Dyer has cast pastiche as "a kind of imitation that you are meant to know is an imitation."[2] He identifies pastiche as a form of combination that operates across many different fields—language, needlework, cuisine—in which "mixtures . . . preserve the separate flavor of each element, not melting ingredients together indissolubly, nor taking bits so small that any other identity is lost."[3] Waters' movies employ this second notion of pastiche in merging different narrative and formalist elements from midcentury television in ways that provide evidence of the director's well-established desire to reverse aesthetic hierarchies, champion social outcasts, and applaud deviations from established cultural norms. Paying attention to how the films of John Waters draw upon midcentury television reveals a great deal about the movies themselves as well as the medium and history on which they comment.

SPECTACLE, CELEBRITY, AND THE VARIETY SHOW

In *Hairspray*, *The Corny Collins Show* recalls variety programs produced by local television stations like *American Bandstand* (WFIL, Philadelphia, 1952–1957; ABC, 1957–1987, 1992, 2002; Syndicated, 1987–1988; U.S.A., 1989) and *The Buddy Deane Show* (WJZ, Baltimore, 1957–1964), which targeted teen audiences with broadcasts scheduled in the afternoon built around teens dancing to popular music. But the fantasies that *Hairspray* yokes to early television and Baltimore are at once broader and grander than can be explained by its references to that subgenre alone. *The Corny Collins Show* is the vehicle through which ordinary people—in the case of *Hairspray*, "ordinariness" is signified by an overweight, charismatic white teenaged protagonist—are brought into the medium's symbolic order and invited to participate in its status conferral functions. In its plot about black teens trying to appear on the program alongside their white peers, *Hairspray* raises the specter of the racialized dynamics of power at work in U.S. cities during the postwar period. Here, "ordinariness" is whiteness, specifically, and nothing else. In narrating how television station managers sought to erase blackness for the purposes of attempting to guarantee the comfort of advertisers, *Hairspray* animates a hopeful vision of television's ideological labors in U.S. culture: if black teens can dance on *Corny Collins*, it is a small victory for basic human decency in the world in which the program circulates.

At the same time, the movie underlines important disconnects between the world as constructed by television and the world off-screen. In *Hairspray*, television's representational regime is no neat mirror of reality; rather, it is one rooted in the painful material struggles of race and class. Caetlin Benson-Allott characterizes this ideological sleight of hand as a "critical mousetrap" that asks "viewers to identify with a nostalgic vision of the 1960s while it simultaneously camps that nostalgic mode to reveal the depoliticizing impulses that drive it."[4] In doing so, the movie emphasizes how U.S. television's multiple discursive registers can make for uneasy bedfellows, where tensions between the medium's mission to communicate for the public good sit in pointed conflict with, in the context of the postwar U.S., its private ownership structure and commercial funding model.

Hairspray accomplishes this commentary on midcentury television most plainly in the sequences wherein it establishes the characters as viewers of *The Corny Collins Show*. Throughout the narrative, action moves between the studio space of the program and characters watching the program on their television sets. In one scene, Tracy and her best friend Penny Pingleton (Leslie Ann Powers) dance in the Turnblad family living room as if they were at the studio themselves. In another scene, Tracy's mother Edna (Divine) watches the program as an acquaintance—a white middle-aged woman—criticizes how *Corny Collins* features white teens dancing to music performed by black singers. In a third scene, Edna watches Tracy perform on the program and worries about her daughter's hair and whether or not she is too young to be dancing on television. These scenes encapsulate how *Hairspray* casts television as a site of struggle over social norms related to race, class, gender, and sexuality. The movie narrates the spectacle *of* the program in the diegesis but, in doing so, it problematizes spectacle *on* the program as well. Tracy Turnblad is an unlikely star even by local television standards; her working-class parents cannot afford the detached suburban homes or cars or closets full of clothing that the other teens who appear on *The Corny Collins Show* enjoy. In addition, her overweight body further marks the character as "Other" in the diegesis; the other

Figure 11.1 In *Hairspray*, teenage protagonist Tracy Turnblad (Ricki Lake) and her friend dance in the family living room while watching an afternoon variety program that targets teen audiences.

female characters are petite, demure, and more conventionally feminine. But in *Hairspray*, Tracy displays confidence and pluck—especially on the dancefloor. So in the scenes in which Tracy dances amongst the other, richer, thinner teens in *The Corny Collins Show*'s studio, *Hairspray* literalizes the cultural work of a television variety show.

In scenes devoted to the program, the movie triangulates between shots of the dancing teens who star in the program, the teens in the studio who attend tapings, and the audiences watching the show from home. In doing so, the movie highlights how variety programs do not necessarily render as spectacle some event happening beyond the realm of the televisual. More precisely: it manufactures an event and invites viewers to participate, collapsing the space between being in the program as a regular star, appearing on the program in the background, and watching the show from your home television set. However tacitly, the logic suggests: anybody at all can appear on the program; its fantasies of publicness are open to everyone. In her work on the relationship between spectacle and democracy as they operate in variety as a genre that crosses different media (television, theater, and so on), Meghan Sutherland suggests that representations of the audience make concrete the ideological labors of popular entertainment: "variety's . . . reputation as a popular medium takes a . . . literal form in its emphasis on the populace that sanctions and consumes it."[5] The program as constructed by *Hairspray* highlights the democracy of variety as a genre insofar as it makes room for an unconventional teen girl in its representational regime and champions her in doing so. At the same time, the movie's insistence on applauding a young white girl highlights the limits of its source material where matters of race are concerned.

Hairspray's narration of historical events through a plot that revolves around a midcentury television variety program looks back at the past in the interest of criticism. But I see Waters' engagement with the variety show elsewhere in his oeuvre in less extant though still pointed ways, for different though still distinctly Watersian ideological ends. In *Female Trouble*, teen girl protagonist Dawn Davenport (Divine) attacks her parents after they refuse to buy her cha-cha heels for Christmas, gets pregnant while hitchhiking in an attempt to run away from home, and ends up working a series of dead-end jobs in an attempt to make ends meet: waiting tables, stripping, prostitution. Dawn falls in with the owners of the beauty shop she frequents, Donald (David Lochary) and Donna Dasher (Mary Vivian Pierce), after marrying the man who does her hair, Gater (Michael Potter). After Dawn and Gater divorce, she convinces the Dashers to fire him. In response, they recruit her to become part of "an artistic experiment" in which they cajole Dawn to perform crimes by assuring her that doing so will bring her notoriety and acclaim—much like the fantasies that Tracy Turnblad associates with television stardom in *Hairspray*. Where Tracy's fantasies of transcendence are wholesome and moral, Dawn's fantasies of transcendence are outrageous and criminal. Over the course of *Female Trouble*, Dawn descends into mania and psychosis; the Dasher's promise of celebrity is accompanied by changes in appearance that feature Dawn wearing increasingly bizarre hairstyles and outfits designed by her Svengalis. Both movies play with ideas about gender and bodies, the fantasies attending stardom and celebrity, as well as how media culture stages spectacles for audience pleasure.

Female Trouble's play with ideas about midcentury television is less obvious than the one offered in *Hairspray* but no less vital to the commentary it offers on celebrity and spectacle; it also uses the formalist characteristics of variety programs to do that work. The logic of the variety show—which foregrounds the overlap between the people depicted on screen and the people in the audience—is also at work in Waters' use of the Dreamlanders, the regular cast and crew the director culled from his friendship circle in Baltimore. As Chris Holmlund argues of her status as a fan of *Female Trouble* upon its initial release in the 1970s, "Waters' hippie-radical fans, like me . . . viewed the Dreamlanders as fellow 'freaks' and 'comrades' . . . We, too, often imagined that, as Mink Stole put it, everyone was 'just hanging around, taking acid, going out shooting stuff and making it all up.'"[6] Where *Hairspray* foregrounds the democratizing logic of television's showcasing of ordinary people, *Female Trouble* problematizes who and what is representable in variety formats. That is especially the case in one scene, in particular. The movie's denouement occurs when Dawn's delusions of violent crime as providing her a route to stardom culminate in her staging a nightclub performance where she presents a series of strange, inexplicable routines: jumping on a trampoline, shredding a telephone book with her bare hands, sitting in a baby crib filled with dead fish and then tossing them into the crowd. The sequence moves between a series of shots in which Dawn's weird stage performances are interspersed with shots of audience members cheering and clapping. Its formal resemblance to how *Hairspray* stages *The Corny Collins Show* is noteworthy here because *Female Trouble* renders Dawn a spectacle via the same narrative logics and formalist paradigms of television variety programs. The scene also underlines Waters' commitment to showcasing unruliness: corpulent bodies that are flamboyantly costumed and captured in exaggerated motion.

In shots that move between Dawn and her audience—who she eventually opens fire upon with a gun she brings into her final act—*Female Trouble* stages a spectacle in ways that resemble the logic of television variety programs. Meghan Sutherland argues that the audience plays a central role in all variety-themed entertainment: "watching others watch the show is part of the spectacle."[7] But in this movie, the spectacle is lawless and weird. Dawn's nightclub act results in her getting convicted of murder and sentenced to death by electrocution. As a marker of just how far she has descended into the delusion of celebrity, Dawn is excited about getting electrocuted because she understands it as bringing her more of the fame she has sought all along. She delivers her final words as though she were being honored in a televised awards ceremony—yet another spectacle that, in the mind of the protagonist, will make her dreams come true. In Waters' hands, Dawn's descent into madness and fixation on stardom-via-criminality are as humorous as they are shocking. Where *Hairspray* and *Female Trouble* offer different though also overlapping commentaries on celebrity, the ways that they stage spectacle are notable for how similar they are—and how closely they parallel stylistic paradigms familiar to television in doing so.

The narrative and formalist attributes of variety programs in *Hairspray* and *Female Trouble* were most common in U.S. television's earliest decades. Programs like *The Colgate Comedy Hour* (NBC, 1950–1955), *The Ed Sullivan Show* (CBS, 1948–1971), *Your Show of Shows* (NBC, 1950–1954), and *The Arthur Murray Party* (ABC, NBC, CBS, DuMont, 1950–1960)—just a few examples of the many variety programs that aired on television in the 1950s and 1960s—are best understood as descendants of radio and vaudeville. In the medium's earliest years, before the genres we now so firmly associate with television (for example, the sitcom or the police procedural) became *de rigeur* programming practices, writers and producers borrowed heavily from other forms of popular entertainment in trying to court audiences. As Susan Murray notes in her work on early television stardom: "The influences of Broadway, nightclub revues, and vaudeville were vital to the delineation of effective performance models for television as they all utilized liveness, direct audience engagement, broad physicality, fast pacing, verbal dexterity, and common, deeply rooted cultural and historical references. Television reimagined many traditional forms of popular culture, adapting them to suit its particular needs and strengths."[8] Variety programs featured a range of performers and acts that spanned everything from music, standup, and sketch comedy to magic, acrobatics, and ventriloquism. In that sense, Dawn Davenport's bizarre yet diverse nightclub act in *Female Trouble* has more in common with midcentury variety programs than it might appear at first glance. I see in Waters' movies parallels with these television shows in terms of how their modes of address do not romanticize the past or the texts that circulated then. Rather, they invoke them to comment on the cultural fantasies they mobilize and to offer altered fantasies in their place. Crucially, Waters does this work without ever relying on pat moralization. Instead, the attention his movies pay to television asks viewers to think about texts from the past in new ways.

MISERY, VILLAINY, AND THE SOAP OPERA

Many of John Waters' movies are interested in the trials of femininity, particularly the labors of marriage and motherhood. While the relationship that *Polyester* and *Serial Mom* have with midcentury film melodramas is a well-excavated topic in scholarship on Waters and his filmography, there is something distinctly televisual about his interest in femininity, patriarchy, and the frequently derided cultural texts that document the miseries of being a cisgender heterosexual woman. Both *Polyester* and *Serial Mom* combine the stock characters of soap operas—heterosexual matriarchs—with the genre's emphasis on endless narrative complication via plots about infidelity, childrearing, and other travails of nuclear families. In both movies, the narrative complications become increasingly wacky and the matriarchs embody—in different ways and to different ends—what Tania Modleski identifies as the imagined "subject/spectator of soap operas," which she casts as "a sort of ideal mother: a person. . . . whose sympathy is large enough to encompass the conflicting claims of her family (she identifies with them all), and who has no demands or claims of her own (she identifies with no one character exclusively)."[9] For Modleski, one of the primary viewing pleasures of soap operas lies in the "desire for a just conclusion to the story [even as it] constantly presents the desire as unrealizable, by showing that conclusions only lead to further tension and suffering."[10] Thus, soap operas feature endlessly delayed resolutions—and when they do occur, these plot points further complicate situations rather than resolve narrative problems. Modleski casts this generic convention as being the means by which soap operas engage with femininity; soap operas are endless in much the same way that the labors of womanhood never cease.

In *Polyester*, the character Francine Fishpaw (Divine) wants nothing more than to be in a loving relationship with her husband and to see her son and daughter happy and successful. Alas, her husband's ownership of an adult movie theater has made them pariahs in suburban Baltimore, and an extramarital affair with his secretary results in Francine seeking a divorce. Her promiscuous teen daughter Lulu (Mary Garlington) gets pregnant and seeks an abortion, and her glue-sniffing son Dexter (Ken King) has an unlikely fetish that makes him a tabloid star when he begins seeking erotic thrills by stomping on the feet of unsuspecting women in public places. If, as Modleski suggests, "soap operas convince women that their highest goal is to see their families united and happy," they also "consol[e] them for their inability to realize this ideal and bring about familial harmony."[11] In *Polyester*, these plots are played for humor rather than pathos. Divine plays the role of Francine Fishpaw to excess as well; the actor's crying is histrionic and her physical presence—theatrical faces, screamed dialogue, an overweight body—makes the movie a study in excessiveness. Close-ups on Divine's face and a soundtrack featuring exaggerated organ music punctuate plot points in ways that underline the movie's play with formalist features long associated with soap operas. When Francine falls in love with a handsome stranger named Todd Tomorrow—played by Tab Hunter, an actor who was perhaps more famous in the 1950s for his looks than his talent—who ends up being in cahoots with her cocaine-addicted, witheringly critical mother, the pair conspire

Figure 11.2 Francine Fishpaw (Divine), the long-suffering mother and housewife in *Polyester*, is the quintessential "ideal mother" of television soap operas.

to embezzle Francine's divorce settlement and prostitute her children. Because *Polyester* is a filmic take on the soap opera, these various narrative threads actually do reach a conclusion, one that results in Francine finding the peace and happiness with her children that has eluded her all along. But the hysterics of the movie's final scene—the children murder their father and his mistress; Francine's boyfriend and mother get run over—is further testament to the movie's play with the generic conventions of soap opera. The movie concludes with Francine embracing her children—who have reformed and become artists; one paints, the other does macramé—as the dead bodies of those who have wronged her lie on the ground around them. In that moment, *Polyester* realizes the promises of the soap opera, making Francine's dreams come true in an homage to a distinctly televisual genre.

Yet the miseries of motherhood are not the only viewing pleasure afforded by the soap opera. As Modleski points out, soap operas feature different kinds of mothers. On one hand, a character like Francine Fishpaw is akin to the ideal subject/spectator constructed by soap operas. She is the ideal mother who understands, tolerates, and loves all despite their wrongdoings; she is nothing if not selfless. On the other hand, a character like Beverly Sutphin (Kathleen Turner) in *Serial Mom*, who manipulates and murders those who cross her, is a villainess who operates as "the negative image of the spectator's ideal self" and points to spectatorial "resentment at being constituted as an egoless receptacle for the suffering of others."[12] Soap opera villainesses are thus the flipside of the ideal mother; where protagonists on these programs are often overwhelmed and disheartened by the trials of heterosexual womanhood, antagonists are emboldened by cheating spouses, pregnancies, and other sources of gender and sexual conflict. The hardships associated with being a wife and mother are thus not destabilizing for villainesses. Rather, these characters "seiz[e] those aspects of a woman's life which normally render her most helpless and tr[y] to turn them into weapons for manipulating other characters."[13] Much like *Polyester* uses increasingly hyperbolic narrative complications for the purposes of comedy, *Serial Mom* features an excessiveness in its plot points. As with *Polyester*, these events are of the domestic sort in *Serial Mom*: Beverly's daughter has an unfaithful boyfriend, Beverly's son gets in trouble at school. But whereas the sad, put-upon housewife/mother of *Polyester* is repeatedly disappointed and even punished by her attempts to parent her children, Beverly Sutphin does so successfully. In *Serial Mom*, the protagonist murders those who cross her family; she disembowels her daughter's cheating boyfriend with a fireplace poker and uses the family station wagon to run over the high school principal who disciplines her son.

Serial Mom's version of the soap opera villainess and the character type as delineated by Modleski diverge in the realm of affability. For Modleski, one of the viewing pleasures of the villainess is despising her: "the extreme delight viewers apparently take in despising the villainess testifies to the enormous amount of energy involved in the spectator's repression and . . . resentment."[14] Because the villainess causes pain and suffering in the narrative worlds of soap operas, she becomes a site of disidentification. Further, she becomes a way of working out the anger and irritation that attend being a wife and mother in patriarchy. But in *Serial Mom*, Beverly Sutphin is eminently likeable. In between the scenes in which she violently murders the people who cross her and her family, Beverly is warm and friendly. The character is beloved by the trash collectors in her upper middle-class neighborhood because she organizes her garbage and recycling so neatly. She is quick to laugh with her husband and children, and lovingly, cheerfully prepares meals and tends house. Thus, in Waters' hands the villainess does not just weather the trials of womanhood, she becomes the hero of the narrative. The movie celebrates the stock character for her deceitfulness and cunning. In a culminating courtroom scene, Beverly Sutphin outwits the processes of law and order that seek to punish her for wrongdoing, acting as her own attorney and winning over the jury to get acquitted.

Historical shifts in both the medium's political economy and consumer capitalism more broadly make the soap opera more closely aligned with prior eras in television's history, especially midcentury, given that the genre was self-consciously borrowed from radio broadcasting during television's infancy. When television was introduced to the consumer marketplace in the U.S., suburban families were targeted by advertisers and network executives,

Figure 11.3 Beverly Sutphin (Katherine Turner) meets actress Suzanne Somers (playing herself) as she is interviewed by a television journalist after being acquitted of murder charges in *Serial Mom*.

with housewives being singled out for special courtship given the wide latitude they were thought to have over household spending. Lynn Spigel argues, the medium's earliest years featured executives and producers "aggressively attempt[ing] to colonize the housewife's workday with regularly scheduled network programs."[15] Soap operas and their stock character types have deep connections to midcentury and the memories that persist about that era in the decades since. Over time, shifts in population and economy have made women working outside the home and two-income heterosexual nuclear families more familiar, constitutive elements of television's business practices and representational regime. As Elana Levine has written of soap opera: "shifting conceptions of femininity and the cultural forms best suited to address feminine interests and concerns [make] soap opera seem to many a holdover from an earlier era."[16] Daytime television programming built around the long-suffering heterosexual housewife—and the villainess who torments her—are thus, to many, relics of a bygone epoch. As such, women like Francine Fishpaw and Beverly Sutphin and the narrative worlds constructed by *Polyester* and *Serial Mom*, respectively, invoke prior moments of television to look back at its forms and archetypes with fondness and humor. While the takes on soap operas and their generic conventions differ in these movies, they both trade on audience familiarity with midcentury television in similar ways, reconstructing it for the purpose of mordantly witty commentary.

PUBLIC AND PRIVATE IN TABLOID NEWS

If *Serial Mom* has one televisual forebear in the soap opera, it has another in tabloid news. As Beverly Sutphin's body count grows, she becomes a news sensation. Over the course of the movie, she repeatedly eludes arrest even as she continues to kill people who cross her and her family. Reporters begin following her around trying to get interviews with her and/or capture her on video. The movie's title is derived from the nickname the protagonist is given in the press as reporters from the scandal-hungry news media seek to further sensationalize the housewife-murderer. Beverly's media-obsessed son fields requests for talk show interviews and the murder trial features television cameras and reporters angling for a statement from her. As Beverly's trial concludes, television actress Suzanne Somers—famous for her role in the 1970s sitcom *Three's Company* (ABC, 1977–1984) and her status as a star who promoted the "ThighMaster," aerobic equipment heavily promoted in television informercials—appears for the verdict because she plans to star in a television miniseries based on Sutphin's life. These plot points provide humorous observations on sensationalism in broadcast journalism and the blurring of entertainment and news during the time of *Serial Mom*'s release. In the late 1980s and early 1990s, as broadcasting faced new competition for advertising dollars from cable, network television in the U.S. responded with a series of programming efforts to keep viewers tuned in.[17] Tabloid journalism was one such attempt, and programs like *A Current Affair* (Syndicated, 1986–1996), *Hard Copy* (Syndicated, 1989–1999), and *America's Most Wanted* (Fox, 1988–2011, 2021–; Lifetime, 2011–2012), which fuse reportage and melodrama via a focus on deviance, luridness, and criminality, became mainstays of broadcast schedules during the era in which *Serial Mom* first circulated amongst audiences.[18]

Yet it is imprecise to historicize tabloid news on television in a way that situates it too neatly in the shifts that occurred on network television in the U.S. during the rise of cable. Genres are dynamic categories whose narrative and formalist qualities are both fixed and fluid; their influences and antecedents are nothing if not multiple. In the case of tabloid news, its televisual predecessors include news formats associated with local television at midcentury. In seeking to differentiate themselves from national news broadcasts and the news broadcasts of their local competitors, postwar-era local television stations developed different news formats: "action" and "eyewitness."[19] Where the former features short segments and personality-driven reportage, the latter emphasizes visuality and on-location reporting.[20] While the formats developed in contrast with one another as different stations used them in the interest of increasing their market share, the legacy of both formats can be seen in tabloid news, which are built around a strong voice in the form of a charismatic host and fast-paced editing that is rich with graphics.[21] In that sense, the tabloid news to which *Serial Mom* refers has as much to do with local television of the postwar era as it does with the transformations on U.S. broadcasting associated with cable in the 1980s and 1990s. Viewed from that vantage point, the many references that John Waters' movies make to television news constitute a thematic trope that problematizes relationships between public and private, as well as fame and criminality.

References to television news in *Polyester* and *Pink Flamingos* underline the issues at stake across his filmography: aberration and deviance, the cultural fringe, and the championing of characters who run afoul of social norms. In *Polyester*, protagonist Francine Fishpaw is tormented by the news media at her home repeatedly: first, when a protest by anti-pornography protesters against her husband's adult theater is covered by reporters, and then when her son becomes a tabloid star after getting arrested for being the "Baltimore Foot-Stomper." Francine's routines in the family home are interrupted by reporters seeking a statement from her about her dysfunctional family members. When crews from television news programs appear at the Fishpaws' front door, Francine dissolves into tears. In *Polyester*'s diegesis, tabloid news is a source of shame for Francine; television cameras are the means by which her private failures as a mother and wife become fodder for public consumption. But in *Pink Flamingos*, such infamy is mobilized for different narrative ends. In the diegesis of this movie, characters compete for tabloid stardom, actively seeking out the publicness from which Francine hides. The central narrative conflict involves Divine playing an eponymous criminal who is named "the filthiest person alive" by a tabloid newspaper. The movie's antagonists, Connie (Mink Stole) and Raymond Marble (David Lochary), covet this title and set out to take it from her. *Pink Flamingos*' plot revolves around the bitter rivalry between these bizarre characters; where Divine has a sexual relationship with her adult son, the Marbles run a black-market baby ring that involves the kidnapping and rape of women for the purpose of selling the babies they conceive to lesbian couples.

The plot of *Pink Flamingos* is secondary to the showcasing of eccentric characters and their bizarre sexual fetishes. In one scene, Divine and her son, Crackers (Danny Mills), break into the Marbles' home, at which point they lick and rub the furniture and ultimately have sex with one another. In another scene, Crackers involves a live chicken in the sexual assault of a woman who the Marbles have sent to spy on them. When the Marbles bait Divine into fearing that the title of "filthiest person alive" will be taken away from her, she sets out to kill them and thus eliminate her competition. The movie's denouement occurs when Divine and Crackers kidnap the Marbles and stage a phony trial for committing the crimes of "first-degree stupidity" and "assholism." Significantly, Divine summons the news media to observe and report on the Marbles' conviction and execution. The character gives interviews to journalists, who are depicted reporting on and recording the Marbles getting tarred, feathered, and then shot in the head. Divine—who, in *Pink Flamingos*, uses the alias "Babs Johnson"—courts the same publicness and infamy that Francine Fishpaw fears in *Polyester*. The plot of *Pink Flamingos* is a series of non sequiturs involving violent crimes and sexual offenses, which its characters engage in as they seek stardom for being depraved. Crucially, *Pink Flamingos* takes glee in this eccentricity, using tabloid journalism as a way of underscoring just how debauched the characters are—in an effort to find humor in it.

While Waters' references to variety shows and soap operas are more explicit, perhaps, than are his references to tabloid news, the points of intersection between his movies and tabloid news are persistent and pervasive. With their shared emphasis on shocking events and sensational modes of address, tabloid news and Waters' movies mine the underbelly of respectable culture for the purposes of spectatorial pleasure. The commentary that Waters offers on tabloid news in *Polyester* and *Pink Flamingos* is not as specific to television as the one offered in *Serial Mom*. In *Serial Mom*, microphones with television affiliate branding appear throughout the movie, and the main character is pursued by an eager band of television cameramen as she eludes the police. In contrast, the "media" Divine refers to and courts in the narrative of *Pink Flamingos* does not feature cameras, per se. Even so, tabloid news is central to all of the movies insofar as it provides a discursive register through which unscrupulous acts become matters of public record—a turn of events which the characters in *Polyester* fear and those in *Pink Flamingos* envy. As such, tabloid news provides Waters' movies with a key set of references and associations for the observations they make about the public lives of private people.

CONCLUSION

Waters' filmography can be characterized by an increase in production budgets over time, as well as greater use of established stars, and circulation via more mainstream distributors. These material changes make it tempting to identify vast aesthetic and political differences across his oeuvre. Movies that Waters made during the 1970s, like *Pink Flamingos* and *Female Trouble*, "embrace all manner of marginal subjects in his beloved Baltimore—eccentrics, the downright mad, transvestites—and seek to embrace these figures by sharing in their delight in disregarding customary notions of good taste, normative sexuality, and racial identities."[22] Critics often contrast these movies with Waters' releases from the decades after, like *Hairspray* and *Serial Mom*. For instance,

Nathan Koob suggests that the more orthodox funding and distribution of his later movies resulted in "Waters start[ing] to abandon the notorious content which made him famous . . . Many of his themes remained similar and his films still had some gross or shocking content, but to a much more limited degree."[23] Similarly, Pat Aufderheide refers to Waters' later movies as featuring "a kinder, gentler approach" from the director, which "leav[e] behind many of the shock-till-you-drop effects that once won John Waters the title of Prince of Puke."[24] Thus, a common theme in writing about Waters involves characterizing him as having his more salacious tendencies tamed and tempered by the practices of commerce that moved his movies towards the cultural mainstream over the course of his career.

At the same time, critics have taken great pains to identify progressive political commitments in the director's more mainstream releases. For instance, Dana Heller casts *Hairspray* as a movie in which affection for the 1960s "and a message of racial equality coexist harmoniously with the transgressive energies of the underground film circuit, the DIY ethos of the punk and independent film movements, and the deconstructive sensibilities of gay culture's camp politics."[25] In casting Waters' most conventional "success" in this way, Heller cuts across familiar ways of categorizing his filmography and characterizing the politics of his movies. Of the outsiders, eccentrics, and other "freaks" Waters features in all of his movies, Walter Metz writes: "The middle-class child's fantasy of being adopted and belonging in an upper-class family is queered in a Waters film such that communal radicals replace the nuclear family as the normative site on which narrative is built. Waters films celebrate the triumph of this [as a] utopian reorganization."[26] Thus, Metz sees parallels across seemingly disparate epochs in Waters' movies and identifies common threads that unite texts that are more predictably differentiated from one another.

Like Heller's and Metz's interventions, attention to how Waters' movies remember television provides evidence of aesthetic similarities and political consistencies across even the most disparate texts in his filmography. In their references to variety shows, soap operas, and tabloid news, Waters' movies offer commentaries on race, class, gender, and sexuality that are by turns amusing and absurd. In some movies, like *Hairspray*, these references are pointed and explicit in the attention they pay to television's generic conventions and representational paradigms. In other movies, like *Pink Flamingos*, these references are diffuse and/or brief, but provide a crucial avenue for interrogating ideological preoccupations of Waters' oeuvre nonetheless. As a heuristic, questioning how Waters' movies remember television provides new insights regarding the cinematic legacy of midcentury television and breaks new ground for understanding the role of television as an issue related to film authorship.

NOTES

1. Fredric Jameson, "Postmodernism or the Cultural Logic of Late Capitalism," *New Left Review* (1984): 65.
2. Richard Dyer, *Pastiche* (New York: Routledge, 2007), 1.
3. Dyer, 9.
4. Caetlin Benson-Allott, "Camp Integration: The Use and Misuse of Nostalgia in John Waters' *Hairspray*," *Quarterly Review of Film and Video* 26, no. 2 (2009): 143.
5. Meghan Sutherland, *The Flip Wilson Show* (Detroit: Wayne State University Press, 2008), 79.
6. Chris Holmlund, *Female Trouble* (Vancouver: Arsenal Pulp Press, 2017), 91.
7. Meghan Sutherland, *The Flip Wilson Show* (Detroit: Wayne State University Press, 2008), 77.
8. Susan Murray, *Hitch Your Antenna to the Stars: Early Television and Broadcast Stardom* (New York: Routledge, 2005), 42.
9. Tania Modleski, "The Search for Tomorrow in Today's Soap Operas," in *Popular Fiction: Technology, Ideology, Production, Reading*, edited by Tony Bennett (New York: Routledge, 1990), 193.
10. 193.
11. 193–194.
12. 195.
13. 196.
14. 195.
15. Lynn Spigel, Lynn, *Make Room for TV: Television and the Family Ideal in Postwar America*, (Chicago: University of Chicago Press, 1992), 77.
16. Elana Levine, *Her Stories: Daytime Soap Opera and US Television History* (Durham, NC: Duke University Press, 2020), 280.
17. John T. Caldwell, *Televisuality: Style, Crisis, and Authority in American Television* (New Brunswick, NJ: Rutgers University Press), 2020, 12.
18. Ibid., 328.
19. Craig M. Allen, *News Is People: The Rise of Local TV News and the Fall of News from New York* (Ames: Iowa State University Press, 2001), 131–132.
20. Charles L. Ponce De Leon, *That's the Way It Is: A History of Television News in America* (Chicago: University of Chicago Press, 2015), 135–138.
21. S. Elizabeth Bird, "Tabloidization: What Is It, and Does It Really Matter?," in *The Changing Faces of Journalism*, edited by Barbie Zelizer (New York: Routledge, 2009), 40.
22. Matthew Tinkcom, *Working Like a Homosexual: Camp, Capital, Cinema* (Durham, NC: Duke University Press, 2002), 157.
23. Nathan Koob, "The Gentrification of John Waters," *Film Criticism* 43, no. 1 (2019): 1.
24. Pat Aufderheide, "The Domestication of John Waters," in *John Waters: Interviews*, edited by James Egan (Oxford, MS: University of Mississippi Press, 2011), 118.
25. Dana Heller, *Hairspray* (Malden, MA: Wiley-Blackwell, 2011), 3.
26 Walter Metz, "John Waters Goes to Hollywood: A Poststructural Authorship Study," in *Authorship and Film*, edited by David A. Gerstner and Janet Staiger (New York: Routledge, 2003), 157–174, 173.

CHAPTER 12

An Audience with John Waters

Jane Giles

Author's note: As its main source, this chapter quotes from unpublished transcripts of original interviews with John Waters and others conducted between May–August 2021 for the documentary SCALA!!! Or, the Incredibly Strange Rise and Fall of the World's Wildest Cinema and How It Influenced a Mixed-up Generation of Weirdos and Misfits (dir. Jane Giles and Ali Catterall, U.K., 2023, 96 mins).

For their film to "find its audience" is the holy grail of most creatives and a challenge, given what lies between a completed work and people watching it. Everything from the programming preferences of the gatekeepers of physical or virtual exhibition spaces, prohibitive or restrictive legislation (the rating systems of the Motion Picture Association in the U.S. and the British Board of Film Classification in the U.K.), and the prescriptive aversion meted out by film critics whose criteria include concepts of good and bad taste in addition to judging professionalism, artistry, and innovation. Camp ironist John Waters is an independent filmmaker whose outrageous low-budget "laugh 'n' barf" American comedies came from the Underground into the studio mainstream and circuit cinemas while remaining loved by loyal audiences of self-proclaimed misfits and weirdos. This audience has been described by Waters as "outsiders that were thrown out of their own outsider world. Gay people that didn't fit in with other gay people. Bikers. Straight bikers used to come to my films. You couldn't tell the difference between a leather queen and a biker until they spoke. They had the same outfit on. It was always a mixture of gay men that liked women, and lesbians who hung out with straight guys. It was completely mixed. Nobody fit in their own minority and that's what made it so exciting, and powerful."[1]

This essay comes from an industrial perspective, the nuts and bolts of exhibition and distribution, to consider the role of the audience for John Waters' films. Our prism is the Scala repertory cinema in London, operative between 1978–1993 during which time it repeatedly showed Waters' films, from *Mondo Trasho* (1969) to *Cry-Baby* (1990), and attracted a particular type of audience response. As Waters said, "I was only in the audience in the Scala for one of my films once, and I remember being shocked, and I had been all over the country to midnight movie audiences everywhere."[2] Focusing on an actual audience rather than a generalized idea, or even no idea, of who was watching the films provides a framework for illustrative evidence to support the theory that group behavior contributes to the impact of a film, and that future creatives may be inspired and influenced by experiencing it in a heightened environment.

Located first in Fitzrovia (1978–1981) and then in King's Cross (1981–1993), the Scala showed roughly 4000 movies throughout its fifteen-year history, a mix of Hollywood classics, arthouse, cult, horror, kung fu, LGBTQ+, and unclassifiable oddities, in daily changing double-bills and Saturday All-Nighters with a smattering of live music and club nights. The Scala's programme was published monthly in an iconic fold-out calendar based on a format used by American cinemas including the Roxie (San Francisco), NuArt and Vista (Los Angeles). With space to contextualize the unclassifiable through programming comparative movies, the design of the calendar sheets conveyed equal import to both high and low art. Critic-proof, the idiosyncratic copy on the back of the calendar sheets sold the films without relying on superlatives or positive press reviews. Providing audiences with an alternative curriculum, the calendars had an estimable role in the evolution of film culture.

The Scala's first iteration was a newly built 300-seat cinema on the site of the former Scala theatre (1905–1969). Its audience was largely comprised of students from the nearby art and fashion school, Central St. Martins, many of whom lived locally in the undeveloped Warren Street squats. Post-punk, the Scala found itself at the epicentre of the flamboyant, gender-bending New Romantic music and fashion scene. It particularly attracted young people discovering themselves and culture outside of home for the first time. Moving venues in 1981 to the former circle area of a down-at-heel but exceptionally atmospheric 1920s picture palace, the second version of the Scala cinema in cruisy, druggy King's Cross was ideally situated for an expansion of LGBTQ+ programming and audiences. Artist, filmmaker, and university Professor of the Arts Isaac Julien describes the Scala's significance as follows:

> I have particular memories of going to the Scala located in Pentonville Road because it was also a place where it converged with a lot of gay subcultural activities. I don't mean to sound too scientific about that,

> I just want to say that one of the most important venues that I went to was The Bell [pub], literally just 50 yards away from this cinema, and that was a venue that had the Pet Shop Boys, Derek Jarman, Jimmy Somerville. I mean everybody really involved in the pop alternative scene. That kind of queer group would also come to the Scala, would all come here to see John Waters films but also other films. And so I think there was a certain oppositional counterculture which existed in the audiences which attended the Scala and I think we saw them as being part of our cultural identity.[3]

The Scala cinema in King's Cross was a cathedral-like space with a cavernous, mysteriously rumbling auditorium, dark corridors, and restrooms that lent themselves to raucous behavior, what was happening on-screen mirrored by audience participation like some kind of expanded cinema, albeit in a fundamentally safe space. Film writer Alan Jones described the Scala audience in terms of a 42nd Street grindhouse:

> I mean, having been in them at the height of the '70s I can tell you that it was sort of similar. You know, people with their legs over the front of the seats. Seats slamming. The gents toilet door revolving. And the dark bits at the back of the auditorium. You didn't go there just in case you might trip over somebody having a shag on the carpet. I mean that was part of the atmosphere, part of the theatre of it all. When you went to 42nd Street, like when you went to the Scala it wasn't just to go and see the film, it was to see the people who turned up, you know, the bonkers guy who's down the front screaming at the screen every time a woman took a top off, stuff like that. So if that's what you wanted then the Scala was the perfect place for that. Sure, you know, you're not going to get that sort of person at an Agnes Varda quadruple bill, are you? But for a John Waters double-bill or Russ Meyer, it's a perfect audience to watch it with.[4]

And in the words of John Waters, "The Scala had magic. It was like joining a club, a very secret club like a biker gang or something. It's like they were a country club for criminals and lunatics and people that were high. Which is a good way to see a movie."[5]

Describing the Scala audience, musician and filmmaker Douglas Hart said, "If you came here to see John Waters films, the people that were coming to see it were not just dressed up like that for the night. That was their lives. They were total outsiders . . . these people lived those films."[6] Musician and DJ Mark Moore was one of them, and has since recalled his most vivid memories of watching films at the Scala:

Figure 12.1 John Waters onstage at the Scala, May 1988.

> Every time *Pink Flamingos* was on, you would go again, or *Female Trouble*, they were usually on together. And you would take someone else who'd never seen it, and just watch with joy as they experienced it for the first time. The bit at the end of *Pink Flamingos* where Divine eats dog shit, you would hear mass screams of disgust from the entire audience, except for the people who'd seen it before, it'd be screams of joy. The floor show at the end of *Female Trouble* where Divine does her performance art act was incredible . . . In the film's world the audience were going wild and in the audience we were all going wild.[7]

The Scala audience yelled at the screen and along with the film in a joyous call and response, but also paid attention, according to musician and actor Barry Adamson:

> As soon as the movie started, it would go quiet. Because everybody was totally focused on, for example, a John Waters All-Nighter, as raucous as that was, seeing *Pink Flamingos*. Everybody was glued to what was going on here, because this movie is from someplace else, that we would probably not see anywhere else except here.[8]

And so, the Scala cinema became synonymous with the films of John Waters.

*

Inspired by the American Underground avant-garde films of Andy Warhol and Jack Smith, Waters' early, self-financed films famously employed a repertoire of Baltimore associates, the Dreamlanders. Their friends and family made up Waters' first audiences in screenings held in non-theatrical alternative exhibition spaces:

> Churches were where underground films opened. My movies *Roman Candles* [8mm, 1966], *Eat Your Makeup* [16mm, 1968], *Mondo Trasho* [16mm, 1969], and *Multiple Maniacs* [16mm, 1970] opened in a church, in both Baltimore and Provincetown, if you can imagine that. The Reverends had never even seen the movie, but they thought "If we can get these people in a church . . . this is a real feat, right?!" At that time churches showed underground movies, in New York too. It was where you had anti-war rallies, the Black Panthers. Churches supported that kind of thing. It's hard to imagine that today. Judson Memorial Church in New York always showed underground movies, and the Unitarian churches in Baltimore was where I showed my movies too. It was great because you got to keep the money. They didn't even want rent money, I think it was free, I don't remember if I paid rent or anything. But yes, it's odd to know that churches used to be a real outlet to see weird underground movies.[9]

Waters also marketed the screenings by approaching people on the street with flyers, targeting those who looked like they may be up for his unique brand of humor and shock value. In this way Waters' microbudget films covered their costs and began to build a following as he worked towards the world premiere of his third feature-length film, *Pink Flamingos* (1972), produced, directed, shot on 16mm and edited by Waters himself on a total budget of $10k (roughly $75k in 2024). Editing your own film, watching the same footage over and over until you can't see the woods for the trees, leaves a filmmaker particularly nervous and unsure of what they have until the film is tested with an actual audience. The screenwriter William Goldman's maxim "Nobody knows anything"[10] is true at every level of filmmaking, from no-budget experimental work to blockbusters. *Pink Flamingos* had its world premiere at the University of Baltimore in late 1972, and as John Waters recounts, "As soon as the film began, I knew I had a hit. The audience roared with laughter in the right places and shrieked in horror in others," while the final shot of Divine eating dog feces guaranteed that people would stay until the end and leave reeling, generating a tidal wave of word-of-mouth.[11]

Pink Flamingos was given a standing ovation, and Waters knew this local response could be replicated nationally but still had to convince his distribution company, New Line. They tried the film out in a Boston gay porn cinema, where "There was more action in the bathroom than the theatre" and Waters pleaded instead for an arthouse opening.[12] As a dedicated cinemagoer he knew where his film would work best.

> I would go to all the art cinemas that were in Baltimore. They played the Bergman movies, and they were shocking. When Bergman first played in Baltimore, it was advertised as a sex film. They renamed *Monika* "The Sins of Monika," cut out all the dialogue, repeated the breast scenes, and showed it in a nudist camp movie theatre. That's how I first saw Bergman, which was hilarious. I would go to see the exploitation movies at the downtown theatres. I saw underground movies in weird little festivals in Baltimore, but mostly I had to go to New York. That's where I got my education, not in film school, but from going to see every kind of movie. I still think that's the only way you learn how to make movies, just watch movies with the sound off and you see how they're made. It's obvious. I remember the Bleecker Street Cinema. I even had sex there, watching *The Blue Angel*. That is something that I'm shocked by when I look back on it.[13]

Pink Flamingos sat on the shelf for a year until it was given a single midnight screening at the Elgin in Manhattan. The auditorium was only half-full, but the response was great, and the film was rebooked for the following week with queues around the block. Word of mouth continued to grow the audience for the film, along with press that picked up on the film's humor as well as its shock value.

New Line then made an inspired trailer, which atypically showed nothing of the film, but rather featured a vox pop of audience reactions. Whereas mainstream film trailers generally show the story in miniature, making sure to include its most dramatic, visually strongest scenes and universally glowing press quotes, New Line did the opposite. The *Pink Flamingos* trailer opens with a full screen title, "WHAT ARE THESE PEOPLE LAUGHING AT?" and the sound of a whooping crowd, followed by opinions ranging from "Great!" to "Garbage" intercut with a few press quotes, ending in a massive round of applause. By withholding information, the trailer piqued curiosity and decades later would be given pride of place in the exhibition *John Waters: Pope of Trash* at the Academy Museum in Los Angeles, to mark his induction into the Hollywood Walk of Fame in 2023. The trailer showed on loop inside a replica of Babs Johnson's pink trailer home, memorably burned down in *Pink Flamingos* by her rivals, the villainous Connie and Raymond Marble.

The trailer sold the film to prestigious arthouses and universities, where the film continued to run and run. Waters says:

> In most of the theatres that showed weird movies, like the Elgin in New York which really was where *Pink Flamingos* got very, very famous and played for a long time, and the Nuart in Los Angeles where it played at least one night a week at midnight for ten years, that's a pretty good run.[14]

New Line screened *Pink Flamingos* in the Cannes film market in 1976, selling it to other territories. The U.K. rights were acquired by nascent independent distributor Mainline Pictures, best known for their Screen circuit of cinemas. The company was run by Romaine Hart (1933–2021), who came from a family of cinema owners dating back to the silent era. Having worked as a booker from the age of sixteen, Romaine transformed one of their run-down fleapits, the Rex in Islington, into a groundbreaking type of arthouse cinema: The Screen on the Green. Unveiled in 1970, this venue almost single-handedly took British cinemagoing out of its postwar doldrums by setting a new standard, specializing in must-see first run movies with a bit of rep around the edges. Furthermore, Romaine's young assistant, Roger Austin, brought in his music industry friends, and in August 1976 The Screen on the Green hosted a seminal gig by punk bands Sex Pistols, The Clash, and The Buzzcocks at a time when they were not welcome elsewhere due to the audience violence that typically broke out at their shows.

Set up in the late 1970s to give their cinemas priority bookings, the distribution arm of Mainline Pictures had noted the growing success of *Pink Flamingos*. The U.K. didn't have a Midnight Movie scene comparable to that of the U.S., but it did have a thriving independent repertory cinema scene and a post-punk audience up for seeing a version of themselves on screen. Waters recalls:

> *Pink Flamingos* was punk before it ever happened, and I think that's why it went over so well. Matter of fact, later, when *Female Trouble* came out that image of Divine with the mohawk was on all those Vivienne Westwood T shirts without any credit to *Pink Flamingos*, without knowing who Divine was, or *Female Trouble*, or anything. I think that it was the punk aesthetic before it even happened. And *Pink Flamingos* still works, it still joyously makes people feel rebellious. It was a movie made as a joke of exploitation, "What could shock an audience that thought they had seen everything?" And it did! I think Londoners always had a great sense of humor about cinema and it spoke to them.[15]

It was in repertory rather than first run where *Pink Flamingos* really made its mark, first shown at the Scala in August 1979 as the lead film in a double-bill with the thematically similar *The Honeymoon Killers* (Leonard Kastle, 1970). Hitting a sweet spot somewhere between punk, gross-out comedy, rock 'n' roll Americana and B-movie schlock horror, it became one of the top ten films most often programmed at the Scala. It was a film that had to be seen to be believed and had to be seen with a cinema audience. Before home entertainment, there was no other way, but even once VHS took off, audiences for *Pink Flamingos* grew and grew as the films regularly appeared on the Scala's monthly calendar programmes, usually triple-billed with *Female Trouble* and *Desperate Living*, or as part of an All-Nighter.

The Scala's vibrant monthly programmes provided not only an unofficial film studies curriculum, but a badge of honor, something to be pinned up on countless adolescent bedroom walls or on the walls of student flat shares, everything circled that people wanted to see:

> The Charles in Baltimore had one of those programmes. I still have the Scala programmes in my film archive. I looked at the [Scala] book of them and it's amazing to see what they paired my movies with and everything. Everybody had them. They were great. You could pore over them. You could look at the ads. Everybody had them on the refrigerator or hanging up in their kitchen or everything. I miss that. I miss advertising. I miss paper. I miss posters. I miss wild posting. We used to go out and paste stuff up illegally. Hang stuff up. I miss all that. That was effective advertising too.
>
> I'm still for giving out handbills on the street. People don't even know what they are. If you hand them something, they're afraid of you. I don't even know if internet ads register on me. I guess I see them. I mean, I get notified by many movie theatres about what's playing, and I do look on the internet. But it's not as much fun as having a poster or a handbill, or something you can hang up in your house or keep. I miss all that. I miss marketing. I miss display ads in the newspapers.
>
> People used the Scala's Christmas programmes as gift wrap? See. That's great, though. That meant everybody's talking about them. They're saving them. They're keeping them. They became collector's items. Probably some of them are worth money today. That's the kind of thing that if you give somebody, they will be a loyal customer. They'll be such a loyal fan, that they are participating. They want you to make money. They're not mad you made money. They're happy to pay because they want it to continue. They want to be in that cult. In that weird audience.[16]

The Scala mailed its monthly programmes to John Waters, who later commented, "It was delightful for me to keep seeing it on those great Scala calendars, playing over and over again. I was thrilled that I had such a great audience."[17] And in return, Waters sent the Scala his annual Christmas card.

The Scala was a club membership cinema, which meant it could, with the permission of its local licensing authority, show unclassified and uncut films, circumnavigating the strictures of the BBFC:

> London was a tough market because you had very strict censorship there. *Pink Flamingos* was banned for a long time at first. The censors even got back to us about it and said, "We'll be honest, we do not know

> how to deal with purposeful bad taste, we do not know how to handle that." That was a smart censor. I'm used to dealing with dumb censors, but this was the only country that had a smart censor.[18]

It was a club than anyone could join if they were over eighteen, or said they were. Many under that age had their first experience of wild movies at the Scala. Annual membership cost 50 pence, and the cards made excellent roaches.

Mainline Pictures went on to acquire the U.K. rights to *Female Trouble* (1974) and *Desperate Living* (1977). New Line had blown both films up from the 16mm on which they originated to 35mm so they could be shown in bigger cinemas. As a repertory cinema the Scala itself had both projection formats. *Female Trouble* cost $25k and had been launched in New York at the RKO on Fifty-Ninth Street. As Waters said, "It seemed I had finally climbed out of the underground."[19] In the U.K. *Female Trouble* was launched at the Scala in February 1980, in a double-bill supported by vintage exploitation featurette *The Cocaine Fiends* (William A. O'Connor and Norton S. Parker, 1935).

Desperate Living had a budget of $65k, but the popularity of the film suffered from an absence of key Dreamlanders, including Divine, contractually tied up onstage during the filming, and the recently deceased David Lochary. It first showed at the Scala in May 1980 double-billed with *Pink Flamingos*, and by

Figure 12.2 *Female Trouble* flyer, February 1980.

August 1980 had fitted neatly into the All-Nighters, which ran from 11pm until 7am the next morning and became the Scala's most enduring legacy. According to Waters:

> Yep, dusk to dawn. We had dusk to dawn shows in Maryland, they were at drive-ins, and it was free to get in, but you had to pay to get out. That was the gimmick of the whole thing and I always loved that concept. The longer you stayed, the more money they made on the concession stand. Dusk to dawn, yeah, I think that's a great idea. At the Baltimore Museum of Arts, we did a dusk to dawn showing of all my movies a couple of years ago, and some of them did stay all night. You could sleep there and everything. It's an exciting concept. Warhol's 25-hour movie, *Four Stars*, was shown once. But the people that went, what an experience. What a memory.[20]

There was now a critical body of work, with the belated addition of 16mm prints of *Mondo Trasho* and *Multiple Maniacs* temporarily brought over for a run at the Scala in April 1982 and never before seen in the U.K.

Polyester (1981) was a massive jump, its $300k budget reflecting that it was Waters' first film shot on 35mm. A romantic melodrama, it was also his first film to receive a lower age classification and not to be released via the Midnight Movie scene in the U.S. *Polyester* is also notable for its "Odorama" Scratch 'n' Sniff cards, an extrasensory gimmick in the style of marketing showman William Castle. The film was not released by Mainline Pictures in the U.K. but by GTO, an independent film distribution company set up in 1974 by music industry maverick Laurence Myers. *Polyester* first screened at the Scala as a "sneak preview" in May 1982, the same month that the Scala programmed "10 Days of Trash," a season including both John Waters' films and *Thundercrack!* (Curt McDowell, 1975), *Color Me Blood Red* (Herschell Gordon Lewis, 1965), *Eraserhead* (David Lynch, 1977), *The Wild Women of Wongo* (James L. Wolcott, 1958), *A Bucket of Blood* (Roger Corman, 1959), *Andy Warhol's Bad* (Jed Johnson, 1977), *Flesh* (Paul Morrissey, 1968), a Russ Meyer All-Nighter, and a shorts programme celebrating the malicious intent of the Three Stooges, which the Scala dedicated to the yet-to-be-deceased George A. Romero. There was also a "John Waters and Friends" All-Nighter of *Pink Flamingos*, *Female Trouble*, and *Desperate Living* interspersed with 1930s archive featurettes *Reefer Madness* (Louis J. Gasnier, 1936) and *Sex Madness* (Dwain Esper, 1938), and music promos including 'London Calling' (The Clash), 'Broken English' (Marianne Faithfull), and The Slits Pictures (directed by Don Letts). Perhaps inadvertently swept into the footprint of "10 Days of Trash" was a Sunday matinee screening of *India Song* (Marguerite Duras, 1975). In his essay "Guilty Pleasures," John Waters described Marguerite Duras as making "the kind

Figure 12.3 May 1982 ("10 Days of Trash").

of films that get you punched in the mouth for recommending them to your closest friends."[21] Waters calls her "the ultimate eccentric" creator of maddeningly boring arthouse films that no one likes.[22] "But then I showed *The Truck* [Le Camion] at the French Academy in New York and we had a packed audience. Everybody was howling and clapping along with *The Truck*, which is a very difficult film to watch. I loved her."[23]

Polyester was next shown at the Scala in April 1983, double-billed with the deeply peculiar science-fiction horror comedy *Phantasm* (Don Coscarelli, 1979), also distributed by GTO Films. Thereafter it showed with tonally similar films including Paul Bartel's *Eating Raoul* (1982) and *Lust in the Dust* (1984), *Attack of the Fifty Foot Woman* (Nathan Juran, 1958), *Harold and Maude* (Hal Ashby, 1971), and many more. Whereas John Waters' more extreme films seemed to belong entirely in their own world, *Polyester* was programmed with a range of oddities with which it shared a sensibility if not a director. Comedian Adam Buxton and his childhood friend, the filmmaker Joe Cornish, were amongst those who saw *Polyester* at the Scala. As Buxton remembers it,

> One of the first double-bills that I went to with Joe was *Polyester*, a John Waters film, and something called *Thundercrack*. I didn't know anything about either of these. Joe sold *Polyester* to me on the basis that it was the

> world's first scratch and sniff movie. It was this technique that John Waters had created called Odorama and it represented a huge leap forward in cinema technology because, at various points in the film a number would come up on the screen. And when the number came up, you looked at a card that you were given when you entered the cinema, when you bought your ticket, and it was a scratch and sniff card and it had eight or ten little circles of odour that you would scratch but because it was a John Waters film, it wasn't strawberry or bubblegum. The nice scratching smells. It was things like vomit, shit. I'm guessing sperm. And none of them really smelt like the things but it was just the idea of it was, oh wow, this is great, we're gonna smell some shit now. Coffee. I think there was coffee, that was quite good. The rest of them . . . Is this really sperm? And so that was good, and quite fun, and by John Waters standards, fairly accessible.[24]

Polyester relied on the provision of its Odorama Scratch 'n' Sniff cards, but the Scala continued to schedule the film even after they had run out in the U.K.

It would be John Waters' next film, the universally loved and charming musical comedy *Hairspray* (1988), with its theme of anti-racism sitting alongside classic bad taste tropes, that represented a sea change in terms of his popularity. Made on a budget of $2.7m, *Hairspray* is based on *The Buddy Deane Show* (1957–1964), Baltimore's version of *American Bandstand*, a teenage dance party broadcast live on television to a home audience who longed to be on the show. *The Buddy Deane Show* was racially segregated and in Waters' version, *The Corny Collins Show*, these boundaries are broken down. It's a film directly about racism but also the achievability of visibility, whatever your dress size.

Grossing over $8m, *Hairspray* was a huge hit and a joyous film, although its release was shot through with sadness following the sudden, unexpected death of Divine on March 7, 1988. Well-known on the London club scene, Divine had played a sold-old solo gig at the Scala in December 1982 as part of a European tour of gay venues and student unions. As British writer and activist Paul Burston said:

> I saw Divine as a musician. I didn't know that Divine was an actor, and an actor with John Waters. I discovered that by coming here, to the Scala [. . .] I think one of the important things to me, being a regular at the Scala was seeing stories on screen that were untold stories until that point for me. Because when I grew up, there weren't stories that reflected the life that I lived or fantasized about or wanted. They just didn't exist. There were no gay characters on soap operas, there was nothing. So, coming here and seeing these stories on the screen, whether they were outrageous stories like John Waters films or whether they were sexy stories, or whatever they were, they gave me this inspiration.[25]

The Scala's April 1988 programme was emblazoned with Divine's face and featured a raucous All-Night tribute screening *Pink Flamingos*, *Female Trouble*, *Polyester*, *Trouble in Mind* (Alan Rudolph, 1985) and Bartel's *Lust in the Dust*. The event was hosted by "Little Taffy" and promised fabulous prizes for the most Divinely Dressed Person, a close contestant for which was the Scala's own box-office cashier. The programme copy concluded, "Show some respect: wear a wig!"

Hairspray had been acquired for U.K. distribution by the Scala's parent company Palace Pictures, established in 1982 by Stephen Woolley and his business partner Nik Powell, primarily to capitalize on the burgeoning home video entertainment industry. *Pink Flamingos* was one of the first titles they released on VHS before moving into film production with *The Company of Wolves* (Neil Jordan, 1984). Palace often used the Scala to test screen its acquisitions or preview new releases to build word of mouth, and in May 1988 brought John Waters to London to promote *Hairspray*. Ever the showman, the director had always traveled extensively with his films to do introductions, Q&As and press interviews building audiences and loyalty, his wit and personality part of the brand.

For its first public screenings in the U.K., the Scala's ever-eccentric programme copy for May 1988 declared: "Surprisingly the film makes a social statement of sorts on 60s racism and is technically Waters' best movie to date. But don't despair, while having achieved, at last, mainstream appeal, Waters still serves us up a trashy piece of high camp. Recommended."

From the first to the last show that day, the reaction grew increasingly wild as the Scala's hardcore audience turned out in force, with Waters present to witness "the most insane vocal partying great audience I ever saw."[26] That night ended with celebratory drinks at the Wag Club in the West End of London, during which Scala cinema programmer Mark Valen was put in a headlock and tossed onto the street by an over-zealous bouncer. Famous for his love of violence, Waters was suitably impressed, and in Valen's telling,

> John was so excited by this that he said, "If you ever want to come and visit me in Baltimore, you're welcome to. Here's my card." Which eventually I did. But it wasn't meant to be that kind of a night though. It just sort of happened spontaneously.[27]

The Scala subsequently programmed *Hairspray* with retro movies *Grease* (Randal Kleiser, 1978), *Shag* (Zelda Barron, 1989), and as part of the Mix, an enduringly popular club night with live drag acts and films including *ABBA: The Movie* (Lasse Hallström, 1977), *Barbarella* (Roger Vadim, 1968), and *Can't Stop the Music* (Nancy Walker, 1980). It also showed with *The Big Meat Eater* (Chris Windsor, 1982), *Superstar: The Karen Carpenter Story* (Todd Haynes, 1987), and *Heathers* (Michael Lehmann, 1989), in addition to Waters' other films.

The success of *Hairspray* naturally attracted the major studios' interest, to whom John Waters delivered *Cry-Baby* (1990), an $11m budgeted rock 'n' roll juvenile delinquent musical starring Johnny Depp and featuring appearances by cult figures including Traci Lords, Patricia Hearst, Joe Dallesandro, and Iggy Pop. The Scala had history with the latter. In July 1972 music promoter Tony Defries had hired the Scala, then known as the King's Cross Cinema, for the weekend for two of his artists to play their first U.K. solo gigs: first Lou Reed and then Iggy Pop. The photographer Mick Rock was there both nights, and the pictures he took became the famous album covers for Reed's *Transformer* (1972) and Iggy and The Stooges' *Raw Power* (1973).

Citing the success of its *Hairspray* previews, Scala requested a special advance screening of *Cry-Baby* for John Waters' fans as part of major distributor UIP's marketing campaign. Chris Hedges, MD of UIP, came in person to inspect the suitability of the cinema. He asked for the auditorium house lights to be turned up—and promptly turned down the request. Nonetheless, the Scala programmed *Cry-Baby* as soon as it became available for repertory bookings, in November 1990, double-billed with a brand new 35mm widescreen print of *The Girl Can't Help It* (Frank Tashlin, 1956). The Scala later experimented by programming *Cry-Baby* with *Pee Wee's Big Adventure* (Tim Burton, 1985) and *Lonesome Cowboys* (Paul Morrissey and Andy Warhol, 1968).

Waters later commented, "Although *Cry-Baby* was not my best movie—a fact I'm well aware of—more people saw it than any other movie I've made in my life."[28] In the U.S., the film opened wide on 1229 screens. It would be the last of Waters' films to screen at the Scala, which closed in June 1993 amidst a perfect storm of the bankruptcy of Palace Pictures the previous year, a year-long court case over an illegal screening of *A Clockwork Orange* (Stanley Kubrick, 1971), and the expiration of its King's Cross cinema lease during a period of both recession and local urban redevelopment. Asked if he was aware of the Scala's closure, John Waters replied:

> It was very sad. Every time I hear any movie theatre that I love is closed down, it's like an end of an era. Also, for me, it was financial. It was where my movies played all the time. You hate it when one of the greatest places that plays your films over and over closes. Are you kidding? It was terrible news. It's still terrible news. I wish it was open now.[29]

*

The repertory cinema audience, and particularly the audience for double-bills and All-Nighters, largely migrated to home entertainment as VHS was overtaken by DVD, hardware and digitization both fell in price, and streaming technologies emerged. Simultaneously, Waters' films *Serial Mom* (1994, $13m budget), *Pecker* (1998, $6m budget), *Cecil B. Demented* (2000, $10m budget), and *A Dirty Shame* (2004, $15m budget) can be seen to have experienced diminishing returns, despite their pleasures.

The final room in the *John Waters: Pope of Trash* exhibition neatly summarized how he himself has entered popular culture, with appearances in many different shows, from *The Simpsons* (Syndicated, 1989–) to *Chucky* (Syfy, 2021–), to the Baltimore-shot *Homicide: Life on the Street* (NBC, 1993–1999). There's also a selection of amateur fan art. It's easy to trace the legacy of the Scala cinema, because we know the names of some of the young people who were in its audience and went on to become filmmakers, including: Danny Boyle, Jonathan Glazer, Mary Harron, Isaac Julien, Beeban Kidron, Martin McDonagh, Steve McQueen, Christopher Nolan, Richard Stanley, Peter Strickland, Sam Taylor-Johnson, Jake West, and Ben Wheatley. We've yet to understand the legacy of the Scala audience's films in terms of who their films may have influenced, the new generation of filmmakers. We've also yet to understand the difference between the influence of films seen on the big screen with an audience, and those watched on small screens, usually at home. Without laughs, cheers, applause, shrieks of horror, or cries of disgust, what does it mean? Here's John Waters with his final word on the subject:

> Whenever you say to young people "Oh you don't have it as good as we did" that means you've become an old fart. Yes, they're having just as much fun as we had. They're doing it a different way. They're celebrating movies a different way. And to be honest, I'm not sure young people even like art films that much anymore. Mostly it doesn't seem that they're looking for controversial films. Whenever I go to art films in America, art theatres, it's all old people. Everybody in the audience is over sixty. So, it is a different world.
>
> When we went to the Scala, the video wasn't even out yet. You couldn't watch a movie over and over. Now you can watch a movie ten times in one night. In the Underground, in those days, you had to go to these theatres to see it again. You might have seen it once when you were young, but you couldn't see it again unless they got a print. So, all that's changed. It's much less rarefied. It's so much easier to see anything today. But maybe that's better. You don't have to move to New York, you don't have to move to London to be able to see every single weird movie in the world. You can get it online. So, in a way, it has made way more people able to see weird movies.
>
> But people always want to be the only one who knows about it and really loves it. It's a great way to be a film snob. If only you have ever seen this

one movie. Now everybody can see it. You can't really be as effective a film snob as you used to. Which was so much fun, to be a film snob.

I made my first movie with my friends, just like kids make movies today with their cell phone. It's a lot easier. All they have is that little thing. I'd have those big heavy things with a neck brace that you had to carry around, with sound on film. It was harder then, but we would have done it the same way.[30]

NOTES

1. John Waters, interview by Jane Giles and Ali Catterall, August 18, 2021.
2. John Waters, interview by Jane Giles and Ali Catterall, August 18, 2021.
3. Isaac Julien, interview by Jane Giles and Ali Catterall, August 3, 2021.
4. Alan Jones, interview by Jane Giles and Ali Catterall, June 29, 2021.
5. Jane Giles, *Scala Cinema 1978–1993* (FAB Press, 2018), 10.
6. Douglas Hart, interview by Jane Giles and Ali Catterall, May 26, 2021.
7. Mark Moore, interview by Jane Giles and Ali Catterall, July 6, 2021.
8. Barry Adamson, interview by Jane Giles and Ali Catterall, June 29, 2021.
9. Waters, interview by Jane Giles and Ali Catterall.
10. William Goldman, *Adventures in the Screen Trade*.
11. John Waters, *Shock Value* (Running Press, 2005), 20.
12. Ibid., 20.
13. Waters, interview by Jane Giles and Ali Catterall.
14. Ibid.
15. Ibid.
16. Ibid.
17. Ibid.
18. Ibid.
19. Waters, *Shock Value*, 109.
20. Waters, interview by Giles and Catterall.
21. John Waters, *Crackpot* (Fourth Estate, 1990), 110.
22. Ibid.
23. Waters, interview by Giles and Catterall.
24. Adam Buxton, interview by Jane Giles and Ali Catterall, June 15, 2021.
25. Paul Burston, interview by Jane Giles and Ali Catterall, June 11, 2021.
26. Waters, interview by Giles and Catterall.
27. Mark Valen, interview by Jane Giles and Ali Catterall, August 12, 2021.
28. John Waters, *Film Threat* (April 15, 1994): 41.
29. Waters, interview by Giles and Catterall.
30. Ibid.

PART III

Interview

CHAPTER 13

Interview with John Waters Conducted by Michelle E. Moore and Brian Brems at His Home in Baltimore, November 2, 2023

BB: Tell me what you love about Baltimore.
John Waters: What I love about Baltimore—I've written about it so much. It's like a character in my movies. I just stayed where I grew up. And I say it now—when I go all over the country and do my shows, I say to all the kids, "Stay where you are. You don't have to"—it used to be you had to move to New York or L.A. if you lived in America to be in the movies or anything. I didn't. I knew what was going on there. I went there, and I got my movies shown there, and I knew the places I had to go, but I just stayed here and made Baltimore a character and made Baltimore—which people had an inferiority complex about then. I don't think they do now, but then they did. And so I just embraced all the things about Baltimore that was used against it. That's how you always change things, if you embrace what they use against you. Like when Trump came out against Baltimore not that long ago and said rats and roaches, I said, "are you kidding me?" Ricki Lake had a roach dress in *Hairspray*. We had rats. She kicked off her shoes when she was in love. You embrace what they use against you and then it doesn't hurt them. You can't use it. And also, it was always an eccentric city. I mean, even Mayor Schaefer, who was a loved mayor here, he was not a hipster at all or knew anything about the arts hardly. And this was when all my movies were getting arrested and everything. I hadn't made *Hairspray*. And he said, "I don't know what they are, but just keep making them here." That was kind of the attitude.

BB: What was it like when you first started making films here?
Waters: I didn't even know how to make one. I lived in my parents' house. I made one in high school called *Hag in a Black Leather Jacket*. Well, that was in '64, yeah. And I just learned from doing it because I had read about Jonas

Mekas and all the underground movies in New York, and I used to go on the Greyhound bus and go watch them. And so I didn't know what I was doing. I didn't know there was editing. I was very *Dogme 95*. I didn't even know it. *Hag in a Black Leather Jacket*, I filmed it in order of shots, and that was the movie. So I just learned from doing it and seeing movie after movie after movie. That was the main thing. I went to the movies really a lot. All kinds. But I saw all the foreign movies that broke the censorship laws. And exploitation movies, they tested them here. We were the exploitation capital of the world, I think. So I saw all of them and then the underground movies which never showed here. I had to go to New York City and put them all together, which were never together kind of.

BB: Why did you decide to stay here as opposed to going to New York or L.A.?
Waters: Well, I have an apartment in New York now, but L.A. would be the worst place for—would have been the worst thing for my career because they would have gotten used to me. They're still not used to me. I come there, they listen to what I'm going to do, they listen, they got a week I'm here, blah, blah, blah. If they were going to see me every week at a party, I'd be like everybody else there. So I never wanted to live there. And L.A. is incredibly seductive when things are going well, which they certainly are now; I have this whole Academy Awards Museum show, I got the star, it couldn't be better, my profile couldn't be higher. But when things are going bad, it's kind of the worst place to be. And in show business, you will always have both. It's never all of one. It's always like the stock market; hopefully it goes up.

BB: What do you think your attitude towards Baltimore is in your movies? How do we see the movies reflect that?
Waters: In my movies, it's praised. I mean, I shot in all kind of the worst neighborhoods but made them look great because everything's sort of reversed in my movies. The villains are the heroes. It's always kind of worse, and the normal people are usually either the villains or the oppressors in some way. So I mean, Baltimore, in *Cecil B. Demented*, I showed every movie theater. I'm really glad that I got that, every marquee and inside everyone. So if you look back, even in *Pink Flamingos*, when Divine is walking around at the top of Harbor Place there, that was before they restored it. Now it's bad again. It got good. But you can see Baltimore all through it, different places. I mean, how it's Divine walking downtown in *Pink Flamingos* or in *Female Trouble* and stuff, those buildings aren't even there. So it is a history of it in some ways.

BB: Do you think there's a definitive film about Baltimore?
Waters: No, I think if you look at Barry Levinson's movies, he captured something very different than I did. And Barry and I didn't meet till we were on the cover of *Baltimore Magazine* together way later, and we became friends, and we talked about it. He lived maybe 10—we both lived in—I lived in Lutherville, he

Figure 13.1 John Waters in Baltimore, November 2023, interviewed by the editors. © Mark Weissburg, 2023.

lived in Pikesville. It's on the Baltimore Beltway, 10, 15 miles apart. He said he never met anyone that wasn't Jewish 'til after high school, and I never met a Jew 'til after high school, and we lived 15 miles away. So that's the thing about Baltimore; the neighborhoods are strong, but people don't leave them, and that's why racism is here.

MM: Congratulations on your honorary doctorate from the University of Baltimore.
Waters: Oh, that was that one, but I've gotten many other doctorates. . . . I got one at RISD. I got two at School of Visual Arts, but I didn't go there. I did go to University of Baltimore because I got thrown out of Catholic high school, and then I failed, and then I had to go to summer school at this private school that my parents knew that my brother went to, and they passed me. I don't even know where I got my high school diploma. I don't even know. I guess I have one. But then I couldn't get in anywhere, so I went to University of Baltimore, which at that time, anybody could go actually. I mean, I'd just been thrown out of school and failed. But there, I was on a literary magazine, and then I got in NYU just from talking, and then I got thrown out of NYU for pot. So basically, school was never great for me because I knew what I wanted to do. That's the thing, you go to school because you don't know what you want to do, I think.

If you know what you want to do, don't waste time with school. I mean, you can meet people, and you can learn. You can learn how to get along and how to negotiate in school. That's why I'm against homeschooling. No matter what hell is for a kid, you have to learn how to negotiate. You can't just be protected from assholes. I mean, they're everywhere. And in high school was the peak. And they are the ones that are accepted in high school, and then their life is downhill afterwards, where the people that weren't, their life goes uphill if they know what they want to do. [laughter]

MM: You have said there was a teacher at the University of Baltimore that taught you how to write.
Waters: Yeah. Miss Norris was her name. Yeah. And there was a magazine called—she didn't teach me what to write. I knew how to write. There was a magazine called *Welter*, and I wrote a story, and it got in there. So that was the first thing I had published. But I had published something else in *Fact Magazine* that was supposed to be exposés. It was a national magazine. But I made the whole thing up, and I got published there. That might have been first. The first thing I was ever published [in] was *Life Magazine*. I wrote a letter sticking up for Andy Warhol when I was a kid in high school. And I always think—they don't have letters to the editor anymore in magazines. And if they do, it's an email. But I always thought before, it would be a good high school exercise; get in print. How can you get in print? And a letter to the editor is probably the first way you can.

MM: And then you transferred up to NYU.
Waters: Yeah. But I only went to two classes. I went to the movies all the time, but University didn't throw me out. I was thrown out of the dorm for marijuana, and then they recommended extensive psychiatric treatment. Anyway, so I came home and made *Roman Candles*. [laughter]

MM: What movies did you see?
Waters: I saw everything on 42nd Street. I saw all the exploitation movies. But I also saw all the Warhol early movies and all the underground movies and Kenneth Anger and all that kind of stuff. So I saw the underground stuff. I saw the foreign movies. But on 42nd Street, I was seeing all the definite exploitation movies that then, no one wrote about except *Variety*. They reviewed them all. But they weren't written about. Intellectuals did not write about those movies then. They had no fan base except crazy people that went to 42nd Street, but they were just to make money. They weren't even written about in a serious at all way or even a comic way, really, except in *Variety* that did review them.

MM: What were the foreign movies?
Waters: Oh, Fellini and Bergman. And Bergman, in Baltimore, was shown as a sex movie. They cut out a lot of the dialogue and kept the tits in, basically. And it was *Sins of Monika*! I can show you, downstairs in my kitchen, an ad that was "forget the Monika hot Sunday in the concession stand." Can you believe

that? And that was not an art theater. [laughter] And we had a censor board too, one of the only three states in the country that do. And we did, so I was always battling with her.

BB: How do you think audiences have shifted with the release of films from theaters to VHS to DVDs to streaming? How does this affect the way audiences watch your movies?
Waters: Well, it helped me in some way. I mean, first of all, in the old days, when *Pink Flamingos* came out, there was no video or DVD. So that's why it could play for 10 years in a theater at midnight, which I did in Los Angeles. And when I was young, a movie opened downtown, first-run, and it played six weeks. And then two weeks later, it opened in suburbia maybe to five second-run theaters, and that was it. You could never see it again unless it was on television, late-night. There was no such thing as—so when video came out, first of all, it was great for porn. That's what first started people getting it. But it gave away all the magic tricks. You could rewind. You could see how they did something, which in a way I was against. But then it helped my movies very much. The videos and everything got them so everybody could see them. You didn't have to go to some weird theater and go to New York to see it. If you lived in Duluth or anywhere in America, they were available all of a sudden. And then with DVDs, completely. And nowadays, it's so switched that art movie theaters where I did—I did exploitation movies for art theaters, which there was no such thing. And there still isn't really. But I did, and it worked. And the richer the neighborhood, the smarter the neighborhood, the better I did. The closer it was to a real grindhouse, the worse I did. They bombed at drive-ins. They didn't work because they smelled a rat, me. Because they were jerking off watching those movies. They were screaming. They thought they were sexy. They didn't think they were funny. They didn't see them ironically in any way.

And now they try to make ironic ones, and it doesn't work because they're trying too hard. You don't have to wink at us. We get it. So, no one was winking in those exploitation movies. And in all the Bergman movies, I just loved them because they were so raw and about depressing material and all that, which I always liked. I always say my favorite genre is feel-bad French movies with frontal nudity. But growing up, I mean the art cinemas here, we had three, and you got espresso coffee when you went. That was so radical. No one had ever heard of espresso coffee. And they played movies sometimes for forty weeks, they would play. And it would be the same gross, 3000 a week or something, I remember. But movies were hits here. Art hits had a very specific audience, and they still do. But after COVID, old people didn't come back. And young people don't like art movies that much. They want to go to a mall and see a comic book movie and then riot afterwards. That's what they want to do. So it's a very different thing now. And streaming, to me, I don't know. I need three assistants to turn on my television. But I watch them. I watch them anyway. To me, right now, there's more people that can say yes to a movie because we've got Netflix. I just want people to see them. How they see them, I like them in a theater, but I don't always go to the theater anymore. Especially when I have to watch a million movies for my top 10 list or something. They stream them for me. It's easy. Sometimes I just have to watch them when I can.

But I do like to go to the movies. And the movie theaters here have been the same for a long time, struggling. And where I appeared this week, I was in Duluth, I was in a lot of places, and it's the one art theater that's in that town, that's been there forever, and they lasted because they have a niche audience. They've built a community, where—it was like the bookstores in America. When all the Borders came out and everything, they thought they're going to put all the little ones out of business. The opposite happened. They stayed in business, and the chains went out of business because they didn't know how to—people go to the movies, they want to meet people, they want to have fun, they want to—yeah. So they kept that niche audience, and I think that's what I always was after, and I've had a very loyal audience for fifty years. But there's still—young people come too now, really young, and they're like twenty. Wouldn't have been born when I made my last movie. So that's why I do all my spoken word shows and keep out. I'm always on the road because I'm a carny, and you have to meet your audience. We've got it all, and we show it all.

BB: Can you describe for me some of the differences in the way you worked early on with a lot of Dreamlanders and then movies later that you made for studios?

Waters: Well, it was completely different because I knew what I was doing. I learned each time. Each time we got a little more money, we got a little more, bigger crew and everything. But people always helped me. Even in the early days, I just had one person, you know? And we would rent the equipment from—and this was big heavy cameras that had magnetic film on them, so it's filming the sound. It was what they used for news teams then. But the news teams would illegally rent it to us. They'd sneak the camera. And these would be teamster types that would come with the equipment, and I'd pay them, and they would teach me how to do it. We'd be in the woods making *Pink Flamingos*, and if you think about that, it was amazing how much they went along with it because I'm sure their politics was probably very, very different than—that was a time of hippies and craziness, and they were great. They really helped me do it and everything. So I learned from them, and then each time I got a little more, and I always got Variety, so I knew the business. I knew how to get distributors. I tried to. And I wrote a lot about that in my book, Mr. Know-it-all. In all my books, I tell the stories of what happened to them.

MM: In the beginning, what were you doing behind the camera?

Waters: In the beginning, in the first round, everything. *Hag in a Black Leather Jacket*—in *Hag*, *Roman Candles*, *Eat Your Makeup*, and *Mondo Trasho*, there was no lip sync dialogue. So we filmed them silent, and then I put in music that unfortunately I didn't pay for, and that's why they're not out today. I didn't even know you had to. I mean, later I did, but it was too late. So they were silent films, only the music was the narrator. The music told the story by the dialogue and everything, by using the words of the song. So I would shoot them silent, and then I would edit them with a hot splicer. You put the glue down and did it. And so you could see the cut on everything. I never even made a print, I don't think. I think on *Eat Your Makeup*, I played the sound on all those movies on reel-to-reel tape recorder, and I had to go, "One, two, three, start it." So sometimes, I'd have to stop the film for it to catch up because it wasn't on the—there was no print to this day. Well, the Academy did restore it, but of a real movie print of those movies with the soundtracks even on the film. They were always on reel-to-reel tape. And I would have to show them. I would go to the theater if I got a booking, set up the cameras in the theater—or tape recorder, and I was the projectionist.

MM: Was there anything from those days that you continued to do as a holdover, as a filmmaker?
Waters: Write them.

I never made a movie I didn't write. I never would ever do it, and I would have no interest. I always cast them. I worked with people like Pat Moran and Vince [Peranio] from the very beginning. And certainly, Pat went on, she's won Emmys. Vince went on, he did The Wire. He did a lot of stuff. But the core group we kind of started with was just my friends. The same way every kid starts to make movies today. They take their cell phone, and they go with their friends and make a movie. I maybe had a little weirder friends, and maybe we were a little more driven, and we were a little more terrorist, and it was in a way it was—I look back on it to realize it was a political act against the tyranny of good taste. But certainly, we weren't saying that when we did it. We were just trying to make a movie that would make us laugh. And we were rebelling against the rules that outsiders live by. Just like today, I make fun of politically correct rules, even though that is my audience. Hippies, same thing. I made *Multiple Maniacs*, the opposite of a peace and love movie. So I was always making fun of that, but those people, my audience that came, they wanted to be outraged by it. They weren't mad at me for doing it. They were hippies that didn't get along with other hippies. They became punks. So it was always one step ahead in a weird way of—like all humor is political. I mean, I say that in my show. In a way, it is because you're getting people to laugh and then to listen and then change. I think I didn't realize—people come over to me now crying saying, "You saved my life with those movies," which is amazing to me. I'm flattered, but I certainly didn't think I was doing that when I made them. It wasn't.

MM: Do you have any thoughts on Maya Deren and her do-it-yourself [aesthetic]?
Waters: Maya Deren, no. I knew who she was, but she wasn't—no, she was part of that Jonas Mekas club, but that was more the experimental side. I liked Kenneth Anger, the Kuchar Brothers, the Warhol. As far as the whole other crowd, Stan Vanderbeek and all that, I like them today more than I liked them then. They were the other ones. We didn't sit with them. They didn't sit with us. I mean emotionally.

MM: What changed for you now that you look at them from this vantage point?
Waters: Well, I see that they were radical technique, but technique I make fun of. I always said that in *Cecil B. Demented*, technique is nothing more than failed style, which is true. Because people look at—I didn't know what I was doing when I made those movies, but if you like them, you call it raw. If you don't, you say amateur. It's the same thing. And I always say if you come from a movie and say the cinematographer was great, that means it's a bad movie if that's the first thing you say when you leave the thing. And I think cinematography can be great, but that shouldn't be the first thing you say. Cinematography is a part of the whole movie. So to me, it's always the script and the people in it.

BB: What kind of experiments would you say that you did in your filmmaking that worked, that didn't work, that you would change?
Waters: I don't know that I'd call it an experiment. Just making it was an experiment. What worked and didn't work? Well, what I say to every kid today, if you think it's too long, cut it. They're all too long. At first, when you first make a movie, you don't want to cut anything. But also, I was influenced then by the Warhol movies that were purposely boring and long. So people say in the beginning of *Mondo Trasho*, "Why does it take her 10 minutes to get on the bus?" Because it was Sunday, the bus didn't come as much [laughter]. So we just would—what I learned is that audiences have some trouble with surrealism. They don't basically like it. They always recognize a star, and the Hollywood system has worked the same way it did with me. When people first saw Edith [Massey], you could tell they loved her. I gave her bigger parts, Divine too. You could just tell audiences hook on to some people that have it. They like to be surprised, but shock is easy, but making them laugh is harder, and most everyone always laughed in my movies, I think, with them, not at them. And they liked that other people were nervous around them; they liked that. They liked that it was a test. Nowadays, people say, "My parents gave me your movies." I think, "They did?" [laughter] When I was young, they called the police and stuff. So it was then an us versus them thing, but that was going on in the '60s. The critics were all straight, but straight didn't mean sexual; straight meant you didn't smoke pot. So there was that world always fighting. And the establishment, I made all bad reviews we used in the ads because they were from critics that we hated them. They never liked what we liked. So to

put Rex Reed, a negative review, which helped. [laughter] You couldn't do that today, it wouldn't work. Well, there's not many critics left, but there's not that many that have that power, but they would be too smart to know. They would know not to do that, yeah.

MM: Your films are partly documentaries of Baltimore, of earlier times, of fashions, of dances. Do you think of them as in any way documentary?
Waters: No, I don't think of them as documentaries. I think, though, that people that were on the real *Buddy Deane Show*, when they saw *Hairspray*, they said to me, "I felt like I was in the Twilight Zone." It was so accurate of what it looked like and what it felt like. Documentary, well, they are certainly—they're saying write what you know. Certainly, and I want to show that, what we did in Baltimore, and what we had here, and that was normal here. People forget all those giant hairdos; that was totally normal in Baltimore. That wasn't a rebel look. Your mother got her hair done the same way. But it was this class issue. Where I grew up, it was not cool to do that. In working-class neighborhoods, it was. So it was a class issue. And then when overnight they ironed their hair, that's when hippies started, and everybody changed, and all the girls with teased hair, it was over. Their life was over. That was the end if they didn't switch over to the flat hair.

MM: Do you see your films as educational? Is that a motive?
Waters: Yes. I think they're educational, yeah. I mean, there was a book called *The Erotic Minorities* by Dr. Lars Ullerstand, the *Grove Press* put out in the '60s. That was a huge influence because it had—it was like *A Dirty Shame*, it had like every kind of weird sexual thing. I read Freud; I love Freud. I read Dr. John Money, who was a Baltimore sexologist who went on to great notoriety, and Oprah wrecked his career. But anyway, so I always read about that kind of thing and was interested in it. And I went to the Kinsley Institute, which was amazing. So that was part of it, and it was educating people. And I always said I made movies for minorities that couldn't even fit in their own minorities, like gay people. The first time I went to a gay bar, I thought, "I ain't this." I'm gay, but this was so square. And I say in my show now, "Why is gay music so bad?" And everybody freaks, and then they laugh because it is. [laughter] But so I'm always trying to use humor to get you to think about things maybe you hadn't thought about before.

MM: You're an avid collector. Your films can [also] be seen as collections.
Waters: Well, they're still available too. That's the most amazing thing. The ones that were from *Multiple Maniacs* on, they're probably more available now than they ever were. I mean, they play on Turner Classics. How could that be? And that's my favorite quote ever, that *Pink Flamingos* played on Turner Classics, which is amazing to me. But the little thing in the program, it just said, "Fat woman lives in trailer." [laughter] And that's my favorite review I ever got in my

whole life. Well, that gets right down to it. Fat woman lives in trailer. Who came up with that? What brilliant publicist came up with that blurb? It just made me laugh so hard when somebody sent it to me, "Look how they're pushing it." This was in the program.

MM: And each individual film is a collection of perversions, of hairdos—
Waters: Perversion, I guess, is a word I use. It sounds harsher than the way I use it. In the movies, they aren't perverted to the people that have it; it's normal. That's the thing. I don't present it—I present it as normal. Now, I saw all the Mondo movies, *Mondo Cane*, all that, which was showing, "This is how people live." And that's why I made *Mondo Trasho*. It was a joke on that. But the people in the film don't think they're perverse. Same way in *Hairspray*, it still doesn't get attacked for drag, even in the South when it's done in grade schools, because Edna is a man, but that's a secret between the audience and the actors. Tracy doesn't think her mother's a man. So they don't know how to attack it. So to me, I was always trying to confuse people, even hipsters and even people that were so liberal, to make them be nervous in a humorous way. Including myself. I wanted stuff that would make me nervous.

BB: Do you think you are a part of the avant-garde?
Waters: No, that word always sounds pretentious to me, and it always sounds—I mean, that word, if people use it again—no, to me, avant-garde would be Stan Vanderbeek, that kind of thing. Or—no, I don't think I'm part of the avant-garde. I'm a commercial.

BB: Why do you think not?
Waters: Because avant-garde sounds to me pretentious, that anyone would say, "I'm the avant-garde," would be an asshole.

BB: A little self-important.
Waters: Yeah, yeah. If someone else said that about me, I'd say that's a compliment, but you're wrong.
Waters: I mean, I'm not *not* that, but to me, that sounds a little too effete. It sounds a little too precious. I hate whimsy.

BB: What do you think was attractive about film as a medium to people in your position?
Waters: I don't know. I just always was drawn to that. I always was a storyteller, and that's what I am as a writer. I'm a better writer than a filmmaker because I do everything. Not only do I—I write books, I write movies, I write shows, I write everything. I am a writer first, but movies was always a great way for me to tell a story. And I was drawn to that from the beginning, being a movie buff, because there were so many different niches of movies and so many genres. And all my movies make fun of a genre. I mean, *Mondo Trasho* was a shockumentary joke. *Multiple Maniacs*, a gore movie. *Pink Flamingos*, a shock

movie. *Female Trouble*, a biopic. *Desperate Living*, a medical movie. *Polyester*, gimmicks of Smell-O-Vision, William Castle. *Hairspray*, a dance movie. *Cry-Baby*, a musical. *Serial Mom*, a true crime movie. *Pecker*, an art pic about an artist. *Cecil B. Demented*, a political movie. And *A Dirty Shame*, sexploitation. So there they are. The only thing I haven't done is science-fiction because I don't know the genre. And a Western because you can't say Indian anymore, so you'd have to say cowboy and indigenous. I thought indigenous, when I was young, meant people that didn't have arms or legs.

BB: Do you consider yourself a provocateur?
Waters: Yeah, sure. But I think I wouldn't say that word either. But yes, that would be way closer than avant-garde.

BB: Why? Why do you think that's closer?
Waters: Because I'm trying to do that to myself. I'm trying to make myself laugh, and what can I get away with that's still humor that isn't just offensive? It has to be not offensive. That's easy to do. It's so easy to do that today, especially. But to make you laugh and be unsure, be nervous if you're laughing, I think is the best kind. That's why Lenny Bruce went to jail for saying cocksucker in 1961. Now, if you called someone a cocksucker in San Francisco, they'd say, "What's the matter with that?" They would be mad that you were using that derogatorily. So words have power to change, and that's what always fascinates me. What can you and can't you do in the supposed outlaw world?

BB: Who ought to be most provoked or shocked?
Waters: I don't know. Everybody should just—the self-righteous are the kind of—for the first time, my whole new show was about this, that basically the right wing gave up on me. They don't hassle me. And the left wing, if I'm ever going to get it, I'd fear it from there, but I haven't gotten it from them. I haven't. But I'm weary of the self-righteous of the left and the closed mind of the right. So I'm a middle-of-the-road maniac now, and that's the first time I've ever been middle of the road. But that's my whole show.

BB: What would you say that used to shock you that doesn't shock you anymore?
Waters: I mean, nudity started. First, you could see a woman's ass, then her breast, then her vagina, then a man's ass, then a man's dick, then fake fucking, then real fucking, then oral sex. That was how it fell, the worlds of censorship. And I witnessed all of that. I saw every film, and you could see like *I Am Curious (Yellow)*, *Mona*, the different movies that broke each thing. And that was fascinating to watch. And once it was over, there was no more exploitation movies because you could do everything. Hollywood has gore in the movie. They have real sex. The only exploitation movie I think that even came out this year would be *Cocaine Bear*. And that was an old-fashioned exploitation movie. But they don't work anymore because all that stuff you can do. So that's

the thing. You can see any—porn's free now. You can just google "Clarence Thomas' anus," and it comes right up without even buffering. So free porn, I mean, it's over. That whole thing, there is no more of those kind of battles anymore. Before, Jackie Kennedy went to see *Deep Throat* when it came out and *I Am Curious (Yellow)*; it became this huge thing. But nowadays, it's just nothing. I mean, porn's free. As soon as porn was free, it was over. You have to have a guilt tax. You can't have free porn. And there's no porn stars anymore because why? Because it's amateur.

So all that, and Herschel Gordon Lewis always said that. He always said, "I make what Hollywood can't show." When they got where they could show frontal nudity, I did gore because there wasn't a law, but that's why we did eating shit in *Pink Flamingos*, as a joke on that. What's left? And I would say Johnny Knoxville's the only one that would have done that after me. So what is left? And what is left is to make fun of—I guess of everyone's rules now, except the obvious ones that everybody thinks they're beyond. So I always said I used to be an outsider, now I want to be an insider. I always want to be what everybody else doesn't want to be, and that's where the humor comes from, kind of. But with movies, it's the same thing. My movies don't work at midnight anymore, they work better at 9 o'clock at night. Even young people don't go to midnight movies anymore, I don't think. They're even home earlier after COVID. I didn't used to go out 'til midnight.

BB: Do you think cinema is still a valuable art form to do that?

Waters: Sure, yeah, it's a still—a movie, yes. And I usually think it's the foreign directors that—and I read a really sad article on Variety or *Deadline* somewhere recently that even the French, the government gives money for those movies, right? Gaspar Noé, Bruno, all those movies. If they were in America, the government would try to stop them. But they're stopping to. They're stopping to because not enough people are going to see them even in France. And so that's scary because without that European cinema that always broke laws and came up with new things and the kind I really like, it'll really be bland, and it'll just be all commercial. I don't hate all commercial movies, but I must admit the number one movie in America, I've never even heard of it because we don't have movie marketing anymore. I miss that. I miss display ads and papers. The ads used to be so great, they were better than the movies. And I always had an ad campaign. I always had a unit photographer. I had stills when I didn't even have a sound person because that's what people remember. You can't get your film shown if you don't have stills. And that one with Divine with a gun, I mean, that's been copied. Balenciaga did the same dress this year. Isabelle Huppert wore it to the Met Ball. So *From Here to Eternity*, that picture of them making out on the beach, nobody remembers that movie. They remember that picture. So I always had a still. I always had stills. So I was always an exploiter. I don't mean that badly. I always was a carny. I knew that I had to sell the movie.

BB: What is offensive to you in filmmaking?
Waters: Offensive is whimsy or hackneyed sentimentality or such political correctness that I feel like I'm getting lectured at in a movie.

BB: You have said that movies saved you from becoming a mass murderer.
Waters: Well, I don't know if a mass murderer. It kept me from being—because I'm not a violent person, but—

BB: But you have anger, right?
Waters: Yeah. Yes, all the stuff that I put in all those movies. If I had done all that stuff in real life, I would be in—death penalty I would have gotten. So yes, I think it definitely did help that I had an outlet for this rage and this anger. Yes.

MM: Is that why so many people die from the death penalty in your films?
Waters: I think that came from always being interested in going to trials and stuff. And so when I made *Pink Flamingos*, I had just been to the Manson trial. So that was a huge, huge influence. And certainly, you can see a trial scene in *Pink Flamingos*, *Serial Mom*. But by then I had gone to a lot of trials. I taught in prison and everything. So that has always been—notoriety, I guess, has always been something in my movies that was an achievement, not a bad one. Even though, even at my mother's funeral, she used to always say to me, "Fools' names and fools' faces always appear in public places," meaning you should never be in the newspaper except when you're born, married, and die. Well, I really fucked that up. And so I think I did make fun of that. And I always liked the press. I always watched the headlines. I always liked the tabloid press. I still get all the tabloids. And just because I like to see their craziness, and the headlines are so berserk and crazy.

BB: Would you say that it was a desire to get to a wider audience in the 1980s?
Waters: I always wanted to have a wider audience. I always wanted to make hit movies in whatever marketplace I was in, which was first underground movies, then midnight, then independent, then Hollywood. And now I'd say I make Hollywood underground, if I make anything. So I always, in that particular world, wanted to make money. And I wanted them to look better. I wanted them to—yes, I mean, whenever I made my own stars, because I couldn't, and then even when I had them and I started using other people, the old stars I created with my friends became part of it too. And so it was all the stars, and it was all a Hollywood kind of thing, only just done on a cracked nutcase version of it. But I respected the rules of it, what you could and couldn't do. I mean, you have to have somebody—I always say someone has to like your movie besides your mother and who you're fucking. When you have the third person, your career begins.

BB: Do you think of yourself as an *auteur*?
Waters: Well, that word is—the French have been so great to me always right from the beginning, so I'm flattered by that word. I certainly would never call

myself that unless I was doing it in a humorous way. But yeah, because I write and direct, yeah. So I don't think anybody else thinks someone else made my movie. I don't think you could say, "Well, that was either him or—", so yeah. But I think, yeah, I love the French. And I can't speak a word of French except *auteur*. I can't even say "*oui*" in public. But they've been so great to me always. And they were with the book too. I just did a book tour there.

MM: What did you think film could help you express that other mediums of art cannot?
Waters: Well, I couldn't sing, or I would have exploited that because I was obsessed by early rock 'n' roll. Painting, I tried being an abstract painter when I was in my beatnik days. But film just seemed—when I first heard about underground movies, that appealed to me the most because it was showbiz, and it was the same time anybody could do it. You didn't have to have money. And I could create a whole world of crackpot kind of movie stars and plots and everything. And they were, in the beginning, very much influenced by the Theater of the Ridiculous, which was then the Theater of the Absurd, which was Edward Albee and all that, and then Theater of the Ridiculous. But I always read about the Theater of Cruelty or terror and all that kind of crazy stuff. But I just wanted to come up with my own version of it.

MM: And your own version of Theater of the Absurd, Theater of Cruelty?
Waters: All of it, of just a group of people that—there's a French word for group madness [*folie à deux*]. That's what I was always searching for.

MM: Did you wrestle with concerns about independence when you began to work within the system?
Waters: No, I was thrilled because—I always say to kids today, "If you don't want notes, if you don't want studio things, then go make a film with your friends and your camera. If you want a house, you're going to get notes." Plain and simple. So it all happened—nothing was overnight, it happened gradually. Each time it got bigger. So yes, I was drawn to New Line, and we grew up together. I mean, in the Hollywood thing, I knew that—I went through the test screenings, I went through all the bad parts of it, but I ended up putting out the movie I wanted. I learned how to negotiate my way through it. And I could buy a house. When I made *Cry-Baby*, I bought this house for the first time ever when I got a real Hollywood salary. I didn't pay for the whole thing. I got enough to—you know? And so I always was—the business of it, I knew too. And that's the thing. You do have to know the business of anything you're getting in. And I did development deals really from *Cry-Baby* on. Every one of those movies, I got a development deal to do, which meant you had to go in to pitch it. I had an ad campaign ready. I convinced them that these movies could make money. And I wanted them to. And I was always shocked when they didn't.

BB: Obviously, you consider yourself a writer. Do your films have room for the performers to ad-lib and improvise? Do you work with them together?
Waters: No.

BB: No, they have to say it exactly?
Waters: Yeah.

BB: Really?
Waters: And I actually said that when I got the lifetime achievement award of the writers. I said, here's what I have when the actors show up and say, "The first thing I do is throw out my script." Well, then join the Writers Guild! No, I mean, if we work it out, it's in rehearsal. I'm not saying I never don't change anything. But no, they don't just—and Stephen Dorff even said to me, I usually always want to change everything, but your words just seem right. If you're doing one of your movies, they seem—and people still quote a lot of the stuff, the dialogue in it. So yes, I expect you to say the dialogue. I don't have time. I'm trying to come in on budget. I'm not like *Cecil B. Demented*, "I have a vision." That was a joke. That's the worst thing you can say when you're making a movie. Have the vision before you get there on the set because you only have so many hours a day to get what you've got to get.

MM: What is the role of the actor in your films?
Waters: Well, the people that always get the part are stars, the ones that come in, that I haven't even told them how to play it in any way. And I've been playing every part in my head the whole time I wrote it, and they just do it the way in my head I had it. And that can happen from the words themselves. So the only direction I always give them is never wink. Say every ludicrous thing as if you believe every word of it, and then it'll be funny. Don't tell the audience it's funny. Let them say it's funny.

BB: Is that how you worked then with Pat Moran, your casting director?
Waters: Well, a lot of people read, and sometimes I'll say "try it" to see if they take direction. Otherwise, if they don't, well, they're not going to take direction. But I can tell immediately when they come in. I mean, I'm polite, so I let them do the whole thing, but I can tell right away. First of all, how they look does matter. But then somebody can be so good they can change that, and they become that person. So it's just their comic timing. And that's why I never hired comics except for Tracey Ullman because then they bring the shtick to it. I don't want you—it is funny, let's hope. If you took this role, you have to think it's funny anyway. You don't have to let them know, the audience, it's funny. It is funny if it works. Don't wink. And comedians often do.

BB: What do you think they [Vincent Peranio and Van Smith] bring to your films?
Waters: Well, first of all, knowledge. They know what I want. They know because they grew up here, and they know—well, Van didn't grow up here, but

he went to college here. So he knew what I was after. And they brought stuff to me, really. Certainly, Van did about fashion, definitely. And Vincent just could make a dollar holler, as we used to say in Baltimore. But also, he made a whole set out of garbage. Mortville, the whole thing was made out of garbage. So they just got it. That's all. They just got it. And we hooked up together. They worked together well. It was like a commune in a way. We hung around with each other all the time too. It wasn't just we made movies. That was our life. I mean, Mink's boyfriend used to be Vincent Peranio. People were all together.

MM: So when you have a finite budget and you have to prioritize, right?
Waters: Well, you never have enough money. No matter what, you never have enough.

MM: How do you make those choices?
Waters: Well, when you're shooting, you just have to. You have to make those choices. You have to hurry up. You have to make two shots into one. You have to be able to have it well-produced. So there's a cover set, so if it rains, this kind of thing. It's never as good as you want it to be, never. When you see the first assemblage of a movie, it's never the movie that you wanted to make. But that's what you have. And now, you make a movie out of that, the best you can. And that's the reality of it.

BB: What are you looking for in a director of photography?
Waters: Somebody that knows my limitations, that also can be fast, can work with me and not take over because I have all the say, but knows how to, "Let's move it along here." This is not about every shot being Elvira Madigan.

BB: So primarily moving quickly and—
Waters: Yeah. And getting it, telling the joke in an economic way. There's no such thing as a good long joke. Let's hit the beats. And that's an editing thing too.

MM: How much of the editing did you do?
Waters: Always. I mean, I edited them all myself up to *Female Trouble* was the first one I think I didn't. I always sat with the editor every day on all of them, even right up to the end. Not at every day at the end, but they would do a cut. I'd give the notes and come back and watch. I always was heavily involved in that. Yeah.

MM: So what does a John Waters film look like then, in your mind? What is the special look?
Waters: It has three reels. I'm still three 30-minute reels, 16-millimeter. A beginning, a middle, and an end. You have to have something at the end because that's when they're deciding in their mind what they're going to say if they liked it or not. That's when word of mouth starts. And I always say when you turn in a script to the studio, the first twenty pages get it made, but the

last twenty pages are what make it a hit. So you just have to move it along. And then that's why I'm not against all test screenings. You just need one shot, and it makes the whole thing work. But when they say, "Who didn't you like?" and they picked the villain, and how do you change that? Well, you're not supposed to like that person. Or if test screenings really worked, every movie would be a hit because they could fix every movie.

BB: Do you think that's the primary purpose of plot, then, too, is to just keep moving?
Waters: Plot is the heart. In writing, plot is the most important thing. It's what makes a hit and the hardest thing. I can think of a million characters, but the plot is the most important, yes. And there's great art films that don't have plots. I'm just saying for a hit, a movie, a hit needs a good plot, yeah. And one critic said that my plots were merely the clothesline to hang my filthy wash, which I always thought was funny [laughter]. And it was a very negative review. [laughter]

BB: Almost a compliment, though.
Waters: Yeah, yeah. No, he was right. He was 100 per cent right.

MM: What's the look you're going for with the composition of one of your films?
Waters: Always, I want it to look like a '50s Hollywood movie. I always wanted to look slick. I never could. I mean, *Cry-Baby* looks really a lot like—I wanted to look like an Elvis movie. I think *Serial Mom* looks like a Hollywood movie, so that's what, yeah. *The Girl Can't Help It*, I want it to look like that.

MM: Are there scenes in your films that you look at now and you wish you could redo to make them look different?
Waters: Oh, everything. I never sit around and watch my own movies, but if I do, what I notice the most is, "Oh, I should've cut that." But I'm happy with it. I don't want to go back and do that. When Criterion redid a lot of them, restored them, it was a thin line. I don't want that scratch there; it was an accident. But don't make it look like something it isn't. Don't leave the dirt in if there's one shot, but still don't make it look too good. [laughter]

BB: Is there a difference in cinema between good bad taste and bad bad taste?
Waters: Sure, I mean, good bad taste is sometimes completely accidental. I mean, really great bad movies didn't mean to be bad. When they're trying to be, they're never that good. It's too obvious. You're winking. But bad taste today, I always say Trump ruined it. I mean, his wife ruined it with those Christmas decorations. That was the final nail because they were so horrible, you couldn't describe them. They weren't funny. It was just over. It was no point anymore, the bad taste thing. So I don't know that what I do anymore is bad taste. I pick subjects that make people nervous. That's what I think I'm more. And I never said camp. That was like old queens talking about Rita Hayworth movies under

a Tiffany lampshade in 1963. That was good then. But then trash was good, but then that got—and then filth was more edgy, that was more punk. And now what is the word? It's just funny. I think all those words are American humor now. You don't have to say any of those words anymore. I mean, I guess edgy usually is good to me. If somebody said it's an edgy movie, that's good. That can be funny, dramatic, that can be anything. It can just be it makes you a little nervous about watching.

MM: What is visually arresting to you?
Waters: It can be a whole style. It can be something radical that makes you look at something in a different way. It's also how it's edited. If the director—I mean, when I saw *Maestro* really, I just realized that—was that the editor or the director? It was the director because he set up the shots to cut that well to it. So I noticed that kind of thing. You can just turn sound off from a movie and you see how it's made. Then you can watch it. You see they cut back, there's a master, they do all that. That's the best exercise to learn how to make movies. Just the sound disguises it all. It's the magic trick.

BB: Do you think that you use sound in your films to do that?
Waters: I use sound to hide mistakes, yeah. Definitely.

BB: How?
Waters: It's fine-tuning it. It's just going over a cut or something that makes you not notice this thing, you notice this. Sound to me, it's a whole part of the thing, but music, it's the narrator. You can always tell if a movie has a narrator it tested badly, so they had to cut out parts that the plot doesn't make sense anymore. So I use music to do that always, even when it did make sense. Like that song "Flying Saucer," that was the first thing in the '50s where they took sampled musical lyrics and told a story out of the original concept of the words. Well, that's what I—I never got over that. I still do it.

MM: I've noticed that in your films, that the music actually is advancing the plot.
Waters: Yeah, it's a narrator.

MM: Which is a really interesting use of music and actually not how most film works.
Waters: I have a score too, but that's different, but the source material, which you have to hear where is that music coming from, always is part of telling the story. It's advancing it. And I think it makes comedy work better. I think it makes it not slow. I think it speeds things up. And it makes you always interested.

BB: What role do you think cinema played in advancing political causes of queer people?
Waters: Well, gay people always watch movie stars. The parody of drag queens were really mimicking movie stars usually. I think there was always a gay undercover spying when you watch movies to think, who did that hair?

Who did that? Where was the queerness in there? It was always in the movie business, always. But hidden. It was also backstage. It was in all the different departments. So I think gay people were always looking for that, trying to figure out what it was. And if it was an exaggerated woman movie star, that is what drag was, exaggerating. Or an exaggerating man, in a way, was this hypermasculinity. And so gay people were always noticing that, I think, way before other audiences did.

BB: Do you think the highly visible representation of queer people in mainstream films like romantic comedies is—?
Waters: Well, that's brand new. I mean, that's what I'm saying. That took centuries, when trans has been accepted in a year. It's truly amazing in a way. Yes, the gay thing in movies has really made it be more accepted, led to gay marriage and everything, but it happened not that quickly. I mean, if you look back, there was always first you had to die if you were gay in a movie, you had to pay for it, and then—like *The Children's Hour*. And all these kind of movies that—I saw every one of them, and we knew every one of those movies—but we rolled our eyes at them because you had to pay for your sins at the end, or it was always the tragic hidden world of some sort. But now, I love those movies. I mean, if you watch *The Children's Hour*, oh my God, it's just like so staggering.

MM: What do you think are your best films?
Waters: *Serial Mom*, I think is my best movie.

MM: Why?
Waters: It's got everything I want. It looks good, it's got a good plot, it was ahead of its time. Kathleen's great in it. She made everybody be even better. Mink's I think great in it. I don't know. It's just, I think it's my best movie. I think it's the best script. I don't know, I just like it best.

MM: It ends with that great courtroom scene and the performance in the courtroom? It makes me think of the film noirs.
Waters: Film noirs were important to me, but I think that movie *Serial Mom* was more of a true crime thing, *In Cold Blood* and that kind of kind of plot because even at the end, it says—it confused people. It said Beverly Sutphin refused to participate in the making of this film. And people then thought it was real. And people were angry at the test screenings that they wanted her to be convicted. They were furious that she wasn't. But then it would have been a normal movie. So film noir, I think in all my movies, I can tell you a different influence of certainly Kenneth Anger's use of pop music before anybody in *Scorpio Rising*. I think Andy Warhol—drugs and gay people finally together on the screen where they belonged. *Girl Can't Help It*, The Lurid Technicolor, and Jayne Mansfield was certainly the biggest influence on Divine. *Texas Chainsaw* because of horror. Divine always said he wanted to be Godzilla, not Elizabeth Taylor. He wanted to be a frightening kind of thing to scare hippies.

That's what he was talking about. What are we talking about, oh influences. What was the beginning? Sorry.

MM: We started with film noir.
Waters: Oh film noir. Oh, okay. And then in *Female Trouble*, certainly Isabel Sarli's movies with Armando Bó looks exactly like Isabel Sarli, who I finally interviewed right before she died in Argentina. Very little known in America. Huge influence on me. Russ Meyer, huge influence. Herschel Gordon Lewis, a huge influence. The Kuchar brothers, how their Technicolor lurid colors looked.

BB: Why did you take the long break from filmmaking after *Dirty Shame*?
Waters: I made four other movies. I wrote, had development deals offered that never got made. I didn't take a break. I had *Fruitcake* out now, and so that's six. So I didn't take a break. I was paid to write every one of them. They just didn't get made.

MM: Why do you think that is?
Waters: Because the last one didn't make money. And also, there's always different reasons. Right now, the strike. I mean, there's no point I can say why they did or why they didn't. The *Hairspray* ones because then they went to the TV version. I mean, different with that. You know what I mean? Or maybe they weren't good. I don't know. They were to me all fine, and who knows? But I didn't really take a break, and then Criterion put them all out. So I'm still just as involved in the movie business as I always was in a weird way. Yeah.

MM: You returned to your roots in a *Dirty Shame*, and then, of course, but *Liarmouth* is a return as well.
Waters: To what?

MM: To—
Waters: Well, it's just crazy sex.

MM: —just the full-throttle absurdity.
Waters: Yeah, definitely, definitely. Yeah. I guess I'm just exploiting. I'm just like a carny. We show it all. We've got it all. So I want to do something that would delight me and would make an audience laugh today. And from the reaction—when I turned in that book, I thought, "This could go either way. I have no idea how this is going to be received." And we got mostly all great reviews, by women too, by anybody that you might have thought, maybe with political correctness and everything. And we gave it to a sensitivity editor, and she never called back. We don't know if she died or something. I don't know. We never know what happened. So we just put the book out.

MM: Why do you think it's so well received now?
Waters: I don't know. Because I guess it's not like any other book, and it makes people laugh. It made them laugh. And that's what everybody comes to me for is basically that's why they're coming, that I can make them laugh.

Figure 13.2 John Waters in conversation. © Mark Weissburg, 2023.

BB: I think they might also come to you for moments of kindness and compassion in your films.
Waters: Yeah, kindness. I'm not mean. I make fun of things I love, including the sexual ludicrousness. I mean, in all my movies, nobody's jerking off to watch my movies. If they are, they're in trouble. But the sex is ridiculous in all my movies. It's comedy, too. Everything is comedy. The human condition is a comedy in my movie. That we have to do these things that we didn't think up. I've always said I was mad at instinct because it wasn't my idea. We have to eat. I didn't think that up. That's a control freak. Right? Which all directors are.

MM: I was so struck in rewatching your films in preparation of how there are these little tender moments, particularly in the early films. In *Pink Flamingos*, they're so kind to their mother.
Waters: To Edie, yeah, yeah.

MM: To Edie. And then once you see that—once I saw that, I began to realize that there's kindness. There is that in all of the films in some regard.
Waters: And there's understanding within this tight community that they're in that is rejected by everybody else. They have a love and a kindness that makes them comfortable to being there. And that's what I think young people mean when they say, "Oh, you saved my life." Because it made them feel comfortable the same way I wrote a whole book called *Role Models*, which is about

the people that gave me that feeling that I knew, "Oh, there's Bohemia, there is other things. You don't have to do this." So everybody's looking for that. And when they find it, those people are important to them. And everybody remembers it. I always say with music, the first record you buy that your parents hate is the beginning of the soundtrack of your life.

MM: That's wonderful. Thank you.
Waters: It really is. Yeah.

Filmography

1964 *Hag in A Black Leather Jacket*
1966 *Roman Candles*
1968 *Eat Your Makeup*
1969 *Mondo Trasho*
1970 *The Diane Linkletter Story*
1970 *Multiple Maniacs*
1972 *Pink Flamingos*
1974 *Female Trouble*
1977 *Desperate Living*
1981 *Polyester*
1988 *Hairspray*
1990 *Cry-Baby*
1994 *Serial Mom*
1998 *Pecker*
2000 *Cecil B. Demented*
2004 *A Dirty Shame*

Selected Writing by John Waters

"Blackboard Jungle." *American Film*. April 1985, 42–46, 48.
Carsick: John Waters Hitchhikes Across America. New York: Farrar, Straus and Giroux, 2014.
"Casting for the Heavies." *Oui*. November 1978, 37.
"Commencement Speech." Rhode Island School of Design. May 30, 2015. *YouTube*. https://www.youtube.com/watch?v=Hl05XGifKb4.
Crackpot: The Obsessions of John Waters. New York: Vintage, 1986.
Director's Cut. Zurich: Scalo, 1997.
"Flock Shock." *American Film*. January/February 1986, 38–41.
Hairspray, Female Trouble and Multiple Maniacs: Three More Screenplays. New York: Thunder's Mouth Press, 2005.
"Hard Traveling." *American Film*. November 1986, 44–47.
Liarmouth: A Feel-Bad Romance. New York: Farrar, Straus and Giroux, 2022.
"Look Back with Anger." *American Film*. January/February 1985, 53–55.
Make Trouble. New York: Algonquin Books of Chapel Hill, 2017.
"Mondo Video." *American Film*. June 1982, 17–20, 64.
Mr. Know-It-All: The Tarnished Wisdom of a Filth Elder. New York: Picador, 2019.
Role Models. New York: Farrar, Straus and Giroux, 2010.
Shock Value: A Tasteful Book About Bad Taste. New York: Thunder's Mouth Press, 2005.
"Out on the Edge." *Index on Censorship* 24, no. 6 (1995): 9–19.
"Silver Screen." *The Red Brick* 1, no. 1 (October 1969): 12, 15.
Trash Trio: Three Screenplays: Pink Flamingos, Desperate Living, Flamingos Forever. New York: Vintage Books, 1988.
"Troubled Waters." *Oui*. August 1979, NP.
Unwatchable. New York: Marianne Boesky Gallery, 2006.
"Water's." *The Red Brick* 1, no. 1 (October 1969): 11.
With Hinley Bruce. *Art: A Sex Book*. London: Thames and Hudson, 2003.
With Hilton Al. "The Duke of Dirt." *Grand Street* 53 (1995): 10–23.

MANUSCRIPTS AND COLLECTION:

John Waters Collection. Reid Cinema Archives, Wesleyan University, Middletown, CT.

Bibliography

"300 Films Screened, 300,000 Attend First Rio Film, TV, Video Festival." *Screen International*. December 22, 1984, 14, 40.
Academy Museum of Motion Pictures. "*John Waters: Pope of Trash*, Exhibition Trailer." Posted September 28, 2023, by Academy Museum of Motion Pictures. *YouTube*, 02:32. https://www.academymuseum.org/en/exhibitions/john-waters-pope-of-trash
Adams, Jason. "Looking Back on John Waters' 'Pecker' on its 25th Anniversary." *Mashable*. September 22, 2023. https://mashable.com/article/pecker-john-waters-25-anniversary
Advertisement. *American Film*. March 1982, 75.
Advertisement. *Boston Phoenix*. November 8, 1983, sec. 3, 18.
Advertisement. *Daily Cougar*. February 3, 1977, 9.
Advertisement. *The New York Times*. November 16, 1986, BR22.
Advertisement. *The Retriever*. March 1, 1976, 9.
Advertisement. *Twin Cities Reader*. October 6, 1982, 28.
Aletti, Vince. "Photo: John Waters." *The Village Voice*. May 9, 1995.
Altman, Dennis. *Coming Out in the Seventies*. Boston: Alyson Publications, Inc., 1981.
Anselmo, Diana W. "Picture Pain: Anti-Heteronormative Female Fandom in Early Hollywood." *JCMS: Journal of Cinema and Media Studies* 62, no. 1 (Fall 2022): 7–35.
Arnold, Gary. "Film Notes." *Washington Post* [*Weekend*]. July 8, 1983, 18.
"Arrest Weirdo in Tate Murder." *Daily News*. December 2, 1969, 1.
"Art in the Movies." *WordPress*. November 12, 2013. https://artinthemovies.wordpress.com/2013/11/12/pecker-1998/#:~:text=Pecker's%20big%20opening%20is%20the,Marks %20flash%20on%20the%20%20%20%20%20%20screen
Astore, Mireille. "The Maternal Abject." Dissertation, Sydney College of the Arts, The University of Sydney, 2002.
Aufderheide, Pat. "The Domestication of John Waters." In *John Waters: Interviews*, edited by James Egan. Oxford, MS: University of Mississippi Press, 2011, 116–124.
Balsom, Erika. *Exhibiting Cinema in Contemporary Art*. Amsterdam: Amsterdam University Press, 2013.
Balsam, Rosemary H. "The Embodied Mother: Commentary on Kristeva." *Journal of the American Psychoanalytic Association* 62 (2014): 87–100.
Banks, Taunya Lovell. "Troubled Waters: Mid-Twentieth Century American Society on Trial in the Films of John Waters." *Stetson L. Rev.* 39 (2009): 153–182.

Benson-Allott, Caetlin. "Camp Integration: The Use and Misuse of Nostalgia in John Waters' *Hairspray*." *Quarterly Review of Film and Video* 26, no. 2 (2009): 143–154.
Benson, Sheila. "Telluride Festival Finds Time for Renewal." *Los Angeles Times* [*Calendar*], September 13, 1987, 32–33.
Bersani, Leo. *Homos*. Cambridge, MA: Harvard University Press, 2009.
"The Best of *American Film*." *American Film*. June 1985, 9, 11–12, 15–16, 19, 92–93, 95.
"The Big Picture." *American Film*. June 1985, 76–77, 79, 81–83, 85, 87–90, 105.
Bird, S. Elizabeth. "Tabloidization: What Is It, and Does It Really Matter?" in *The Changing Faces of Journalism*, edited by Barbie Zelizer. New York: Routledge, 2009, 40–50.
Bolter, Jay David and Richard Grusin. *Remediation: Understanding New Media*. Cambridge, MA: MIT Press, 1999.
Bordwell, David, and Kristin Thompson. *Minding Movies: Observations on the Art, Craft, and Business of Filmmaking*. Chicago: University of Chicago Press, 2011.
Bourdieu, Pierre. *Distinction, A Social Critique of the Judgement of Taste*. New York: Routledge, 1984.
Bowen, Peter. "Flash in the Pan." *Filmmaker Magazine*: Fall 1998. Archives. https://filmmaker magazine.com/archives/issues/fall1998/flash_pan.php#:~:text=And%20 Pecker%20 was%20based%20on,I%20was%20never%20like%20Pecker
Braver, Rita. "John Waters, Conoisseur of Quirky Art." *CBS News.com*. March 12, 2023. https://www.cbsnews.com/news/john-waters-art-collector-baltimore-museum-of-art/.
Brooks, Brian. "John Waters Looks Back and Forward Prior to His Film Society Retrospective." *FilmlincDaily*. September 5, 2014. https://www.filmlinc.org/daily/john-waters-interview-retrospective-film-society-2014/
Brown, Joe. "Baltimore's Master of Bad Taste." *The Washington Post*. February 6, 1985, C7.
Buchloh, Benjamin H.D., and Hal Foster. *Exit Interview*. New York: no place press, 2024.
Bugliosi, Vincent. *Helter Skelter: The True Story of the Manson Murders*. London: Arrow Books, 2018.
Byars, Jackie. *All That Hollywood Allows: Re-reading Gender in 1950s Melodrama*. Chapel Hill and London: The University of North Carolina Press, 1991.
Caldwell, John T. *Televisuality: Style, Crisis, and Authority in American Television*. New Brunswick, NJ: Rutgers University Press, 1995/2020.
"Camp John Waters 2024." *Events.com*. September 22, 2024. https://events.com/r/en_US/registration/camp-john-waters-2024-kent-september-915361
"Cecil B. Demented." *Irish Film Institute*. https://ifi.ie/film/cecil-b-demented/
Cedrone, Lou. "Museum Honors John Waters." *Baltimore Evening Sun*. February 7, 1985, D1, D6.
Cedrone, Lou. "'Tai-Pan' Is an Old-Style Epic; 'Something Wild' Is New and Strange." *Baltimore Evening Sun*. November 7, 1986, B4.
Celenza, Andrea. "Maternal Erotic Transferences and the Work of the Abject." *Journal of the American Psychoanalytic Association* 70, no.1 (2022): 9–38.
Cills, Hazel. "Teenage Girls Assaulted by Wild Animals! An Interview with John Waters." *Rookie*. February 17, 2012. https://www.rookiemag.com/2012/02/teenage-girls-assaulted-by-wild-animals-an-interview-with-john-waters/
"Cinémathèque Française Exhibitions, Homages and Special Events (1937–1986)." *Variety*. October 1, 1986, 40, 42.
Clark, Rob. "John Waters." *This Week in Texas*. July 12–18, 1985, 64–69.
"Cleveland." *Boxoffice*. April 10, 1978, ME-1.
Cohen, Stanley. *Folk Devils and Moral Panics*. St. Albans, Paladin, 1973.
Cooper, Dennis. "Interview: John Waters." *Bomb Magazine*. April 1, 2004. https://bombmagazine.org/articles/2004/04/01/john-waters/

Cotter, Holland. "Art Review: In Photos as Well as Films, John Waters Blithely Puts His Worst Foot Forward." *The New York Times*. February 6, 2004. https://www.nytimes.com/2004/02/06/arts/art-review-photos-well-films-john-waters-blithely-puts-his-worst-foot-forward.html

Creed, Barbara. "Horror and the Monstrous-Feminine: An Imaginary Abjection." *Screen* 27, no. 1 (1986): 44–71. https://doi.org/10.1093/screen/27.1.44

Cummins, James. "Bone to Pick." *Fangoria* 108. New York: September 1991.

Cunningham, Daniel Mudie. "The 'Film' on Whiteness: Depicting White Trash in U.S. Film, 1972–2002." Ph.D. diss., University of Western Sydney, 2004.

Daniel, Drew. "Experience & Innocence." *FREIZE*. June 1, 2012. https://www.frieze.com/article/experience-innocence

Danto, Arthur. "The Artworld." *The Journal of Philosophy* 61, no. 19 (October 1964): 571–584.

DeCaro, Frank. "The Empty 80s." *Detroit Free Press*. December 31, 1986, 1C–2C.

Dafoe, Taylor. "'Contemporary Art Hates You': John Waters, the Prince of Puke, on His New Retrospective." *Art net* (dot com.). October 31, 2018. https://news.artnet.com/art-world/contemporary-art-hates-you-john-waters-the-prince-of-puke-on-his-new-retrospective-1383673

De Leon, Charles L. Ponce. *That's The Way It Is: A History of Television News in America*. Chicago: University of Chicago Press, 2015.

DeLibero, Linda. "John Waters: Indecent Exposure." *ASAP/Journal*. February 5, 2019. https://asapjournal.com/review/john-waters-indecent-exposure-linda-delibero/

DeMello, Margo. *Animals and Society: An Introduction to Human-Animal Studies*. New York: Columbia University Press, 2012.

Denerstein, Robert. "Telluride Film Fest to Tribute Frears, Two Others in '87." *Hollywood Reporter*. September 4, 1987, 1, 22.

de Voogd, Barend. "Things That Should Be Illegal." *The Flashback Files*. September 2009. https://www.flashbackfiles.com/john-waters-interview

del Barco, Madalit. "'Here I Am, Closer to the Gutter than Ever': John Waters Gets His Hollywood Star." *NPR Weekend Edition*. September 24, 2023. https://www.npr.org/2023/09/24/1200624382/here-i-am-closer-to-the-gutter-than-ever-john-waters-gets-his-hollywood-star

Didion, Joan. *The White Album*. New York: Simon & Schuster, 1979.

Doherty, Thomas. *Pre-Code Hollywood: Sex, Immorality, and Insurrection in American Cinema 1930–1934*. New York: Columbia University Press, 1999.

Doherty, Thomas. *Teenagers and Teenpics: The Juvenilization of American Movies in the 1950s*. Boston: Unwin Hyman, 1988.

Doty, Alexander. *Flaming Classics: Queering the Film Canon*. New York and London: Routledge, 2000.

Doty, Alexander. *Making Things Perfectly Queer: Interpreting Mass Culture*. Minneapolis and London: University of Minnesota Press, 1993.

Dunn, Jancee. "Q&A: John Waters." *Rolling Stone*. June 12, 1997. https://www.rollingstone.com/culture/culture-news/qa-john-waters-236819/

Dyer, Richard. *Pastiche*. New York: Routledge, 2007.

Ebert, Roger. "John Waters, the Father of Odorama." *Daily Sentinel* [*Entertainer*]. September 11, 1987, 13.

Edelman, Lee. *No Future: Queer Theory and the Death Drive*. Durham, NC: Duke University Press, 2004.

"Edward Furlong & Jacqueline Domac Affair Is the Scandal Hollywood Forgot." *Eighties Kids*. N.D. https://www.eightieskids.com/edward-furlong-jacqueline-domac-romance/

Egan, James. *John Waters: Interviews*. Jackson: University Press of Mississippi, 2011.

Eleftheriadis, Konstantinos. *Queer Festivals*. Amsterdam: Amsterdam University Press, 2018.
Elsaesser, Thomas. "Tales of Sound and Fury: Observations on the Family Melodrama." In *Home is Where the Heart Is: Studies in Melodrama and the Woman's Film*, edited by Christine Gledhill. London: BFI Publishing, 1987.
Engstrom, John. "John Waters: 'Sleaze King of Cinema?'" *Boston Globe*. September 17, 1986, 42.
Everette, Dennis Wayne. "The Filthiest People Alive: Productions of Urban Spaces and Populations in the Films of John Waters." MA thesis, Miami University, 2011.
Farber, Manny. "Underground Films; A Bit of Male Truth." *Commentary* (November 1957). https://www.commentary.org/articles/manny-farber/underground-filmsa-bit-of-male-truth/
Ferrante, Anthony C. "The Market where Evil Dwells." *Fangoria* 103. New York: June 1991.
"Film: Revivals." *The New York Times*. December 14, 1986, G20.
"Film Reviews: Female Trouble." *Variety*. February 5, 1975, 22.
"Film Reviews: Pink Flamingos." *Variety*. December 11, 1974, 18.
"Flash in the Pan." *Filmmaker Magazine*. Fall 1998. https://filmmakermagazine.com/archives/issues/fall1998/flash_pan.php
Freund, Charles Paul. "John Waters, Filmdom's Bad Boy, Getting a 'Career Retrospective.'" *Baltimore Sun*. August 5, 1983, C1, C5.
Gallagher, Mark. *Another Steven Soderbergh Experience: Authorship & Contemporary Hollywood*. Austin: University of Texas Press, 2013.
Garder, Chris. "John Waters Salutes 'Desperate Showbiz Rejects' at Hollywood Walk of Fame Ceremony: 'Here I Am, Closer to the Gutter than Ever.'" *Hollywood Reporter*. September 18, 2023. https://www.hollywoodreporter.com/news/general-news/john-waters-salutes-desperate-showbiz-rejects-hollywood-walk-of-fame-ceremony-1235593112/
Garvey, Ellen Gruber. *Writing with Scissors: American Scrapbooks from the Civil War to the Harlem Renaissance*. New York; Oxford: Oxford University Press, 2013.
Gieskeke, Winston. "Getting Steamy with Traci Lords." *Palm Springs Life* 2019. https://www.palmspringslife.com/traci-lords/
Goldstein, Patrick. "Crackpot." *Los Angeles Times Book Review*. November 16, 1986, 4.
Gorfinkel, Elena. "Cult Film or Cinephilia by Any Other Name." *Cinéaste* 34, no. 1 (2008): 33–38.
Gorfinkel, Elena. "*Polyester*: The Perils of Francine." *Polyester*, Criterion Collection Blu-Ray edition essay, 2019.
Griffin, Chloé. *Edgewise: A Picture of Cookie Mueller*. New York: b books, 2014.
Grossman, Dave, and Gloria DeGaetano. *Stop Teaching Our Kids to Kill*. New York, Crown Publishers, 1999.
Grosz, Elizabeth. *Sexual Subversions*. Sydney: Allen & Unwin, 1989.
Guerra, Joey, "Filmmaker John Waters Comes to Houston to Discuss the Original 'Hairspray,' His 'Most Devious Movie.'" *Houston Chronicle*, November 12, 2024, accessed February 24, 2025, https://www.houstonchronicle.com/entertainment/movies_tv/article/john-waters-hairspray-houston-q-a-tickets-1988-19905618.php
Gunts, Ed. "Baltimore Gets Very Own Walk of Fame: Hampden's Newest Attraction Is a John Waters Star Walk." *Baltimore Magazine*. May 29, 2019. https://www.baltimoremagazine.com/section/arts entertainment/baltimore-john-waters-hampden-star-walk-of-fame/
Gunts, Ed. "John Waters Introduces the World to His 'Roommates.'" *Washington Blade*. May 8, 2022. https://www.washingtonblade.com/2022/12/08/john-waters-introduces-the-world-to-his-roommates/
Hainley, Bruce. "John Waters." *Artforum*. September 1995.
Halberstam, Jack. *The Queer Art of Failure*. Durham: Duke University Press, 2011.

Hall, Trish. "John Waters' Films Have Low Budgets, Large Leading Lady." *Wall Street Journal*. March 31, 1983, 1, 20.
Halle, Howard. "John Waters, 'Director's Cut.'" *Time Out New York*. November 28, 1996.
Halley, Peter, and Bob Nickas. "John Waters." *Index* (1997). http://www.indexmagazine.com/interviews/john_waters.shtml
Halperin, David M., and Valerie Traub, eds. *Gay Shame*. Chicago: University of Chicago Press, 2009.
Halter, Ed. "*Female Trouble*: Spare Me Your Morals." *The Criterion Collection*. June 26, 2018. https://www.criterion.com/current/posts/5767-female-trouble-spare-me-your-morals.
Hamilton, Neil. *Rebels and Renegades: A Chronology of Social and Political Dissent in the United States*. New York: Routledge, 2002.
Hampton, Howard. "*Pink Flamingos*: The Battle of Filth." *The Criterion Collection*. June 28, 2022. https://www.criterion.com/current/posts/7845-pink-flamingos-the-battle-of-filth.
Hartl, John. "Sleaze and Sex Get a Showing." *Seattle Times*. January 18, 1985, 19.
Harvey, Dennis. "The Godfather of Gross-Out." *Film Comment* 36, no. 4 (2000): 34–36.
Hawkins, Joan. "Sleaze Mania, Euro-Trash, and High Art: The Place of European Art Films in American Low Culture." *Film Quarterly* 53, no. 2 (1999): 14–29.
Hays, Matthew. *The View from Here: Conversations with Gay and Lesbian Filmmakers*. Vancouver: Arsenal Pulp Press, 2007.
He, Jenny. *John Waters: Pope of Trash*, edited by Jenny He and Darra Jaffe. New York: DelMonico Books, 2023.
Heiferman, Marvin. "Everything Always Looks Good Through Here! John Waters and Photography," in *John Waters: Change of Life*. New York: New Museum of Contemporary Art, 2004, 20–41.
Held, Isabelle. "John Waters: Pope of Trash." *Fashion Theory*. 2024. https://doi.org/10.1080/1362704X.2024.2350754
Heller, Dana. *Hairspray*. Malden, MA: Wiley-Blackwell, 2011.
Hendricks, Nancy. *Daily Life in 1950s America*. Santa Barbara: ABC-Clio, 2019.
Herbert, Daniel. *Maverick Movies: New Line Cinema and the Transformation of American Film*. Oakland, CA: University of California Press, 2024.
Hileman, Kristen. "Inappropriation," in *John Waters: Indecent Exposure*, edited by Kristen Hileman. Berkeley, CA: University of California Press, 2018, 16–27.
Hileman, Kristen. *John Waters: Indecent Exposures.* Baltimore: The Baltimore Museum of Art in association with the University of California Press, 2018.
Hirsch, Foster. *Hollywood and the Movies of the Fifties*. New York: Alfred A. Knopf, 2023.
Holmlund, Chris. *Female Trouble*. Vancouver: Arsenal Pulp Press, 2017.
Hoberman, J., and Jonathan Rosenbaum. *Midnight Movies*. New York: Da Capo Press, 1983.
Hunt, Joshua. "Sure, It Won an Oscar. But Is It Criterion?" *The New York Times*. February 29, 2024. https://www.nytimes.com/2024/02/29/magazine/criterion-collection.html
Hunter, Stephen. "John Waters: Never Quite Gone, He's Back Again." *Baltimore Sun*. October 5, 1986, 1M, 6M–8M.
Hutcheon, Linda. *The Politics of Postmodernism*. London: Routledge, 1989.
Ives, John G. *American Originals: John Waters*. New York: Thunder's Mouth Press, 1992.
Ives, John G. *John Waters*. New York: Thunder's Mouth Press, 1992.
"I Want to Live!" *AFI Catalog of Feature Films*. https://catalog.afi.com/Catalog/moviedetails/52606
Jameson, Fredric. "Postmodernism or the Cultural Logic of Late Capitalism." *New Left Review*. 1984, 53–92.
"John Waters." C. Grimaldis Gallery. https://www.cgrimaldisgallery.com/john-waters

"John Waters." Marianne Boesky Gallery. https://marianneboeskygallery.com/artists/64-john-waters/biography/waters
"John Waters New Film *Eat Your Makeup* Also *Short Circuit*. . . ." Boohooray. August 3, 2024. https://www.boo-hooray.com/pages/books/6477/john-waters/john-waters-new-film-eat-your-makeup-also-short-circuit-teenage-mutant-ninja-turtles?soldItem=true
"John Waters (& Divine) on Letterman, Part 1 of 3: 1982." Video, February 16, 2018. https://www.youtube.com/watch?v=AIPF8mk1a4Q
"John Waters on Letterman, Part 2 of 3: 1983–86." Video, February 20, 2018. https://www.youtube.com/watch?v=Rn96HXDGboo&t=0s
"John Waters on Letterman, Part 3 of 3: 1987–1992." Video, February 22, 2018. https://www.youtube.com/watch?v=Ii34WyuAGLg&t=0s
"John Waters: Pope of Trash." N.D. *Academy Museum*. https://www.academymuseum.org/en/programs/series/john-waters-pope-of-trash
Kael, Pauline. "Trash Art and the Movies," in *Going Steady: Film Writings, 1968–1969*. London: Marion Boyars, 1970, 87–129. Originally Published in *Harper's Magazine*, February 1969.
Kaltenbach, Chris. "Divine Fans Want to Build a Monument to Late Actor." *The Baltimore Sun*. January 18, 2016. https://web.archive.org/web/20170829074341 /http://www.baltimoresun .com/features/baltimore-insider-blog/bs-ae-divine-20160115-story.html
Kane-Meddock, Derek. "Trash Comes Home: Gender/Genre Subversion in the Films of John Waters," in *Gender Meets Genre in Postwar Cinemas*, edited by Christine Gledhill. Urbana, Chicago, and Springfield: University of Illinois Press, 2012, 205–218.
Keller, Alexandra, and Frazer Ward. "Matthew Barney and the Paradox of the Neo-Avant-Garde Blockbuster." *Cinema Journal* 45, no. 2 (Winter 2006): 3–16.
Kelley, Mike. "Cross-Gender/Cross-Genre," in *Foul Perfection: Essays and Criticism*, edited by John C. Welchman, 106–120. Cambridge, MA: The MIT Press, 2003.
Kelly, Oliver (ed.). *The Portable Kristeva*. New York: Columbia University Press, 1997.
Kendall, John. "'Family' Member Says Life Was a Game with Manson." February 4, 1971. https://www.cielodrive.com/archive/family-member-says-life-with-manson-was-a-game/
Kennedy, Tammie M., Joyce Irene Middleton, and Krista Ratcliffe. "The Matter of Whiteness: Or, Why Whiteness Studies Is Important to Rhetoric and Composition Studies." *Rhetoric Review* 24, no. 4 (2005): 359–373.
King, Jennifer. "John Waters." *Artforum* 50, no. 10 (Summer 2012).
Kinon, Richard, dir. *Love Boat*. Season 9, Episode 3, "Hidden Treasure/Picture from the Past/Ace's Salary." Aired October 12, 1985, ABC.
K.L.E, Marissa. *Discourses of Neoliberalism in Singapore's Higher Education Context: Individualist and Communitarian Perspectives*. New York: Routledge, 2023.
Klinger, Barbara. *Melodrama and Meaning: History, Culture, and the Films of Douglas Sirk*. Bloomington and Indianapolis: Indiana University Press, 1994.
Koob, Nathan. "The Gentrification of John Waters." *Film Criticism* 43, no. 1 (2019).
Kozlovic, Anton Karl. "DeMille, Cecil B." *Senses of Cinema*. Issue 66, March 2013. https://www.sensesofcinema.com/2013/great-directors/cecil-b-demille/
Krauss, Rosalind. *Under Blue Cup*. Cambridge, MA: MIT Press, 2011.
Kristeva, Julia. *Powers of Horror*. New York: Columbia University Press, 1982.
"Landmark Theatres." *American Film*. May 1985, 71.
"Landmark Theatres." *American Film*. July–August 1985, 69.
"Landmark Theatres Series of Note." *American Film*. June 1984, 77.
"Landmark Theatres Series of Note." *American Film*. July/August 1984, 78.
LaRocca, Lauren. "Cult Classic." *Baltimore Magazine*. October 2018. https://www.baltimoremagazine .com/section/artsentertainment/john-waters-shares-highlights-from-upcoming-bma-retrospective/

Lescaze, Zoë. "How Chelsea Became the Unlikely Center of the Art World." *The New York Times*. September 28, 2023. https://www.nytimes.com/2023/09/28/t-magazine/chelsea-new-york-art.html

Levi, Pavle. *Cinema by Other Means*. Oxford: Oxford University Press, 2012.

Levine, Elana. *Her Stories: Daytime Soap Opera and US Television History*. Durham, NC: Duke University Press, 2020.

Levine, Lawrence. *Highbrow, Lowbrow: The Emergence of Cultural Hierarchy in America*. Cambridge, MA: Harvard University Press, 1990.

Levy, Emanuel. *Gay Directors, Gay Films?: Pedro Almodóvar, Terence Davies, Todd Haynes, Gus Van Sant, John Waters*. New York: Columbia University Press, 2015.

Lodge, Sally A. "John Waters." *Publishers Weekly*. July 17, 1981, 6–7.

Loory, Stuart H. "Nixon Says Manson Is Guilty, Hits Press." *The Los Angeles Times*. August 4, 1970, 1.

Lyons, Ingrid. "Unapologetic Protagonist." *Irish Arts Review* 36, no. 3 (2019): 82–83.

MacDonald, Scott. "John Waters' Divine Comedy," in *John Waters: Interviews*, edited James Egan, 71–92. Jackson: University Press of Mississippi, 2011.

Macnab, Geoffrey. *J. Arthur Rank and the British Film Industry*. New York: Routledge, 2013.

Mareth, Paul D. "Muddy Waters." *American Film*. September 1982, 6.

Maslin, Janet. "The Screen: 'Polyester,' An Offbeat Comedy." *The New York Times*. May 29, 1981, C6.

Maza, Erik. "John Waters and Patricia Hearst on Covid, the Met Gala, and 30 Years of Friendship." *Town and Country*. October 29, 2020. https://www.townandcountrymag.com/society/tradition/a34395567/john-waters-patricia-hearst-conversation/

McCauley, Mary Carole. "Baltimore Museum of Art Opens Its John Waters Exhibit Sunday—And It Is as Weird as You Might Expect." *The Baltimore Sun*. October 5, 2018. https://www.baltimoresun.com/entertainment/arts/bs-fe-waters-exhibit-20180926-story.html

McClintock, John. "How A Crackpot Sees Hollywood." *Times Tribune* [*Calendar*]. October 26, 1986, 2.

McLane, Betsy. *A New History of Documentary Film*. 2nd Edition. New York: Bloomsbury, 2012.

McLane, Betsy. *High Camp: A Gay Guide to Camp and Cult Films Volume 2*. San Francisco: Leyland Publications, 1997.

McDonagh, Maitland. "The State of Horror Nation." *Fangoria* 103. New York: June 1991.

"M.D. on Manson's Sex Life." *Los Angeles Free Press* 7, no. 4, issue 288 (January 23–29, 1970): 1, 8.

Melnick, Jeffrey. *Creepy Crawling: Charles Manson and the Many Lives of America's Most Infamous Family*. New York: Arcade Publishing, 2018.

Mercer, John, and Martin Shingler. *Melodrama: Genre, Style, Sensibility*. London and New York: Wallflower Press, 2004.

Metz, Walter. "John Waters Goes to Hollywood: A Poststructural Authorship Study," in *Authorship and Film*, edited by David A. Gerstner and Janet Staiger. New York: Routledge, 2003, 157–174.

Modleski, Tania. "The Search for Tomorrow in Today's Soap Operas." *Popular Fiction: Technology, Ideology, Production, Reading*, edited by Tony Bennett. New York: Routledge, 1979/1990, 189–207.

Moon, Michael, and Eve Kosofsky Sedgwick. "Divinity: A Dossier, A Performance Piece, A Little-Understood Emotion." *Discourse* 13, no. 1 (1990): 12–39.

Muir, John Kenneth. *Horror Films of 2000–2009*. Jefferson, NC: McFarland, 2023.

Muñoz, José. *Cruising Utopia: The Then and There of Queer Futurity*. New York: New York University Press, 2009.

Murray, Susan. *Hitch Your Antenna to the Stars: Early Television and Broadcast Stardom*. New York: Routledge, 2005.

Nair, Kartik. *Seeing Things: Spectral Materialities of Bombay Horror*. Oakland, CA: University of California Press, 2024.

New Museum. "John Waters Change of Life." Archive. https://archive.newmuseum.org/exhibitions/412

Ngai, Sianne. *Theory of the Gimmick: Aesthetic Judgment and Capitalist Form*. Cambridge, MA: Harvard University Press, 2020.

"No Smoking in This Theater." Special Features, *Polyester*, directed by John Waters (1981; New York, NY: Criterion Collection, 2019), DVD.

Nwonka, Clive. *Black Boys: The Social Aesthetics of British Urban Film*. New York: Bloomsbury Publishing, 2023.

Oliveira, Rui Trindade. *Supranational Horrors: Italian and Spanish Horror Cinema since 1968*. Lanham, MD: Lexington, 2022.

"Openings." *Baltimore Sun* [*Maryland Live*]. April 24, 1987, 14.

Osborne, Peter. *Anywhere or Not at All: Philosophy of Contemporary Art*. Brooklyn, NY: Verso Books, 2013.

Osborne, Robert. "Rambling Reporter." *Hollywood Reporter*. February 24, 1987, 5.

Padilla, Elisa. "The Baltimore Artist: Taste, Class, and Distinction in John Waters' *Pecker*." *Quarterly Review of Film and Video* 39, no. 2 (2022): 341–359.

Pagnoni Berns, Fernando Gabriel, and John Darowski (eds.), *A Critical Companion to Wes Craven*. Lanham, MD: Lexington, 2023.

Pagnoni Berns, Fernando Gabriel, John Darowski, Canela Ailén Rodriguez Fontao, and Mariana Zárate. "From Traditional Slasher to Fourth Wave: Fantastical Reconversion in *The Final Girls* and *Happy Death Day*," in *Fourth Wave Feminism in Science Fiction and Fantasy, Volume 1. Essays on Film Representations, 2012–2019*, edited by Valerie Frankel. Jefferson: McFarland, 2019, 77–87.

Palis, Eleni. "The Economics and Politics of Auteurism: Spike Lee and *Do The Right Thing*." *Cinema Journal* 57, no. 2 (Winter 2018): 1–21. https://doi.org/10.1353/cj.2018.0000

Peary, Gerald. "John Waters and His Dreamlanders in P-Town." *Provincetown Arts* 13 (1997–1998). http://www.geraldpeary.com/interviews/wxyz/waters-p-town.html "*Pecker* review." *Siskel and Ebert*. 1998.

Penwarden, Charles. "Of Word and Flesh: An Interview with Julia Kristeva," in *Rites of Passage: Art for the End of the Century*. London: Tate Gallery Publications, 1995.

Perini, Lorenza. *Giving Feminism a Bad Name: The Uprising of the Anti-Feminism Instances in Times of Populisms*. Milano: Ledizioni, 2021.

Pousner, Howard. "Director Waters' Films Have a New Generation to Offend." *Atlanta Journal*. January 29, 1985, 1B, 11B.

Proctor, William and Mark McKenna. "Introduction: The Death and Resurrection Show: Horror Franchise Cinema and the Romanticization of Cult," in *Horror Franchise Cinema*, edited by William Proctor and Mark McKenna, 1–28. New York: Routledge, 2021.

Puglia, David. *Tradition, Urban Identity, and the Baltimore "Hon": The Folk in the City*. Lanham, MD: Lexington, 2018.

Pulido, Javier. *La década de oro del cine de terror español (1967–1976)*. Madrid. T & B Editores, 2012.

Rea, Steven. "A Look at John Waters and His Bizarre Films." *Philadelphia Inquirer*. March 27, 1985, 4G.

Reeves, James A. "Wild About Waters." *American Film*. January 1983, 8.

Reichstein, Gail. "The Bizarre John Waters." *34th Street* [*Daily Pennsylvanian*]. March 21, 1985, 5.

Richardson, Brenda. "John Waters: Stop, Look, and Listen," in *Unwatchable*. New York and Zürich: Marianne Boesky Gallery and de Pury & Luxembourg, 2006, 77–84.

Riefe, Jordan. "Bieber, Pimples, Lassie with a Facelift: John Waters on His L.A. Art Exhibition." *Los Angeles Times*, February 16, 2021.

Roen, Paul. *High Camp: A Gay Guide to Camp and Cult Films Volume 1*. San Francisco: Leyland Publications, 1994.

Russell, Kate J. "The Cinematic Pandemonium of William Castle and John Waters," in *ReFocus: The Films of William Castle*, edited by Murray Leeder. Edinburgh: Edinburgh University Press, 2018, 237–254.

Ryan, Tom. "Sirk, Hollywood, and Genre." *Senses of Cinema*. Issue 66, March 2013. https://www.sensesofcinema.com/2013/feature-articles/sirk-hollywood-and-genre/

Salvato, Nick. "Tramp Sensibility and the Afterlife of 'Showgirls.'" *Theatre Journal* 58, no. 4 (2006): 633–648.

Sanders, Ed. *The Family: The Life and Crimes of Charles Manson and His Followers*. New York: Hachette Books, 2023.

Sanders, Julie. *Adaptation and Appropriation*. 2nd edition. London and New York: Routledge, 2016.

Schaefer, Eric. *"Bold! Daring! Shocking! True!" A History of Exploitation Films, 1919–1959*. Durham and London: Duke University Press, 1999.

Schatz, Thomas. *Hollywood Genres: Formulas, Filmmaking, and the Studio System*. New York: McGraw-Hill, 1981.

Schatz, Thomas. "The New Hollywood." *Movie Blockbusters*, edited by Julian Stringer. New York: Routledge, 2003, 15–44.

Schmitz, Anthony. "Crackpot: The Obsessions of John Waters." *The New York Times*. November 9, 1986. BR33.

Schnurmacher, Thomas. "Comedy Returns to the Bar Scene." *Montreal Gazette*. July 7, 1984, H-6.

School of Visual Arts. "John Waters Keynote Address: Make-up Commencement for Classes of '20 and '21." Posted August 2, 2022, by School of Visual Arts. *YouTube*, 18:03. https://www.youtube.com/watch?v=YGLvzIhKthg&t=1s

Sconce, Jeffrey. "XXX: Love and Kisses from Charlie," in *Swinging Single: Representing Sexuality in the 1960s*, edited by. Hilary Radnor and Moya Luckett. Minneapolis; London: University of Minnesota Press, 1999, 207–223.

Scott, Vernon. "Reporters Who Would Interview 16-Year-Old Edward Furlong, the Charismatic Young Costar of 'Terminator 2' and Other Hit Films, Are Asked to Sign an Agreement." *UPI Archives*. April 20, 1994. https://www.upi.com/Archives/1994/04/20/Reporters-who-would-interview-16-year-old-Edward-Furlong-the-charismatic/5404766814400/

Seabrook, John. *NoBrow: The Culture of Marketing, the Marketing of Culture*, 1st ed. New York: A.A. Knopf, 2000.

Shaw, Oliver. "That Time John Waters and Andy Warhol Unknowingly Parodied JFK's Assassination at the Same Time." *Interview*. August 21, 2019. https://www.interviewmagazine.com/film/that-time-john-waters-and-andy-warhol-unknowingly-parodied-jfks-assassination-at-the-same-time

Shklovsky, Victor. "Art as Technique," in *Modern Criticism and Theory: A Reader*, edited by Nigel Wood and David Lodge. London: Langham, 2013.

Silverman Kaja. "The Female Authorial Voice." *The Acoustic Mirror: The Female Voice in Psychoanalysis and Cinema*. Bloomington: Indiana University Press, 1988.

Singer, Ben. *Melodrama and Modernity: Early Sensational Cinema and Its Contexts*. New York: Columbia University Press, 2001.

Slavtcheva-Petkova, Vera. *Young People, Media and Politics in the Digital Age*. New York: Routledge, 2023.

Sloman, Larry "Ratso." "High Times Greats: Interview with John Waters." *High Times*. April 22, 2020 (originally published 1983). https://hightimes.com/culture/high-times-greats-john-waters/

Smith, David E. and Alan J. Rose. "The Group Marriage Commune: A Case Study." *Journal of Psychedelic Drugs* 3, no. 1 (September 1970): 115–119.

Solondz, Todd. "Interview with John Waters," in *John Waters: Change of Life*. New York: New Museum of Contemporary Art, 2004, 102–115.

"Soviet Film Is Highlight of Festival." *Daily Sentinel*. September 6, 1987, 3A.

Spigel, Lynn. *Make Room for TV: Television and the Family Ideal in Postwar America*. Chicago: University of Chicago Press, 1992.

Staff/BMA Stories. "Coming Attractions: John Waters in Conversation with Catherine Opie and Jack Pierson." *BMA/Stories*. January 27, 2023. https://stories.artbma.org/coming-attractions-john-waters-in-conversation-with-catherine-opie-and-jack-pierson/

Stallybrass, Peter, and Allon White. *The Politics and Poetics of Transgression*. Ithaca: Cornell University Press, 1986.

Stevenson, Jack. *Desperate Visions: The Films of John Waters & the Kuchar Brothers*. London and San Francisco: Creation Books, 1996, 119–136.

Stockton, Kathryn Bond. *The Queer Child, or Growing Sideways in the Twentieth Century*. Durham, NC: Duke University Press, 2009.

Stoppard, Lou. "The Photographer Behind John Waters' Cult Classic 'Pecker.'" *Aperture*. March 27, 2019. https://aperture.org/editorial/john-waters-chuck-shacochis/

Stuart, Jamie. "John Waters on 'Pecker,' Retrospective Trailer." Promotion. Posted August 28, 2014, by Film at Lincoln Center. *YouTube*, 0:58. https://www.youtube.com/watch?v=JTrDtoBpwXE

Stevenson, Jack. "From the Bedroom to the Bijou: A Secret History of American Gay Sex Cinema." *Film Quarterly* 51, no. 1 (1997): 24–31.

Sutherland, Meghan. *The Flip Wilson Show*. Detroit: Wayne State University Press, 2008.

Szczepaniak-Gillece, Jocelyn. "Smoke and Mirrors: Cigarettes, Cinephilia, and Reverie in the American Movie Theater." *Film History* 28, no. 3 (2016): 85–113. https://doi.org/10.2979/filmhistory.28.3.05

Taylor, Robert. "John Waters Film Festival Is Not For the Faint of Heart." *Oakland Tribune*. April 6, 1984, D-8.

Thomas, Adelosa. "Bad Influence: John Waters Reflects on His Unabashedly Filthy Filmography." *Letterboxd*, May 10, 2024. https://letterboxd.com/journal/john-waters-retrospective-interview/

Thomas, Jonathan. "Absentee Landlord." *ARTFORUM*. December 6, 2011. https://www.artforum.com/events/absentee-landlord-191473/

Thomas, William V. "The New Catholic Ratings Look Beyond Sex in Movies." *Baltimore Sun*. February 14, 1982, D1, D9.

Thompson, Bill, and Andy Williams. *The Myth of Moral Panics: Sex, Snuff, and Satan*. New York: Routledge, 2013.

Tillmans, Wolfgang. "Wolfgang Tillmans in Conversation with John Waters," in *John Waters: Indecent Exposure*, edited by Kristen Hileman. Berkeley, CA: University of California Press, 2018, 154–167.

Timpone, Anthony. "The Lean Season." *Fangoria* 103, New York, June 1991.

Timpone, Anthony. "Return of the Indie." *Fangoria* 101, New York, April 1991.

Timpone, Anthony. "Summer Screams." *Fangoria* 114, New York, July 1992.

Tinkcom, Matthew. *Working Like a Homosexual: Camp, Capital, Cinema*. Durham and London: Duke University Press, 2002.

Todd, Antony. *Authorship and the Films of David Lynch: Aesthetic Receptions in Contemporary Hollywood*. London and New York: I.B. Tauris, 2012.
Turner, Jim. "Desperately Seeking Scares." *Fangoria* 106. New York: September 1991.
Turnock, Bryan. *Studying Horror Cinema*. Liverpool: Liverpool University Press, 2019.
Uricchio, Marylynn. "Director John Waters Serves Up Humor with Shock Value." *Pittsburgh Post-Gazette*. February 13, 1986, 20.
Vanderbeek, Stan. "The Cinema Delimina: Films from the Underground." *Film Quarterly* 14, no. 4 (Summer 1961): 5–15.
Vigil, Luis. "Malos tiempos para el terror." Madrid: Zinco Editores, February 1994.
Vigil, Luis. "Reponso." *Fangoria* 17. Madrid: Zinco Editores, March 1993.
Waldron, Abigail. *A History of LGBTQ+ Survival Through the Lens of American Horror Cinema*. Jefferson, NC: McFarland, 2022.
Walcott, Ellison. "Waters' World: 'Demented' and Disappointing." *Ace Magazine*. August 24, 2000. https://www.acemagazinelex.com/Backissues_ACEWeekly/000824/index.html
Walley, Jonathan. "The Material of Film and the Idea of Cinema: Contrasting Practices in Sixties and Seventies Avant-Garde Film." *October* 103 (Winter 2003): 15–30.
Walker Art Center. "John Waters to Take Over Walker Galleries as Absentee Landlord." Press. April 1, 2011. https://walkerart.org/press-releases/2011/john-waters-to-take-over-walker-galleries-as
"Waters Fest Skedded." *Hollywood Reporter*. October 15, 1987, 8.
"Waters Films: Tasteless, Vulgar, Campy." *Provincetown Advocate*. August 9, 1979, 5, 25.
"Waters Retro in Philly." *Variety*. January 5, 1983, 28.
Walters, Ben. "John Waters: Why the Auteur of Outrage Won't Joke About the Manson Murders." *The Guardian*. November 8, 2018. https://www.theguardian.com/film/2018 / nov/08/john-waters-homotopia-festival-liverpool-manson-murders
Weintraub, Alex. "Divine Wisdom: Polyester and the Return of Trash Cinema." *Los Angeles Review of Books*. December 21, 2015. https://lareviewofbooks.org/article/divine-wisdom-polyester-and-the-return-of-trash-cinema/
West, Alexandra. *The 1990s Teen Horror Cycle: Final Girls and a New Hollywood Formula*. Jefferson, NC: McFarland, 2018.
White, Diane. "The King of Sleaze." *Boston Globe*. November 6, 1986, 93, 95.
Willemen, Paul. "Distanciation and Douglas Sirk," *Screen* 12, no. 2 (Summer 1971): 63–67.
Williams, Linda. "Film Bodies: Gender, Genre, and Excess." *Film Quarterly* 44, no. 4 (Summer 1991): 2–13.
Williams, Linda. *Playing the Race Card: Melodramas of Black and White from Uncle Tom to O. J. Simpson*. Princeton and Oxford: Princeton University Press, 2001.
Wood, Robin. *Hollywood from Vietnam to Reagan*. New York: Columbia University Press, 1986.
Wyrick, Craig. "Maker of 'Pink Flamingos' Will Be Riverfest Speaker." *Daily Iowan*. April 12, 1984, 12B.
Yablonsky, Linda. "*Multiple Maniacs*: Genuine Trash." *The Criterion Collection*. March 21, 2017. https://www.criterion.com/current/posts/4467-multiple-maniacs-genuine-trash
Zupancič, Alenka. *The Odd One In: On Comedy*. Cambridge, MA: MIT Press, 2008.

Index

Adamson, Barry, 203
aesthetics
  budgetary constraints, 98, 234
  good taste/bad taste relationship, 18, 19, 67, 73, 78, 83–4, 170, 175, 200, 207–8, 235–6
  of guilty pleasures, 65–6, 67–8, 76, 78–9
  the nobrow aesthetic, 66–7, 78, 110
  see also trash aesthetic
Almodóvar, Pedro, 16, 97
American Film, 31, 32
Anger, Kenneth, 4, 16, 34, 97, 226, 237
Anselmo, Diana W., 154
Arbus, Diane, 71–2, 84, 120
art *see* contemporary art
auteurism
  commodification of, 83
  melodrama, 16
  in the 1990s, 63–4
  reputational analysis, 32
  of Waters, 16, 83, 231–2
avant-garde film, 4, 228, 229

Bergman, Ingmar, 108, 205, 222–3
Bersani, Leo, 164
Beyond the Valley of the Dolls (Meyer), 22
body genre, 17, 173, 174, 178, 189
Bordwell, David, 107
Burston, Paul, 211
Buxton, Adam, 210–11

camp
  aesthetic in *Female Trouble*, 22, 24, 139
  camp humor, 65–6, 88–9
  of the little movies, 114
  nobrow aesthetics, 67, 87
  parody in *Polyester*, 26, 27, 148
  readings of melodrama, 16, 18
  and the trash queen aesthetic, 170
  Waters' rephotographed stills as, 75
  Waters' use of campness, 6–7, 156, 198, 200, 212, 235
  see also queerness
Castle, William
  influence on Waters, 16, 34, 38, 43, 97, 112
  marketing-gimmick cinema, 38, 104, 105, 112–13, 122–3
  referenced in *Serial Mom*, 58

The Tingler's buzzing seats, 104, 124
visceral, physical response of the audience, 105
Waters' photographed stills from, 112

Catholic Church
film-ratings system, 34
the Mansons alongside Catholic imagery, 154, 155, 156, 157
in *Multiple Maniacs*, 156–7
transgressions of in Waters' films, 155–6
Virgin Mary imagery, 69, 73, 88, 89–90, *89*, 93, 155–6
Waters' Catholic upbringing, 2, 65, 66

Cecil B. Demented
actor performances, 100
Baltimore setting, 220
and Cecil B. DeMille, 105–6
David Lean book, 113
DVD menu, 99
dying for art, 107–8
the movie within the movie, 99–100
plot, 97–8, 99
resonances with Waters' little movies, 113–14
Steadicam shots, 101, 102, 103–4
verité style, 98, 100–2, *102*, 106, 107
visual style, 98, 99–100, 226
Waters' cinematic values and principles, 5, 53, 97–8, 108, 114

contemporary art
art vs non-art in *Pecker*, 68–9, 91–2, 120
gimmickry of, 121–3
retrospectives and exhibitions of Waters' art, 64–5, 75–7, 120–1
space for humor, 65, 121
Waters' love-hate relationship with, 43, 63, 64, 68, 76–7, *77*, 81–2
see also Pecker; photography

Cooper, Dennis, 120
Cornish, Joe, 210–11
Cotter, Holland, 75
courtroom trials
death penalties, 231
Female Trouble, 22, 107, 159, 161
the Manson trials, 151–2, 155, 156, 158–9, 231
Pink Flamingos, 54, 196–7, 231
Serial Mom, 160–1, *194*, 195, 231, 237
trial-as-spectacle, 107, 160–1
Waters' fascination with, 22–3, 54, 159–60, 231

Craven, Wes, 60; *see also Scream* (Craven)
Crowe, Cameron, 81
Cry-Baby, 5, 63, 82, 88–9, 213, 232, 235

Deluxe, Delores, 131–5
DeMille, Cecil B., 105
Deren, Maya, 4, 226
Desperate Living
as a body genre, 17
the Mansons referenced in, 158, *158*
re-worked nuclear family, 162, 163
Scala screenings, 208–9
transgressive characters, 171
within the Trash Trilogy, 4, 82
Waters' visual style, 98

Diane Linkletter Story, The, 3
Dirty Shame, A, 5, 53, 82, 83, 105, 227, 238
Divine (Glen Milstead)
attendance at screenings, 37
as a grotesque "drag queen" figure, 25, 170, 175–6, 180–1
London audiences for, 211
in *Pink Flamingos*, 4, 149
rephotographed still from *Multiple Maniacs*, 75, 111–12, *111*, 115–16, 120

Divine (*cont.*)
  and the trash queen aesthetic, 170–1, 173
  vocal qualities, 137
  Waters' friendship with, 2–3, 85, 144
  see also Female Trouble; *Hairspray*; *Pink Flamingos*; *Polyester*
Doherty, Thomas, 19, 105
Doty, Alexander, 18
drag artists
  Divine as a grotesque "drag queen" figure, 25, 170, 175–6, 180–1
  Lady Zorro, 85, 86
  in *Pecker*, 85
Dreamlanders
  collaborative approach, 3, 4, 132, 133–4, 147, 224–5, 233–4
  marketing stunts and campaigns, 140
  role of Waters' friends, 131–2, 148, 154, 204
  in *Shock Value*, 35
  visual style, 99–100
  Waters' control of the script, 135, 136, 141, 142–3, 144, 146, 147, 148, 233
  see also Deluxe, Delores; Figgs, George; Moran, Pat; Pearce, Mary Vivian; Peranio, Vincent; Stole, Mink
Duras, Marguerite, 209–10
Dyer, Richard, 185

Eat Your Makeup, 3, 137, 204, 224
Ebert, Roger, 38, 86
exploitation movies, 19–21, 220, 222, 223, 230

Faith, Karlene, 152
family
  in *Desperate Living*, 162, 163
  in *Female Trouble*, 13, 162–3
  non-normative communities, 161–3
  parodied in Waters' films, 161
  in *Pink Flamingos*, 162, 163–4, 176–7
  re-worked nuclear families in the Trash Trilogy, 162–4
  see also Manson Family; motherhood
Fangoria, 51, 52–3
Fassbinder, Rainer Werner, 16, 34, 97
Fellini, Federico, 222
Fellini's 8 ½, 123–4
Female Trouble
  audience affective reactions to, 175, 203
  Baltimore setting, 220
  as body genre, 17, 189
  camp aesthetic, 19, 22, 139
  commercial and critical success, 135
  Dawn's "bad girl" narrative arc, 19–20, *20*, 21, 22–3, 107, 156, 159, 162–3, 188–9
  Divine's performance, 142, 143
  dying for art, 22, 107, 159, 189
  flyer, *208*
  interviews with cast and crew, 131
  melodrama of, 13–14, 19–24
  midcentury television in, 188–90
  motherhood in, 16, 23, 169–70, 175–6
  references to the Mansons, 158–9, *159*
  re-worked nuclear family, 13, 162–3
  Scala screenings, 208
  script, 136, 143, 147, 148
  set design, 141
  teen exploitation mode, 19–21
  transgressive characters, 171

within the Trash Trilogy, 4–5, 82
trial-as-spectacle, 22, 107, 159, 161
violence-showbiz confluence, 21–3
Waters' visual style, 98, 107
Ferrante, Anthony C., 52
Figgs, George
on the Dreamlanders, 136–7
on the early films, 137, 138
in *Female Trouble*, 136
on *Female Trouble*, 139
friendship with Waters, 136
interview, 131–2, 136–9
in *Multiple Maniacs*, 113, 138–9, *139*
music career, 137–8
in Waters' films, 131
in *Wizard of OD*, 137, 138
film festivals, 37–9, 43, 212
film noir, 237–8
film studies, 5
filmmaking practice
of Cecil B. DeMille, 105–6
colorization, 116
continuous shots in *Polyester*, 99
dying for art, 22, 107–8, 159, 189
early films collaborative nature, 224–5, 233–4
professionalization of Waters' visual style, 98–100
remakes, 122–3
role of the actors, 233
role of Waters' friends, 131
sound, 7, 91, 236
Steadicam shots in *Cecil B. Demented*, 101, 102, 103–4
the table read, 116, 119
verité camerawork in *Cecil B. Demented*, 98, 100–3, *102*, 106, 107
verité camerawork of the early films, 98
verité style in mainstream productions, 106–7
visual style of *Cecil B. Demented*, 98, 99–100, 226
Waters' control of the script, 135, 136, 141, 142–3, 144, 146, 147, 148, 233
Waters' editing, 204, 220, 225, 234
films
audiences at the Scala, London, 200–1, 202–3, *203*
autobiography in Waters' films, 7, 70–2, 81
Baltimore settings, 173, 175, 219, 220–1, 227
big screen-small screen differences, 214–15, 223
as a business, 232
in The Criterion Collection, 108, 115, 118, 151, 235, 238
definition of a John Waters film, 234–5
early films, 3
educational function, 227
filmography, 3–5
generic playfulness, 228–9
increased budgets for, 197–8, 232, 234
influences on Waters, 237–8
kindness in, 239–40
lack of filmic production of the 1980s, 31–2, 36, 238
learning by making and watching, 98, 132, 205, 219–20, 222, 236
marketing stunts and campaigns, 17, 36, 135, 140, 150, 204, 226–7
restorations of, 108
retrospectives, 2, 37, 205
Waters' status within the film industry, 64, 78, 93, 97–8, 99, 118–19, 220, 221, 233
see also individual films
Furlong, Edward, 85, 90–1, 93

Garvey, Ellen Gruber, 154
genres
  body genre, 17, 173, 174, 178, 189
  generic multiplicity of Waters, 7, 16–17
  soap operas, 191
  see also horror
gimmicks
  Castle's marketing-gimmick cinema, 38, 104, 105, 112–13, 122–3
  Hardy Har, 124
  Odorama screenings of *Polyester*, 27, 37, 38, 123, 209, 211
  referenced in Waters' films, 123
  The Tingler's buzzing seats, 104, 124
  use of bad reviews, 134–5, 226–7
  in Waters' artworks, 121, 123–4
Goldin, Nan, 72, 84
Gorfinkel, Elena, 67
Grosz, Elizabeth, 179

Hag in a Black Leather Jacket, 3, 137, 148, 219, 220, 224
Hainley, Bruce, 110, 112
Hairspray
  Baltimore setting, 219
  characters watching TV programs, 187, *187*
  commercial and critical success, 5, 42, 43, 63, 73, 82, 198, 211, 212
  The Corny Collins Show, 184, 186, 211, 227
  gimmickry in, 123
  in the National Film Registry, 2
  and the "The Nicest Kids in Town" article, 42–3
  remakes of the stage version, 122
  Scala screenings, 212
  TV's transcendent promise, 184, 186, 188
  valorisation of failure, 73
  variety show genre, 186–9, 190, 211
Halberstam, Jack, 67, 68, 84
Hart, Romaine, 206
Hearst, Patty, 101, 142, 160, 213
Held, Isabelle, 179
Heller, Dana, 198
High School Hellcats (Bernds), 20–1, *21*
Holmlund, Chris, 189
horror
  as body genre, 17
  classic horror cycle, 55
  in the early 1990s, 48
  the Final Girl figure, 49
  global decline in of the 1990s, 50–3, 60
  the monstrous-feminine, 180
  sanitization of, 48–9, 51, 53, 56, 60
  on-screen violence/real-life behavior links, 56–9
  slasher formula, 49–50, 53
  as a video medium, 50, 51, 52, 53, 58–9, 60
  see also Scream (Craven); *Serial Mom*
Houten, Leslie Van, 151, 152
humor
  camp humor, 65–6, 88–9
  in contemporary art, 65, 121
  Liarmouth, 238–9
  satiric observation in Waters' writing, 33–4, 35, 43
  transgressive laughter, 155–6, 225, 226
  in Waters' films, 134, 171, 227, 229, 233, 238
  see also gimmicks
Hutcheon, Linda, 6

I Want to Live! (Wise), 23

Jameson, Frederic, 185
Jones, Alan, 202
Julien, Isaac, 201–2, 214

Kane-Meddock, Derek, 161
Keller, Alexandra, 117
Kelley, Mike, 176
Koob, Nathan, 83, 198
Kristeva, Julia, 169, 179

Lean, David, 113–14
Lee, Spike, 32, 63, 97
Levi, Pavle, 110
Levinson, Barry, 220–1
Levy, Emmanuel, 6, 31
Lewis, Herschell Gordon, 16, 97, 230
LGBTQ+ film production, 28
Lochary, David, 22, 100, 132, 137, 140, 149, 154, 157, 159, 163, 188, 196, 208
Lords, Traci, 93
Lynch, David, 32, 97

Manson Copies Divine's Hairdo, 112, 160
Manson Family
  alongside Catholic imagery, 154, 155, 156
  in American cultural life, 152, 153
  court trials, 151–2, 155, 156, 158–9, 231
  murders by, 152
  references in the early films, 22, 33, 112, 151, 156–7
  as a re-worked nuclear family, 161–2, 164
  Waters' advocacy work, 38, 152–3
  Waters' changing perspective on, 151–2, 153, 158, 165
  Waters' recognition of, 164–5
  and Waters' scrapbooking practice, 153–5, 160
Massey, Edith, 19, 25, 31, 35, 41, 143, 146, 154, 163, 176, 226
McDonagh, Maitland, 51–2
McLane, Betsy, 100
Mekas, Jonas, 3, 4, 220, 226
Melnick, Jeffrey, 152
melodrama
  as a body genre, 17
  camp readings of, 16, 18
  definitions, 14–15
  emotional excess, 27
  exploitation movies, 19–21, 220, 222, 223, 230
  of *Female Trouble*, 13–14, 19–24
  filthy behavior in, 18
  1950s family melodrama, 13–14
  Polyester, 23–7, 99
  post-Hays Code, 21–2
  queer readings, 18
  Waters' transposition of queerness into, 13–14, 28
  Waters' use of the melodramatic, 14, 15–19, 28
Mercer, John, 14–15, 27
Metz, Walter, 6, 161, 198
Meyer, Russ, 22
midnight movie culture
  audiences for Waters' films, 200–1, 202
  contemporary, 230
  dusk to dawn showings, 209
  Pink Flamingos, 31, 36–7, 78, 82, 98, 170, 205, 223
  and the trash aesthetic, 16, 33, 170
Milstead, Glen (Divine) *see* Divine (Glen Milstead)
Modleski, Tania, 191, 192, 193
Mondo Trasho
  black-and-white aesthetic, 17
  Catholic imagery, 155–6
  as an early film, 3, 204
  filmmaking practice, 98, 224–5
Moore, Mark, 202–3

Moran, Pat
at demonstrations, 142
on the early films, 140
friendship with Waters, 139–40
interview, 131–2, 139–43
later career, 225
marketing stunts and campaigns, 140, 150
payments, 143
on *Pink Flamingos*, 141
as trouble-shooter *cum* producer, 131, 138, 143
motherhood
in *Female Trouble*, 16, 23, 169–70, 175–6
maternal abject, 168–9, 174–5, 179–80
parodies of distraught motherhood, 16, 23
in *Pink Flamingos*, 98, 168, 169, 174–6, 181, 239
in *Polyester*, 25, 26, 169, 190–2, *192*, 193, 194, 196
in *Serial Mom*, 55–6, 168, 190–1, 192–4
soap opera villainesses, 192–3
Waters' interrogation of maternal roles, 168, 169, 170
Mottola, Greg, 81
Multiple Maniacs
black-and-white aesthetic, 17
Catholic imagery, 155–6
as an early film, 3, 14
early screenings, 204
Jesus-as-hunk representation, 113, 138–9, *139*
references to the Mansons, 151, 156–7
rephotographed stills, 75, 111
set design, 157
Waters' visual style and use of *verité* camerawork, 98
Murray, Susan, 190
New Line Cinema, 5, 14, 69, 204, 205, 206, 208, 232
New Queer Cinema, 64
Ngai, Sianne, 120, 121

Oliveira, Rui Trindade, 50

Padilla, Elisa, 72, 82, 84
pastiche, 6, 24–5, 185–6
Pearce, Mary Vivian
in *Female Trouble*, 22, 148, 149, *149*
interview, 131–2, 148–50
in *Pink Flamingos*, 149
in Waters' films, 131
Pecker
art morality tale, 69–71
art vs non-art, 68–9, 91–2, 120
autobiographical elements, 70–2, 81, 84, 85–6, 87, 93–4
camp humor, 65–6
commercial and critical success, 94
within film history, 63, 64
film's origin, 71–2
Fudge Palace, 70, 84, 86, 88, 89
guilty pleasures framework, 65–6, 67, 79, 84
mainstream appeal of, 73, 79, 86
Pecker's photographs, 68–9, 84–5, 87–90, *88*
queer and nobrow camp aesthetic, 67, 87
the queer art of failure, 73–4, *74*
the "real" photographer, 72–3, 120
satirisation of the New York art world, 63, 64, 67–8, 69, 71, 92
sincerity of the actors performances, 88–9, 90, 91–2
sound track, 91
T-Bone, 69, 85–6, 90
title, 69, 82, 86
within Waters' filmography, 82–3
and the work of Arbus and Goldin, 71–2, 84, 120

Peckinpah, Sam, 97
Peranio, Vincent
at demonstrations, 134
filming of *Female Trouble*, 134
filming of *Polyester*, 134
friendship with Waters, 132–4
interview, 131–5
later career, 225
Lobstor, 132
in *Multiple Maniacs*, *139*
payments, 135
set designs, 22, 133, 134–5, 141, 234
trailer for *Pink Flamingos*, 133
and Waters' filmmaking practice, 233–4
performances (by Waters)
cameo in *Something Wild*, 41–2, *41*, 43
Divine Waters, 40–1
film appearances, 43
film festival lectures, 37–9, 43, 212
Late Night with David Letterman, 40
no-smoking public service announcement, 39–40, *39*
Waters' persona, 43–4, 83, 131, 214
photography
Divine in Ecstasy, 111–12, *112*, 115–16, 120
Illusion-O, 112–13
Leader, 114, 126
Liz Taylor's Hair and Feet, 125–6, *125*
Manson Copies Divine's Hairdo, 112, 160
Mark series, 74–5
materiality of cinema in, 114
Movie Star Jesus, 113, 114
rephotographed stills, 18, 75, 76, 111–16, *111*, 120, 123, 125–6, *125*
Santa Molester, 113
Sullen Cookie, 112, 115
Walters' photography, 74–5
see also Pecker
Pink Flamingos
the abject in, 173
actor performances, 100
audience affective reactions to, 17, 27, 174, 175, 203, 204, 205
Babs Johnson's trailer, 145, *172*, 173
Baltimore setting, 173, 220
as a body genre, 17, 173, 174, 178
continuity-driven style, 17–18
court trials, 54, 196–7, 231
critique of societal norms, 178–9
early screenings, 204–5
and the façade of respectability, 170
the grotesque/obscene, 98, 169, 173, 196–7
infamous closing scene, 4, 82, 87, 98, 118, 149, 173, 175, 180, 203, 204, 230
influences, 141
Kiddie Flamingos (video art), 116–17, 118–20, 122, 123
London screenings, 206
as a midnight-movie classic, 31, 36–7, 78, 82, 98, 170, 205, 223
motherhood, 98, 168, 169, 174–6, 181, 239
in the National Film Registry, 2, 78
queer empowerment, 178–9, 181
re-worked nuclear family, 162, 163–4, 176–7
script, 135, 141, 142–3, 144, 145, 146, 147
set design, 157–8, *157*
spectacle-celebrity relationship, 196
synopsis on Turner Classics, 227–8
television tabloid news, 196–7
transgressive characters, 171, 177
Waters' visual style, 98

Polyester
Divine in, 148
emotional excess, 27
and the façade of respectability, 25–6, 169, 170, 196
gimmickry in, 123
intertextuality with Sirk's melodramas, 24–7, *24*, 99
melodrama, 23–7, 99
motherhood in, 25, 26, 169, 190–2, *192*, 193, 194, 196
non-normative communities, 161
Odorama screenings, 27, 37, 38, 123, 209, 211
Scala screenings, 209, 210–11
as soap opera, 190–2, *192*
spatial symbolism, 25–6
television tabloid news, 196, 197
Waters' visual style, 99
pornography
as a body genre, 17
free porn, 229–30
in *Pink Flamingos*, 177–8
in *Polyester*, 25, 123, 196
referenced in *Cecil B. Demented*, 104, 114
referenced in Waters' lectures, 38
Preminger, Otto, 97
Prince, Richard, 75, 76

queer theory, 28, 66–7, 164
queerness
affinities with the melodrama, 13–14, 16, 18, 28
anticommunitarian impulses, 164
Divine as a grotesque "drag queen" figure, 25, 170, 175–6, 180–1
Divine in Ecstasy, 111–12, *111*
dress and gender performativity, 179
LGBTQ+ programming and audiences in London, 201–2
non-normative communities, 154, 155, 161–2
queer art of failure, 67, 68, 73–4
queer empowerment in *Pink Flamingos*, 178–9, 181
queering effect of Waters' films, 6, 7, 175
queering of the American family, 13–14, 161–2
reactionary protests against in educational settings, 118–19
reflected in movies, 236–7

Reagan, Ronald, 49
reputation-studies approach, 32
Roen, Paul, 18
Roman Candles, 3, 137, 148, 204, 222, 224

Salvato, Nick, 171
Sanders, Julie, 23
Sayles, John, 42
Scala repertory cinema, London
the All-Nighters, 209
audiences for Waters' films, 201, *203*, 206, 212, 214
celebration of Divine, 211–12
Cry-Baby screenings, 213
Desperate Living screenings, 208–9
Female Trouble screenings, 208
Hairspray screenings, 212
iconic fold-out calendar, 201, 207, *210*
legacy of, 214
LGBTQ+ programming and audiences, 201–2
as a membership cinema, 207–8
Pink Flamingos screenings, 206
Polyester screenings, 209, 210–11
"10 Days of Trash" season, 209–10, *210*
Schatz, Thomas, 15, 49

Scream (Craven)
dark side of suburbia, 54–5
on-screen violence/real-life behavior links, 56–7
similarities with *Serial Mom*, 48, 49, 54, 57, 58
video rental store, 58, 59
Scream 2 (Craven), 60–1
Screen on the Green, Islington, 206
sculpture
Awful David Lean, 113–14
Fellini's 8 ½, 123–4
Looser Gift Basket, 124
Serial Mom
Beverly as soap opera villainess, 192–3
Beverly Sutphin character, 55–6, 168, 192
commercial and critical success, 63, 83
dark side of suburbia, 54, 55, 160
and the façade of respectability, 54, 160
glamorization of crime, 160
gory horror of, 49, 59–60, *59*
horror cinema in, 55–6, 57, 58, *58*
within the horror genre, 17, 48–9, 53, 60–1
Manson Family references, 160
meta approach, 49, 54, 59
motherhood, 55–6, 168, 190–1, 192–4
on-screen violence/real-life behavior links, 56–9
similarities with *Scream*, 48, 49, 54, 57, 58
soap opera matriarchs, 190–1
tabloid news, *194*, 195, 196
trial-as-spectacle, 160–1, *194*, 195, 231, 237
video rental store, 58
visual style, 235
as Waters' best movie, 236–7
Shacochis, Chuck, 72–3, 120
Sherman, Cindy, 75, 121
Shingler, Martin, 14–15, 27
Short Circuit, 3
Singer, Ben, 27
Sirk, Douglas
All That Heaven Allows, 24, 25, 26
courtroom drama, 22
critical reception, 28
family 1950s melodrama, 15
juvenile delinquent melodramas, 19
Polyester as homage to, 24–7, 99
within the studio system, 99
use of *cliché*, 26
Written on the Wind, 18, 22, 25, 26
Smith, Jack, 16, 204
Smith, Walter Avant (Van), 22, 132, 133, 138, 141, 146, 147, 154, 233–4
Something Wild (Demme), 41–2, *41*
spectatorship
audience affective reactions, 101, 105, 201, 204
audience affective reactions to *Female Trouble*, 175, 203
audience affective reactions to *Pink Flamingo*, 17, 27, 174, 175, 203, 204, 205
audiences at the Scala, London, 200–1, 202–3, *203*, 212
audiences for art house movies, 223–4
marketing-gimmick cinema, 104–5
and television in *Hairspray*, 186–8, *187*
in Waters' visual arts, 116–18
see also gimmicks
Stallybrass, Peter, 17
Stole, Mink
acting career, 146–7
in *Desperate Living*, 145, 147
drug culture, 143
in *Female Trouble*, 133, 136, 144
Figgs' friendship with, 136

Stole, Mink (*cont.*)
friendship with Waters, 144, 148
in *Hairspray*, 43, 145
interview, 131–2, 143–8
in *Multiple Maniacs*, 111
in *Pecker*, 91
in *Pink Flamingos*, 100, 144, *145*, 146, 147
in *Polyester*, 146
professionalism, 137
in *Serial Mom*, 55, 56
at special screenings, 37
voting, 143–4
in Waters' films, 131
style *see* filmmaking practice

television
advertising and daytime programming, 193–4, 195
in *Female Trouble*, 188–9
as site of sociocultural struggle, 186–8
soap opera villainesses, 192–3
soap operas, 185, 190–4, 197
spectacle-celebrity relationship, 187, 188, 189–90, 196
tabloid news, 185, 195–7
TV's transcendent promise in *Hairspray*, 184, 186, 188
unruly bodies, 188
variety shows, 185–90, 197, 211
in Waters' films, 184–6, 197–8
Theater of the Ridiculous, 232
Thompson, Kristin, 107
Timpone, Anthony, 51, 52
Tinkcom, Matthew, 16
trash aesthetic
the abject mother figure, 168–9
Baltimore settings, 172–3, 175
in *Cecil B. Demented*, 114
Divine and the trash queen aesthetic, 170–1, 173
and the façade of respectability, 78, 173–4
the grotesque/obscene, 168
and the midnight movie culture, 16, 33, 170
of the 1960s and 70s, 170
the Scala's "10 Days of Trash" season, 209–10, *210*
shock's parameters over time, 229–30
as sociopolitical commentary, 171–2, 175
transgressive characters, 171, 177
Waters as the Pope of Trash, 16, 78, 82, 83, 170
White trash studies, 172
Trash Trilogy, The, 4–5; *see also Desperate Living*; *Female Trouble*; *Pink Flamingos*
trials *see* courtroom trials

Ullman, Tracey, 5, 233
underground films, 3–4, 5

Valen, Mark, 212
Van Houten, Leslie, 165
VanDerBeek, Stan, 3, 4, 226, 228
video art
Faux Video Room, 117–18, *117*, 120, 121
Kiddie Flamingos, 116–17, 118–20, 122, 123
visual arts
art world/cinematic world contrasts, 116–18, 119–20, 124–6
the cinematic in Waters' visual art, 110–12, 114, 115
Hardy Har, 124
and lowbrow cinema, 110
remakes in, 123
scrapbooks, 153–4, 160
Secret Movie, 118
of Waters, 5–6
see also photography

Ward, Frazer, 117
Warhol, Andy
  career, 66
  films, 98
  influence on Waters, 4, 75–6, 97, 204, 226, 237
  leader in the screen tests, 114
  opening party for *Female Trouble*, 135
  white trash aesthetic, 170
Waters, John
  advocacy work and the Manson family, 38, 152–3
  art films as his guilty pleasures, 67–8
  and the avant-garde, 228, 229
  Baltimore house, 1, 34
  biography, 2–3
  education, 221–2
  filmography, 3–5
  Hollywood star, 78, 93, 221
  images of, *221*, *239*
  oeuvre, 1–2, 63
  parodic reworking of Hollywood, 2, 3, 6
  as provocateur, 229
  sartorial style, 38, 39, 83
  scholarship on, 2, 5
  status within the film industry, 64, 78, 93, 97–8, 99, 118–19, 220, 221, 233
  teaching in Maryland's Patuxent Institution, 2, 153
  see also films; performance; photography; visual arts; writing
White, Allon, 17
White trash studies, 172
Williams, Linda, 15, 17
Wilroy, Chan, 137, 139–40, 141, 147
Wise, David, 3, 4
Wizard of OD, 137, 138
writing
  American Film magazine, 31–2, 34–5, 38, 43
  Art: A Sex Book, 110, 112
  Crackpot, 32, 35–6, 38, 40, 43, 97–8
  essays, 32, 37
  "Guilty Pleasures," 209–10
  "Hard Traveling," 31–2
  humor and satiric observation, 33–4, 35, 43
  "Leslie," 152
  Liarmouth, 5, 44, 238–9
  magazine articles, 32, 33–4, 42–3, 222
  Mr. Know-It-All, 108
  "The Nicest Kids in Town," 42–3
  oeuvre, 65, 228
  Role Models, 239–40
  screenplays, 31, 33
  Shock Value, 33, 35, 159–60

Zagarrio, Vito, 40–1
Zeffirelli, Franco, 81

EU Authorised Representative:
Easy Access System Europe Mustamäe tee 50, 10621 Tallinn, Estonia
gpsr.requests@easproject.com

Printed and bound by CPI Group (UK) Ltd, Croydon, CR0 4YY
08/09/2026
02213211-0013